OXFORD STUDIES IN DEMOCRATIZATION

Series editor: Laurence Whitehead

....

HUMAN RIGHTS AND DEMOCRATIZATION
IN LATIN AMERICA

OXFORD STUDIES IN DEMOCRATIZATION

Series editor: Laurence Whitehead

....

Oxford Studies in Democratization is a series for scholars and students of comparative politics and related disciplines. Volumes will concentrate on the comparative study of the democratization processes that accompanied the decline and termination of the cold war. The geographical focus of the series will primarily be Latin America, the Caribbean, Southern and Eastern Europe, and relevant experiences in Africa and Asia.

OTHER BOOKS IN THE SERIES

The New Politics of Inequality in
Latin America: Rethinking Participation and Representation
Douglas A. Chalmers

Citizenship Rights and Social Movements:
A Comparative and Statistical Analysis
Joe Foweraker and Todd Landman

Regimes, Politics, and Markets: Democratization and
Economic Change in Southern and Eastern Europe
José María Maravall

Democracy Between Consolidation and
Crisis in Southern Europe
Leonardo Morlino

The Bases of Party Competition in Eastern Europe: Social and
Ideological Cleavages in Post Communist States
Geoffrey Evans and Stephen Whitefield

The International Dimensions of Democratization:
Europe and the Americas
Laurence Whitehead

Human Rights and Democratization in Latin America

Uruguay and Chile

....

Alexandra Barahona de Brito

OXFORD UNIVERSITY PRESS
1997

Oxford University Press, Walton Street, Oxford OX2 6DP
Oxford New York
Athens Auckland Bangkok Bogota Bombay
Buenos Aires Calcutta Cape Town Dar es Salaam Delhi
Florence Hong Kong Istanbul Karachi
Kuala Lumpur Madras Madrid Melbourne
Mexico City Nairobi Paris Singapore
Taipei Tokyo Toronto
and associated companies in
Berlin Ibadan

Oxford is a trade mark of Oxford University Press

Published in the United States
by Oxford University Press Inc., New York

British Library Cataloguing in Publication Data
Data available

Library of Congress Cataloging in Publication Data
Data available
ISBN 0–19–828038–6

1 3 5 7 9 10 8 6 4 2

Typeset by Graphicraft Typesetters Ltd., Hong Kong
Printed in Great Britain
on acid-free paper by
Bookcraft (Bath) Ltd
Midsomer Norton, Somerset

This book is dedicated to Jonathan Becker
and to the memory of my friend
Diogo de Mello.

Acknowledgements

I would like to thank the ESRC, the Henry Trust Fund, the Chigusa Fund, St Antony's College, the Politics Applications Committee, the Cyril Foster Peace Fund, and the Norman Chester Fund, for sponsoring my doctoral research.

I received help from innumerable people in both Uruguay and Chile and am grateful to them all. Special thanks in Uruguay to Romeo Pérez and the Centro Latino Americano de Economía Humanística (CLAEH), Héctor Acosta at the Political Commission of the Frente Amplio, Luís Eduardo González of Equipos Consultores and the staff at Serpaj. In Chile thanks are due to the Academia de Humanismo Cristiano (ACH), to Jaime Valenzuela and to Cristián Gazmuri and Julio Faúndez for their support and friendship. Thanks also to the Instituto de Estudos Estratégicos e Internacionais in Lisbon who gave me a 'sabbatical' from work to edit the thesis for publication.

I would like to acknowledge the support of my thesis supervisor, Alan Angell, without whom this thesis would not have been possible. He suggested the topic of research in the first place and played the dual role of academic advisor and crisis counsellor to myself and his other Chileanist 'Alan's Angels'. I also gratefully acknowledge the encouragement and attention I was accorded by Professor Juan Linz who was a great source of inspiration. Despite his very busy schedule he was, as with all his students, unfailingly generous with his time, expertise, and support. Thanks are due also to Laurence Whitehead for his support, insightful comments, and for checking a tendency towards 'purple prose' and 'wishful analysis'.

Thanks to Anthony Kauders and Rodrigo Amaral for help with editing and translation and to Pilar Domingo, Paula Alsonso, and Pam Lowden for their friendship and support throughout. Last but not least, thanks to my parents for their support and encouragement.

Table of Contents

Abbreviations

AAPP	Asociación de Abogados de Presos Políticos
AD	Alianza Democrática
ACC	Alianza de Centro Centro
AFDD	Agrupación de Familiares de Detenidos Desaparecidos
AFDE	Agrupación de Familiares de Detenidos Ejecutados
AFPD	Agrupación de Familiares de Prisioneros Desaparecidos
AFPJM	Asociación de Familiares de Procesados por la Justicia Militar
AFPP	Asociación de Familiares de Presos Políticos
AHC	Academia de Humanismo Cristiano
AI	Amnesty International
ANC	African National Congress
ASCEEP–FEUU	Asociación de Estudiantes de Enseñanza Pública-Federación de Estudiantes Universitários
AW	Americas Watch
BS	Bloque Socialista
CAPE	Comité Asesor Político Estratégico
CAS	Comando Anti-Subversivo
CBI	Corriente Batllista Independiente
CC	Comando Conjunto
CCDH	Comisión Chilena de Derechos Humanos
CDU	Grupo de Convergencia Democrática Uruguayo
CEDH	Coordinadora de Entidades de Derechos Humanos
CHIP	An internet news summary service
CODEPU	Comité de Defensa del Pueblo
COMASPO	Comisión de Asunto Políticos
CONAPRO	Concertación Nacional Programática
COPROPAZ	Comité Pro-Paz

CNT	Confederación Nacional de Trabajadores
CNI	Central Nacional de Inteligencia
CNPDHJ	Comité Nacional Pro-Derechos Humanos Juveniles
CNH	Consejo Nacional Herrerista
CNVR	Comisión Nacional de Verdad y Reconciliación
CPPD	Concertación de Partidos Por la Democracia
CS	Convergencia Socialista
CVDC	Comités Voluntarios de Defensa Civil
DA	Democracia Avanzada
DICAR	Dirección de Inteligencia de Carabineros
DIFA	Dirección de Inteligencia de la Fuerza Aérea
DINA	Dirección de Inteligencia Nacional
DINARP	Dirección Nacional de Relaciones Públicas
DINE	Dirección de Inteligencia Nacional del Ejército
DSCD	Diario de Sesiones de la Cámara de Diputados (Chile)
DSCRROU	Diario de Sesiones de la Cámara de Representantes de la República Oriental del Uruguay
DSCSROU	Diario de Sesiones de la Cámara de Senadores de la República Oriental del Uruguay
DSCS	Diario de Sesiones de la Cámara de Senadores (Chile)
DSVS	Double Simultaneous Voting System
DYP	Democracia y Progreso
ESMACO	Estado Mayor Conjunto
EU	European Union
FA	Frente Amplio
FASIC	Fundación de Ayuda Social de las Iglesias Cristianas
FFCCU	Fuerzas Conjuntas Uruguayas
FMLN	Frente Farabundo Martí de Liberación Nacional
FUCVAM	Federación Unificada Cooperativa de Viviendas y Ayuda Mútua
GAL	Grupos Anti-Terroristas de Liberación
HA	Herrerismo Autentico
IACHR	Inter-American Commission for Human Rights

IACHR	Inter-American Court for Human Rights
IC	Izquierda Cristiana
ICJ	International Commission of Jurists
IDI	Izquierda Democrática Independiente
IELSUR	Instituto de Estudios Legales y Sociales del Uruguay
IFP	Inkatha Freedom Party
ILO	International Labour Organization
IU	Izquierda Unida
JCJ	Junta de Comandantes en Jefe
JOG	Junta de Oficiales Generales
LSE	Ley de Seguridad del Estado y Orden Pública
LTTE	Liberation Tigers of Tamil Eelam
LYC	Libertad y Cambio
MIR	Movimiento de Izquierda Revolucionaria
MMYFPJM	Movimiento de Madres y Familiares de Procesados por la Justicia Militar
MNR	Movimiento Nacional de Rocha
MPP	Movimiento Por la Patria
MPS	Medidas de Pronta Seguridad
NSD	National Security Doctrine
MYFDU	Madres y Familiares de Desaparecidos Uruguayos
MYFUDA	Madres y Familiares de Uruguayos Desaparecidos en Argentina
NP	National Party
OAS	Organization of American States
OCOA	Oficina Coordinadora de Operaciones Anti-Subversivas
ONUSAL	Misión de Observadores de las Naciones Unidas en El Salvador
PAC	Partido Alianza de Centro
PAIS	Partido Amplio de Izquierda Socialista
PCCh	Partido Comunista Chileno
PDC	Partido Demócrata Cristiano
PDN	Partido Democrático Nacional
PGP	Por El Gobierno del Pueblo
PH	Partido Humanista
PIT–CNT	Plenario Intersindical de Trabajadores–Confederación Nacional de Trabajadores
PL	Partido Liberal
PN	Partido Nacional
PPD	Partido Por la Democracia

PR	Partido Radical
PR	Partido Republicano
PRSD	Partido Radical Socialista Democrático
PS	Partido Socialista
PSA	Partido Socialista Alianza
PS-A	Partido Socialista Almeyda
PS-B/N	Partido Socialista Briones/Nuñez
PSD	Partido Social Democracia
PU	Popular Unity
RPF	Rwanda Patriotic Front
RN	Renovación Nacional
SERPAJ	Servicio de Paz y Justicia
SDL	Socialismo Democracia y Libertad
SICAR	Servicio de Inteligencia de Carabineros
SID	Servicio de Inteligencia de Defensa
SIDE	Servicio de Inteligencia del Ejército
SIFA	Servicio de Inteligencia de la Fuerza Aérea
SIN	Servicio de Inteligencia Naval
SADF	South African Defence Forces
SPO	Special Prosecutor's Office (Ethiopia)
SWAPO	South West Africa People's Organization
UC	Unión Cívica
UCB	Unión Colorada y Batllista
UDI	Unión Democrática Independiente
ULD	Unión Liberal Democrática
UN	Unión Nacional
UN	United Nations
UNECOSOC	United Nations Economic and Social Council
UNH	Unión Nacional Herrerista
UNO	Unión Nicaragüense de Oposición
UNRG	Unidad Revolucionaria Guatemalteca
UP	Unidad Popular
UPD	Unidad Por la Democracia
UPD	Unión Popular Democrática
UPS	Unión Popular Socialista
UYR	Unidad y Reforma
VB	Vanguardia Batllista
WOLA	Washington Office on Latin America

Justice is the first virtue of social institutions, as truth is of systems of thought. A theory however elegant and economical must be rejected or revised if it is untrue; likewise laws and institutions no matter how efficient and well-arranged must be reformed or abolished if they are unjust . . . Being the first virtues of human activities, truth and justice are uncompromising.

John Rawls, *A Theory of Justice*, 1971

When we toss into the midst of a society of men a principle divorced from all the intermediary principles that bring it down to us and adapt it to our situation, we create great disorder; because when this principle is torn from all its links and deprived of all its supports . . . it destroys and overthrows. But it is the fault not of the first principle but of our ignorance of the intermediary principles.

Benjamin Constant, *Des Réactions Politiques*, 1797

Introduction

This book analyses Uruguay's and Chile's attempts to resolve the human rights violation conflicts inherited from military-state repression. It focuses on how the post-transitional democratic governments handled social demands for an official recognition of the truth about human rights violations committed by the outgoing military regimes, and for the punishment of those guilty of committing and ordering those violations. The aim of the book is to shed light on the political conditions which permitted, or inhibited, the realization of policies of truth-telling and justice under these successor regimes. Here the objective is not to moralize politics or to politicize ethics, but rather to examine how far truth and justice can be realized in restricted political conditions.

It has been noted that 'Intellectual efforts to conceptualize the unfortunately rich and complex reality of violation of human rights may be equated with providing an alibi [for] those directly responsible for them' and that furthermore, 'any intellectual differentiation with the purpose of allowing a deeper understanding of the causes of human rights violations runs the risk of being perceived as implying a loss of righteous moral indignation against all and every single act of inhumanity.'[1] Yet the demand for truth and justice is simultaneously 'a problem located in the sphere of the ideological and symbolic' and 'a battle situated in a political plane.'[2] Moreover, while such demands are absolute and ethical and operate in the realm of black and white, political reality is coloured in shades of grey; while the call for truth and justice focuses on principles, political struggle is about power.

It is therefore necessary to assess how the demands of a black and white world are accommodated by the politics of transition and incipient democratization which are 'a matter of infinite gradations.'[3] Without detailed empirical research of how accountability for past abuses operate within specific political contexts, it would be impossible to strengthen our understanding of the politics of transition as well as to address the concerns of those whose full participation in a democratic society can only occur if the issue of accountability is dealt with.

Interest in the subject of accountability for past abuses has grown over the last few years due to the recent experiences of a number of countries in this area. Attempts at transitional justice undertaken in the former Communist countries in the early 1990s were responsible for sparking off widespread interest in processes of truth-telling and justice. El Salvador's record as the first country to have a truth-telling report undertaken by the United Nations as part of a general international peace mission in 1993 and the recent establishment of a Truth and Reconciliation Commission by President Mandela in South Africa has also reinforced this trend.

Latin America was a percursor in this field. Before the wave of transitions from authoritarian rule were well underway in the region and long before this question had become a matter of concern in the wider intellectual and political community, a group of individuals headed by the Archdiocese of São Paulo in Brazil and the Geneva-based World Council of Churches had begun to elaborate a report to 'tell the truth' about the human rights violations committed by the Brazilian Armed Forces. The military were still in power and what was to become the world's first *Nunca Mais* (Never Again) report had to be worked on in absolute secrecy.[4]

Ten years after the its publication in 1985, truth-telling has become a demand echoed around the world and is now part of the official politics of transition in many countries. Truth-telling has been undertaken by presidentially appointed commissions in Bolivia (1982), Argentina (1984), Zimbabwe (1985), Uganda (1986), the Philippines (1986), Chad (1990), Chile (1990), Ethiopia (1992–3), Sri Lanka (1995), South Africa (1995); by parliamentary commissions in Uruguay (1985–6), Paraguay (1989), and in Germany after re-unification (1992); by international bodies, such as the United Nations and the Red Cross, in co-operation with national governments in El Salvador (1993), Guatemala (1995), and Namibia (1991);[5] by international war tribunals in the case of the former Yugoslavia; and finally, through reports written by national non-governmental organizations in Brazil (1985) and Uruguay (1986–9) and by international non-governmental organizations in Rwanda (1992) and Honduras (1993).[6]According to one study, at least fifteen truth commissions were set up between 1974 and 1994 and six were established in the space of only a year and a half, between March 1992 and late 1993.[7]

The Southern Cone of Latin America has served a model, be it positive or negative, for all of these initiatives. El Salvador's commission was based on the experiences of Argentina and Chile. The Southern Cone of the 1980s, as well as Portugal, Greece, and

Spain in the 1970s, were examples studied with great interest by East European scholars and politicians. The South African commission is modelled directly on its Chilean counterpart, and other Latin American and Eastern European experiences were studied by South African activists and scholars in the period leading up to the formation of that country's truth commission.

Truth-telling is invariably accompanied by demands for justice. Without being exhaustive, attempts to do justice have included the official establishment of special national tribunals as in Argentina and some Eastern European countries; international tribunals such as the Nuremberg and Hague tribunals set up to judge the Nazis and war crimes in the former Yugoslavia and genocide in Rwanda respectively; individuals taking their cases to court as in Chile, Paraguay, and Uruguay; non-governmental groups in regional or international courts in the cases of Honduras, Uruguay, and Paraguay; processes of disqualification or purges as in the Portuguese and Eastern European transitions in the 1970s and 1990s respectively. However, successful experiences with prosecution for past abuse or other forms of punitive action have been few, posing numerous political as well as legal problems. Many countries, such as El Salvador, Uruguay, Brazil and post-Sandinista Nicaragua, have opted for blanket or successive amnesties. Others have opted for selective pardons or laws limiting prosecution, as in the case of Argentina.[8] Yet others, such as Chile and South Africa, have inherited constitutionally enshrined amnesties from the dictatorial or transitional periods, and have attempted to formulate innovative policies which link immunity from prosecution or the definitive application of amnesties with confession to a truth commission.

Whatever the outcome of each experience with truth and justice, it is easily demonstrated that the issue of accountability for past abuses has received increasing recognition. In 1974, when Southern Europe gave rise to the second wave of transitions, this problem had not 'been researched in a systematic and comparative fashion.'[9] Throughout the 1980s, when Latin America experienced the demise of military authoritarian rule, literature on these processes began to refer to the importance of repressive legacies for the politics of transitions.[10] A number of studies emerged from then on mostly undertaken by international lawyers and human rights organizations. These have discussed the legal and political problems rooted in the nature of transitional justice and the concomitant national and international judicial, juridical, and constitutional problems involved in the implementation of human rights policies.[11] Since the early 1990s and the transitions in Eastern

Europe and in some African countries, a number of international conferences and study projects have been held which focus on the issue of transitional justice.[12]

Despite the interest in this issue, there are few books based on detailed empirical research which examine comparatively how repressive, constitutional, and political legacies and specific transitional contexts as well as democratizing political conditions shaped the ability of democratic governments to deal with the issues of truth and justice.[13] This is certainly the first book which assesses the cases of Uruguay and Chile in this comparative fashion. The experiences of these countries are not merely a matter of concern for specialists in the politics specially of those two countries: they are formative examples of attempts to deal with a fundamental aspect of the politics of transition and democratization. The value of this book therefore lies primarily in the fact that it makes an original contribution to our understanding of the key political, legal, and moral issues involved in the process of regime transition and democratization. The decision to adopt a comparative approach was based on the numerous commonalities between the Uruguayan and Chilean transitions, making comparison feasible. While respecting what is unique to each country, a comparative methodology allows the identification of the key variables permitting or inhibiting the implementation of truth and justice policies. The choice of region was determined by my own specialization and by the formative impact of the Latin American experiences in this field.

Four arguments are put forward in this book. The first is that a policy which provides for 'total' truth and justice is impossible. A brief counter-factual exercise is useful to illustrate this point. Assuming for a moment that an unambiguous truth and total justice were possible, what would an 'ideal' truth and justice policy consist of? Ideally, truth and justice would reverse the symbolic, political, and moral balance of power between the repressors and their victims, rob the repressors of political and moral legitimacy, destroying their power and restoring moral and political power to the previously unrecognized victims. The truth would be both individual and global, consisting of a detailed account of each and every act of injustice and denial on the one hand, and the sum total of individual truths as well as the global assignation of political and moral responsibility for injustice and denial on the other. The repressors would also acknowledge their guilt, repent, and accept the legitimacy of the victims' suffering. Justice would ideally be similarly both specific and global, including both individual prosecutions and a political official tribunal which would demonstrate institutional or collective and not only individual guilt. Thus, catharsis would be total.

Clearly, the ideal is mediated by the constraints imposed by reality. Purely physical limitations render such an ideal impossible. Limited time and human and material resources means that policies of accountability will have to be partial, selecting and prioritizing the abuses that can be dealt with.[14] A report of each and every violation would take years to compile. The guilty often refuse to acknowledge their guilt or to repent because they feel they have done the truthful and just thing. Two competing versions of the truth will continue to exist even when the facts have been proved beyond a shadow of doubt.[15] Recent revisionist exercises by the right in Germany demonstrate this, as does the argument in the United States which has arisen surrounding the issue of the historical justification for dropping the bomb.[16] Similarly, the trial of each and every violation would be impossible.

Thus, even in ideal conditions in which the courts can dedicate themselves full-time to the successful resolution of these cases, in which the passage of time and financial limitations are not a consideration in the compilation of a 'total truth-telling report', and in which the violators have no power to resist these measures, 'total' truth and justice are impossible. Even in the ideal or most favourable of circumstances, the uncompromising nature of truth and justice are compromised.

The intensely political nature of the pursuit of accountability as well as the legal problems involved introduce an immediate tension between the absolute and ethical nature of demands for truth and justice, and the political conditions in which attempts to fulfil those demands are made.

Two further points can be made in this respect. As noted by Whitehead, in situations of regime transition, what is often sought is not a total truth but rather a selective version of the latter, to serve as a well-functioning foundational myth which can legitimize the post-transitional balance of forces.[17] Moreover, on a more abstract or philosophical level, demands for total truth do not take into account that the concept or nature of truth itself is not unambiguous even if it is uncompromising as a value.

This brings us to the second argument put forward in this book: namely, that the nature and success or failure of truth and justice policies are determined by the particular national political conditions and the institutional, constitutional, and political limitations operating during the transitional period and under the successor democratic regimes.

Uruguay and Chile, for example, experienced restricted, negotiated peaceful transitions to democratic rule. This type of transition poses a series of problems. A first restriction is that the repressors are not defeated and are even given a degree of political legitimacy by their voluntary withdrawal from power and their participation in the transitional negotiations with the democratizing civilian élites. This means that successor democratic governments must avoid a backlash which may endanger the stability of the transition when pursuing accountability for past abuses.

Transitions which are peaceful democratic restorations also mean that truth and justice have to be pursued within the framework of the rules of the democratic game. Democratic pluralism, which ensures a continued voice for the violators and their allies, forces successor governments to negotiate politically rather than just impose solutions to the human rights legacy. The voice of the victims and their demands have to be accommodated in a pluralist context, and are thus inevitably forced to coexist with the counter-demands of the military and their allies.

Peaceful transitions to democracy imply the continued existence and survival of the state institutions which existed both prior to and under military rule. In both Uruguay and Chile the most systematic violators were members of the most powerful institution of the state, namely the military. If violations are committed by a party or a social group, it is possible to imagine that punishment and truth-telling may pose less of a threat to the structure of these states. Similarly, if violations are mere excesses committed by individuals within an institution of the state, their prosecution may also be less of a threat to these structures.

In Uruguay and Chile, however, human rights violations were committed by modern hierarchical military institutions which were an integral part of the state apparatus, and which had been the backbones of long-lasting regimes, and they were institutionalized and condoned by the military hierarchy. The successor regimes were thus faced, on the one hand, with the question of how to punish institutionalized crimes without destroying the state institution which had perpetrated them, and on the other hand, with the fact that individual prosecution of institutionalized crimes would sustain the 'legal' fiction that crimes were committed by individuals for individual reasons, as individual prosecution cannot reveal the political fact of institutional criminalization.[18]

Transitions to democracy have a further implication: policies for accountability have to comply with judicial due process and with recognized standards of due process in the pursuit of accountability.[19]

The names of the perpetrators of violations, for example, a part of the truth, are often left out of truth-telling reports in order to avoid trial by publicity before formal legal charges can be made in the courts.[20] Inevitably, the exigencies of due process mean that in many cases the courts will not be able to legally establish the guilt of those who 'everyone knows' have committed atrocities. Democracy cannot permit indiscriminate purges and mass or collective trials because, even if they may be seen to be 'just' in that they enable the punishment of those who 'everyone knows' are guilty, this kind of 'rough' justice debilitates the rule of law. In most cases where 'total' truth and justice are attempted, new injustices are invariably perpetrated.

Ironically, non-democratic successor regimes may be philosophically and psychologically better prepared for policies which attempt 'total' justice due to limited or absent pluralism and a lack of concern for due process. Yet whilst liberal democratic systems of justice may never succeed in proving the guilt of individuals whom everyone 'knows' are guilty, this morally unsatisfactory situation is ultimately more life-affirming because it strengthens the institutions and procedures which are indispensable for a functioning democratic order.

Successor democratic regimes are therefore faced with a tall order. In the words of one author, 'the quest for a yardstick with which to judge the actions of predecessors in power is fraught with legal difficulties'. It is difficult 'to determine values that transcend the lifetime of a political regime against which acts can be judged . . . to relate the attitude of individuals to the sum total of the record of the regime served, [and] to determine a precise point at which action in the service of past political goals turns into criminal conduct'.[21] Faced with the complexity of the problems surrounding transitional truth and justice, it is not surprising that a South African observer facing these questions in her country confessed to be alarmed by 'the magnitude of the task ahead and the depth of understanding required.'[22]

The third argument put forward in this book is that accountability for past abuses or backward-looking policies which deal with the legacy of a previous regime are not, in and of themselves, necessary or able to consolidate democracy. It is only in so far as they form a part of a wider process of fundamental, forward-looking institutional reform to promote present and future accountability—namely, a reform of the principles and the procedures governing the judiciary and the forces of repression—that they can become a key to democratic consolidation. Accountability for past abuses may go a long way towards initiating that process. Indeed, attempting to pursue accountability may make a vital contribution to setting in motion a dynamic for wider reform, while worrying too much about stability can lead to a reform immobilism which halts the social, institutional, and political transformation necessary for the process of democratic consolidation. In the words of one observer, 'anyone who has ever tried to learn how to ride a bicycle knows that the secret of staying on top is to keep moving. If one applies this mechanical metaphor to the context of a transition, the idea would be that if you worry too much about maintaining your stability, you freeze the transition and go backwards.'[23] In the final analysis, however, it is the fundamental overhauling of these institutions which is indispensable.

It has been argued that accountability for past abuse is fundamental to the process of democratic consolidation and because it may act as a deterrent.[24] This is difficult, if not impossible to prove. Attempting to argue in favour of truth and justice on the basis of predictive criteria leaves us on shaky ground. One can only assess how key events affect a nation's future, its self-image, political culture, and collective myths with greater historical hindsight. Even with hindsight, problems remain. Although it is possible to claim that political culture is shaped by processes of truth-telling and justice and that the nature of that culture is fundamental to consolidation, attempting to understand how political culture shapes the process of consolidation is either elusive or falls into the banal (the more democratic the culture the more consolidated the democracy). Furthermore, it is almost impossible to know whether truth and justice were in fact the 'critical factors' which led to the consolidation of democracy. Once consolidation is a *fait accompli* how to assess the significance of the input of truth and justice in bringing about that desirable state of affairs? Other, often unexpected, intervening variables may come into play which actually democratize repressive forces unaffected by trials more than others which have been prosecuted. Moreover, if one bases the value of truth and justice on these criteria, were it to be proved that punishment does not benefit democratization or deter future violations, the apparent 'utility' of accountability would disappear.

This brings us a fourth and final set of related arguments made in this book: namely, that reliance on a purely instrumental logic would be insufficient justification for these policies of accountability. They derive their strength and legitimacy from an appeal to more fundamental intuitions about the just treatment of all citizens in a civilized society. In other words, the pursuit of truth and justice should not be justified merely because it consolidates democracy or acts as a deterrent; that accountability should be pursued as an end in itself, because it is fundamental independently of its contribution to democratization; and finally that, truth and justice are not merely peripheral issues among the many which are dealt with in the transition from authoritarian rule but the key ethical as well as political problem of regime transition. Demands for truth and justice are about reclaiming history in the face of denial and the restoration of accountability and equality before the law in the face of impunity. As such they are at the heart of the politics of transition to democracy, the latter essentially characterized by accountability, equality before the law, and a political culture based on a common understanding of the past which is affirmative of democratic values. Furthermore, as noted above, these demands attack those who lead the repressive apparatus of the state, and as such have the greatest capacity for destabilizing the processes of authoritarian withdrawal from power and subsequent democratization.

It is necessary here to separate the two related policies of truth and justice which make up accountability for past abuses. While claiming that both are politically and ethically central, this book sustains that while the first is always possible and necessary, the latter, while desirable, is often not possible and is sometimes unnecessary.

There is much debate about whether punishment is preferable to forgiveness or whether forgiveness can occur without punishment. Some would argue that there is an obligation under international law to prosecute crimes against humanity. Others claim that the setting of too high a standard can backfire: national governments may be unable to live up to these standards and thus they may both weaken the authority of incipient democracies as well as the force of international law.[25]

Fundamental philosophical differences regarding the ends of punishment lie at the heart of this debate. Arendt pointed out that people are apparently only able to forgive that which they can punish. If one considers the statements of many victims of repression and their relatives, however, it is possible to claim that people are also willing to forgive when there is acknowledgement. In other words, to forgive one needs to know who and what one is forgiving. Although punishment is preferable to impunity for both political and ethical reasons, it is argued that the absence of punishment is admissible only when there has been an official acknowledgement of the truth and when a national consensus exists for non-prosecution.[26] This claim not only echoes that of the victims but also the conviction that punishment can neither be imposed from the outside nor simply willed into existence: it must stem both from the ability and the common desire of societies to carry it out.

On the other hand, unlike justice, officially sponsored truth-telling is always possible, necessary, and desirable for a number of reasons. One author has pointed out, 'in contrast to ordinary justice, transitional justice implies arguments addressed to the public at large and to future historians . . . it seeks to achieve moral and political regeneration . . . it pre-figures the uncertain verdict of history. Transitional justice is in this sense half constitutive and half symbolic, partly performative and partly a morality play.'[27] If justice is not possible, however, this kind of effect can be achieved with an official truth-telling exercise.

Truth-telling is the key to the reconstruction of collective identity and memory at a critical juncture of a country's political history and it is a struggle for control of the future: 'When the past is resignified so as to explain (and thus legitimate) the present, what is at stake is more than the here and now. To the extent that the resignification bears on the projects and possibilities of the actors in question, a dispute over the past is a struggle for control over the future.'[28] Reconstructing collective memory after a repressive period during which reality is manipulated by the repressors is critically important if a nation's collective memory is to do justice to the oppressed and to make them full members of society. As one observer has noted, had the Croatian state publicly disavowed the fascist Ustache state and acknowledged its participation in the extermination of thousands of people in the gas ovens when it was proclaimed in 1990, the Serbs and the Croatians might be 'ending the past' rather than living it over and over again. Instead, 'the Serbs in Croatia were manipulated by Belgrade and their local leaders into believing that the new Croatia was the Fascist Ustache come again'.[29] A similar point has been made about the Boers and their continued self-image as people under siege and their concomitant difficulty in coming to terms with a modern multi-racial democracy in South Africa in the absence of a coming to terms with British repression.[30]

Thus, officially sponsored recognition of the truth is politically fundamental since it permits the banishing of dangerous ghosts and makes a new democracy legitimate and credible in the eyes of the victims, their relatives and all those allied to their cause. As this is a significant number of people, responding to their aspirations is as much a matter of efficacy as it is of ethics. Moreover, as the Croatian example demonstrates, such experiences affect the whole of society and not just the victims and their allies. Many governments have argued that forgetting the past is the only way not to upset a delicate transition by alienating former repressors, but as Rosenberg notes, 'reconciliation at gunpoint should not be confused with the real thing.'[31] Moreover, just because the issue is not overtly on the political agenda, this is no reason to ignore it. It may be 'boiling underground, waiting to erupt.'[32]

A national, officially promoted acknowledgement of the truth about repression is also necessary for imminently practical reasons which have an ethical basis. It is the first step towards a series of necessary measures: namely, establishing responsibility for crimes organized by the state; pinpointing the institutional causes of abuses, a first step towards necessary structural reform; counteracting the social effects of denial by recognizing the suffering and dignifying the victims and allowing for their proper mourning; extending material and moral measures of compensation and reparation; resolving legal and material issues such as the collection of life insurance with official recognition of death. Thus, the plight of the victims and their relatives are pending social problems which must be dealt with even in the absence of judicial prosecution.[33] Furthermore, as courts can only prosecute individual crimes, they may not reveal collective institutional responsibility. A truth report, on the other hand, can undertake a necessary global political–institutional judgement.

In addition to the four key arguments outlined above, this book proposes a framework of what may be considered a successful policy of truth and justice, particularly in restricted settings such as those found in Uruguay and Chile. Generally speaking, such a policy must be ethically and politically informed, simultaneously addressing the needs of the victims of repression, ensuring that the military remain subordinated to civilian authority, as well as strengthening the institutions and principles which sustain a democratic polity (the latter two are not one and the same thing—the first is a short-term consideration, the latter a long-term aim.) It must find a balance between maximalist moral demands, whose tendency is to stretch political limits, and pragmatic minimalist demands, whose tendency is to assert the power of those limits. It must not be a weapon in the struggle for power, but a tool for reconciliation; it should not be used to crush opponents, but as a way to re-establish a lost equilibrium between different social and political forces.[34] Given the likelihood that the sectors of society which carried out and supported repression will not accept the truth as it is told by their victims, the temptation to somehow 'force' them to accept that vision is always present; yet, if societies confront their past under conditions of democratic pluralism, they neither can nor should do so. Victims and their relatives will have to coexist with former repressors in a pluralist context and therefore should not treat a new democratic regime as 'an enemy' when the latter is unable to fulfil all their demands. As Sachs says of South Africa, 'to wallow in the impossibilities is to disclaim responsibility for what is the historic task of our generation.'[35] On a more practical level, policies must be timely and sustainable: the truth cannot wait a few years before it is addressed, and the policy adopted must be carried through or it may lead to the loss of legitimacy of the government implementing it.[36] Making it sustainable usually means it will be limited.

More concretely, a successful human rights policy must minimally produce a national, officially promoted acknowledgement of the truth about repression, its nature, extent, the identities of the victims, of those responsible for planning and directing, carrying out, and covering up gross violations.[37] It must recognize the suffering of the victims and offer material and moral measures of compensation and reparation. Depending on the repressive legacy, this may include the liberation of political prisoners, reversal of purges, restitution of lost property. In all cases the building of monuments or decreeing national days of mourning for the victims are possible. Compensation should never be offered as a replacement for truth.[38]

As far as justice is concerned, it is easier to say what should not be done. Governments should not place any further obstacles in the path of justice than those which already exist; they should not pass amnesties without a full official accounting of the truth; they should not become victimizers in the pursuit of justice and should therefore comply with internationally recognized standards of due process of law. On the positive side, governments must ensure that they do all that is possible, given the circumstances they find themselves in, to prosecute human rights violators, in order to permit the redress of the legacy of impunity and to affirm the principle of the rule of law and accountability.[39]

Placing truth and justice in a wider context, governments should undertake the necessary measures of institutional reform and prevention, such as policies to democratize the military, strengthen the judiciary, and promote a culture of human rights.[40]

A final reminder: neither truth-telling nor prosecution is a miraculous remedy to solve what are deep wounds and often irreconcilable differences. They merely represent the beginning of a long and arduous process of a society's attempts to come to terms with its all too well-developed capacity for self-destruction. As pointed out by a member of the Centre for the Study of Violence and Reconciliation in South Africa, truth commissions can be 'a psychological healing process by aiding a much-needed truth recovery, giving survivors the space to recount past abuses and by providing some form of reparation' but 'establishing a truth commission is not sufficient in itself to meet these psychological needs'.[41]

The book is organized chronologically so as to permit a better understanding of the ability or willingness of democratizing élites to pursue policies of truth and justice, by previously examining the legacies of authoritarian rule and the politics of transition prior to the inauguration of democratic rule.

The book is divided into four parts. The first, 'Problems of Transitional Truth and Justice in Comparative Perspective and Human Rights Violations Under Military Rule in Uruguay and Chile', consists of two 'stage-setting' chapters. The first places the Uruguayan and Chilean cases in a wider context, by examining various experiences of truth and justice for past abuses in Latin America and elsewhere.

The second chapter examines comparatively the breakdown of democratic rule, the repression, and the justification for the methods used by the military. The description of the nature of the repressive legacy faced by democratizing élites allows for an understanding of how the latter shaped the demands of its victims and created different needs and problems for the designing and implementation of legacy policies. The analysis of the military's attitude towards the human rights issue and the nature and reasons for military resistance to truth and justice during the transitions and beyond, permits an understanding of the political and ideological dynamics of the struggle between the armed forces and the civilian élites attempting to implement such policies.

The second part, 'Truth and Justice in Transition', consists of two chapters, examining how the issues of truth and justice evolved in the transitional period in Uruguay and in Chile. The aim of these chapters is to show how the political nature and dynamics of the transition and negotiations shaped the political élites' ability to pursue truth and justice in the democratic period, as the transitional period is seen to represent a 'critical juncture' during which the stage is often set for what comes in the democratic period.[42] The third part of the book, 'Truth and Justice under

Democratic Successor Regimes', examines how the issues of truth and justice were dealt with under democratic rule. It consists of two chapters: the first dealing with the Uruguayan case and the second with the Chilean.

The fourth and final part, 'Assessing Truth and Justice in Uruguay and Chile: The Road to Democratic Consolidation?', consists of one chapter and my conclusions. The chapter is divided into two sections: the first assesses the two cases comparatively in the light of the preceding empirical study and in the light of the 'ideal' human rights policy outlined above. The underlying question in this analysis is whether everything possible was done after taking the political situation into account. The conclusion represents a departure from the main body of the book, consisting of a reflection on the links between accountability and democratic consolidation.

The bulk of the research is based, first, on numerous interviews carried out in Uruguay and Chile between April 1991 and September 1991. Secondly, a systematic survey was made of all the major newspapers in Uruguay between 1983 and 1987 and a selection of press articles from the period between 1980–3 and 1987–9. The same was done for Chile, covering the period between October 1988 and January 1996. Thirdly, all relevant debates in the Chamber of Deputies and in the Senate in both countries were reviewed. Finally, a survey was conducted of the major political and legal periodicals from both countries as well as from the United States which focused on the general issues of transitional and democratizing politics or matters relating to human rights violations, truth, and justice.

PART I

Problems of Transitional Truth and Justice in Comparative Perspective and Human Rights Violations under Military Rule in Uruguay and Chile

Dictatorship is much more than brutal repression or a lack of political expression. It is something that is there day after day, year after year, impregnating everything until it invades the most intimate life of human beings . . . surrounded by the webs of a system which determines what we do and do not do, what we think, what we believe, what we dream and what we do not speak out.

Patricia Politzer, *Miedo en Chile*, 1990.

For the twelve years of the military dictatorship, the word *libertad* referred to nothing but a plaza and a prison . . . one in every eighty Uruguayans had a hood tied on his head while the rest, doomed to isolation and solitary confinement even when spared the pain of torture, wore invisible hoods as well. Fear and silence were mandatory. Hostile to any and all living things, the dictatorship poured cement over the grass in the plazas and felled or whitewashed every tree within its reach.

Eduardo Galeano, *The Hidden Wounds*, 1993.

*

If asked what they want, their answer will be: a decent country, respectful of family life and patriotism. But ask them what they don't want and you'll soon be able to understand their view of the world and the difficulties they encounter when they must govern in accordance with such hatreds.

Jacobo Timmerman, *Prisoner Without a Name, Cell Without a Number*, 1981.

Life is black or white. We chose it to be black, and that is it.

Military Refrain in Coronel Regino Burgueño, *Guerra No Convencional y Acciones Irregulares*, 1980.

1

Confronting Legacies of State Repression: Uruguay and Chile in Comparative Perspective

In Uruguay and Chile demands for truth and justice were a product of the experience of repressive military-authoritarian rule. In 1973 the military had seized power, determined to 'wipe out' the subversive threat which they saw as responsible for the breakdown of democratic order in both countries. The collective social impact of the repression which ensued was devastating. Seemingly arbitrary state violence and the use of repression deliberately to create a 'culture of fear' eroded collective identities, alienated the population from the public sphere, shrunk vital social and psychological spaces to a bare minimum, and produced a generalized 'social autism'.[1] These societies became paralysed by an 'inertia of fear'.[2]

Paradoxically, however, although a widespread policy of human rights violations initially has the effect of paralysing protest and dissent, eventually it brings about the initiation of the dynamics of opposition against its perpetrators. It was precisely under the 'reign of terror' that the universal 'metapolitical' language of human rights sowed the seeds for the destruction of fear, for the resurrection of civil society, and for the growth of opposition to repressive rule.[3] If the military coups of 1973 expressed 'a loss of the juridical meaning of society and not just a loss of the juridical sense of the military',[4] it was precisely the recovery of this 'juridical sense', of a commitment to the minimal definition of democracy, to the rule of law, and to basic human rights as ends in themselves, which represented the silver lining in the cloud of repressive rule.

If these regimes are subject to 'continuous processes of change and transformation',[5] one of the main triggers for their transformation is the response of the victims of human rights violations to the facts and the impact of violence. Focusing on violations makes the opposition both revolutionary and universal or non-partisan:

on the one hand, the defence of human rights indicts the regime system as a whole, not only the specific government committing the violations.[6] An opposition which is driven by a concern for human rights ultimately aims to defeat these regimes and not merely to reform them. Thus, the legal defence of basic rights becomes subversive of the authoritarian order: it is a political weapon in the struggle to limit violations under military rule by raising the political cost of repression, but it is also a tool to defeat the system of rule itself.[7] On the other hand, the human rights issue, being the non-partisan, non-violent, universal discourse of opposition *par excellence*, is crucial in uniting the opposition forces and giving them political force in the face of repression.[8]

The need to defend basic rights, once taken for granted, fundamentally changed pre-existing attitudes towards those rights and towards democracy. This was particularly true of the left, which altered its stance from rejecting the natural law concept of rights in favour of a socialist view of rights only realizable in a radically transformed socio-economic setting, to accepting and defending the concept of universally held rights and of liberal democratic rule.[9] Thus, the legacy of repressive rule was not only the unhappy assortment of cruel and inhumane acts described above, but the desire to overcome the horror of those acts.

The oppositions in both Uruguay and Chile were empowered by their countries' democratic tradition: the oldest and strongest in Latin America, comparing favourably with their most advanced European contemporary counterparts. The modern democratic political system in Uruguay was inaugurated at the end of the civil war between the rival Colorado and Blanco factions in 1904. These became the traditional parties which have dominated Uruguay's political life to the present. From 1904 onwards, Uruguay experienced almost uninterrupted civilian democratic rule up to the military coup of 1973. Even during the exceptional authoritarian Terra regime (1933–42), 'there was no torture, no murder, no political prisoners and little censorship'.[10] Similarly, the Uruguayan military was amongst the most innocuous in Latin America, demonstrating no political prominence from the end of the Civil Wars onwards.[11] Uruguayans took pride in their tradition, as the popular refrain 'como el Uruguay no hay' (there is no place like Uruguay) demonstrates.[12] They saw themselves as living in the Switzerland of Latin America, in 'a little world apart' from their more violent undemocratic neighbours.[13]

In Chile limited élite republican rule was inaugurated in 1830 with the 'Conservative Republic' of Diego Portales. Despite the authoritarianism of the 1833 Constitution, the limited and often repressive nature of early constitutional government, and sporadic armed conflicts, Chile saw the progressive consolidation of a disciplined competitive party system whose boundaries for participation became more democratic until the military coup of 1973. By the 1930s it was arguably a 'complete' democratic party system.[14] According to one study, Chile ranked fifth among the world's most democratic nations between 1900 and 1950.[15] Although more powerful and autonomous than in Uruguay, the military was similarly subordinate and loyal to the constitutional order.[16] Furthermore, the judiciary and the Supreme Court were among the most fiercely independent in the region; it is unique as the only self-selecting judiciary in Latin America.[17]

This tradition of which the military was also a part meant that as they tortured and disappeared 'enemies of the nation' the Armed Forces claimed to be defending the same values that the opposition represented. 'Had there been no tradition of the rights of man, no constitutional or statutory commitments for the right to security from torture, the practice of torture would not have constituted a violation.'[18] The military was backed by a complex system of beliefs based on traditional notions of the Armed Forces as an embodiment of the Nation and guarantors of national constitutions providing for military intervention, as well as on the more recently developed concepts of the National Security Doctrine (NSD), which, in their view, justified their repressive actions. None the less, they were also forced to respond to the moral opposition of human rights organizations, the Catholic Church, democratic parties, and the international community.[19] The self-proclaimed 'democratic' militaries in Uruguay and Chile found it increasingly difficult to legitimize arbitrary and illegal violence in the name of Christian and national democratic values.

It was also as a result of this tradition that demands for truth and justice were powerful and became central to the politics of transition and democratization. With the demise of these repressive regimes, the democratic opposition and successor democratic governments were confronted with the need to take on board the victims' demands for accountability.

The brutal repression unleashed by the military represented a radical departure form traditional peaceful methods of conflict mediation, even breaking the mould of 'traditional' authoritarian repression. This 'new' repression was illegal and clandestine. It violated even the stringent laws of the regimes. It was based on the systematic violation of human rights. It was covered by the protective mantle of official denial and impunity for the repressors. Thus, denial called for truth, impunity for justice.

Although there are an infinite number of ways in which these objectives can be pursued, much depends upon the histories and traditions of the peoples involved, and much depends on the power possessed by those who pursue these ends when the historical opportunity to redress past injustices arises. If the best way to reverse the balance of power between repressed and repressor is through truth-telling and justice, ironically the degree to which demands for truth and justice can be translated into political realities depends ultimately upon the power that the repressed possess *vis-à-vis* the repressors.

The historical opportunity arises when the deniers of truth and justice are defeated. However, the demise of the repressive regimes of Uruguay and Chile occurred in less than ideal conditions, namely through peaceful transitions consisting of a negotiation between equals. The outgoing military authorities which had violated human rights withdrew from government voluntarily and retained a high degree of power and autonomy. As a result, telling the truth and prosecuting human rights violations had a great potential for de-stabilizing the process of the violating authorities' withdrawal from power. Compromises were therefore inevitable.

An overview of various experiences with transitional truth and justice demonstrate that it is not only Uruguay and Chile which face difficulties in the pursuit of accountability. They are present even in the most favourable political circumstances.

Truth and Justice in Transitional Periods: An Overview

The most favourable transitions are those which impose insignificant political constraints on the pursuit of accountability. They may result from defeat of the repressive forces or regime in a war culminating in external occupation, from revolution, civil or guerilla war, spontaneous mass insurrection or regime collapse stemming from ideological disintegration. The nature of the armed conflict or collapse, the successor governments, and the policies selected to deal with the issue may differ, but in all cases the threat of reaction is minimal. Most of these cases demonstrate that where resistance is very weak and the new victors have massive political resources, an over-zealous pursuit of either truth or justice leads to the violation of due process. The defeat of the Vichy regime in France, of Germany and Japan at the end of

World War II, the collapse of *Salazarismo* in Portugal in 1974 and of *Somocismo* in Nicaragua in 1979, as well as the collapse of the communist regimes of Eastern European are examples.

In France, the Gaullists judged the whole Vichy State as illegitimate. Any material or moral help to the enemy was liable to attract the death penalty. All due process procedures were violated when punishing and persecuting collaborators. Moreover, in 1944 40,000 French citizens were killed by their compatriots and 150,000 were interned.[20]

Even these 'ideal' cases of absolute defeat did not make total truth and justice possible. In the case of Germany and Japan, only a minority of those guilty of crimes against humanity were actually tried and sentenced.[21] The crimes were barely matched by the punishment. Between 1959 and 1969 of the 1,000 cases presented in the German court, only 100 received life sentences, and by 1981, of the 6,000 convictions only 154 received life sentences.[22] De-Nazification was not very successful: as a Liberal Party parliamentarian in Germany recently claimed in 1985, of the 410 deputies elected in 1949, 57 were ex-Nazis, and before the October 1994 elections there were still Nazis in the Bundestag. Over 50 years later, the Israeli state is still attempting to prosecute Nazi war criminals and the task of Nazi-hunters continues. Furthermore, although the trials were politically and morally 'just', many observers have noted that they exercised *ex post facto* justice.[23] The War Crimes Tribunal for the Former Yugoslavia set up in May 1993 is legally sound, based on the Nuremberg precedent. Yet, the absence of full external occupation makes a difference as it 'will be difficult to gain custody over many of the accused'.[24] The genocide of the Tutsi and the slaughter of thousands of Hutu who worked with the Tutsi by the Hutu-led regime is also being investigated by the Yugoslavia War Crimes Tribunal, whose mandate was widened to include the Rwandan genocide. Again, the arrest of those against whom international arrest warrants have been issued will be difficult. Moreover, the upper echelons of the Hutu regime who planned the genocide have not been indicted because the collection of hard evidence is an arduous process.[25]

In Portugal and Nicaragua prosecution depended on the internal national balance of forces between the violators and the victims. The total defeat of the previous regime led to widespread purges in Portugal and the prosecution of thousands of people who had served the Somoza regime in Nicaragua. In the former case, the purges affected all sectors of public administration as well as the nationalized private sector. While institutionalized and administered from above, political parties were actually quite cautious on the issue, and it was the workers' and students' movements which pressed on with the process, leading to what were called the 'savage' or extra-judicial purges, dealing a very severe blow to the leading cadres of *Salazarismo*.[26] In Nicaragua, the Junta of the Government of National Reconstruction set up Special Tribunals in November 1979 which were dissolved in February 1981, having convicted 4,331 of the 6,000 charged with crimes under the Somoza regime. The trials suffered from a series of due process irregularities incompatible with Nicaragua's 'commitments under the American Convention on Human Rights'.[27]

In Eastern Europe similar processes were initiated with the collapse of Communist rule, also leading to a violation of due process.[28] In the former Czechoslovakia, despite President Vaclav Havel's opposition to purges, a commission was set up in February 1991, to review 15,000 StB (Statni Bezpečnast; the secret police) files and uncover the 140,000 secret police agents active between 1948 and 1989. A Lustration Law was passed in October 1991, which led to a purge more extensive than any 'since the aftermath of the Soviet invasion in 1968, when between 70,000 and 100,000 people were expelled from the Czechoslovak Communist Party and lost their jobs'. Both the commission and the law were criticized by the ILO for violation of international labour law standards.[29]

In Bulgaria and Poland only a milder 'creeping de-communization' took place, because of splits within the ruling UDF over the issue in the first case, and because of the return to power in 1993 of former communist forces in the latter case. Both processes suffered from due process problems. In Bulgaria, three disqualification laws passed in 1992 were heavily criticized because they were based on 'a concept of collective guilt, providing that people are to be punished not for specific acts but for belonging to specific groups'. Only one law was upheld by the Supreme Court, and it is estimated that it led to the removal of several thousand former communists from managerial positions.[30] In Poland, four of the six presented were rejected by the parliamentary commission concerned for legal reasons.[31]

As Rosenberg points out, these regimes were 'criminal regimes' in contrast to Latin America's 'regimes of criminals'.[32] Individualizing crimes thus becomes extremely difficult, particularly when whole societies were 'complicitous' with the former regime. Proving whether collaboration was forced or willing is well nigh impossible as it involves the discovery of people's intimate motivations. As one reporter put it: 'Should the cleaning lady who spied on her employer be punished? How about the people, and there were many, who played along with the secret police, acting as "informers", but relaying only worthless information?'[33]

Abuse of notoriously unreliable secret police files can turn truth-seeking into a farce, it can create unjust situations for innocent people when they are used in a struggle for power, and discredit the process of democratization. In Poland, for example, President Lech Wałęsa and the Speaker of the Parliament were among those named as police informers by the Minister of the Interior.[34]

Despite massive political resources to undertake this kind of process, the justice systems of these countries are often in dismal conditions, thus contributing to irregularity in prosecutions.[35] Furthermore, in the zeal to try to judge past leaders some charges have been so absurd that faith in the judiciary has been undermined.[36] In Germany, a *Study Commission for the Assessment of History and Consequences of the SED Dictatorship in Germany* was set up in March 1992 to study violations between 1949 and 1989.[37] Although initially unclear whether the findings would serve as a basis for prosecutions, these were subsequently undertaken. Thus, 'super-spy' Markus Wolf was put on trial for running agents in West Germany and charged with treason. Yet, as Rosenberg has noted, treason 'is usually interpreted as the betrayal of your country, not the failure to anticipate which will be your country so you can avoid betraying it.'[38] Romania's trial of four of Ceausescu's former aides initiated just five weeks after the revolution was also less concerned with procedure and more with satisfying a public desire for revenge.[39]

It is often difficult to deal with the worst period of violations most of which occurred immediately after the Communist takeover, and again prosecutions can be unjust.[40] Since it is often impossible to establish individual guilt for political crimes, leaders are judged on corruption charges. This is the case with prosecution of former President Todor Zhivkov and other leaders of the former Bulgarian regime. In Romania, defendants were actually expressly limited to testifying about their acts during the 1989 revolution in order to protect still powerful people involved in repression under Ceausescu.[41] Hungarian President Arpad Goncz refused to sign a bill to prosecute those suspected of crimes during the 1956 Revolution and the Constitutional Court declared that such a bill was unconstitutional for its retroactive punitive effects. None the less, the bill was passed.[42]

Transitions by collapse do not necessarily have to create further injustice, but justice may take years to achieve. The Bolivian attempt to deal with the legacies of repression of the García Meza regime, which collapsed in 1981, was more successful on juridical grounds. In April 1993, nine years after the initiation of proceedings against dictator General García Meza, the Bolivian Supreme Court found the General guilty on 36 charges, including sedition, insurrection, organizing armed groups, murder, and fraud. In March 1995, García Meza was extradited from Brazil to serve his sentence. He was sentenced to 234 years (meaning a maximum of 30 years) together with 47 collaborators with sentences ranging from one to 30 years. Six were acquitted. This was the first time in Latin American legal history that members of a *de facto* military government have been held accountable for usurping power and violating constitutional norms.[43]

At the opposite end of the spectrum to the situations outlined above, one finds transitions which offer little or no political latitude for the implementation of truth and justice policies. These may be gradual transitions in countries where violations were committed long before the transitions so that demands for accountability are not paramount. In Spain, for example, amnesties were passed, as human rights violations had been committed during the Civil War both by the forces of the outgoing regime and the forces in opposition to it, and so neither side wanted to explore the issue further. With few exceptions violations had practically ceased long before the transition took place and 'memories of previously costly conflicts seem to have been important in convincing decision making élites that the creation of a stable democracy was vastly more important than revenge or the narrow pursuit of partisan interests.'[44]

Brazil is another example of this kind of transition. The Sarney government, although elected, presented a high degree of continuity with the previous military regime, ruling 'in association' with elements of the Armed Forces to whom it was beholden. The military had withdrawn slowly and gradually and still retained a high degree of power. There was no desire on the part of the political élite or of the population to overturn the self-proclaimed military amnesty of 1979. Moreover, the worst violations had been committed fifteen years before and had affected only a small group in society. No official truth-telling was undertaken, a task which was left to Church leaders and an international religious organization.[45]

Although not a negotiated transition as the two above cases, the military in the Philippines played an important role in overthrowing the Marcos regime so that the Aquino government was not in a strong position to prosecute those who were effectively allies.

The government set up a Presidential Committee on Human Rights under Senator José Diákono. It carried out meticulous investigations, but it had no power to prosecute. After the military killed unarmed protesting farmers in 1987, the commissioners resigned, the commission lost credibility, and a subsequent commission fared even worse.[46]

Transitions which take place after prolonged armed conflict also present special problems. In some cases situations of armed conflict persist. In others, the new political authorities are still subordinate to, associated with, or dependant on the outgoing repressive authorities or military violators. Thus, there is often no clear break with the past. Civilian authorities may concentrate more on subordinating the military to their authority than on prosecuting human rights violations which may—or may not—be committed by both sides.

The problem of the continued presence of the repressive forces is apparent in the case of Namibia. Following the election of Nujoma of the South West Africa People's Organization (SWAPO) to the presidency in 1989 and the Declaration of Independence in 1990, the government attempted to deal with the issue of accountability and truth but faced great difficulties, having only a tenuous command over its Armed Forces. These, in the form of the People's Liberation Army of Namibia (PLAN), the armed wing of the SWAPO, were responsible for the violations committed during the war together with the South African Defence Forces (SADF).[47]

Often dealing with a massive task in a context of very limited resources, truth-seeking policies drag on and lose their impact. In Uganda, the National Resistance Army government of Yoweri Museveni, succeeding the genocidal regimes of Idi Amin (1971–9) and Milton Obote (1980–5), set up the Oder Commission of Inquiry in 1986 which was to investigate all crimes committed from independence in 1962 to 1986. After nine years and plagued by financial restraints, it has yet to complete its task which is now regarded with some popular scepticism and apathy.[48] Lack of credibility due to an absence of due process is a problem exemplified by Ethiopia, where truth-telling and prosecution have been attempted through a Special Prosecutor's Office (SPO) operating under the aegis of the Transitional Government which assumed power in May 1991 after the overthrow of Mengistu Haile Mariam. The trial of 1,315 former Dergue regime officials for their role in the 'Red Terror' is underway, and a historical record of the repression during the seventeen-year rule of Mengistu is being prepared.[49] However, one of the tasks of the SPO has been to review cases of people who have been held for over a year without formal charges or trial since the transition, and who are accused of human rights violations.[50]

In other cases, given guilt on both sides, amnesties are adopted to avoid uncomfortable revelations. In Nicaragua, where the Esquipulas Accords and Organization of American States (OAS) played an important role in the peace process, three amnesties were passed during the transition period in 1990 and 1991 by the Sandinista-led National Assembly and by the Chamorro government, leading to the release of over 1,000 prisoners of the Contra War. In this case, prosecutions were avoided in part due to the continued political weight of the Sandinista Army, which has also been accused of human rights violations during the Contra War and since. Thus, if the first Nicaraguan transition, resulting from total victory in internal war, led to excesses on the side of 'justice', the second transition, a negotiated one in which the Chamorro-led Unión Nicaragüense de Oposición (UNO) coalition won and shared power with the Sandinistas, has led to an excess on the side of impunity.[51]

The search for truth and justice in transitions occurring after or even during prolonged armed conflict can be further complicated by the ethnic or religious nature of past or ongoing conflicts. The previous violating regime may have been identified with a particular ethnic or religious group and the victims will have been members of opposing groups. Prosecution may exacerbate divisions and lack impartiality, or solutions may consist merely in a reversal of who represses whom. Given that transitional truth and justice are often sought by civilian/military groups connected with or responsible for violations, given that these policies may be undertaken in contexts of continued strife, and given, moreover, that the outcome of the transition is often a far cry from democracy, the political use and abuse of truth commissions and trials is frequent and their credibility concomitantly questionable.[52]

An example of conflict divided along ethnic lines is in Sri Lanka, where Tamils, Sinhalese, and Muslims have fought since 1956. This strife culminated in a civil war in 1983, with government forces and civil militias of Sinhalese and Muslims pitted against the Liberation Tigers of Tamil Eelam (LTTE). Both sides are responsible for committing human rights violations. The electoral victory of the People's Alliance (PA) in August 1994 on a platform of accountability for human rights and an end to the civil war led to negotiations and the formation of three Truth Commissions in November 1995 to investigate disappearances and other violations.

The latter have been criticized for not being comprehensive enough, for omitting the consideration of a variety of violations. At the time of writing, the outcome of these investigations and the question of prosecution is still to be determined.[53]

In the case of Rwanda, the defeat of the Hutu regime by the Rwanda Patriotic Front (RPF) in July 1994 led to a national attempt to undertake trials. As in Uganda, justice has suffered from a lack of resources in the face of a monumental task. An estimated 145,000 people were involved actively in the killings. Lack of human resources has led the Rwandan government to request the European Union to send 600 judges to assist in the process. Given these severe limitations, minimum standards of detention have been violated, with an estimated 27,000 people imprisoned by mid-1995, and there has been a failure to comply with due process.[54] Moreover, the new Rwandan Patriotic Army (RPA) is itself guilty of violating the rights of the Hutu not only during the war against the genocidal government forces but also after taking power.

Externally monitored solutions to armed conflict and legacies of human rights violations can have a real impact as well as avoid some of the pitfalls of national solutions, which may be hostage to the difficulties outlined above. Rwanda's truth-telling process, for example, is the only example of such a process undertaken and financed solely by international non-governmental organizations. The Commission of Investigation on Human Rights Violations in Rwanda since October 1990 was set up in 1993, and the release of its report in Europe and Rwanda had a great impact on French and Belgian policies towards the country and the conflicts they had also been involved in.[55]

In El Salvador, the issues of truth and justice were dealt with by a United Nations-sponsored peace process which included a comprehensive human rights accord signed in July 1990 and provided for the establishment of an Ad Hoc Commission to purge the military of corrupt and abusive officers and of a Commission on the Truth to investigate past abuses. The report issued in March 1993 was unique in that it included the names of over 40 officers and eleven members of the Frente Farabundo Martí de Liberación Nacional (FMLN) responsible for gross human rights violations, because it was a part of the process of ending armed insurgency and not undertaken once power had been transferred to new authorities, and because it represented 'the first time since the Nuremberg and Tokyo trials following World War II that foreign, rather than national figures, investigated past episodes of violence in a sovereign country'.[56]

Only days after its release, the Salvadorean Assembly voted a Law of General Amnesty for the Consolidation of Peace, placing all those named beyond the reach of the law. President Cristiani rejected it as unfair and the Supreme Court claimed it lacked objectivity. The military closed ranks after the publication of the report and when Misión de Observadores de las Naciones Unidas en El Salvador ONUSAL finally left the country in May 1995, no reparations had been made because of their refusal to co-operate with enquiries.[57]

In Guatemala, an estimated 50,000 mostly indigenous people have been killed and another 45,000 disappeared since 1980, the highest such toll in Latin American. 'On a regional scale, for every victim in Uruguay there were 10 in Chile, 100 in Argentina and 300 in Guatemala.'[58] The human rights issue was also at the heart of the UN-mediated negotiations between the government and the Unidad Nacional Revolucionaria Guatemalteca (UNRG). In March 1994 both parties signed an agreement to create a UN-monitored human rights team, the Misión de las Naciones Unidas en Guatemala (MINUGUA), to constrain the activities of security forces and strengthen domestic human rights institutions. The government promised not to promote an amnesty, to modify the penal code to include human rights violations, not to initiate prosecution of violations, but to permit individuals to take their cases to court. An agreement not to publish the names of the violators was reached. Attorney-General Valladares began to investigate human rights violations in 1994.

With the failed *auto-golpe* (self-coup) by President Serrano in May 1993, the human rights ombudsman León Carpio was elected to complete the Presidential term. Initially, he vigorously investigated and denounced human rights violations, a first in Guatemalan history. However, 'lacking a political party base, the new president appears to have felt so strong a debt to the officers who allowed him to assume the presidency that he [was] loath to confront them on these issues'.[59]

The Honduran transition also involved internationally sponsored solutions and monitoring. The Esquipulas Accords governing the Central American peace process provided for the creation of a National Commissioner for the Protection of Human Rights through the National Reconciliation Commission. The Commissioner published a report on disappearances under military rule between 1981 and 1984 with the support of non-governmental organizations, of President Callejas and his successor in 1994, President Reina, a respected human rights lawyer.[60] The Inter-American

Court of Human Rights (IACHR) also took up Honduran cases of disappearances due to pressure from Honduran and US non-governmental human rights organizations. It found Honduras responsible for a deliberate plan to disappear people which claimed 140 victims between 1981 and 1984 and ordered the government to pay damages to the families of the disappeared. This unprecedented litigation represented an 'enormously valuable experience in the use of inter-governmental mechanisms for the protection of human rights and reflected prolonged co-ordinated efforts by relatives of the disappeared and local and international human rights organizations.'[61]

What the three cases outlined above also demonstrate, however, it that externally monitored solutions can be a double-edged sword, particularly when the repressors are not defeated. On the one hand, international participation can ensure impartiality and yield positive results. In El Salvador, for example, 'the fallout from the report combined with the pressure by the UN and the Clinton Administration, prompted Cristiani to inform the Secretary General of his decision to remove the remaining officers by the end of June 1993'. On the other hand, solutions which are not totally generated from within and lack a strong domestic élite constituency may not endure once international monitors have departed.[62]

In Guatemala, for example, the military are still extremely powerful and violence has not ended with the transition. Guatemala's military have successfully fended off investigations and prosecutions by selectively killing judges and police officers.[63] In 1994 an estimated 14,156 people suffered from human rights violations mainly at the hands of the Comites Voluntarios de Defensa Civil (CVDC), a 500,000-strong paramilitary force.[64] The Honduran military also continues to resist attempts to do justice, and is suspected of murdering key witnesses.[65]

Moreover, truth-telling and prosecution in particular are particularly thorny issues in the cases of Guatemala and Honduras and in other Central American countries, as they implicate US intelligence officials who were directly involved in the policy of disappearances.[66] This highlights the importance of international support for truth and justice policies in less powerful countries. Coalitions between truth- and justice-seeking domestic and international constituencies can produce very positive results. These coalitions are, of course, less likely to occur if international powers are themselves implicated in the violations.

All of the above cases also demonstrate another fundamental point: namely, that 'fair' policies of truth and justice depend upon the answer to the question 'Transition to what?' The less democratic the regime arising from the transition, the more likely it is that accountability for past violations degenerates into revenge and produces further injustice. As noted above, in many of these cases the capacity to implement positive truth and justice policies is severely limited by the nature of the regime implanted after the transition. Clearly, the further one gets from a stable and minimally functioning democratic outcome, the more likely it is that truth and justice policies become instruments of revenge or power politics, causing further abuses.

Restrictions on the search for truth and justice are also found in transitions where the forces of the violating regime suffer only a partial collapse or defeat, are replaced by opposition successor regimes, but still retain control of armed power. Collapse can occur by defeat in an external war and/or by a powerful opposing faction within the military élite defeating the previously dominant ruling faction. The two cases that fit this category are the Argentine and the Greek cases. Both were also transitions to democracy. Interestingly, these are the cases which have, at least initially, gone furthest in the prosecution of those responsible for directing human rights violations.

In Argentina, the national humiliation of defeat in the Malvinas War in 1982 led to the demise of the military government and its replacement with the opposition Radical government of President Alfonsín. The military's self-amnesty was annulled, a truth-telling Nunca Más (Never Again) commission was appointed by the President. Finally, a special tribunal was established which tried and sentenced the leaders of the ruling military juntas. After military rebellions which reached a pitch in December 1986, however, the Alfonsín administration passed a Punto Final or Full Stop law which placed a 60-day limit on initiation of new cases. This did not resolve the problem, as 400 new cases were taken to court in that period. In April 1987 the so called Easter Week Rebellion took place, in which an amnesty was called for. In June of that year the Due Obedience Law was passed. In October 1989 President Menem pardoned 280 military officers and accused left-wing subversives. The Junta members were finally pardoned in May 1990.[67]

In Greece, defeat in the Cyprus war in 1974 also led to the collapse of the Colonels' regime. Unlike Argentina, however, the punishment of the regime leadership was condoned by the generals in the Armed Forces who had been politically subordinated to the colonels. The first trial in 1975 convicted 32 officers with sentences ranging from 5 months to 28 years. This is the single most successful case of accountability. There was no amnesty and some of these criminals are still in gaol.[68]

Finally, much less favourable to those pursuing truth and justice than the above, are those transitions which are negotiated between the outgoing authorities and the opposition. In these situations the repressors are not defeated and retain a high degree of control over the successor regime. In the words of one observer, these are situations where the powerful are weak and the powerless influential.[69] Paraguay and South Africa as well as subjects of study of this book, Uruguay and Chile, fall into this category.

In Paraguay, the fall of Stroessner and the transition to elected rule led the House of Deputies and Senate to create human rights commissions to investigate old abuses and new crimes in June 1989. They also called on the Attorney-General to initiate trials against those responsible for torture, disappearances, and other crimes, as well as those who covered up the crimes. President General Rodríguez did not co-operate with these initiatives despite an initial commitment to truth and justice; in 1990 he vetoed two bills which proposed to give the commissions the power to subpoena witnesses. Moreover, the Minister of Justice and Labour was removed from his post after promising the UNHCR full co-operation in the prosecution of human rights violations.

Gratitude to Rodríguez for getting rid of Stroessner, the continued political influence of the Armed Forces, the lack of independence of the judiciary, and the fact that Paraguay has little experience with democracy and the expectations that experience generates in people, has made prosecution difficult. On the other hand the fact that most of the violations were committed by the police and not the military means that prosecutions will not appear as threatening to the armed institution as they otherwise would. In May 1992 four high-ranking police officers were convicted of the torture and murder of an individual in 1976 and sentenced to 25 years' imprisonment. A retired army general was convicted of covering up the crime and sentenced to five years. With the election of Wasmosy in 1994, there was renewed hope for prosecution, as the President was opposed to an amnesty.[70]

In South Africa, the African National Congress (ANC) did not pass the two-thirds threshold for a majority in Congress; the transition was negotiated by the Transitional Executive Council which also negotiated the Constitution, creating a partnership between National Party (NP) and ANC moderates. An amnesty was agreed to in large part because the ANC also committed crimes, and even though most of the violence of the past years is the responsibility of the security forces, trials would also affect ANC members.[71] In Mandela's words 'The whole spirit of negotiations would be against taking revenge on any particular individual. You think of a settlement as involving the entire community in support of the settlement. Otherwise it will be an intolerable situation.'[72]

President Mandela announced the establishment of a Commission of Truth and Reconciliation in May 1994. After wide-ranging consultations with different social sectors, the National Reconciliation and Unity Act became law in July 1995 with the support of the National Party and the abstention of the Inkatha Freedom Party permitting the formation of the Commission.[73] The Commission will work for 18 months which can be extended by another 6 months. A report must be issued within the 3 months following the end of its work. It will consider all crimes committed between March 1960 and December 1993.[74]

In an innovative solution to the problem of silence and amnesty, the South African process has made a linkage between truth and justice: it ensures an amnesty for all involved in the crimes including the ANC, but only if confessions are made to the Commission.[75] The powers of the Commission are also more wide-ranging than those found in either Uruguay or Chile, as it can subpoena witnesses and carry out searches and seizures and legal action can be taken against those who refuse to declare before the Commission.[76] This will ensure that the code of silence among perpetrators will be broken and the fate of the victims can be known by all.[77] Moreover, names of perpetrators will be published in the *National Gazette*. Although these measures will ensure that the truth is known, the commission generally removes the right of victims to make civil claims against those who apply for amnesty. The positive influence of this model is already apparent: in January 1996 a number security force and former government officials, including former Defence Minister Magnus Malan, were indicted for training a force responsible for the massacre of a number of people in 1987 in KwaZulu-Natal.[78] These individuals will have to go before the Truth Commission for the amnesty to be applied.[79]

Semi-Restricted, Peaceful Transitions to Democratic Rule: The Cases of Uruguay and Chile

Understanding the nature of different types of transitions and their outcomes is necessary for an *a priori* assessment of the limitations imposed on successor governments in dealing with the legacies of state repression. Yet it is in and of itself insufficient. Given the unique historical and political-cultural characteristics of each country, there are ultimately as many real transitions as there are transition types. This discussion therefore needs to move from the realm of the general to the realm of the particular, focusing on the dynamics of the struggle for truth and justice within the context of the specific processes of transition and democratization in Uruguay and Chile. It does not attempt to construct an overarching theory of transitional truth and justice, but rather to tell two parallel stories in detail.[80]

While both Uruguay and Chile fit into the category of negotiated transitions, they met with differing levels of success in their attempts to implement policies of truth and justice. Each attempt to deal with such legacies was ultimately shaped by historically and country-specific conditions. Any examination of attempts by successor regimes to come to terms with the past therefore has to take into account the specific and different political, institutional, and legal legacies of repressive rule and the varying specific political conditions prevailing both in the transitional period and under the first successor regime.

As far as the legacies of military rule are concerned, the following elements have to be taken into account:

- the differing nature and strength of the human rights movement inherited from that period;
- the differing amount of international support for truth and justice received by each country under military rule;
- the differing power of state autonomous institutions in favour of truth and justice;
- the differing nature of inherited constitutional legislation as it affected the human rights issue;
- the judicial precedents for prosecution inherited from military rule.

All of these inherited factors conditioned future options.

Regarding the dynamics of the transition processes themselves and the articulation of the human rights issue within them, the following factors conditioned the ability to deal with the issue:

- the nature of the relationship of the opposition parties with the human rights organizations during the transition;
- the degree of political party opposition unity, links with the human rights movement, and commitment to the human rights issue in the transitional period as shaped by restored or transformed party systems;

- the transitional legal and constitutional setting;
- the nature and power of the military institution in the process of withdrawal;
- the role played by state autonomous institutions such as the Catholic Church in the human rights movement during the transition;
- the articulation of the issue of human rights violations by the main actors shaped the progress of truth and justice in the period;
- the nature of the military's relations with the party or coalition which won the transitional democratic elections and their ability to resist truth and justice.

All of the above provide a necessary background to understanding the issue in the democratic period.

Under democratic rule, varying performance in a number of key areas shaped the success or failure of truth and justice in Uruguay and Chile. Differing degrees of success and failure were conditioned by the differing ability to neutralize the power of those who committed the violations and their allies, not allowing their resistance to be permitted to cross the fragile line from predictable opposition to institutionally threatening contestation; on the differing ability of the government to neutralize those who demanded the realization of 'total' justice and truth, a demand impossible to realize in the best of circumstances, a demand which must be given a voice and at the same time be politically contained.

The level of commitment of the democratically elected executive to pursuing such policies actively and the presidential commitment to truth and justice were also extremely important. This is particularly the case in such politically restrictive situations where skilful political craft and leadership qualities become essential, where leadership is 'about making things happen that otherwise might not happen, and preventing things from happening that ordinarily would happen'.[81] Similarly, the unity of the parties committed to truth and justice was also very important, as was the support of strong human rights organizations or a committed church hierarchy in eliciting success. Thus, for example, a lack of party unity in the Uruguayan context and the presence of party discipline and unity in Chile helped to bring about a more successful outcome in Chile.

It is important to note at this stage that in the case of Uruguay, the restoration of the electoral and party system promoted fragmentation, discouraged parties of principle, and reduced internal programmatic consistency. The political parties represented not so much coherent ideological groups as agglomerations of simultaneously common and conflicting interests. The electoral and party system, unique and veritably baroque, is governed by the Double Simultaneous Voting System (DSVS) and the Ley de Lemas or 'factions' law introduced in 1910.[82] The law permits the creation of sub-parties under the umbrella of the two traditional parties. The Colorado and Blanco or National parties were *lemas*, and all subparties within them *sub-lemas*. Each of these *sub-lemas* is permitted to present individual lists for the presidential and primary elections. According to the DSVS system, legislative and executive elections are held at the same time, so that participating parties present *listas* or lists including presidential and legislative candidates simultaneously. The winner in presidential elections is the leader of the *sub-lema* winning the most votes. It is possible for the *lema* which wins most overall votes to lose to the opposition, if one of the latter's *sub-lemas* receives a higher number of votes than any of the *sub-lemas* under the other *lema*.[83] This resulted in increased fragmentation as each *lema* contained innumerable *sub-lemas* which, although generally identified with the greater party, represented specific and particularistic interests.[84] Because of its peculiar nature, the Uruguayan party system has been seen as a two-party system, a multi-party system, and even, because of the electoral domination of the Colorado party, as a dominant party system.[85] The first real challenge to the two traditional parties only emerged in the early 1970s with the formation of the left-wing coalition, the *Frente Amplio*.[86] None of the above mentioned characteristics boded well for an issue whose successful resolution required party unity, adherence to principle, and programmatic clarity.

Chile's party system by contrast, which was not restored but transformed under military rule, is dominated by disciplined programmatic parties, which eventually brought about the creation of a united opposition to authoritarian rule, not least because victory in the 1988 plebiscite depended upon such unity. The need to unite to defeat the regime, the nature of the electoral law, the ideological approximation between the two major opposition parties, the Socialists and the Christian Democrats, and finally the impact of the political culture of left pragmatism on the opposition during exile, promoted a cohesive, unified, programmatically consistent opposition. Furthermore, the electoral law of 1989 encouraged coalition-building, unification, and cohesion among the major parties, and discriminated against minor parties.[87]

Related but separate is the issue of political culture. Although often hard to pin down, political culture is extremely important in day-to-day political management.[88] Skidmore, for example, emphasized the importance of the 'conciliatory strain in Brazilian political culture' as a factor leading to a popular acceptance of the military's self-amnesty.[89] In Uruguay and Chile the inherited political culture was democratic. Hence the importance attached to truth and justice in the transitional and democratizing periods; hence the attachment to due process and the rule of law. In Uruguay, however, pact-making traditions formed and reflected a political culture with an aversion to extremes: accommodation and compromise in the *sociedad amortiguadora* were prized political virtues.[90] It has been said of the Uruguayan political system, that it tends not to provide solutions but rather accommodations.[91] This tendency is largely a product of a long tradition of pact-making and accommodation between the two traditional parties, a hallmark of Uruguayan élite politics, which permitted the Colorado party to consistently win elections and the Blancos to none the less consistently share power.[92] Thus, 'the institution of the pact facilitated co-existence on a basis of division of the prerequisites of power'.[93] In this small *país de cercanías*, élite politics were privatized, almost as if between members of the same extended family.[94] Yet, despite accommodation, politics were intensely fought. Political campaigns were seen to be 'excessively open, noisy and bothersome.'[95] Thus, the Uruguayan political culture of accommodation and pact-making was perhaps less conducive to truth and justice than the Chilean emphasis on legalism and formality.[96]

The constitutional, juridical, or judicial context must also be taken into account. Policies were harder or easier to implement depending on the existence of legal or constitutional impediments to truth and justice, the ability or willingness of the government to get rid of any such constraints, and of the judiciary to pursue justice. In Chile, for example, the implementation of truth and justice policies was made more difficult (and in some areas impossible) due to this kind of restriction. The constitution passed by the military limited the democratizing government's power to pursue truth and justice, as did other authoritarian legislation, such as the amnesty law of 1979 and varied anti-terrorist legislation.

The power and role played by extra-governmental institutions in favour of truth justice and policies was also critical. The role of the Catholic Church—which, as noted by some authors, can play a central role in pressing for respect for human rights under military rule, creating a powerful truth and justice lobby, and contributing to the 'resurrection of civil society' and the power of the human rights movement—is examined.[97] In Uruguay, for example, the capacity of the Church to press effectively for truth and justice was very limited due to the historical domination of Batllismo, the secular, anti-clerical political philosophy of Uruguay's dominant political leader. The latter reduced the influence of the Catholic Church in the political arena from the beginning of the twentieth century.[98]

In Chile the reverse was true. The Church has been extremely powerful and has legitimately intervened in politics throughout the history of the Republic. The historically prominent role of the Church in Chile survived and even thrived under the dictatorial regime. It played a crucial role in the human rights drama, enabling the democratic opposition to respond to human rights violations and encouraging it to form a commitment to truth and justice.[99]

The presentation and the nature of the human rights policies themselves were also very important, as this affected their success or failure. In Uruguay, policies were not clear-cut and did not have pre-determined and defined objectives. They did not separate truth-telling, which aimed at a political, moral, and institutional judgement, from judicial prosecution, which aimed at the prosecution of individuals. Thus, the failure of one was linked to the failure of the other. Attempting institutional judgement in the courts or prosecution by truth raised the levels of dangerous military contestation unbearably. No time-limit was set on the truth-telling policy. The truth must be known quickly if it is to have the desired effect of reconciliation. It has been noted that once the euphoria of democratic restoration wears off, people are less willing to tolerate uncertainty stemming from backward-looking policies when they are preoccupied with living standards and other more 'immediate' pressing issues.[100] The judicial policy did not define which cases were to be prosecuted and the criteria for judgement. This is necessary to prevent the loss of political control over the judicial process.[101] All the factors outlined above shaped the outcome of the truth and justice sagas in Uruguay and Chile. The next chapter will turn to the repressors and examine the legacy which Uruguay and Chile faced on the eve of the transition to democracy.

2

The Dynamic of Military Repression in Uruguay and Chile: Ideology and Resistance to Truth and Justice

Introduction

When the Armed Forces of Uruguay and Chile seized power in 1973, they came armed with a military–political project to restore order through the elimination of a 'subversive threat' which, in their view, had brought their countries to the brink of chaos.[1] The presence of this arbitrarily and nebulously defined subversive threat provided the justification for an extensive and illegal repression for which there was no precedent in these countries. It resulted in human rights violations which were 'systematic, institutional, massive, and unheard of' in the history of both countries.[2]

Military intervention received crucial support from civilian élites. The inability of past civilian governments to resolve political as well as economic crises and to respond to escalating social demands, led to the growing abandonment of democratic values by the political élite and the emergence of disloyal oppositions. Intense fears and hatreds generated by political polarization and the emergence of armed violence broke down the previously immutable limits on political action. Thus, the tacit pact to exclude the military from conflict resolution effectively came to an end.[3]

The interventions of 1973 demonstrated a 'boundary change' in military aims; they transcended the 'moderating pattern' of temporary mediation between conflicting civilian élites.[4] The Armed Forces shared the widespread doubts about the capacity of the traditional political systems to restore economic growth and put an end to political violence. Buttressed by the 'new professionalism' resulting from long-term processes of institutional modernization, growing institutional autonomy, and ideological homogeneity, liberated by the concomitant 'emancipation from civil society', increased material capacity and ideological self-confidence, and the material and moral backing from the United States, the military responded to the breakdown of democratic order with an autonomously defined repressive agenda.[5]

Thus, despite civilian backing for and participation in the authoritarian regimes, these élites had no control over the military's definition of what constituted subversion, nor over the systems and methods used to repress that threat. The 'brumairean moment' gave the military a free rein to define the aims of their rule according to their own institutional logic. In the words of the Uruguayan military, 'The mission of the Armed Forces is, in the final instance, political. It is not party political, not class oriented or partial: it consists fundamentally in the defence of essential and permanent values which lie are at the heart of the existence of the Homeland.'[6] Civilians may have thought that intervention was totally democratic, aiming only at saving the countries from 'marxist totalitarianism'. But the military 'went to war against marxism and the most important thing was to annihilate, I repeat, annihilate marxism and not to restore democracy. And the annihilation of marxism could not be achieved in a democratic climate; the annihilation of marxism and of everyone that considered themselves pro-marxist, neutral, luke-warm, undefined, was carried out with the brutal methods of a repression which knew no limits.'[7]

This will be a stage-setting chapter. It will describe the nature of the repression unleashed by the military in Uruguay and Chile, and it will examine why the Armed Forces chose to implement a repressive strategy based on the systematic violation of human rights and the military's justification for this repression. The aim is to permit an understanding of the nature of the danger faced when attempting to implement policies of truth and justice by understanding the military's ideological and institutional resistance to truth and justice in the transition to and consolidation of democratic rule in each country.

Repression under Military Rule

The reasons for military intervention in Uruguay and Chile were multi-causal and very complex, and it is not the aim of this chapter to describe them in detail. Briefly, the crisis in the Uruguayan welfare state stemming from the stagnation of the economy from the 1950s onwards and the failure of the increasingly fragmented traditional party system to deal with its effects led to a general loss of faith in the political system, an increase in ideological extremism, trade union mobilization and armed violence.[8] In the early 1960s armed violence emerged with the Tupamaro guerrilla movement, becoming 'a source of trauma and insecurity in a country where political violence had all but disappeared in the course of the twentieth century.'[9] In the labour sector, strikes and mobilization escalated with the creation of the Confederación Nacional de Trabajadores (CNT) in 1966, and with the unification of the unarmed left within the FA coalition in 1971 which challenged the political hegemony of the traditional Blanco and Colorado parties.[10]

The authoritarian civilian Colorado governments of Pacheco Areco (1966–71) and Bordaberry (1971–3) responded to these challenges with increasingly militarized repressive policies which led to growing military intervention in political life. Although the Armed Forces were involved in repression from 1968 onwards, the militarization of the state made a qualitative leap in September 1971 when, after the mass escape of over 100 Tupamaros from the Punta Carretas gaol, Pacheco Areco decreed that the military should have total control over the battle against subversion.[11] The Estado Mayor Conjunto (ESMACO), and the Fuerzas Conjuntas (FFCC), were created to centralize military and intelligence operations between the three branches. From December 1971 the Junta de Comandantes (JCJ), was charged with directing the anti-subversive operations.[12]

The process of militarization was consummated in February 1973, when the Boisso Lanza Pact between President Bordaberry and the military command gave the military direct power with the creation of the Consejo de Seguridad Nacional (CSN), composed of the President, the Ministers of Defence, Interior, Foreign Relations and Economy, by the JCJ and by the ESMACO. Military power and autonomy grew, abetted by an authoritarian executive and unfettered by a severely debilitated judiciary.[13] The legislature was unable or unwilling to challenge this process. Despite resistance from the Frente Amplio, the traditional parties approved the repressive legislation which contributed to bringing the military to power. The parliament was easily dissolved when, in an act of democratic defiance, it refused to comply with the military's demand that one of its Frente representatives be stripped of immunity for subversive activities. Thus, with the dissolution in June 1973, the rule of law had ceased to exist, torture had already become systematized in the military prisons, and power was entirely in the hands of an executive under military tutelage.[14]

Unlike the 'slow motion' coup in Uruguay, military intervention in Chile took the form of an extremely violent 'lightning' coup. Despite the absence of an armed guerrilla force, the level of perceived threat was much greater in Chile as the process of political radicalization and polarization had penetrated deeper into the social fabric. The political system, already strained by a long-term process of substantive democratization and economic reforms, made the transition from 'partial to total crisis' with the 1970 election of a radical socialist government.[15] Between 1970 and 1973 the Popular Unity government ruled with a commitment to pursue the peaceful road to socialism, implementing ambitious programmes of agrarian reform, nationalization, and social mobilization which challenged the very foundations of the capitalist state. It expanded the limits of liberal democratic legality to breaking-point, bringing it into conflict with the judiciary, the Constitutional Tribunal, and the increasingly ideologized and disloyal opposition of the right and centrist PDC, finally provoking the breakdown of the state of compromise.[16] The government was caught in the cross-fire between an increasingly aggressive reaction from a traditional élite which 'felt itself on the verge of extinction', and a radical minority which favoured the faster and less peaceful armed path to socialism.[17] The Armed Forces became involved in the conflict. They were called on by the government to put down strikes, to repress illegal armed activity on the left. President Allende requested that they mediate the conflict between the government and the opposition in Congress. The right actively encouraged them to depose the PU government.

When the military intervened in September 1973, they therefore claimed that they were doing so 'with the patriotic commitment to restore the Chilean essence, justice and the institutions . . . destroyed by the intromission of a dogmatic and excluding ideology, inspired by the foreign principles of marxism–leninism'. Although there was no overt armed guerrilla force, they were convinced that they faced a powerful but hidden subversive army and were ready to take radical action to destroy it.[18]

In both Uruguay and Chile, military repression was made possible through the creation of a coercive legal framework which eliminated judicial protection and guarantees of due process, destroyed executive accountability, abolished legislatures, and established military jurisdiction over a wide range of civilian offences. More or less permanent states of exception were used to 'bypass legal limits on [military] power without ever departing from formal constitutional rule'.[19]

In Uruguay, four basic measures permitted the institutionalization of a 'permanent state of exception in which the Executive acted with impunity, and which gave the systematic violation of human rights a legal framework'.[20] These were the Medidas de Pronta Seguridad (MPS), the suspension of individual guarantees, the continuous declaration of a state of internal war and siege, and the Ley de Seguridad Interna del Estado y Orden Pública (LSE). The MPS were decreed in 1968 and 1969 by the government of Pacheco Areco to repress strikes, permit the implementation of a harsh economic stabilization programme, and to put down the guerrilla movement. They limited the right to strike, to hold meetings, and freedom of speech, restricted the right to judicial due process, habeas corpus, and increased police powers and weakened those of the legislature. The judiciary lost the right to review executive orders for arrest for 'reasons of national security' and it became impossible to know who had been detained and where. Individual guarantees were suspended in August 1970, in September and November 1972, and March 1973 to facilitate the defeat of the Tupamaros.

The state of siege was first decreed in August 1970, and renewed in April 1972 and May 1973. This state permitted preventive detainment, limited habeas corpus, derogated the inviolability of domicile, the right of assembly, association, and speech, and extended the time that an individual could be held before being presented to a magistrate. In April 1972 the parliament voted through the state of internal war, a juridical concept not contemplated in Uruguayan constitutional law, in response to the murder of four policemen accused by the Tupamaros of belonging to the right-wing death squad or Esquadrón de la Muerte. Under the state of war the judiciary and the parliament lost all control over arrests and ordinary courts ceased to have jurisdiction over civilians accused of subversion. The state of war ended in June 1972, and was replaced by the LSE in July 1972. This law also gave the military courts jurisdiction over civilians. All these measures were used abusively, far beyond the letter of the law. Their application 'annulled or rendered ineffective all the procedures established by law to protect human rights and fundamental freedoms'.[21]

With the coup in June 1973, the parliament and the CNT were dissolved, all parties and movements considered to be of the left were declared illegal, and the military intervened in the state university. The Armed Forces consolidated the repressive legal framework through a series of Institutional Acts. These suspended the elections planned for November 1976, declaring 'the incompatibility of social peace and the free activity of the Political Parties'. They gave the military the 'direct competence and responsibility for the preservation of Internal Security', allowing them to appoint the President and the members of the Supreme Court, the Electoral Court, and the Administrative Tribunal. They put the 19 departmental governments under the control of the executive. They prohibited all candidates and elected officials belonging to party lists labelled marxist or pro-marxist, those electorally associated with the latter, all presidential and vice-presidential candidates and parliamentarians and finally, members of all the party committees which had participated in the elections of 1966 and 1971 from participating in political activities for 15 years.

10,000 citizens were thus deprived of their political rights. The civil service was purged, civil servants were deprived of security of tenure, and police records were kept on everyone. In a country in which more than 200,000 out of 2,700,000 inhabitants worked for the public sector, this political control acquired a totalitarian character and had a devastating impact on civil and political freedoms. Finally, the judicial system was subordinated to the executive, following the dictum that when it is not possible to 'conquer judges, one changes the Law'.[22]

In Chile, the authoritarian legal framework was set up after the coup. As in Uruguay, it was based on the extreme concentration of power in a military-controlled executive and the continuous application of various states of exception, through which the 'democratic orientation of the state was replaced by another which buttressed the coercive apparatus of the state and reinforced authoritarianism as a system of government'.[23] Power was concentrated in the executive immediately after the coup, when the Government Junta assumed constituent, legislative, and executive powers.[24] Unlike Uruguay, where power was administered collegially by the three branches, the army and its commander General Pinochet progressively ruled supreme over the Junta, gradually eliminating all military opposition to one-man rule.[25] In June 1974 General Pinochet was made President of the Junta and Supreme Chief of the Nation, and in December 1974 he became President. By 1975 General Pinochet had the power to legislate and to determine the application of a state of siege. The government's intelligence service answered only to him, becoming a 'praetorian guard'. Thus, the Executive was personalized in the dual figure of the President and Commander-in-Chief of the Armed Forces.[26]

The regime's first measures were to dissolve the Congress, outlaw the Popular Unity coalition parties, and all other parties were declared in recess. The electoral registers were destroyed and local authorities were taken over by military commanders. The public sector was purged and most employees lost job tenure. The Constitutional Court was dissolved, the military took charge of the universities, and the legal status of the Central Única de Trabajadores (CUT), was cancelled.[27]

For fifteen years the country was continuously under some form of state of exception. The state of siege was maintained from September 1973 to March 1978, between November 1984 and June 1985, and finally between September 1986 and January 1987.[28] The state of emergency ruled from 1978 to 1988. In April 1979 this state was supplemented by an anti-terrorist law which penalized attacks on morality and the social order, and in March 1981 a new 'state of risk of disturbance to internal order' was created. Both permitted harsher penalties than the milder state of emergency. The prior constitutional interpretations of these states was expanded so that penalties increased and emergencies could be defined preventively.

The Junta and later the President were solely responsible and unaccountable for actions undertaken under these states of exception. Personal freedoms and guarantees were severely restricted. In 1975 the period of arrest prior to appearance before a court was extended from 48 hours to five days.[29] Moreover, the state of siege was declared to signify a state of war, giving wartime military courts jurisdiction over civilians. The Consejos de Guerra, or War Councils, provided no guarantees of due process and were used to systematically repress the left between 1973 and 1977.[30]

After March 1978 the ordinary courts assumed jurisdiction over political cases. But the Supreme Court, given its hatred of the Allende regime, saw military rule 'as a lawfully based government, and that the military authorities were exercising a necessary ultimate power to uphold the law'.[31] It did not differentiate between the legality of a democratically elected government and one originating by force, and it was in agreement with the ideological foundations of the military regime.[32] From 1976 onwards, for example, the newly created preventive *habeas corpus* or the *recurso de protección,* although legally applicable, was consistently rendered impotent by the Supreme Court. Moreover, the courts renounced the right to review sentences passed by the military tribunals.[33]

The Chilean regime also altered the country's fundamental constitutional laws. The decrees contradicting the Constitution were legalized by a law which stated that all future legislation would have the force of modifying constitutional norms.[34] Between 1975 and 1976 the Junta passed four Constitutional Acts as part of a gradual and permanent progress towards establishing an institutional system which would strengthen the regime. The four acts served to codify existing practices and to broaden the powers of arbitrary decision-making. The concept of 'latent subversion', for example, was created so that it became unnecessary to prove the existence of a real armed threat.

Finally, in 1981 a new Constitution was inaugurated which created the legal framework for a 16-year transition to a 'protected democracy'. Unlike Uruguay, therefore, the Chilean military were able to transform the constitutional regime of their country. Despite the fact that both the Constitutional Acts and the 1980 Constitution guaranteed rights and access to due process and judicial protection, the continued application of states of exception, the wide powers of detention, and the ineffectiveness of the courts meant that rights were in no way protected. The judiciary were not permitted to question the 'foundations of the measures adopted by the authorities in the exercise of its faculties'. Under a state of siege *habeas corpus* was invalidated. From 1981 onwards, the military courts were again given wartime jurisdiction over civilians deemed to have committed acts of terrorism. In these courts there was no right to appeal. This brief analysis is perforce schematic because of the immense legislative undertaking of the regime. After only four months in power, for example, the military had passed almost 250 decree laws.[35] Overall, however, 'the broad powers assumed by the authorities enabled them to carry out a thorough reorganization of the institutional structure of the state. Those authorities were not subordinated to the Constitution and its laws, which enabled them to significantly limit the functions of the Judiciary and to remove from the political arena any groups that could represent divergent points of view.'[36]

Unlike Uruguay, where the repressive apparatus was integrated into the structure of the Armed Forces, in Chile repression was undertaken by centralized and autonomous security services which answered only to the President. In June 1974, the Dirección de Inteligencia Nacional (DINA) was created to 'properly coordinate repressive activities' and to avoid 'an excessive decentralization of repression which could lead to tensions between the different branches of the Armed Forces'. It was deemed that a 'general involvement of the Armed Forces in that task . . . could lead to a politicization with potentially serious consequences for political stability'.[37] The DINA became immensely powerful. The structures, operation, and laws governing it were secret. It was therefore free of all controls and protected from the interference of the courts, the greater part of the executive, the Junta, and the commanders of the other branches. The DINA answered only to General Pinochet.[38] It investigated and controlled even government and military personnel. The organization was funded both by the state and by its own commercial enterprises. Unlike the other intelligence services, which depended on the command of the different branches of the military, the DINA was a government service. 'It therefore had a greater capacity for centralized action as well as greater State resources and means.'[39] It became 'a superstate within Chile'.[40]

In August 1977 the DINA was replaced by the Central Nacional de Informaciones (CNI), largely as a result of international pressure. The CNI was established by a completely public decree and operated under the Ministry of the Interior. Legal authority for the maintenance of public order resided with the Carabineros or the Policía de Investigaciones (PI). Both of these entities developed its own intelligence services which operated alongside and at times in competition with the CNI.

Repression in Uruguay was characterized by a system of totalitarian control over the population ensured by the widespread use of mass, prolonged imprisonment and the systematic application of torture.[41] The system entailed the 'inviligation of society'. One in six out of the country's inhabitants were imprisoned.[42] Between 1972 and 1983, 50,000 out of 3 million inhabitants were detained and 5,000 were convicted of national security crimes.[43] One out of every five Uruguayans went into exile. All citizens were categorized A, B, or C according to their 'degree of danger'. Only A citizens were free from persecution and given a certificate of 'democratic faith'. Strict ideological controls were imposed on the educational system through centralization under a single government ministry.[44] A National Centre of Public Relations was launched, which carried out an incessant and pervasive propaganda campaign in favour of the military. Between 1970 and 1978 the totalitarian requirements of repression led to an increase in police and military personnel from 42,000 to 64,000.[45] Overall, owing to its extension in time and the number of people it affected, this system 'irradiated its effects throughout the whole of the Uruguayan population, leaving its mark upon each family, work-place and every kind of human group'.[46]

The detention centres used by the military were 'total institutions of a special kind' and were part of 'a larger network of institutionalized repression and intimidation aimed at specialized publics and at the population at large'. The prisons were centres for psychological destruction which aimed to break the inmate as an individual, to experiment with new forms of punishment, and to train their military guardians. Prison rules were militarized and similar to those used in concentration camps: 50 people died in or after release from prison, cancer rates were very high, many prisoners committed suicide, and 80 per cent were on tranquillizers.[47]

Through this system, 'the subjection of society through terror was aimed at, in order to paralyse all acts of opposition and resistance and, in this way, to discipline the social body and ensure a pattern of behaviour of tacit support'.[48] Well over a third of those imprisoned were re-detained. Most of those released were subject to being recalled by the military courts and were controlled by continued parole. Release did not represent a guarantee of future freedom. The families of the detained were for the most part not informed of their whereabouts, prisoners were mostly ignorant of where they were being held, and between 1975 and 1977 over 30 per cent were held incommunicado for the duration of their imprisonment.[49]

'All the people who were detained in Uruguay were tortured. There was nobody who was not tortured.'[50] Torture was used primarily as 'a political instrument. Apart from the immediate aim of extracting a confession of crimes as a means of interrogation, its final aim was the destruction of political opposition to the system.'[51] The military were careful to keep their victims alive: 70 per cent of the detained were subject to medically controlled tortures to ensure that the they did not die and to prepare them for renewed sessions. Doctors played an advisory role in psychological torture.[52]

The victims of repression were mostly members of left-wing organizations. Of those detained by the security forces 62 per cent were active militants, 18 per cent were political leaders, and 9 per cent trade unionists. The first wave of judicially processed detainees (1972–4) primarily affected members of the Tupamaros, the second (1975–7) members of the Communist Party.[53] The seventeen leaders of the Tupamaros were held separately as hostages: any attacks on the military were to result in their deaths.[54] There were, however, many who were detained and subsequently released without being processed. It is estimated that 18 out of every 10,000 inhabitants were processed by the military courts. When taking into account those who were detained without being processed, 31 out of every 10,000 inhabitants were imprisoned.[55]

Detentions were carried out by all branches of the armed forces and in some cases by the police. Before 1972 most operations were carried out in equal proportions by the Army, the Police, and the Fuerzas Conjuntas (FFCC). Between 1972 and 1977 the army undertook the bulk of repression, from 1978 to 1980 the Navy predominated, and finally, after 1980, it was the police and the army which detained suspects.[56] Prisoners were held in one of 52 detention centres all over the country, most of them official military installations. These were administered by middle-ranking officers of all branches of the Armed Forces.[57] From 1975 onwards, due to overcrowding in ordinary military installations, the use of Argentine-style illegal and clandestine interrogation centres increased.[58] According to Julio Cesar Cooper, former member of the Armed Forces and torturer, up to 90 per cent of Uruguayan officers were made to carry out tortures.[59]

The use of detainment-disappearance, assassination, or extra-judicial execution was relatively rare in Uruguay. An estimated total of 160 people were disappeared by the Uruguayan security forces between 1971 and 1981, 127 of them in Argentina. In addition 32 people were killed by torture, and 26 executed extra-judicially.[60] The disappearances in Uruguay took place between 1971 and 1982. Most of them occurred during the wave of detentions following the 1980 constitutional plebiscite. In Argentina they took place between May and October 1976, affecting primarily members of the PVP, and in December 1977, this time affecting members of the Grupos de Acción Unficadora (GAU). The latter disappearances coincided with the repression of the same political groups within Uruguayan frontiers.[61] It was in 1976 that Zelmar Michelini and Hector Gutierrez Ruíz, two famous opposition politicians in exile in Buenos Aires who had done severe damage to the regime's image abroad, were disappeared and assassinated.[62] The Uruguayan direction of this clandestine repression was in the hands of General Amaurí Prantl, head of the Defence Intelligence Service (SID). This organization co-ordinated the activities of all military and police information networks and anti-subversive units under the Oficina Coordenadora de Operaciones Anti-Subversivas (OCOA). The transfer of clandestine prisoners from Argentina to Uruguay required the permission of both General Prantl and the Chief of Army Intelligence (SIDE), General Otto Paladino.[63] These organizations co-operated with the Argentine, Brazilian, Chilean, and Paraguayan military within the framework of the so-called Operación Cóndor which aimed to co-operatively eliminate the enemies of these regimes across frontiers.[64] It was concluded in 1985: 'Sixty one Uruguayan and three foreign military officers are directly involved and responsible for these kidnappings, disappearances, tortures and homicides.'[65]

In Chile repressive methods were more varied, changed over time, and entailed many more disappearances and assassinations as well as the wider use of illegal detention centres. It is estimated that between 1973 and 1990, 2,801 people were murdered, executed, disappeared, tortured, or killed by other methods.[66] The worst period was between 1973 and 1976, when terror reigned, as the intelligence services arrested thousands in stadiums and secret detentions centres, military installations, and camps: thousands were tortured or disappeared, and knowledge of their whereabouts was denied.[67] It is estimated that up to December 1973, 18,000 people were detained, and by December 1975 between 40,000 and 50,000 had been politically detained.[68] Relegations and exile proliferated. The entire Allende cabinet was interned in a prison camp.[69] There were numerous massacres in the provinces, extra-judicial executions, tortures and disappearances.[70]

Between 1974 and August 1977 illegal and clandestine repression in the form of kidnappings, illegal arrests without trial, torture, disappearances, and assassinations reached their peak. 'From February 1974 onwards, the methods changed suddenly and radically. The intelligence services ceased to publicly announce deaths and the persons detained began to disappear.'[71] The DINA was probably responsible for the disappearance of 1,000 to 2,000 people.[72] Despite the fact that there were only three official detention centres, from February 1976 onwards extensive use was made of clandestine detention centres.[73] Repression was carried out by all branches of the Armed Forces and the Carabineros through their intelligence services, often with the co-operation of civilians and overlapping with provincial military authorities. These were the Servicio de Inteligencia de la Fuerza Aérea (SIFA), later renamed Dirección de Inteligencia de la Fuerza Aérea (DIFA), the Servicio de Inteligencia de Carabineros (SICAR), replaced by the Dirección de Inteligencia de Carabineros (DICAR), the Servicio de Inteligencia Naval (SIN), which operated mostly in Valparaíso, and the Dirección Nacional de Inteligencia del Ejército (DINE).[74] Between 1975 and the end of 1976, the Air Force intelligence service gave rise to the clandestine Comando Conjunto (CC) which was also responsible for many disappearances particularly in the Santiago area.[75] Between 1974 and 1976 the DINA set up a network of co-operation between the intelligence services of the Southern Cone in the so-called Operación Cóndor. This operation produced the assassination of opposition politicians and generals in exile, such as the murder of constitutionalist General Prats in Buenos Aires, of Orlando Letelier, Allende's ambassador in Washington in 1976, and the attempted assassination of Bernardo Leighton, leader of the Christian Democrats in Italy.[76] The Letelier assassination, coinciding with the election of the more pro-human rights President Carter in the United States, led to the dissolution of the DINA in August 1977. The official centres of detention were closed, the state of emergency ended, and the level of disappearances declined dramatically.

In 1977 the CNI was created to replace the DINA. Although it was not legally permitted to arrest and detain, it violated its own laws. The number of detainees that were tortured increased as the practice became systematized.[77] From 1979 onwards repression intensified with the emergence of the armed groups, the Frente Patriótico Manuel Rodríguez (FPMR) and the MAPU-Lautaro. Between 1978 and 1981 a few disappearances occurred but they were not systematic and were not carried out by the CNI; other groups, such as the Comando de Vengadores de Mártires (COVEMA) operated illegally. The latter emerged after the assassination of a colonel in July 1980, out of the Comando Anti-Subversivo (CAS) created to detain those responsible for the assassination. The CAS was integrated by the Brigada de Homicídios y de Inteligencia Policial de Investigaciones, the Carabineros' OS-7, and the CNI's Metropolitan Brigade.[78] Torture and illegal detention continued, although the new state of siege no longer permitted indefinite detention without trial. Due to the fear that the courts might not act with sufficient severity, prohibition on entering the country as well as exile and 'cultural exile' replaced judicial prosecution. This period ended with the plebiscite which inaugurated the 1980 Constitution.

Between 1980 and up to the emergence of the first organized opposition protests in 1983, illegal and criminal repression reemerged. After 1981 the CNI carried out disappearances selectively.[79] The military war tribunals began to function again, despite the fact that there was no constitutionally declared state of war. Mass arrests were used, especially in poor neighbourhoods, where a single operation could affect up to 21,000 people.[80] From 1983 to 1986 expulsions, prohibitions on entry into the country, relegations, the use of concentration camps, massive *allanamientos*, and press censorship dominated. The jurisdiction of the military courts was increased through the Ley de Seguridad del Estado.[81]

Between 1986 and 1988 repression declined and exiles began to return. There were five cases of disappearance.[82] Between the plebescite of October 1988 and the inauguration of the democratic government in March 1990, repression declined radically due to the liberalization. The Carabineros were responsible for public order, and there was one final case of disappearance of the leader of the MIR, Oscar Néghme, in 1988.

The victims of repression varied in each period, although the majority belonged to left-wing organizations. Out of the 2,920 cases investigated by the Rettig Commission, 50 per cent of the victims of repression belonged either to the Socialist Party, the Communist Party, or the Movimiento de Izquierda Revolucionaria (MIR).[83] In the early period, victims included members of the Unidad Popular, militants of parties sympathetic to the government, leaders of local community organizations, beneficiaries of the agrarian reform, and simple peasants and workers. From 1974 most of the victims were members of left-wing parties. The MIR and other groups were systematically decimated according to plan. Between 1983 and 1986, during the period of mass protests, all kinds of people, most of them with no political links at all, became victims of repression. Finally, from 1986 to 1988, most of the victims of repression were people accused of terrorism by the military.

The Dynamic of Military Repression

Despite the common policy of systematically violating basic human rights, repressive strategies varied in each country. The military in Uruguay applied the *estrategia del tornillo*, whereas the Chileans opted for the *estrategia del martillo*.[84] A number of factors account for these differences. First, the level of perceived threat differed.[85] In Uruguay, despite the emergence of the FA, the coalition was more moderate than the Popular Unity; it had won only 18.3 per cent of the vote in 1971 and it was far from taking power as the UP had done in Chile.

Moreover, the visible guerrilla threat had, by the military's own admission, been completely defeated by the time they took power. 'Citizens could not accept, whatever the levels of terror reached between 1976 and 1980, that repression should affect men and women belonging to political organizations which they had seen acting legally for many years and against whom accusations of guilty association with armed subversion were less than credible.'[86] In Chile, a profoundly traumatized society and a fearful military were more willing to accept the *mano dura*.[87] The initial level of extreme violence in Chile can be explained by deep polarization, fear, and military uncertainty over the level of resistance to be met.[88]

Secondly, the different repressive structures produced different repressive methods. Assassination and disappearances were a prominent feature of the Chilean repressive policy because of the DINA. The simultaneous centralization under General Pinochet and autonomization in operations permitted the creation of an isolated criminal world which operated according to its own logic and rules. According to the estimates, the DINA had 2,000 uniformed members, 15,000 informers, and 2,000 civilian advisors.[89] In Uruguay the collegial rule ensured the equality of all branches preventing *caudillismo* and guaranteeing greater institutional control over repression. The military chose to implement a repressive strategy within pre-existing, 'official' military institutional structures. A conscious decision was made 'to rotate all officers into and out of intelligence duties in order to familiarize them with the vital tasks of intelligence and to avoid the creation of an autonomous intelligence service.'[90] Army installations and public prisons were the main places for detention and imprisonment.

Thirdly, the size and homogeneity of the country influenced the choice of repressive strategy. In a country as small as Uruguay, 'where everyone lives near one another and where everyone knows each other' a policy of disappearances and assassinations was impracticable.[91] 'In such a small scale society where everyone is connected' such repression would have assumed 'a quality of personalized atrocities.'[92]

Having accounted for the differences, it is necessary to understand the similarities. Why did the Armed Forces of Uruguay and Chile employ methods of repression that were illegal and which violated human rights? Why did they not follow the legal repressive traditions of their European authoritarian counterparts? Although 'no factor, institutional or otherwise, taken in isolation can explain or predict the behaviour of the military', one cannot ignore the importance of ideology in shaping the dynamic of state repression.[93] The 'growing rejection of traditional boundaries to military action',[94] not only reflected the depth of the crises faced, but, more importantly, it resulted from a shift in the principles and ideas which guided, defined, and legitimated the military's vision of their role in society.

All organizations need a set of guiding principles to give coherence to their actions. This is never truer than in an organization where members are asked to risk their lives in the course of duty. The greater the danger to be confronted, the greater the need for an indestructible unity of purpose. According to a Uruguayan war manual, 'For those leading the Revolutionary War, the cohesion of the Armed Forces is the greatest difficulty to overcome . . . Strengthening the morale of the Armed Forces has to be one of the constant preoccupations of the Commanders . . . The ideal is to imbue them with a spirit of "terrorist hunters" . . . a soldier's guiding code of honour should be the ability to demonstrate a mystique equal or superior to that of his enemies.'[95]

The new ideological arsenal which guided military actions came in the form of the NSD developed in the United States and in Brazil in the 1950s and 1960s, and of the model of counter-insurgent war, developed by the French during the Indochina (1945–54) and Algerian (1954–62) wars, and by the United States in the same period.[96] This ideological focus provided the military with a simplified and manichean interpretation of social and political relations and a strategic military response to them. In both countries, this ideology came to dominate the institutions on the eve of intervention. This rigid ideological construct found a perfect breeding-ground in these institutions. The military's capacity for autonomous action, their monopoly on the use of force, their hierarchical structure, their training and *Weltanschauung* already made them more likely to approximate the ideal type of 'total organizations' which have the greatest anti-democratic potential.[97] They are the least porous and most ideologically homogeneous organizations of the state. They cultivate a more than usual amount of 'order worship'. Their concept of chaos is much more wide-ranging than that of civilians who live in a more non-hierarchical and disorderly environment.

Thus, in Uruguay, in the late 1960s 'a sub-group, a real "political party"', took control of the Armed Forces and carried out a new project. 'The control of information and knowledge gained by the group which combated the "tupamaros" began to place them very close to the mechanisms of power.' The military engaged in a process of 'growing elaboration of an autonomous ideology which was directed in principle at the armed corporation itself and which then permeated the whole of society.'[98] Likewise, immediately after the coup in Chile, 'a uniformed group based in the Army came into existence which acted in secret without any desire for protagonism . . . a group of notable coherence in terms of ideology and action which was a determining factor in the human rights problem'.[99] Constitutionalists, men of the 'moderating' tradition such as General Prats of Chile and Admiral Zorrilla of Uruguay, were rendered impotent in the face of the new ideologues.[100]

The innovative aspects of this new geo-political vision were firstly its emphasis on the internal over the traditional external threat. The defence of national sovereignty became synonymous with national security. Given the Cold War context and the emergence of left-wing guerrillas in the region, the internal enemy was communism. 'The South American version of geopolitics considered that everything was war, whether there was an exchange of fire or not. The enemies were now to be found mainly on the internal front.'[101]

The second innovation was the radical re-definition of the nature of the enemy. It was hidden, ever present, the direct or indirect source of all social conflicts and absolutely evil. 'In this century, the communism brought about through the Bolshevik Revolution of 1917 constitutes the direct or indirect, visible or hidden source of all subversion in today's world.'[102] The enemy operated clandestinely and it did not recognize the ethical limits on combat. It used 'blackmail, terrorism, insult, genocide, crimes against the nation, degradation, debasement, drugs and depravity'.[103] The subversives were 'irascible, failed adventurers and delinquents, crafty, treacherous'. They presented 'a repugnantly sordid array of base behaviour, disloyalties, felonies and immoralities'.[104] In the words of Pinochet, 'Marxism is not simply a mistaken doctrine like many others throughout history. No. Marxism is an intrinsically perverse doctrine, which means that everything that springs from it, however healthy it may appear, is corrupted by the poison which eats away at its roots.'[105] Thus, 'a quasi-theological reassignment of meaning took place that erased reference to the real threats, transforming them into demonic forces'.[106]

Thirdly, the war against this enemy was seen as moral, total, and endless. 'We are in a war between democrats and totalitarian communists. It is a war to the death.'[107] This was to be 'the final battle which will determine the fate of civilization, its end or its rebirth. Whoever loves what is ours, our sublime tradition which exalts our high spiritual heritage, cannot be indifferent or removed from this struggle between Good and Evil and has the duty to commit themselves to the defence of the Christian West.'[108] Finally, since 'the "enemy" was not defined according to an opposition to the state but rather opposition to the Armed Forces which . . . defined themselves as the sole representatives of the Nation and the State', all those opposed to military rule were therefore subversives.[109]

The dynamic of repression resulting from this ideology corresponded more closely to a totalitarian logic than a traditionally authoritarian one. Of the ten characteristics Linz attributes to totalitarian repression, eight were present with differing intensity in Uruguay and Chile.[110] The notion of 'possible crimes . . . based on the logical anticipation of objective developments' replaced the tradition of legal prosecution after the commission of actual crimes.[111] Repression was 'used against whole categories of people irrespective of any evidence of guilt or even intention of threatening the political system'.[112] The prophylactic discourse of disease and the concomitant reference to surgical action to remove the cancer from the body politic was also typical of the totalitarian logic.[113] Similarly typical were the seemingly arbitrary repression, torture, propaganda, and censorship aimed at terrorizing the population and immobilize the opposition.[114]

The boundaries between times of war and peace also typically collapsed. In a reversal of the Clausewitzian dictum, politics became the waging of war by other means. 'Force monitored persuasion, might established right, and conflict resolution was sought in terms of the defeat of the enemy—of the "other" looked on as a *hostis*.'[115] 'In effect, according to Lenin's concepts, systematically and effectively applied by international communism, peace is nothing more than the continuation of war by other means.'[116]

No citizen was immune, because there were no limits to the definition of subversion. In Uruguay, the military saw subversion 'as violent or non-violent actions of a political nature in all fields of human activity which are carried out within a State and whose aims are regarded as not convenient for the political system as a whole'.[117] In the words of a former DINA agent, 'First the aim was to stop terrorism, then possible extremists were targeted and later those who might be converted into extremists.'[118] There could no longer be a division between the 'civilian and military fronts: the whole country and nation constitute a single bloc, a single army. The war today imposes absolute unity, the complete cohesion of the country.'[119]

Society therefore became the object of 'an implacable manipulation.'[120] 'Differences were labelled deviation and subversion and were subjected to a process of normalization.'[121] According to a Uruguayan military manual, 'One has to remove the fish from the water in order to fish it, one has to separate the terrorist from the population in order to make him disappear. One needs an efficient system of information which permits the "organization of the population". In each house, each block, each neighbourhood, an informant should be nominated . . . This system can be used for negative ends. But if it is used for the Defence of Democracy, it is invaluable. One must use whenever possible, the weapons of the enemy.'[122] Finally, there were no 'frontiers, ethics or conventional procedures'.[123]

All violations were justified. In a mirror-image logic, the methods putatively used by the enemy justified the use of similar methods by the military, by application of a '"white" marxism-leninism'.[124] Yet, despite this totalitarian logic, repression in Uruguay and Chile did not approximate the extension and intensity of totalitarian repression. Why, it is pertinent to ask, was repression not worse? A number of factors limited the coercive potential of these authoritarian regimes *vis-à-vis* their totalitarian counterparts.

In the first place, 'In the Latin American normative and cultural context, those who held military power [knew] that, whatever they [said], there still exist[ed] above them a superior legitimacy, that of the constitutional order', such that, 'Not only [could] they not claim its support, but they also [had to] ultimately pay lip service to it.'[125] The hegemony of the democratic ideal and of the North American model made these regimes react against totalitarian movements, not in favour of them. The military's claim that they were members of the civilized western international community made the open and massive violation of human rights inconceivable. International hostility and pressure militated against such a course of action. Moreover, within a capitalist context which requires 'a minimum of secrecy and inviolability in order to operate' the conditions necessary for a totalitarian type of repression simply did not exist as 'this requirement creates some sanctuaries for potential opposition'.[126]

Secondly, the contradictory nature of the military's loyalties and therefore of their ideology acted as a brake on ideological repression. The difference between totalitarianism and authoritarianism is not so much based 'on the fact that one has an ideology and the other does not but on the different quality of the two ideologies', the different legitimating discourses, and the concomitant difference in 'respective *potentialities*'.[127] Ideologically less consistent and coherent, their discourse more contradictory and fragmented than that of their totalitarian counterparts, these regimes did not completely reject an 'old order', nor did they explicitly articulate a vision of a brave new world. Although their implicit vision of a conflict-free society rid of all subversion and eternally harmonious did represent an unarticulated vision of a kind of regressive utopia, unlike the European authoritarians of the inter-war period, the Armed Forces of Uruguay and Chile did not aim to create a real alternative to democracy.[128]

These regimes derived their legitimacy primarily for 'restoring order, re-establishing clear and fixed limits, expelling everything foreign, preventing contamination and assuring a hierarchical unity wherein everyone had a "natural" place.'[129] The Latin American crusade substituted Christianity, the Family, Tradition, and the Nation for France's Mision Civilatrice. What therefore made this putative total war less total was partly the military's identification with the democratic traditions of their country, their loyalty to the liberal democratic state within which they had evolved.[130]

Their rhetorical and at times actual adherence to the rule of law was a product of this tradition. Throughout their rule, the military were very careful to disguise the more repulsive aspects of their repressive policy. On paper, human rights were guaranteed in both Uruguay and Chile. The Uruguayan fifth Institutional Act of 1976 declared that human rights were guaranteed in the country. The Chilean Constitution similarly recognized the basic rights.[131]

Although these rights were obviously not respected, the operations of the security forces were covered by a mantle of secrecy in order to maintain the 'democratic fiction'. All members of the repressive organizations were covered by anonymity. They dressed as civilians, and were not identified by name, branch, or organization. Detainees were not permitted to see their interrogators or torturers. Officers appearing in court would do so under assumed names. The membership of the security forces of those accused of violations would be denied by their respective organizations. The repressive services ensured that silence would prevail by threatening those who faltered with death or punishment, by encouraging complicity and participation in tortures and other violations, by getting signed statements from doctors and victims to the effect that no illegal acts had been perpetrated, and by covering up all operations systematically.[132]

The regimes also provided the repressive services with a cover through an iron curtain of denial. 'The most unbelievable explanations' were given for disappearances. They were 'attributed to "uncontrolled bands" or "vendettas between subversive groups arguing that the disappeared are people who have fled from the country"'.[133] According to Almirante Merino in Chile, for example, 'All the assassinations were committed by the Communist Party.'[134] At most, it was admitted that these were 'isolated cases which fortunately happen only very rarely' or 'isolated excesses of secondary level officers'.[135] The regime in Uruguay only admitted to the disappearance of 6 people but it refused to acknowledge the involvement of the security forces.[136] Government legislation ensured the secrecy of operations and later permitted the destruction of all records pertaining to repressive activities.[137]

Thus, the elements missing in the list of characteristics of totalitarian coercion are precisely those which express this adherence to the democratic tradition: the military did not disregard the appearance of legal procedures, the formalities of trial, the opportunity for a semblance of a defence in imposing penalties, nor did they surround their illegal activities with the moral self-righteousness and publicity found under totalitarian regimes.[138] How could a regime claiming to defend democratic western and Christian values proudly publicize such crimes? And how could a regime claiming to uphold the rule of law in the face of totalitarian attacks, openly defy this same rule of law? Hence the denial and covering-up of repression. Hence the enormous body of institutional acts, laws, decrees, and constitution building. And thus too, when all is said and done, the limited—relative to the totalitarian cases—extent of repression.

Finally, the level of 'totalitarian' penetration in these regimes was not uniformly distributed. At one level, these regimes were typically authoritarian given their rhetorical adherence to democratic legalistic values, given their more porous quality, given the presence of limited pluralism, and their daily political and diplomatic confrontation with the values and rhetoric of the opposition and of the international community.[139] It was only sections of the military institution which developed the totalitarian logic more fully in their implementation of repression. One saw a repressive ideological dynamic or 'pockets' within the military which operated according to a totalitarian logic. The 'closer' to the repressive apparatus and the 'further' from the limited pluralism at the regime level, the more the totalitarian elements of the ideology dominated and the more the totalitarian repressive dynamic took hold.

These coexisting tendencies occasioned paradoxical results. On the one hand, the totalitarian dynamic led the Armed Forces, so attached to legal conventions, to violate their own laws; on the other, it led them to attempt to pass constitutions which aimed at 'protecting democracy'. Thus, although the Uruguayan military tortured almost one-third of their population, they forced President Bordaberry to resign for his desire to destroy the traditional parties by abolishing them.[140] In Chile, one could be abducted by an illegal and official non-existent Comando Conjunto, but one's criminal abductors took the trouble to fill out forms with the relevant information.[141]

The more the totalitarian ideology penetrated the Armed Forces, the worse the repression. Thus, the differences in repressive methods were partly shaped by the intensity and extension of the penetration of the totalitarian ideology within the Armed Forces. This is particularly clear when one compares Uruguay and Chile with Argentina. It is widely accepted that the penetration of this ideology in Argentina was the greatest of the three countries.[142] Here, the total institutionalization of repression within the structures of the Armed Forces, together with the intensity of this ideological outlook, made repression the worst in the Southern Cone, as the military became more of a totalitarian institution or organization than it did in any other case.[143]

By contrast, for example, the Uruguayan military 'lived preoccupied with achieving an equilibrium between the National Security Doctrine . . . and the ideological values governing institutions, proportional representative democracy and the political parties,'[144] since repression was not implemented by an autonomous agency with little loyalty to an eventual democratic restoration. Moreover, the military limited their actions, preferring, in a small country and society, to detain, and imprison rather than to assassinate and disappear.

To claim that repression was ideologically motivated does not imply that all within the military were true believers. It is possible for ideology to direct action in the absence of true belief if it is understood 'as a form of discourse or a political language —a body of linguistic propositions expressed as speech-acts and united by the conventions governing them. Its adherents will have varied beliefs about its conventions, yet all will be constrained by them in order to be recognized as competent speakers of their discourse'.[145] Actions were shaped by ideology in so far as the military conformed to its conventions. Ideology may have been cynically adopted by the *golpistas* in order to gain control over the military institution and to provide cohesion to the ranks in the exercise of power. Yet whether they ultimately believed it or not is relatively unimportant. They trained their officers to repress in accordance with it.

The dynamic of state repression was fed by non-ideological factors as well. In Chile, for example, much repression was internally directed due to General Pinochet's struggle for supremacy. 'General Pinochet did not know which army was in control, he did not know how many supported the constitutionalist line of Generals Schneider and Prats. He had to put the house in order, whatever the cost.'[146] In Uruguay the constitutionalists had already been neutralized with the defeat of the Navy by February 1973. Collegiality and the absence of an organization similar to the DINA also meant that the repression of internal dissidence was implemented through institutional purges.[147]

Another dynamic for repression in Chile were the rivalries between the different repressive agencies of the armed forces. The latter were largely the product of General Pinochet's and the DINA's struggle for supremacy.[148] The general's promotion of the DINA as a praetorian guard fuelled the resentment of the repressive apparatuses of the other branches of the armed forces and alienated the other Commanders. Civilians became cannon-fodder in these wars. 'The various military intelligence services fought over the capture and interrogation of prisoners.'[149] The rivalry between the SIFA-CC and the DINA, for example, even led the former to murder two of its members for wanting to 'defect' to the DINA.[150] In Uruguay, the repressive hardcore equivalent was never as strong as the DINA and were in any event defeated after leading a failed internal coup attempt from within the SIDE in 1978.[151]

Finally, the resistance of the autonomous hardcore to liberalization was another dynamic of repression in both countries. In Uruguay, for example, the internal coup attempt by ultra-hardline Generals Prantl and Cristi and Colonel Jorge Nader in 1980, occurred just before contacts began to develop between the regime and the National and Colorado parties in an attempt to begin the process of military withdrawal.[152] The death by torture of Dr Roslik in April 1984, for example, was thought to have been part of the hard-line's efforts to impede the promotion of General Medina, who was in favour of negotiating a rapid democratic exit with civilian élites.[153]

Military Justification for Human Rights Violations and Resistance to Truth and Justice

Whatever the factors feeding repression, on the eve of democracy, the military were faced with the unenviable task of defending their repressive record. Military resistance to truth and justice was articulated according to the ideological discourse of national security. The ideological justification for human rights violations was never direct. Rather, the NSD discourse was used to legitimate the repressive actions of the institution, primarily by emphasizing the military's democratic vocation and the enemy's totalitarian intent.[154]

Their argument developed as follows: they claimed that they

had been at war and that because of the nature of the enemy, the normal laws of conduct could not apply. 'When the ideological war emerged a new form of defence also emerges. One enters the realm different from the traditional one.'[155]

In peace one usually forgets the tragic dimensions of war, which unfortunately often precedes it; one forgets that the 11th of September was a military operation, that is, an act of war . . . the Armed Forces went out to fight . . . this decision implied the use of all the necessary resources to crush the will to fight of those who had brought about destruction and chaos . . . the victory of freedom could not have been obtained without the use of severe and dissuasive force . . . soldiers go to war and when they return victorious they are faced with forgetfulness.[156]

The Plan Zeta played a very important role in justifying the use of force in Chile. This plan, allegedly concocted by the left but actually compiled by the military with the CIA, supposedly contemplated the physical elimination of a part of the leadership of the Armed Forces and of the opposition to the Popular Unity government in an *auto-golpe* which was to take place on the 19 September 1973. General Pinochet claimed that the DINA had found 100,000 subversive weapons in October 1973 and that the paramilitary forces of the Popular Unity government probably numbered 100,000 men trained by the Cubans between 1969 and 1973. Had this been true, this would have represented more than triple the number in the Chilean army and a little less than double the number of the armed forces as a whole. This claim also contradicts the *Plan Zeta*, according to which the communists were planning to kill these leaders with the explosion of floral arrangements previously packed with bombs.

Secondly, the military claimed they acted in defence of democracy. Military rule had never been 'a movement of force opposed to democracy. The opposite was true. It was in defence of democracy that the constitutional president was subsequently replaced, when he tried to eliminate the traditional political parties and the vote as a form of the sovereign expression of the people. It was in defence of democracy that the 1980 plebiscite was convoked, respecting the verdict of the ballot box.'[157] General Pinochet modestly expressed this attitude when he stated that 'Now reconciliation is also talked about but I have been saying this for at least four years in my speeches about national unity. So don't come and steal the eagle's eggs.'[158]

They claimed that they could not be taught lessons by the very same politicians who had contributed to the breakdown of democracy. 'We do not need tutors to sustain the principles of dignity and the protection of human rights . . . the essential idea that the aim of the state is to promote the public good incarnate in the well-being of all humans, disappeared in a thick fog of personal or sectoral bastard interests, of exaggerated power ambitions, selfish electoralism, excessive passions and demagogic manœuvres'. 'We do not want and nor will we permit revanchism because base passions have no place in those who seek national well-being.'[159]

Thirdly, they compared themselves favourably with 'real totalitarians'. In the words of a Chilean general: 'You say we are living in a dictatorship, that one cannot go out into the street without getting killed. I go out into the street and so do you, and we are not dead yet. I am sure that had these people gone for a conference to change the German regime in Hitler's time, Mr. Hitler would have said: "You know what, put them all in the gas chambers", and that would have been the end of the story.'[160] In the words of the Generalissimo: 'Is there any dictator who placed limits on himself when backed up by law and with all the power in his hands? None. And yet this Constitution determined a period of eight years after which the citizenry could pronounce itself upon whether it wanted the government to remain or not.'[161] The Uruguayans also compared themselves favourably with their Southern Cone, particularly their Argentine, counterparts.[162]

Fourthly, accusations of human rights violations were denounced as subversive. Being in the vanguard of the battle against the ultimate evil, the military became the embodiment of all the highest values of the nation. Their discourse indicated that the military existed 'in its own right and needed no justification . . . elevated to a rank of superstitious veneration, as if the world were a poor and insipid place without them'.[163] It was therefore claimed that 'All actions or corporative or individual manifestations which tend to diminish or maliciously object to the behaviour of the members of the Armed Forces in the struggle against subversion, or, what is essentially the same, betray the Nation, constitutes a disguised complicity with the enemies of the regime.'[164] For them, 'behind the facade of justice, these accusations hide the political aim of attacking and persecuting the men who acted in an extremely critical moment in the life of the nation'.[165] 'The army has been the object of attack and insidious propaganda coming from certain sectors and from the same internal and external enemies that it once had to fight.'[166]

Typical of these responses was the argument that accusations were made with 'communist bad faith, to deliberately deceive people and the international bodies concerned with human rights . . . the aim of these accusations is none other than to turn the defeat that the revolutionary war, sedition and communism suffered in Uruguay, into a possible triumph for international public opinion through intentional propaganda and gross deformations'.[167] Pinochet's response to human rights criticisms was that these were 'an annoyance invented by the Communists' who always used 'the famous human rights injection'.[168] Even the United Nations, the US government and various international bodies were seen to be infiltrated by Communists.[169]

Given this ideological outlook, the military were, in the final analysis, quite proud of what they had done, and dismissed criticisms aimed at diminishing the gargantuan task they had undertaken. 'For the military institution, there were no bad military officers. Only soldiers who followed orders.'[170] They felt that 'they participated in a heroic historic act'.[171] The military saw themselves as the representatives *par excellence* of the democratic traditions of the nation. For them democracy re-emerged not despite, but because of them. 'Once the virile decision to defend ourselves and to employ the proper methods to deal with the fierce attack we were suffering had been taken, the military defeat of a terrorist organization until then considered invincible was achieved in only a few months.'[172] Uruguayan General Rapela was proud to say that 'These armed forces have been consulted keenly by other countries to see how we combated sedition and to know the instruments which we used to fight it. If you will forgive the false modesty, we are a school to be consulted by many friendly countries. If you knew the amount of times that people have visited our institute to see the way in which we combated sedition, you might even be astonished.'[173] Pinochet was similarly proud of the fact that they 'practically cleaned the nation of marxists'.[174]

The military were therefore fundamentally unrepentant. 'We are accused of not respecting human rights. We are the ones who said "mercy for the defeated" and if in battle we had to pay with our own blood in order to survive, the innocent blood of our dead who we mourn and who we will always remember to lift our spirit; and if in battle we had to kill enemies who wanted to see us destroyed, we say to our people that nobody will teach us to respect the human rights of the defeated.'[175] They were 'not afraid of the future because [they had] a clear conscience that the measures [they had] to adopt and execute, some of them difficult to accept, were taken with the greater aim of defending the nation'. And they would not 'hesitate to repeat them if the security of the country demanded it'. If the same conditions were to repeat themselves, they would not 'have any alternative' but to carry out another coup.[176]

Military resistance to truth and justice, however, was not only the result of this ideological outlook. More importantly, perhaps, it was a manifestation of institutional fears that such policies would result in the destruction of the Armed Forces. The hierarchy's priority was the 'duty to watch over the prestige of the armed and security forces; to prevent all attempted reprisals against their members for political reasons'.[177] Thus, the secrecy surrounding human rights violations and the ideological discourse which justified them not only served as a façade to deflect international criticism and to permit the smooth implementation of the military's repressive strategy. It was also designed to protect the members of the military from future prosecution. The Armed Forces resisted truth-telling because human rights violations were institutionalized and therefore implicated the hierarchy. The commanders felt compelled to protect their inferiors as they if bereft of protection, might threaten to make revelations which would affect the hierarchy.[178] Although for some it may have been 'an undescribable pain . . . to witness the frustration of all that one most revered throughout one's whole life: the concept of command, doing one's duty . . . and respect for the citizens to place arms in our hands to defend them and not to kill them', in the words of one Chilean general, they could not 'accuse a superior . . . it was necessary to protect the Army from this aberration and. . . . to protect the Junta as well'.[179] In both cases, the hierarchy assumed the responsibility of protecting the lower ranks. In Uruguay 'In accordance with the policy duly outlined, this general command will not permit any form of revisionism of the actions undertaken by the [members of the armed forces] in the war against subversion and if any conflict with Human Rights are attributed to it, the subscriber will take responsibility for having given the first order to that end, in his capacity as Chief of the Joint General Command in the period in question.'[180] General Pinochet was typically less formal and more direct: 'If anyone touches any of my men, rule of law is over'.[181]

Conclusions

In Uruguay, the military's long-standing Republican tradition had led them to reject President Bordaberry's advice that the traditional parties be permanently abolished in 1976. This loyalty, the absence of a strong man, fears of the danger of institutional politicization, the failure to successfully carry out a coherent neo-liberal economic policy which had culminated in the resignation of super-minister Végh Villegas in 1976, and increasing international isolation, led the military to promote an opening of politics much sooner than in Chile.[182] As early as 1978 the military leadership initiated talks with the parties, and between 1977 and 1980 the power of the hard-liners started to wane. Although they hoped to institutionalize authoritarian rule with a new Constitution in 1980, lack of support from crucial entrepreneurial and political élites and the absence of popular support of any kind condemned the military's constitutional plebiscite to failure.[183]

In Chile, on the other hand, the struggle of the opposition was to prove much harder. Military rule was supported by significant sectors of both the population and the right-wing élite. Pinochet had succeeded in institutionalizing his authoritarian political ideology with the 1980 Constitution and in consolidating the regime's economic neo-liberal revolution.[184] Unlike Uruguay, the regime successfully made the transition from the initial reactive phase to undergo a long foundational period.[185]

Whatever the differences, the civilian élites of both countries could expect a high degree of military resistance on the human rights issue. The latter would predictably 'attempt to maintain initially strong positions, recover from previous losses, redress grievances, resist civilian encroachments and seek the best possible terms of accommodation in the new situation'.[186] And they would have the power to do so effectively, because instead of immersing themselves in purely professional matters, they would retain a significant political influence in the newly installed democratic regimes. Regardless of the constitutional arrangement, they would continue with a high level of institutional prerogatives to exercise some kind of power over civilians.

The military, on the other hand, could expect to be confronted with a strong human rights lobby in both countries, given their democratic political culture which meant that political élites were either forced or naturally inclined to take the issues of truth and justice on board.

As will be seen, the military's ideology and concomitant attitude to human rights violations was to remain essentially unchanged, negative, and inflexible. Abandoning their ideological vision would have implied an inability to defend the *raison d'être* of their rule and its repressive methods. It would have implied the complete breakdown of the ideological interpretation of the nature of the subversive enemy and therefore the breakdown of their justification for combat methods. Abandoning the ideology would imply the admission that the institutions had become criminalized.

None the less, their strategies could be more flexible, depending on the ability of the democratic oppositions and governments to force the military to accept truth and justice. Democratizing élites could force the military to strategically accept policies of truth and justice, since their strategies to deal with the issue of violations, were shaped not simply by their ideology, but more importantly, by the legal, institutional, and political context of the transitional period. As one author puts it, it is not necessary that the military become democrats overnight; they can be 'forced, tricked, lured, cajoled . . . into democratic behaviour.'[187]

From the military point of view, the more they were able to make their ideological vision dominate, the more successful they could consider their historical and conjunctural management of the issue. On the other hand, the more they were forced to sacrifice their basic vision on the issue of repression in the implementation of reactive strategies, the more the civilian opposition, human rights organizations, and the victims of repression could consider their strategies successful. For the military an ideal scenario would be one in which the new democratic regime accepted the ideological and historical explanations of the military as justifications, equated criticism, truth-telling and trials as attacks on the honour of the armed forces and by extension on national security, and rejected an amnesty on the grounds that there were no crimes to be punished. On the other hand, the more the democratic governments and opposition challenged these premisses, the more the success lay with the victims of repression. The following chapters will analyse the complexities of this battle as it evolved in Uruguay and Chile.

PART II

Truth and Justice in Transition

It is hard to remember that . . . the time is now and the place is here and that there are no second chances at a single moment.

Jeanette Winterson, *The Passion*, 1987

3

Negotiating Truth and Justice in the Transition to Democracy in Uruguay, 1980–1985

Human Rights in the Transition Process: 'Una Salida Mentirosa'[1]

The Uruguayan transition began with the failure of the military to impose an authoritarian Constitution through a plebiscite in 1980 and ended with the national elections of November 1984, from which the Colorado party and its leader, Julio María Sanguinetti, emerged triumphant.[2]

The plebiscite represented the military's first attempt to extricate the institution from direct rule, institutionalize the political power they had acquired under authoritarian rule, retain their corporate autonomy, and ensure indirect political control over future civilian governments through an authoritarian 'national security' Constitution which severely limited civil and political rights. Surprisingly, given the still dormant and repressed state of civil society and internal opposition, the military regime lost the plebiscite, winning only 43 per cent of the votes. This 'unexpected opening' represented 'the first step of the Uruguayan transition to democratic restoration' and the 'last stage of the military regime'.[3]

Following the regime's defeat in the plebiscite, General Álvarez, who became the first military president of the regime after a bitter internal power struggle in September 1981, presented a *Cronograma* for a controlled liberalization, announcing that the traditional parties could choose new leaders through primaries who would then negotiate with the Armed Forces Political Affairs Commission (COMASPO) and agree on a Constitution which would ensure the military's position as guardians of national security. The military authorities hoped that the primaries, from which the left was excluded, would lead the pro-regime factions of the traditional parties to victory. This would permit the military leaders to agree to a constitution with their authoritarian civilian allies.[4]

The results of the primaries, however, reconfirmed the military's isolation. The anti-regime factions of the Colorado and Blanco parties won 70 and 78 per cent of the vote respectively. The pro-regime factions of the Colorados got 28.7 per cent of the party vote and the right of the Blanco Party 21 per cent. The Unión Cívica (UC), a small catholic party promoted by the military to increase the pluralist credentials of the liberalization won only 1.2 per cent of the vote. Moreover, it was the more radical Blancos who gained an overall majority winning 49 per cent of all votes cast; the left, unable to participate, voted *en masse* for the Blanco leader, Wilson Ferreira Aldunate.[5]

The military overplayed their hand again during their first formal negotiations at the Parque Hotel in April and May 1983 with representatives of the traditional parties. President Álvarez, whose position was still politically dominant within the military, insisted on a withdrawal which would leave the structures of the authoritarian state intact and further his own power ambitions.[6] For their part, the parties refused to accept the military's conditions which they rightly claimed had already been rejected by the majority of the population in the 1980 constitutional plebiscite. As a result of this *impasse*, formal talks and contacts were abandoned between the parties and military representatives.

Between May 1983 and the re-establishment of formal civil–military contacts in June 1984, the opposition mobilized against the regime, prompting the military to reconsider their negotiating strategy. Although the left remained illegal, the traditional parties sought closer ties with its leaders as well as with the recently emerging social organizations united in the newly created Intersectorial. The ensuing mobilizations culminated in the largest demonstration in the country's history on 27 November 1983. It was estimated that 10 per cent of the country's population were present. They also led to the first general strike since the coup which paralysed the city of Montevideo in January 1984.

At the November demonstration, the parties, including figures of the illegal left, made the so-called Proclama del Obelisco or the Proclamation at the Obelisk. With it they became committed to a united inter-party strategy based on the refusal to participate in elections with proscriptions and on the demand for the immediate re-establishment of civil and political rights as pre-conditions for continued negotiations. The Multipartidaria and the Intersocial were created out of the Intersectorial in early 1984, the former representing the parties and the Plenario Intersindical de Trabajadores–Confederación Nacional de Trabajadores (PIT–CNT), and the latter all other social organizations. These organizations aimed to co-ordinate the opposition activities of the parties, the trade unions and the social organizations.

This was the period of greatest inter-party unity. The Proclama constituted the 'greatest effort towards unification ever undertaken.' It was never to be repeated.[7] The traditional parties had tended to diverge on opposition strategies from the outset of the 'unexpected opening'. There was no basic inter-party consensus on which transition strategy to adopt and on what conditions to accept in the negotiations with the military.[8] On the one hand, the Blancos favoured the promotion of radical mobilizations in alliance with the social movement and the illegal left in order to completely defeat the military. The Colorados, on the other, favoured a more conciliatory élite-led approach, discouraged mobilizations, and became increasingly willing to negotiate with continued proscriptions. The Colorados and the UC were, for example, opposed to the General Strike in January 1984 and they withdrew from the *Intersectorial* in protest against the organization's decision to promote it. At the Colorado party convention in July 1984, its leader, Julio María Sanguinetti, made it clear that the party was looking for 'an agreement with a man of the regime who will give the people freedom and democracy and ensure a return to the Constitution, but we have not yet found that man'. According to Sanguinetti, the party was willing to 'reach any agreement if that is the objective, however uncomfortable the situation may be'.[9]

These basic strategic and tactical differences were exacerbated by the 1982 primaries. The latter had both disclosed and encouraged antagonistic partisan strategies. The Colorados, worried about the prospect of an invincible Blanco Party swelled with illegal leftists, made it their priority to eliminate the possibility of a national alliance between the Blancos and the Frente Amplio.[10] Sanguinetti advocated the legalization of the moderate sectors of the FA, knowing that enfranchisement of Frente representatives would naturally encourage the coalition to acquire a political life autonomous from the Blanco Party.

The Blanco Party and Ferreira in particular, on the other hand, interpreted the results of the primaries as a confirmation of popular support for Ferreira's radical opposition strategy, and they saw their majority vote, unprecedented in Uruguayan history, as a sign of likely success in future transitional Presidential elections. This view both encouraged the party to pursue a radical independent strategy and led it to become dependent on Ferreira's directives. Ferreira was determined to become the absolute leader of his party. He wanted to reform its traditional conservative identity, transforming it into a radical, populist, national, and socialistic party. Still in exile, he had attempted and failed to prevent other Blanco leaders from participating in the Parque Hotel so that they should not threaten his pre-eminence.[11]

Finally, the left had voted for Ferreira in 1982 because of its identification with the Blancos in exile. None the less, relations between the parties were volatile due to competition and suspicion among the leadership. The Frente's leadership feared that the continued identification of its supporters with the Blanco Party would threaten the autonomous future of the coalition. With the Frente's leader Líber Seregni still in gaol, its base organizations still operating in semi-clandestinity, and its unity threatened by the divisions created by exile and internal ideological differences, this fear was understandable.[12]

In the face of a united and mobilized opposition, the military underwent a process of internal reorganization and adopted a new transitional strategy which signalled the end of Alvarista hardline domination. The resignation of hardline General Paulós, marked the decline of Alvaristas and the rise of the pro-negotiating faction led by Generals Raimúndez, Buadas, Linares Brum, and Angel Barrios.[13] The military had been initially divided over the conditions for withdrawal to demand from the traditional parties. The Álvarez option had been renewed repression. He had responded to the mobilizations by dictating two acts in August 1983 which decreed the temporary suspension of all political activity and increased proscriptions and censorship.

The Junta de Oficiales Generales (JOG), however, fearing a breakdown in hierarchical authority and increasing internal factionalization resulting from different views on how to negotiate the transition, decided after a process of internal deliberations and bitter power struggles to veto Álvarez's authoritarian plans and adopt a more conciliatory strategy. Thus, when Álvarez recommended continued police street presence in August 1983, in order to repress continued mobilizations, 'to maintain . . . fear' and to put a stop to 'any revisionist attempts' the JOG voted for negotiation instead of confrontation by 12 out of 16 votes.[14]

In late 1983 the military abolished the institutional acts of August and de-proscribed all leaders of the traditional parties with the exception of Ferreira Aldunate. The latter, still in exile, was particularly detested by the military for his denouncing of the regime in co-operation with the communists. Furthermore, he was wanted by the military justice system on charges of subversive association. The military decided to cut their losses, and abandoned attempts to bring the Blanco Party into the negotiating fold. Instead, they decided to isolate the Blancos and accepted the Frente as viable negotiating partners.

In order to permit the left's participation in negotiations, they released Líber Seregni from gaol in March 1984 and in June they legalized the Socialist and Christian Democratic *sub-lemas* of the Frente through Institutional Act 18. The latter derogated the June 1982 party law forbidding parties with international connections. It restored political rights to 6,500 politicians, although 3,000, among them Líber Seregni, were still banned from political activity. It de-proscribed the leaders of the Christian Democrat *sub-lema*, Young and Cardoso, who later participated in the final negotiations with the military. Finally it permitted the 70,000 members of the Armed Forces to vote in the Presidential elections planned for November 1984.[15] Moreover, knowing that the political prisoners were a major concern for the Frente, they made a verbal commitment which promised to release 411 prisoners who had served more than half of their prison sentences.

The pro-negotiating military faction was strengthened in June 1984 when General Medina was promoted against the will of the Alvarista hard-line to the position of Commander-in-Chief, winning the nomination over the Alvarista General Julio Bonelli and replacing the hard-line General Pedro Aranco. Medina consistently resisted President Álvarez's attempts to block the transition and sought an agreement with the politicians.[16]

As the FA, the Colorados, and the UC decided to re-establish official contacts with the military despite the remaining proscriptions, the Blancos, increasingly isolated, made a last bid for an intransigent principled opposition. In June 1984 they withdrew from the Multipartidaria, protesting at the other parties' decision to negotiate in violation of the commitment made at the Proclama. On 16 June, Ferreira returned to Uruguay for the first time since his original departure for exile under military rule. It was hoped that his return would turn the tide against the negotiating parties, that the force of his popularity would overcome the military and force them to de-proscribe him. His return, however, did not have the intended effect. He was immediately gaoled on arrival.[17]

In response to Ferreira's imprisonment, the parties in the Multipartidaria agreed to carry out a national civic stoppage to press for the Blanco leader's release and de-proscription. But on 26 June, the day before the Paro Cívico, or Civic Strike, was scheduled to take place, the parties surprisingly decided to negotiate and to cancel the mobilization.

The Frente's decision to negotiate was one which took the Blancos by surprise and which the party would never forgive. It led to the definitive 'rupture of the opposition front'.[18] The Frente's decision condemned the Blancos's radical position to failure since they could not hope to succeed in their confrontational strategy without the support of the left.

For the Frente, however, moderation and the acceptance of negotiations gave the coalition the opportunity to re-build itself and to acquire political respectability. Participation in the Club Naval permitted the inclusion of the left into the formal political arena in exchange for their acknowledgement of the 'rules of the game'.[19] The Frente also felt that Ferreira, isolated by exile, was misjudging the strength of the military by demanding their total defeat. Finally, 'there was an undercurrent of resentment at the Blancos' hubris and a refusal to grant them favoured status compared with that of the Colorado party.'[20]

Seregni justified negotiating despite Ferreira's proscription on the grounds that the transition could not be sacrificed for one man. He claimed that he, Seregni, had agreed to allow his party to negotiate despite his own continued proscription.[21] But Seregni had little to lose by accepting his own proscription since he, unlike Ferreira, had little chance of winning national elections. Similarly, Sanguinetti argued that it was 'as bad to triumph at the expense of principles as it is to never triumph for never defending them.'[22] But like Seregni he had everything to gain and nothing to lose by accepting Ferreira's proscription. With Ferreira and Seregni proscribed he was conveniently assured electoral victory in November 1984.

The Club Naval talks in which the FA, the Colorados, and the UC participated, and from which the Blancos excluded themselves, were held in August 1984. They marked the end of the negotiating phase of the transition, leading to the passage of Institutional Act 19. The latter validated the continued existence of the National Security Council with military representation, but stated that it could only be convened by the President. It created the new category of State of Insurrection which could similarly only be declared by the President with the approval of the Parliament. The military justice system was limited to military crimes in time of war and, if voted by the parliament, in times of State of Insurrection. The legal mechanism of *habeas corpus* was created, and the system of military promotions was modified. Despite changes in the latter, however, the command still decided who stood to be selected for promotion. The Commanders-in-Chief of the Armed Forces had to be the three most senior generals in the forces, and the President could only promote generals from a selection of six proposed by the institution. Finally the act provided for the possible reform of Institutional Acts 9 and 13 pertaining to social security, Acts 8 to 12 pertaining to the Judiciary, and for the derogation of the Organic Military Law. The act was to remain valid until 1 March 1986, unless a Constituent Assembly proposed constitutional reforms between July and October 1985 and these changes were ratified by a plebiscite on 11 November 1985. Finally, the pact fixed the date for national elections in November 1984, at which time a new democratic executive and legislature would be elected, completing the transition to democracy. Unlike Chile, therefore, the transition implied a virtual restoration of the pre-authoritarian political system and Constitution.

The civil-military Club Naval pact which the talks culminated in was thus consummated through the exclusion of the Blancos from the transitional élite settlement and at the cost of Wilson Ferreira's probable electoral victory. The Blanco Party not surprisingly boycotted the negotiations not only in protest against Ferreira's continued imprisonment and proscription, but also because they believed the pact was inadequate as a foundation for the new democratic era. It was in their opinion, 'a decision to exit an authoritarian regime and not a commitment to build a new society'. It was 'completely useless to lay the foundations or to trace a path for a new form of social fellowship'. It had been 'a merely electoral decision which postponed the task of reconstruction to the future', its attention fixed 'on that which it was desirable to leave behind at the expense of the preoccupation of that which had to be built later on'.[23]

While the Blancos portrayed the Colorados and the Frente as 'opportunists serving their own interests', with the Colorados gaining a guarantee of electoral victory and the Frente political respectability, the pro-accord parties saw the Blancos as 'demagogic free-riders' who were unwilling to pay the political price of accommodation, but were nevertheless willing to participate in the elections which the pact they had rejected guaranteed.[24] The Blancos participated in the elections, threatened with the loss of their *lema* and with the prohibition of participation in the future Constituent Assembly. Despite initial hopes to the contrary, the military refused to de-proscribe Ferreira after the pact. They maintained the fiction that the institution could not interfere with the Ferreira case, since it was a legal issue in the hands of the independent military justice system.[25]

With Ferreira in prison and Seregni proscribed, Sanguinetti was the only 'natural' party leader running for election. Campaigning on the themes of moderation and pragmatism, calling for a Cambio en Paz, or Peaceful Change, the Colorados won 41.2 per cent of the national vote. They were closely followed by the Blancos, represented by Presidential candidate Alberto Zumarán and Vice-Presidential runner-up, Gonzalo Aguirre with 35 per cent. The Frente, which ran under the Christian Democrat *lema*, led by Juan José Crottogini and labour leader José D'Elia, gained 21.3 per cent of the vote.[26]

Predictably, one of the major areas of concern for the military in the transition was the issue of trials for human rights violations. This preoccupation was ambiguously expressed both at the Parque Hotel and at the Club Naval. At the Parque Hotel there was no direct reference to the issue. But according to an Alvarista general, his faction was 'accused of being continuist or pro-coup because it had demanded guarantees. It had wanted what would be done with them when the new government took power to be clear.'[27] Thus, in the debate over the jurisdiction of the military justice system, the Armed Forces representatives argued that the military courts should have jurisdiction over civilians in cases of subversion and over military personnel in times of both war and peace.[28] It was largely due to the unwillingness of the parties to accept the military's jurisdictional demands that the talks first became a *diálogo de sordos* or a dialogue of the deaf and then broke down.[29] According to Sanguinetti himself, the demand was unacceptable because 'the doubtful independence and technical capacity of the military magistrates do not provide sufficient guarantees.'[30]

Both civilians and military negotiators had learnt two lessons from the experience at the Parque Hotel. Public talks were inadequate since they put too much pressure on both sides to 'play to the gallery'. Secondly, the human rights issue would have to be deliberately ignored. The Club Naval talks were therefore reserved and no official records were kept of the conversations. And both General Medina and the civilians deliberately avoided bringing human rights violations to the negotiating table. According to Medina, 'We all knew that the issue of revisionism and of trying the military was pending. We all knew as well that if these issues were placed on the negotiating table things would be complicated and we were all extremely interested in finding a way out.'[31] The military negotiators, however were faced with explicit demands from the hardline. President Álvarez and his allies were particularly preoccupied with the still unresolved issue of human rights violations; 'The military—engaged in a severe internal battle between moderates and hard-liners, although divisions were also based on leadership loyalties which had little to do with the cleavages outlined above—understood that guarantees against revisionism were a *sine qua non* condition for an exit.'[32] Thus, Medina, whose position within the military was internally precarious, had to prove himself capable of preventing 'revisionism' and 'revanchism' if he was to win the compliance of the hard-line with the negotiation and put a stop to internal factionalism.

Initially 'the Commanders in Chief practically proposed a "blank cheque" for all that had gone before.'[33] The Junta made it clear that it would seek 'the reconciliation of all Uruguayans, avoiding all forms of intolerance as well as all acts of revenge or revanchism related with the grave events which characterized the historical chapter now being closed and overcome . . . looking towards the future and taking the past into account only to learn lessons and to avoid making the same mistakes.'[34] The military representatives proposed that military jurisdiction should include military crimes perpetrated not only in times of war or insurrection, but also those committed in peacetime. After much negotiation, however, it was finally agreed that 'Common crimes committed by military personnel in time of peace, wherever they are committed would be submitted to the ordinary justice system'.[35] The hard-line complained to the Junta twice about the lack of guarantees implicit in this solution. According to one Alvarista:

> We wanted an orderly and peaceful transition, but also one which was clearer in terms of what would be done with the military. It was not a question of wanting to continue in government but rather one of wanting guarantees that there would be no revanchism. We wanted all accusations to be directed towards the military justice system and, being unable to obtain that, we asked for guarantees . . . We criticized them for only having obtained promises and because nothing had been clearly established regarding that question.[36]

Responding to this pressure, the Junta decided to order General Medina to propose an amnesty at the Club Naval. Sanguinetti, however, persuaded the General not to do so: were an amnesty to be accepted by the Colorados and the UC, it would have forced the

Frente to abandon the talks. On the other hand, were it to be rejected, it would have led to a hard-line veto of the talks. Thus, before the Junta's demands could be complied with, Sanguinetti and General Medina called an unexpected press conference announcing the successful completion of the talks.[37]

The military had thus apparently handed over power with no guarantees of impunity. Yet immediately after the talks ended, Medina gave a press conference stating that 'the Armed Forces were ready to accept justice over those elements which form a part of the ranks that have demonstrated dishonesty or over elements which are in the ranks that acted on their own account; but for those that acted on orders or on the command of a superior, those will deserve our greatest backing'.[38] He also claimed that 'the normal changes in the jurisdiction of the Military Justice system and the Civil Justice system . . . will not affect the army or its members'. Finally he warned that the military would not accept 'being messed around with or anything of the kind'.[39] Furthermore, only a few weeks later General Medina claimed that the disquiet within the ranks over the lack of guarantees at the Club Naval had been overcome.[40]

How had Medina managed to reassure the ranks and calm the nerves of the hard-line given the lack of formal guarantees at the Club Naval? How could he claim success when even Sanguinetti was making public statements claiming that human rights violations would be judged by the ordinary courts?[41] It can only be assumed that General Medina had decided to put all his eggs in 'a secret Sanguinetti basket'. It is widely believed that Sanguinetti and Medina reached an 'informal gentlemen's agreement' in which the former assured the general that he would personally see to it that the military would be protected. In all likelihood this was the price Sanguinetti was willing to pay to get Medina to support the talks despite the pressure from the hard-line.[42] Sanguinetti was therefore instrumental in gaining the confidence of the pro-negotiating Medina, persuading him that he would not support an unrestricted amnesty for political prisoners and that the issue of human rights violations was better 'settled out of court'.

According to one military source, 'The great architect [of the transition] was Sanguinetti who persuaded some of the military of the best way to engineer the exit.'[43] Together with General Medina he had made the Club Naval talks viable by leaving out guarantees of impunity, allowing Medina to calm fears within the military through a secret promise, and permitting the military negotiators to claim that the Armed Forces were leaving power 'with honour, which is what we had hoped for'.[44] If indeed Sanguinetti and Medina had reached a private understanding, the victory of the former at the polls in November 1984 partially vindicated the General's bet. As Gillespie points out, 'The Colorados offered the military a suitable force to which to hand over power, as well as certain guarantees that their interests would be respected thereafter.'[45]

During the electoral campaign which followed the pact, the problems to arise in the democratic period over the lack of clarity on the human rights issue surfaced with a vengeance. The Blancos accused the Frente of having abdicated from their principles by participating in the Club Naval and indicated that the coalition had pacted impunity with the military.

The Frente, on the other hand, was preoccupied with trying to prove both to its more radical members and to the public at large that participation in the pact had not in any way implied an abdication of principle. There had been a 'strong critical current' within the coalition against Seregni's decision to participate in the talks. The radical factions thought that in doing so Seregni had 'made commitments which transcended the directives imposed by the Executive Desk'.[46] Participation in the pact had been ratified by the leadership by 14 votes out of 31 with 6 abstentions.[47]

According to Seregni, the Frente had made it clear that it would only negotiate if justice were not compromised, and that if such a compromise were to be made between the Colorados and the military the negotiations would have ended 'without the backing of the FA'.[48] It would be a major concern for the Frente and for the radical sectors in particular to prove that participation was not a sign of softness with dictators and violators. Seregni consistently claimed that his coalition had not renounced 'any of its principles, abandoned any of its banners'. He assured everyone that 'the government that takes power will not promote actions of hatred, revanchism or revenge but will promote an absolutely independent justice'.[49]

Predictably, the Colorados had no such problems. Unlike both of the other parties, their executive had with one minor exception, approved the pact.[50] Whatever the secret arrangement between the future president and General Medina, the Colorados also indicated that justice would proceed. According to future Vice-President Tarigo 'the theme of human rights violations was not discussed and the extension of military jurisdiction was not successful. The text of the Act 19 is, with a couple of touches that make no difference to the substance, that of the Constitution itself.'[51]

During the electoral campaign an attempt was made to heal the rifts caused by the transition. The Concertación Nacional Programática was set up in an attempt to arrive at a social and political policy pact between the parties in preparation for the democratic period. It was within the CONAPRO that the first explicit joint party commitment was made to truth and justice. In October 1984, largely due to the efforts of the country's major human rights organization, the Servicio de Paz y Justicia (SERPAJ) a declaration was signed which promisingly stated:

> Keeping Uruguayan society ignorant of the truth of the accusations, and allowing the impunity of the acts which are considered to be illegal constitutes a grave risk for respect for human rights in the future . . . all the organs of the State must seek to clear up the events referred to according to their respective competencies . . . the Judiciary must be provided with the effective and juridical instruments which will permit effective investigation, without impinging upon the powers of the Executive to clear up the facts.[52]

Despite this apparently clear commitment all was not well. The agreement was not personally signed by Sanguinetti, but by a Colorado representative. The CONAPRO basically collapsed as soon as the democratic government had been inaugurated.[53] Finally, in his inaugural speech Sanguinetti made no mention of justice for human rights violations. The President reminded people that the Armed Forces should be treated 'without the spirit of revanchism, with all the respect and dignity which should be accorded to an institution of the State'.[54]

Accounting for the Problems with Truth and Justice

In the Uruguayan transition, the military not only failed to pass an authoritarian constitution to institutionalize a 'protected democracy', but they also failed to extract formal guarantees of impunity from the opposition parties at the Club Naval pact. None the less, a number of factors inherent in the dynamics of the transition process proved to undermine the successful promotion of human rights policies after President Sanguinetti took power in March 1985.

As indicated in Chapter 1, the transition was pacted between equals. The negotiations consisted of a *reforma pactada* or pacted reform, in which the military did not succeed in getting the guarantees they initially sought from the civilians, but in which the civilians were in turn unable to impose a radical *ruptura* with the past.[55] Thus, although the military did not gain new constitutional prerogatives they remained extremely powerful. The experience of power had radically transformed their self-conception. They now aimed to reserve 'autonomy as political actors during the negotiating process and later, after leaving the exercise of power, they would not consider themselves as part of the State but would instead place themselves above it, becoming its guardians'.[56]

Moreover, although the Club Naval pact did not guarantee impunity, and although the only written document to emerge from it, the Institutional Act 19, represented a restoration of the pre-authoritarian political system, guaranteeing the return of the 1967 Constitution and giving the military no greater formal power than they had possessed before the breakdown of democracy, the pact implied the tacit recognition of the military's institutional autonomy. It legitimated the Armed Forces as political actors with the capacity to negotiate. Through it, the parties legitimated them as valid interlocutors. Thus, not only did the parties have limited room to impose policies on the military to which the latter were actively opposed, but it was also unlikely that the future democratic executive would break 'the rules of the game and promote the trial of one of the parties involved in the pact'.[57]

Secondly, the Uruguayan transition was characterized by a dynamic of restoration rather than renovation. No new democratic and consensual symbols were created, and inertia ruled.[58] A conservative, immobilist climate based on a 'Fear of change dominated the political sentiments of a population whose main aspiration was to return to a rosier past.'[59] Uruguayans seemed to want *un ayer mejorado para mañana*.[60] It was to be a *cambio en paz* according to Sanguinetti, Seregni's *salida realista*.[61] The prudence was apparently favoured by the population: despite the proscriptions, 71 per cent of Montevideans thought that the pact had occurred at the right moment and only 22 per cent thought that the politicians should have waited for better conditions.[62] More revealingly, it was the most conservative party which had won the election. Thus, a radical discourse of democratic renovation through truth and justice could hardly fare so well in a conservative climate of this nature.

Notably, one of the key elements of restoration was the re-establishment of the pre-authoritarian party system described in the first chapter, namely the DSVS and *lema* system. Thus, restoration implied party fragmentation, exacerbated intra-party divisions, and promoted programmatic compromise necessary to accommodate different factions with different ideological and political inclinations within the same grouping. Parties were not 'programmatic' or internally consistent and unified regarding either transition strategies or the human rights issue.[63] As Gillespie points out, the electoral law tended to 'punish parties of principle and reward alliances of convenience' and the 'fight between the parties centred on the procedures and personalities as much as on principles'.[64] The FA and the Blanco Party suffered most from this problem. Exile only exacerbated divisions between the internal and exile factions, divisions which in the case of the FA militated against the development of an internally consistent human rights policy in the democratic period.

The transition process by which the parties had regained their political prominence, namely through internal party elections and later through the transitional elections themselves, discouraged inter-party alliances and promoted competitive differentiation. The transition was simultaneously a liberalization and an electoral competition giving the parties little time and incentive to form a solid opposition block.[65] But it was not only the 1982 primaries and the national elections in November 1984 which encouraged competition and division between the parties. The élite negotiations also affected the fragile unity between the parties most committed to truth and justice; the breakdown of the alliance between the Blancos and the FA over the latter's decision to participate in the talks despite the continued proscription and imprisonment of the Blanco's leader greatly diminished the possibility of a long-term co-operation between them under democratic rule.

Furthermore, although the regime in Uruguay lost the plebiscite in 1980, this unexpected victory for the forces of democracy neither gave the opposition parties the need to make alliances, or the time to develop an inter-party practice of human rights defence in co-operation with the nascent human rights organizations.

Thirdly, the transition was characterized by the increasing importance of élite negotiations and the decrease in the importance of popular mobilizations as a means of conquering political space for the opposition. There were three major waves of social mobilization which aimed to oust the military from power, but they were essentially subordinated to the parties.[66] The transition was an affair of the political élites and the military.[67] This had a number of implications. Since the human rights movement was most strongly linked to the social organizations, this lack of power also implied a lack of strength of the most committed truth and justice lobby. Moreover, since the strength of the FA lay within the social movement, its decision to adopt the conservative Colorado path of negotiations led to a weakening of the social organizations and the party most committed to human rights and strengthened the conservative Colorado party, whose links with the social movement were almost non-existent.

Fourthly, it was the party closest to the military which won the elections in 1984. The Colorado party's rhetoric, in keeping with the conservative tendencies of the electorate, encouraged prudence and conservatism above principle and renovation. It was difficult to expect that Sanguinetti would 'make recourse to ethical discourses' or represent radical new symbols of truth and justice in the democratic period, given that the transitional discourse of the party represented 'the anti-values of that possibility'. Sanguinetti, 'in his version of realism maintained one . . . the acceptance of the reality of power and wiped out the reality which the opposition could create'.[68]

Moreover, the nature of the relations between the Colorado party and the military was not favourable to future government policies for truth and justice. The governing party had established an associative relationship with the military command. Sanguinetti had given the military his personal commitment to 'contain' the human rights issue in exchange for a reduction in military institutional demands. The outcome had been an Institutional Act which had not given the military the powers they had desired, but which had produced a hidden and personalized presidential agreement which aimed to protect them from prosecution. Comfortable coexistence at the cost of principle was the name of the game.[69]

Apart from the factors related to the dynamic of the transition process itself, a number of elements regarding the human rights issue itself weakened the chances for truth and justice. In the first place, the human rights movement in Uruguay was a late developer and an isolated *decidor de la verdad* (speaker of the truth).[70] It was weak, fragmented, and had little power to influence the parties.[71] Until 1981 human rights activism occurred only in exile. In 1975 Buenos Aires became the centre of opposition activity. Senators Zelmar Michelini of the FA and Blanco leaders, Hector Gutiérrez Ruíz and Wilson Ferreira Aldunate were the key figures in the exiled campaign against the regime. The most important instances of international denunciations were the testimony of Zelmar Michelini of the FA at the Russell Tribunal in Rome in March of 1974, and the testimony of Ferreira Aldunate at the US Congress Committee for International Relations in Washington in June 1976.[72] The latter had resulted in the passing of the Koch

Amendment which placed an arms sale embargo on the country which Koch had labelled 'the torture chamber of Latin America'.[73]

From 1976 onwards, Mexico City and Caracas became the centres of opposition, following the military coup in Argentina and the assassination of Michelini and Gutierrez Ruíz by the Uruguayan and Argentine security forces. The Frente's Comité Coordinador, or Co-ordinating Committee in exile, the trade union Organismo Coordinador de las Actividades de la Central Nacional de Trabajadores en el Exterior (OCACNTE) formed in May 1979, the Asociación de Familiares de Uruguayos Desaparacidos (AFUDE) formed in Paris in 1979, and individual Blanco leaders became the focus of resistance to the dictatorship. In 1977 the Communist and Socialist parties formally unified their activities, and in April 1979 they co-ordinated with the Blanco Party, forming the pluralist Grupo de Convergencia Democrática Uruguaya (CDU) under the leadership of Ferreira's son, Juan Raul Ferreira. The CDU became the principal voice of the opposition abroad. The aim of the group was to 'contribute to the re-establishment of Uruguayan democracy by collaborating in the preparation and implementation of a responsible political project'.[74] It focused primarily on demands for the liberation of the political prisoners and the immediate restoration of civil and political liberties.[75] As a result of this unification, joint solidarity groups were formed in the different countries of exile carrying out propaganda work against the regime and keeping contact with individual leaders inside the country.[76]

Opposition to military rule within Uruguay itself did not assume institutional forms until after the 1980 plebiscite. Rather, it was limited to a silent or cultural rebellion. The *canto popular*, prison poetry, 'subversive' literature, and isolated forms of symbolic resistance were the main expressions of opposition up to 1980.[77] Thus, for the first seven years of military rule there was no organized internal opposition at all, be it human-rights-focused or otherwise. The first formal human rights group, the Madres y Familiares de los Uruguayos Desparecidos en Argentina (MFUDA), was formed only four years after the beginning of military rule in 1977, in response to the disappearance of Uruguayans in Argentina. It began to pressure the Uruguayan authorities for information on the whereabouts of their relatives in 1979, and the regime found it extremely easy to deny any involvement in disappearances which had occurred in a neighbouring country.

It was only as late as 1981 that the first pluralist human rights organization, which became the leader of the human rights movement, the SERPAJ, emerged. However, lacking any institutional backing, it was easily persecuted by the authorities. It was declared illegal in 1983 after organizing a hunger strike in protest against the stalemate in the talks between the parties and the military, and was only re-constituted in 1984 during the electoral campaign. The SERPAJ promoted the organization of the Movimiento de Madres y Familiares de Procesados por la Justicia Militar (MMFPJM) in 1982, and the formation of the Madres y Familiares de Desaparecidos en Uruguay (MFDU) in 1983.[78]

Similarly, there were no third party legal defence organizations until 1981. The Colegio de Abogados (CA) or Bar Association, the only existing organization capable of undertaking the defence of victims, refused to do so. Its directorate was dominated by the pro-regime factions of the traditional parties. These won the six internal elections between 1968 and 1980, controlled the organization and consistently refused to adopt resolutions in protest against human rights violations. Only in 1981 did the Colegio awaken from 'a long period of lethargy to which successive directorates submitted it'.[79] The first legal defence organizations comparable to the Chilean Human Rights Commission, namely the National Commission for Human Rights and the Instituto de Estudios Sociales y Legales (IELSUR) only emerged in September 1983 and 1984 respectively.[80]

However, unlike its Chilean counterpart, the National Commission 'stayed on the margins of criticism of the military's administration of power . . . it lacked an internal structure beyond the periodic meetings of its members. Its life was ephemeral and its activity was practically paralyzed with the beginning of the electoral campaign towards the end of 1984 and it finally dissolved itself under democratic rule.'[81] The IELSUR, founded by lawyers who abandoned the *Colegio* in protest against the directorate's decision to limit itself to the administrative processing of human rights cases on behalf of the National Human Rights Commission, began to take on human rights cases in co-ordination with the SERPAJ from 1984 onwards, only a year before the democratic government took power.

The co-ordination of the human rights movement was only institutionalized in 1984 with the creation of the Coordinadora de Entidades de Derechos Humanos (CEDH), composed of all the human rights organizations, the three major parties, and the key organizations of the social movement, namely the trade union federation reconstituted in 1983, the Plenario Intersindical de Trabajadores–Confederación Nacional de Trabajadores (PIT–CNT), the Asociación Civil de Estudiantes de Enseñanza Pública–Federación de

Estudiantes Universitarios (ASCEEP-FEUU), and the Federación Unificadora de Cooperativas de Vivienda por Ayuda Mutua (FUCVAM).

The human rights movement did not have deep roots in the country as a whole, and its regional networks suffered from fragmentation and weakness. The first regional, non-metropolitan human rights opposition only emerged in 1983, initially tied to local churches. These organizations encountered 'a "great vacuum" due to the lack of openness to collective expression. The "de-freezing" of social interaction occurred after the mobilization in the capital city of the country and only recently impelled by the mobilization of the political parties.'[82] Likewise, the Comisiones Departamentales de Derechos Humanos (CDDH) in Salto, Paysandú, Rocha, Florida, Durazno, and Maldonado, local pluralist commissions of notables set up along the lines of the National Human Rights Commission, 'gradually lost their functions with the arrival of the democratic government'.[83] None of these groups succeeded in setting up a national or regional co-ordination. Moreover, 'with the installation of the democratic regime in March 1985, a generalized slowdown in the activities of the movement in the interior of the country took place'.[84]

The effective development of a human rights movement in Uruguay was held back for a number of reasons. In the first place, the nature of repression militated against the formation of opposition groups. 'Due to the very characteristics of the country—a homogeneous geography and a scarce and concentrated population—the control and disarticulation of civil society were complete.'[85] The regime successfully eliminated any 'space of opposition' each of them 'discovered and annihilated'.[86] Control of the media in Uruguay was total until 1980.[87] Strict censorship ensured that exile newspapers which publicized human rights violations were not known inside the country.[88] The call for an amnesty for political prisoners, for example, only became public for the first time in 1982, when it was mentioned in a minor opposition paper, *La Plaza*.[89] The first signed petition from the organization of relatives of political prisoners to President Álvarez to release the prisoners was also made in 1982, and it represented one of the first public challenges to the regime over the issue of human rights violations.[90] Similarly, the first public list of the disappeared appeared in November 1983.[91] The first public denunciation of torture and demand for justice was made in June 1983, when the SERPAJ publicized the plight of 25 Communist Youth students in military custody.[92]

Secondly, the absence of state-autonomous institutions like the Catholic Church which were capable of or willing to protect fragile opposition networks was detrimental to the effective development of a human rights movement, since the effectiveness of the Church as moral opposition to regimes which claim to defend Christian values cannot be underestimated.[93] The power of the Catholic Church in Uruguay was limited because of the secular nature of that society. Moreover, the hierarchy maintained 'an official and frightened silence, and did not stimulate or protect those who tried to organize themselves to defend the rights of the victims of repression'. Only individual religious figures undertook such tasks, but always 'without receiving the protection or the institutional cover of their superiors'.[94] The SERPAJ, for example, founded by a priest, was expressly denied the support of the Church hierarchy.[95]

Thirdly, Uruguay suffered from a lack of international attention. The importance that international human rights pressure has in forcing repressive regimes to curb human rights violations, thereby boosting the confidence of the internal opposition, and weakening the legitimacy of the regimes, has been noted by a number of authors.[96] The fifth Institutional Act on human rights decreed in 1976, for example, was dictated largely as a result of the pressure applied by the Carter administration.[97] Similarly, the 1976 US Congressional hearings on Uruguay also had a great impact on the self-confidence of the regime. Yet, according to the International Commission of Jurists, despite the fact that 'the situation of human rights was very serious in Uruguay, comparable in all aspects to that of Chile . . . it [was] much less well known at the international level'.[98] Partly due to the fact that the Uruguayan slow motion coup was eclipsed by the violent coup in Chile, 'The international preoccupation with events in Chile afforded the Uruguayan dictatorship the luxury of silence and anonymity, allowing it to act with impunity while creating a totalitarian regime in a nation with an even more democratic and civil tradition than Chile.'[99] The system of imprisonment and the relative absence of disappearances may also have made Uruguay seem less worthy of international attention. Moreover, Uruguay was never as prominent a member of the international community as the other countries of the Southern Cone. Its traditional parties had no international counterparts or linkages being unique to that country. As there were no human rights organizations until 1980, no natural channels for international support developed. Uruguay thus received fewer visits from international organizations. The only missions to Uruguay were by the International Commission of Jurists and Amnesty International in November 1974 and in December of 1975, by the US Bar Association in May 1978 and by the Red Cross in 1979.[100] The members of the Inter-American Commission for Human Rights of the OAS were never allowed into the country.[101]

As single issue organizations, human rights organizations do not represent a power alternative. If their demands are not taken up in the formal political arena, if the parties do not adopt human rights platforms, there is little hope for a national political solution to the human rights legacy. Uruguay and Chile met with very different levels of success in creating an effective human-rights-focused opposition. Consequently, the ability or the willingness of the democratic parties to press for truth and justice in the transitional period varied.

In Uruguay, the depth of party commitments to truth and justice was very superficial for a number of reasons. For one thing, the autonomous political power of the movement was not great. Up to 1981, human rights activism had not been a reflection of a strong institutionalized movement, but the product of the concern of leading opposition politicians who denounced human rights violations in international forums in their capacity as party leaders rather than as human rights activists. Human rights activism was a part of the general opposition activities of exiled Blanco, FA, and CNT leaders. Individuals undertook to denounce human rights violations not as human rights activists but as representatives of opposition parties and organizations. After 1981, despite the emergence of a number of autonomous groups, the fragmentation and late development outlined above did not permit them much control over party policy formation. Party delegates in the CEDH, for example, lacked representativeness; they reflected individual rather than party commitments.[102] This constant 'trumping' of partisan over human rights activist identities was partly a function of Uruguay's intensely 'partidocratic' traditions, and partly a reflection of the stunted development of the human rights movement. Although the *denuncia* of human rights violations became one of the triggers which weakened the position of the military and promoted the transition process, it did not reflect great organizational strength and cohesion.

Furthermore, the nature of the parties in opposition to military rule also militated against the formation of an effective unified human rights opposition. The Colorado party, which was to lead the future democratic government, had undergone a profound process of authoritarianization throughout the 1960s and 1970s, actively promoting and participating in military rule. It was only with the internal party elections of 1982, a mere two years away from the inauguration of democracy, that the balance of forces within the party shifted. The democratic leaders of the party had no tradition of participation in a human-rights-focused opposition. As a party unique to Uruguay, it had no formalized international connections. It did not suffer from the effects of mass exile so there was no external or international current to encourage it to adopt a human rights platform or to promote policies of truth and justice, so it emerged in the transition with a very conservative agenda.

On the other hand, the parties which were under democratic rule to constitute the opposition to the Colorado executive after March 1985, namely the Blanco Party and the FA, were more committed to human rights. The impact of this activism, however, was hampered due to the isolationism of exile. What is more, both of them laid a greater emphasis on restoration of civil and political rights and amnesty than on truth and justice.[103]

The tendencies outlined above were exacerbated by the timing of the emergence of the movement, and the presentation of the specific demands for truth and justice. These demands emerged relatively late so that they could not reflect a long-term development of consensus on policy and strategy between the human rights groups and the opposition parties. More importantly, however, they also emerged in the period of internal and national party elections, a time in which inter-party competition militated against the undertaking of broad consensus-building activities, tending rather to foster a separation and differentiation between the major parties. The priorities of unifying fragmented parties dominated by the *lema* system, the increasing intensity of competition between the three main democratic contenders, and the necessity of convincing the military to negotiate were issues which took up the greater part of party political energies. Thus, despite the importance of the CEDH in promoting many of the anti-government demonstrations in 1984 and early 1985, and although it was SERPAJ that promoted the first informal meetings between party leaders, the links forged between these leaders and SERPAJ were short-lived and did not engender any deep personal commitments to the causes of truth and justice. Co-operation between the human rights groups and the parties peaked during the electoral campaign in 1984, only to wane soon after.

Fourthly, partly due to the parties' lack of explicit commitment, and partly because of its own radical 'popular' orientation, the SERPAJ forged closer links with the social movement than with the political parties. The SERPAJ constantly emphasized popular mobilization as the only means of achieving truth and justice. In its view, 'under no circumstance will these measures be easily applied without a considerable popular mobilization which will demand that the government put them into practice'.[104] The stress on mobilization which it adopted as part of the social movement also collided with the élite negotiating logic of the transition, thus further distancing the organizations from the parties. The lack of executive co-ordination resulting from this popular 'democratic' approach was felt at CEDH meetings. These were more deliberative than executive, reducing its effectiveness in playing a leadership role.[105] In the words of its leader, the SERPAJ's 'attitude of impassioned "teller of the truth" meant that it had to suffer a certain isolation even from the political sectors which had similar interests but which gave greater priority to other political tactics over a radical demand for the truth'.[106]

In the fifth place, although all the political parties apparently supported justice, investigations of grave human rights violations, and an amnesty for political prisoners, this commitment was beset by a number of weaknesses.[107] The links between the parties and the human rights organizations, for example, were fragile. When SERPAJ carried out a hunger strike and called for a Day for National Reflection on 25 August 1983, in response to the breakdown of the first Parque Hotel talks between the military and the parties, it was only 'faced with the response in solidarity and the mobilization generated that the political parties decided to accompany the protest, calling the population to participate in the mobilization of the 25th of August'.[108]

Moreover, the subject of human rights violations was not a major issue in the transitional process as a whole, nor in the election campaign in 1984. The opposition press which began to emerge in 1981, such as the Blanco paper *La Democracia* and the Colorado's *Opinar* and *Correo del Viernes*, focused primarily on constitutional issues and demands for the recovery of civil and political rights. The issue of amnesty for political prisoners was the focus of the human rights violations debate. It was the constant banner of all the protests and demonstrations against the regime in the transitional period.[109] For Sanguinetti it was 'the theme of national pacification'.[110]

Truth and justice were therefore put on the back-burner. On the whole, there was a conspicuous silence surrounding these issues throughout the whole transition. 'At no time was the issue of human rights violations dealt with and demands were limited to calls for the restoration of the traditional democratic standards ... human rights were reduced to the humanitarian gesture of demanding the liberation of the political prisoners.' Thus, the parties did not in general commit themselves to 'a social content beyond the theoretical benefits of a democratic system whose traditional structures were being restored. The political parties themselves left the demands of the human rights movement out of the political debate and shifted the nucleus of the electoral campaign to the discussion of ... and demand for the liberation of the political prisoners as the essence of social reconciliation.'[111]

Seemingly implicit in this attitude was that the issue of 'revisionism ... was not and should not be posed, given that it is a problem which will only arise in two and a half years. Its discussion at this time would not lead to any positive outcome and would only introduce possible internal conflicts at a time when the parties are engaged in other arduous and urgent tasks'.[112]

As noted above, the issues of truth and justice were not clearly dealt with by the civilians and the military during the two negotiations at the Parque Hotel and the Club Naval. Instead, they were deliberately ignored. As Ferreira later put it 'Nobody wanted to introduce as an unwelcome guest an issue which would have been prickly and would have hurt the negotiations as they unfolded.'[113] Furthermore, the key Club Naval talks were secret. There were no written records of the meetings or of the agreements made. This allowed the Colorado party to pursue a two-track policy: on the one hand it publicly supported truth and justice, while on the other it made private arrangements with the military to prevent just these policies. Sanguinetti probably reached a private agreement with the military on the issue of prosecution outside the confines of the formal negotiations, so that although the transition did not produce any explicit guarantees for impunity, such guarantees were privately conceded by Sanguinetti.

Secrecy increased the climate of mutual suspicion between the Blancos and the Frente, since the absence of the Blanco Party from the transitional pact enabled it to accuse the Frente of having pacted impunity for the military. Lack of policy, ambiguity, and a general silence meant not only that the human rights issue had a very low moral and national profile, but also that it became very easy for parties to renege on fragile commitments. Gillespie points out that when pacting a transition 'ambiguity can be functional when debating highly charged issues'.[114] But it can be deadly when it is combined with a similar ambiguity in the commitments existing outside the confines of the pact itself.

Another feature which hindered the successful resolution of the human rights issue in the democratic period was that individual party platforms suffered from a lack of clear-cut truth and justice policies and concentrated overwhelmingly on the issues of amnesty for political prisoners, exile, and job recoveries in the public sector. No party made explicit the need for the government to undertake specific measures to permit the active promotion of truth and justice. The attitude to justice was *laissez-faire*, in that the government would have to play no active part in the process. Global and officially promoted truth-telling as a distinct policy was not advocated. Moreover, the Human Rights Co-ordinator was unable to 'overcome the conflicting positions of the political parties' and even to achieve an explicit policy consensus on the popular cause of the liberation of political prisoners as well as 'the revision of crimes against humanity committed by the military. The parties preferred to make a generic declaration about the moral duty of the future democratic government to investigate and judge the crimes using all government powers.'[115]

The Colorado platform mentioned only the issues of amnesty and pardon, the return of exiles, and job restorations.[116] While the party supported an amnesty, excepting those cases involving homicide, they rejected the concept of reciprocity, excluding the military from an amnesty. Its programme stated that it was imperative 'to undertake the task of national pacification which can ensure that there will be no-one in the country excluded. There can be no person deprived of their freedom for ideological reasons . . . The pacification aim will be implemented through a number of political and legal initiatives, among them an amnesty law dictated with a broad humanitarian spirit, complemented by the necessary pardons.' Justice or truth were not mentioned as a part of the party's government programme.[117] The Blanco Party manifesto endorsed policies similar to those of the Colorado party. The party was divided with regard to the amnesty for political prisoners. The Wilsonistas favoured an unrestricted amnesty whereas the two other more conservative *sub-lemas* followed the Colorado line. Again the Blanco platform had no position on truth-telling or justice.[118]

The FA and the UC were the only parties which explicitly demanded the 'situation of the detained disappeared be cleared up'.[119] The Frente, however, did not present specific government policies for the official promotion of truth-telling or justice. Finally, the coalition supported a general and unrestricted amnesty, rejecting the Colorado's differentiation between prisoners accused of homicide and prisoners of conscience. In their view, the military courts had provided no procedural guarantees and consequently sentences could not be regarded as legally acceptable. It was felt that whatever crime had been committed had been more than paid for by the inhuman conditions suffered during prolonged imprisonment. Last but not least, most of the prisoners were Frentistas.[120]

This general lack of programmatic clarity was compounded by the fact that public statements by party leaders on the issues of truth and justice were for the most part similarly unclear and ambiguous. Sanguinetti's declarations were the most ambivalent of all. His support of justice was tempered by his 'promotion of a discourse of forgetfulness'.[121] On the one hand, he claimed that 'In the Uruguay of 1985 what we need is justice. An independent justice which must act with serenity and apply the law without signs of weakness.'[122] On the other hand, he repeatedly emphasized that 'the most important thing is that there should be a great capacity for forgiveness, because if we cannot forgive the errors of the past we will remain buried in them'.[123] All the political and social actors should proceed 'without rancour and without a spirit of revenge'.[124] It was useless to insist on 'the memory of past conflicts', and it was desirable to 'turn over a new page, leave all that to historical memory which is always wise and a good counsellor'.[125]

The future government basically adopted a *laissez-faire* attitude to justice and truth. The government would promote neither truth nor justice but neither would it 'forbid a citizen from denouncing criminal acts committed by some public servant before the ordinary penal system'.[126] They did not favour an active government promotion of justice. 'We the politicians will administer or legislate, that is our role, but we will not judge.'[127] Sanguinetti was opposed to a policy of official truth-telling which he dismissed as revisionism. Only the courts could revise 'criminal situations'.[128] The government could not get involved 'in the task of historical revision which is the role of historians anyway or of assigning responsibilities'.[129]

Blanco attitudes to justice were similar to those of the Colorados, although Ferreira Aldunate took a rhetorically tough line on the issue, having narrowly escaped assassination himself in Buenos Aires in 1976. The ordinary courts should judge members of the military accused of human rights violations. Similarly, 'politicians could not carry out trials. They cannot judge if a person committed a crime or not. That is a role exclusive to the Judiciary.'[130] On a few occasions, Blanco leaders also advanced a similar *discurso de olvido*.[131] According to Ferreira 'if the price we have to pay to achieve a climate of national understanding and to reconstruct the country is to sacrifice justice in some way, well, we have to pay it and it will be paid'.[132] These kinds of statements became more frequent with the partial *rapprochement* between the two traditional parties after the national elections in November 1984.[133]

'Though all parties were circumspect in admitting that it might be necessary on pragmatic grounds to bolt shut the Pandora's Box of human rights, it was clear that the left had the strongest feelings on the subject.'[134] None the less, the Frente did not advocate government sponsored truth-telling: 'The FA would not promote the application a policy of revisionism.'[135] Líber Seregni, supported justice and was opposed to an amnesty for the military. He claimed that it was not only those who had ordered human rights violations, but also those who had carried them out who had to be prosecuted.[136] He did not, however, outline a government policy which would permit successful prosecution. On his release from prison in March 1984, Seregni mentioned only the problem of exile and amnesty, claiming that the Frente did not think of 'revanchism or revenge or hatreds. But we do want justice'.[137] Finally, he favoured the independent action of the courts.[138]

As noted above, the only explicit joint party commitment made to truth and justice was signed in October 1984 within the CONAPRO. This was largely due to the efforts of SERPAJ. Yet, this commitment was made within the fragile structures of the CONAPRO, which collapsed with the inauguration of the democratic government.

The human rights organizations represented by SERPAJ were the only ones to produce a clear policy statement on truth and justice. SERPAJ advocated the creation of a parliamentary commission to investigate human rights violations and send the information gathered to the courts. It recommended purging the ranks of those repeatedly implicated in the worst violations. Unlike the parties it explicitly argued that 'the future government must provide real guarantees that will encourage the victims to communicate the information that they have'. This was deemed necessary because 'we are talking about an institution. The isolated citizen lacks the strength to call the Armed Forces to account.' More radically, the organization wanted:

> Not only the punishment of a few transgressors of social norms, but also the trial of the administration of the Armed Forces as an institution during this period and of the National Security Doctrine which they sustained . . . this regime was not a government of a few military personalities but a government of the Armed Forces which did not result from

a gradual domination but which was actually juridically formalized by norms inspired by the National Security Doctrine. We are therefore faced with a Military Power which has to account not only for the conduct of its men but also for the logic of its workings and existence.

They therefore wanted a truth-telling policy which would reveal the institutional and systematic nature of the repression, an objective which could not be achieved merely through prosecution of individuals in the courts. Finally, like the Frente, SERPAJ also supported a general and unrestricted amnesty.[139]

The urgent and critical tone of SERPAJ's most complete statement in the transitional period reflected both its lack of power and the fear that the movement was faced with parties reluctant to assume the necessary responsibility. They criticized the *laissez-faire* attitude of the parties and attacked the position of the 'understanding pragmatists who repeat that "politics is the art of the possible", in order to avoid committing themselves'.[140]

Finally, the military predictably resisted any form of truth and justice. These were dismissed as 'revisionism' and 'revanchism'. As early as 1976, the General Command had made their view on the matter quite clear. The institution would not permit any 'form of revisionism of the actions of its members during the war against subversion'.[141]

In September 1982 President General Álvarez made a terrible gaffe. He stated that 'the Armed Forces are open to any attempt anyone wishes to make regarding [revisionism]. They have nothing to hide. The country went through a war, a state of internal war, which was approved by the General Assembly.' The following day he retracted in a televised statement, claiming that the press had misinterpreted his idea of 'revisionism', and that he wanted to 'discard any thought or attempt to proceed with a revision of the actions and of the difficult and painful contribution of the Armed Forces, be it now or in the future'.[142]

The idea of an amnesty for political prisoners was rejected, except for those who had not participated in 'actions in which they robbed, kidnapped, or killed repeatedly'. However, since the military claimed that all the prisoners were terrorists this acceptance was rendered meaningless.[143]

Last but not least, the military in Uruguay had never been submitted to the ordinary courts under authoritarian rule. In 1983, the Military Justice system had punished the officers who had tortured and killed doctor Vladimir Roslik, and 50 officers had been tried by the military Tribunales de Honor.[144] A precedent of civil jurisdiction over military crimes, and of military acceptance of this jurisdiction, would obviously have made it harder for the Armed Forces to argue in favour of military jurisdiction. Moreover, it would have made it more difficult for them to argue that prosecution for violations constituted a political attack on the institution. Because prosecution for human rights violations under democratic rule could not be regarded simply as a continuation of the pre-existing state of affairs the military were in a better position to oppose trials as signs of 'revanchism'.

Setting the Stage for Conflict: Los Infortunios de la Excesiva Sensatez[145]

The Uruguayan transition 'set a course which left its mark on the period which followed it.'[146] As this chapter has shown, the weakness of the human rights movement, the ambiguity over human rights commitments, and the lack of emphasis on truth and justice, and finally the dynamics of the transition process itself, made progress towards and élite convergence on the human rights issue very difficult. After the elections a further attempt at party unity for future democratic governability was made with the creation of the CONAPRO, where the parties agreed to build consensual economic, social, and human rights policies. Yet the CONAPRO did not overcome legitimate party differences or sectoral divisions, and collapsed with the inauguration of democratic rule. The Colorados were therefore faced with a democratic opposition with which it had few ties of loyalty. It had minority representation within a legislature which was ready to do battle on the human rights and economic policy fronts. The Colorados gained 13 out of 29 senate seats, and 41 out of 99 seats in the Chamber of Deputies. The Frente gained 6 and 21 seats in the Senate and Chamber of Deputies respectively, while the Blancos gained 11 and 35 seats. The Union Cívica won 2 seats in the Chamber of Deputies.

Internal party conflicts could also be expected. The Frente had the worst internal scenario. The election had represented a victory for the moderate factions. The Lista 99 and the Christian Democrats together had gained 51 per cent of the vote. The Communist and Socialist parties as well as the radical left group, the IDI, had gained 49 per cent. The system of weighted internal voting, however, bore no relation to the electoral support given to each group. Seregni's moderate position was therefore internally precarious.[147] This division within the Frente, although not a product of the pact itself, also prevented the coalition from supporting unified coalition policies for truth and justice in the democratic period.[148]

Finally, public opinion was ambiguous. The percentage which had voted for the parties advocating a general and unrestricted amnesty represented only 44.6 per cent of votes. Moreover, 64 per cent of the votes reflected an acceptance of the pacted transition which made truth and justice more difficult.[149] Nonetheless, in May 1985, 44 per cent of Montevideans thought that human rights violations had been the worst feature of the military regime, and a year later 73 per cent of them were still convinced that human rights violators should be tried.[150]

Despite the relatively negative scenario which this chapter has analysed, the outcome was not pre-determined. As Colorado Vice-President Tarigo proudly claimed on television, the parties had succeeded in reducing the Club Naval pact 'to a tiny little thing'.[151] Impunity had not been negotiated and was therefore not inevitable. But the democratic opposition parties most committed to truth and justice would have to overcome partisan differences to resist the President's already apparent lack of commitment; and they would also have to implement a military policy which would quieten the fears of the hard-line and gain the acceptance of the negotiators for truth and justice. Finally, they would have to heed the warning of the human rights organizations that the feasibility of truth and justice policies 'is weakened proportionally to the time which passes before they are applied.' As it turned out, it was the Colorado and Blanco parties which overcame partisan differences, creating an alliance which militated against justice. The government's military policy was never separated from the human rights issue and was based on protecting the hard-line against demands for justice. Finally, it was only after a year and a half of bitter inter- and intra-partisan struggles that the parties resolved the human rights issue. But by then it was too late.

4

Truth and Justice in the Transitional Period in Chile, 1988–1990

Una Salida Constitucional:[1] *A Defiant General and a United Opposition*

The Chilean transition evolved in three phases, and was carried out according to the transitory provisions of the 1980 Constitution, which provided for a step-by-step passage to a protected democracy under the tutelage of the military. The first of these steps was the referendum of 5 October 1988. Chileans were asked to decide whether General Pinochet should continue to rule for another eight years. The regime lost the vote, thus initiating the formal process of transition from military authoritarian rule.

This defeat led to the second phase, between October 1988 and December 1989, which consisted of negotiations between the regime and the opposition for constitutional reforms which were submitted to a plebiscite in July 1989; of the strengthening of authoritarian political and institutional enclaves with the passage of restrictive laws by General Pinochet; and of the national electoral campaign and the elections in December 1989 from which the democratic opposition emerged victorious. During the final phase of the transition between December 1989 and March 1990, General Pinochet passed additional last-minute *leyes de amarre* or 'tying up' laws to further restrict the powers of the new democratic government. The transition ended in March 1990 with the inauguration of the new democratic government led by President Aylwin.

The transition began in 1988 when, by a narrow majority of 54.71 per cent, Chileans voted against the extension of General Pinochet's rule.[2] Unlike Uruguay, however, the democratic opposition had resolved its political and strategic differences and was united from the outset. The regime had been successful in passing a Constitution in 1980 which had institutionalized its concept of a protected democracy and which had radically transformed the juridical and ideological foundations of the political system.

The inauguration of the Constitution had the simultaneous effect of institutionalizing the regime and gradually mobilizing the opposition parties against it.[3] From 1983 onwards, the opposition made successive attempts to unite by overcoming basic ideological differences and diverging opposition strategies.[4] It was divided into two major camps, the moderate Christian Democrats and the radical Socialist-Communist bloc. These groups were wary of an alliance due to the enmity between them caused by the collapse of the Popular Unity government. After the failed attempt to bring the regime down through popular mobilizations under the initial leadership of the newly revived trade union movement in 1983 and 1984, the opposition parties were forced to reformulate their strategies.[5] A year before the *protestas* the Christian Democrats had decided against the possibility of a multi-party coalition to oppose the government, but during the protests the party abandoned its *camino propio* or 'lone path' to make an alliance with the moderate socialists and a number of other parties. Similarly, the moderate Nuñez faction of the socialist camp underwent a process of internal ideological reform, abandoning its revolutionary commitments. It decided to support democracy unambiguously and, realizing that its past unwillingness to form an alliance had contributed to the breakdown of democracy, it decided to ally with its erstwhile enemies.[6]

These changes led to the formation of the Alianza Democrática (AD) in 1983.[7] Although the Alianza signalled an élite settlement between the 'renovated' Socialists and the Christian Democrats, it did not succeed in overcoming the differences between these groups and the far left. In August 1985, under the auspices of Archbishop Fresno, opposition unity was again promoted with the Acuerdo Nacional para la Transición Para la Democracia or the National Agreement for the Transition to Democracy.[8] The Acuerdo, however, also failed to include the far left, now organized within the Movimiento Democrático Popular (MDP). Similarly, despite the attempts to forge a unified programme for opposition in 1986 within the Alianza, with a new programme designed by Christian Democrats and moderate Socialists called the Bases de Sustentación de un Futuro Régimen Democrático or the Foundations for the Future Democratic Regime of 8 September, the radical Almeyda socialists abandoned the alliance in 1987, forming the Izquierda Unida (IU) with the Communists, the MIR, the Christian Left, and the MAPU instead.[9]

It was only with the approaching plebiscite that most of the opposition finally resolved its differences.[10] The popular mobilizing strategy was abandoned, the parties accepted the transitional framework of the 1980 Constitution and decided to oppose the regime according to its own rules.[11] Only the Communists and other fringe left groups, having opted for armed opposition in 1980, were excluded from these alliances, but they were politically weak and isolated. Thus, the Comando por el NO which promoted the plebiscite campaign set up by the Concertación de Partidos por el NO, finally included the radical Almeyda faction of the Socialist Party, which although previously allied to the Communists, had split over the latter's initial decision to boycott the plebiscite.[12]

With the Comando, Pinochet was faced with an opposition whose unity 'put an end to the weakening dispersion of its opponents and assured them an effective political conduct which guided not only the members of the main democratic political parties but also the most representative social organizations in the country.'[13] The aftermath of the plebiscite saw the consolidation of this unity. The moderate socialist camp united in the Partido por la Democracia (PPD) decided to present a joint presidential candidate with the Christian Democrats. The radical left, now united under the Unidad por la Democracia (UD) decided to back the same candidate.[14] The Concertación de Partidos Políticos por la Democracia (CPPD) was set up in 1989, and the leading figure of the Christian Democrats, Patricio Aylwin, was chosen as its leader.

The commitment on the part of the opposition to remain united after the plebiscite and to present a single presidential candidate in the 1989 elections under the CPPD, gave the NO vote real power and credibility. Unlike Uruguay therefore, the opposition remained united throughout this period. Although Pinochet had been defeated, his 43.01 per cent share of the vote was impressive enough. Furthermore, transitory articles 24, 29, and 27 of the Constitution determined that General Pinochet would remain president until March 1989; that whatever the outcome of the plebiscite, General Pinochet would stay in power for a transitional period of one year; that elections should be held in the 90 days before the end of the year. Finally, the regime could waive the prohibition of re-election so that General Pinochet could be the candidate for the elections in 1989.[15]

Unlike the intricate and lengthy behind-the-scenes élite negotiations which occurred in the Uruguayan context, the regime in Chile engaged in a one-sided 'strategy of retreat' by implementing legislation which bolstered the position of General Pinochet, the military, and their allies. In this final 'lame-duck' year of his rule, the General made sure that he left the country *atado y bien atado* or well and truly tied up by passing a series of *leyes de amarre*. 'Just like a real operation of the Joint General Staff, an attack on all the centres of power of the Chilean political system was planned and the policies best suited to place obstacles in the way of the democratic authorities during the transition were designed.'[16]

Nevertheless, the unity of the opposition and a tactical alliance with the moderate right paved the way for a partial reform of the Constitution; the period between 1983 and 1988 had led to a first partial élite settlement between the left and the centre. The plebiscite produced a second partial élite settlement between the unified opposition and the moderate right.[17] Thus, for the first time the moderate right represented by Renovación Nacional (RN) dominated the radical right represented by the Unión Democrática Independiente (UDI), leading to the isolation of the *duros* or hardliners.[18] The RN decided to negotiate constitutional changes with the opposition and not to support Pinochet's renewed candidacy for the presidential elections. Together with the CPPD, it formed a joint technical commission which published a document in April 1989 proposing 33 constitutional modifications.

Pinochet initially resisted these changes. On 10 April 1989, the general issued a statement in response to the proposed reforms, which denounced the proposals as affecting 'the dignity and the future situation of His Excellency the President of the Republic and Commander-in-Chief of the Armed Forces.' These attacks were 'felt as directed at all the members of the institution.'[19] Finally, however, an agreement was reached in June 1989 to make 54 modifications to the Constitution. The reforms lowered the threshold for amendments to a one-off three-fifths vote in both houses for most laws. The powers of the National Security Council were reduced and the influence of the military diluted by greater civilian representation. Article 8 of the Constitution which had prohibited all Marxist or left-wing movements was altered to prohibit any anti-democratic acts or political violence and movements, and organizations of right and left and ideologies were no longer proscribed. The powers of the President were slightly reduced, and the powers of the legislature correspondingly increased. The President could no longer dissolve Congress, exile by executive decree, or censor the press during states of exception. The number of senators was increased from 36 to 48. International human rights agreements were incorporated into Chilean jurisprudence. The right to *habeas corpus* or the *recurso de amparo* could no longer be abrogated under states of exception. Finally, the United Nations Convention Against Torture and the Inter-American Convention to Prevent and Sanction Torture entered Chilean law in November 1988. On 30 July 1989 these reforms were approved by an overwhelming majority of 85.7 per cent of the population.[20]

Despite these reforms, Pinochet succeeded in imposing a number of legal changes which limited the powers of the President and the Congress, consolidated the authoritarian character of the Supreme Court, and widened the powers of the military. A number of these changes were extremely detrimental to the future application of truth and justice policies. Laws were passed, for example, granting security of tenure in the public sector. Only five of a total of 1519 posts in the Ministry of the Interior, and four out of the 115 in the General Secretariat of the Government could be designated by the new government. Thus, within the whole of the government apparatus, the new democratic executive would only be able to nominate 566 people.[21] The powers of the Congress were also severely limited. Despite attempts to remove them during the constitutional negotiations, the nine appointed senators remained in place due to differences between the CPPD and RN.[22]

Moreover, the authoritarian tendencies of the Supreme Court were strengthened. Through the Rosende Law of June 1989, General Pinochet attempted to pack the Court. The law offered US$50,000 to all its members over the age of 75 with 30 years of service to the judiciary who were willing to retire within 90 days. Eleven of the seventeen judges were eligible, but only seven accepted the offer.[23] The same was done with the Constitutional Tribunal. The powers of the Tribunal had been widened under the 1980 Constitution, allowing it to decide on the constitutionality of decrees or resolutions made by the President. Two of its seven representatives—not coincidentally those who had voted against the regime's decision to prosecute Clodomiro Almeyda, the ex-Chancellor of the Allende regime, according to Article 8 of the Constitution in 1987—were replaced by jurists favourable to the regime.

The opposition was also unable to curtail significantly military institutional autonomy or to press successfully for the resignation of General Pinochet. The General stated that he would remain Commander-in-Chief so as to ensure the stability of the transition and because he had 'people in the army who could be harassed'.[24] Pinochet consolidated his own power, restructuring the high command by placing unconditional supporters in top positions and reducing the number of generals from 48 to 42.[25] He warned that his enemies should not forget that 'the army will always cover my back'.[26] In a measure designed to protect himself and the military from truth and justice, Pinochet ordered the destruction of the CNI and DINA archives in 1989.[27]

The opposition quickly realized that to call for his resignation would provoke the hostility of the Armed Forces as a whole. They abandoned this demand and concentrated on cultivating direct ties with the other commanders, hoping to reduce the importance of the dictator. They also made it clear that the new government would not attempt to restructure the armed forces. Their aim was rather to redress the balance of power in the relations between the military and the democratic executive. The CPPD attempted to limit military autonomy. The 1980 Constitution 'placed unprecedented constraints on the power of elected government authorities to intervene in military affairs, while guaranteeing the military an important sphere of intervention in the affairs of the state'.[28] The President, for example, could only select the Commanders-in-Chief from the five most senior generals and, once elected, the latter could not be removed from their posts for the four years of their tenure.

The opposition attempted to cut military power with a proposal for a new Law of the Armed Forces. In a speech on 23 August 1989, celebrating his sixteen years as Commander-in-Chief of the Armed Forces, Pinochet rejected these reforms. He warned that the new government should not attempt to affect the immovability of the Commanders-in-Chief who were still to remain in their posts until 1997. They were to 'refrain from undue intervention in the definition and application of defence policies' and in matters pertaining to the 'command structure, the internal organizations of each institution, the system for acceptance, promotion and retirement of personnel, the planning of war contingencies, and the elaboration of logistical policies'. He also demanded that the military have the right to 'decide on their needs and budget requirements, and on the jurisdiction of military tribunals as established in the present Constitution' and he warned that the new government should respect the opinions of the National Security Council.[29]

In October 1989 the military presented their own draft of an Organic Constitutional Law of the Armed Forces. It gave the military total control over its own education, health, salaries, pensions, retirements, and promotions. The Ministry of Defence and the President could only choose from the small number nominated by the command. The bill set minimum levels for the military budget, which could never fall below the 1989 level and had to be adjusted for inflation. The military also reserved for itself a part of the earnings from copper exports.[30] This law was passed after the elections in December 1989.

Predictably, one of the major areas of civil–military contention was the issue of human rights violations. Unlike Uruguay, the CPPD had a high profile and a well-defined human rights agenda. The Programa Básico de Gobierno of January 1988 committed the opposition to truth, justice, and the liberation of political prisoners. These commitments had led to the creation of specific policies by the coalition's Comisión de Justicia y Derechos Humanos set up in March 1989.[31] The major area of conflict was an initial opposition commitment to abrogate the 1978 amnesty law.[32] The military and right-wing response to this plan was violent.[33] The CPPD therefore abandoned this commitment, and became very cautious in its attitude toward the prosecution of crimes committed before 1978. According to Aylwin, the derogation of the amnesty law was a 'possible way forward which will be subject to the verdict of the people and to the agreements which can be achieved'.[34] Instead of derogation, the Concertación considered proposing a law which would reinterpret the Supreme Court's conservative application of the amnesty, by stipulating that although the amnesty precluded sanctions, it would not preclude investigations. It also contemplated a proposal which made crimes against humanity not eligible for amnesty, so that disappearances could be sanctioned regardless of the amnesty law. None of these proposals were finally taken up.

The CPPD also shifted its initially equal emphasis on truth and justice, to an emphasis on truth. According to Aylwin, justice would be done only *en la medida de lo posible* or 'as far as possible'.[35] In order to defuse tensions created by the confrontation between the opposition's intentions and General Pinochet's defiant warnings against witch-hunts ('if anyone touches any of my men, the rule of law is over'), the CPPD's leaders also underlined that only individuals could be prosecuted through the ordinary courts, and that there would be no institutional trials by special courts. The basic commitment to truth-telling and justice, however, was not abandoned, and the CPPD did not sacrifice its judicial policies for accommodation as the Colorados had done in Uruguay. Thus, in an attack on Büchi, Zaldívar of the Christian Democrats insisted that *no habrá borrón y cuenta nueva*.[36]

Unlike Uruguay, the opposition was strengthened by the active support of the human rights groups and the Church. Both were already busy with the task of compiling and publishing 'the social truth', using their extensive documentation to produce publications recounting the experiences and outcome of military repression. One of the most important publications to emerge at this time was the Vicaría's *La Memoria Prohibida* (The Forbidden Memory), which described the first ten years of repression under military rule.[37]

On 14 December 1989 national elections were held. They were fought between two competing blocs, one represented by Patricio Aylwin leading the CPPD, the other by the right's reluctant candidate, Hernán Büchi, who led the Democracia y Progreso coalition uniting the RN, the UDI, and a few other radical right-wing parties.[38] The Communists and the MIR, although excluded from the CPPD, supported Aylwin's candidacy. Unlike Uruguay, therefore, the elections did not promote further divisions, but rather united the truth-telling and justice opposition in a solid block against the civilian right. Campaigning on the themes of truth, justice, social equity, and reconciliation, the CPPD won with 55 per cent of the vote.[39] The extremely biased bi-nominal electoral law, however, ensured the over-representation of the right. While a winning vote needed 65 per cent to gain a seat, the runner-up needed only 33 per cent. Conservative rural areas were also ensured over-representation. This gave the right a critical number of seats in both houses of the legislature. They secured 49 out of 120 seats in the Chamber of Deputies, RN gaining the greatest number with 34, the UDI winning 13. The right also won 16 out of the 38 elected seats in the Senate; RN gained 11 and the UDI 2. The presence of nine designated senators, however, shifted the balance of power in favour of the right, ensuring an anti-*Concertación* majority. The right had the power to veto legislation, particularly constitutional reform bills which required a two-thirds majority in each house.[40]

After the elections, a few last-minute laws were passed to further protect General Pinochet's position, to shield the Armed Forces from prosecution, and to limit the powers of the new government. In December 1989 the National Security Council, the Supreme Court, and General Pinochet announced their appointments, predictably all ex-members of the outgoing regime. In January 1990, the regime passed the Organic Constitutional Law of Congress. The third article of this law prevented the Congress from bringing Constitutional charges against acts of corruption and treason committed prior to its inauguration in March 1990, prohibiting congressional investigations of the Pinochet government, and thus reducing the power of investigating commissions set up within the legislature. The courts effectively became the only arena in which to sanction official abuses under military rule; if Pinochet could not ensure criminal impunity for the armed forces, he made sure that political impunity was guaranteed.[41]

The CNI was dissolved with no oversight on the part of the *Concertación*. An estimated 19,000 people were incorporated into the army intelligence network, the DINE, which was to be headed by the last director of the CNI.[42] Pinochet also established a dual centre of power to challenge the dominion of the Executive with the creation of a defiantly deliberative body, the Comité Asesor Político Estratégico (CAPE) made up of former members of the General Secretariat of the Presidency, whose function it was to advise Pinochet on political and military matters.[43] In January the law of the Armed Forces drafted in October 1989 was passed. It ensured the autonomy of the services and their freedom from executive control. In a symbolic parting gesture, General Pinochet disbarred one of the few pro-human rights judges, Juez Réné García Villegas, by presidential decree in February 1990.[44]

On the day of the inauguration of the new government, Aylwin's speech set the tone for the years to come. Unlike Sanguinetti, who emphasized pacification and accommodation with the military, Aylwin spoke of the need for reconciliation which, although necessarily inclusive of the military, could not be achieved without a firm national commitment to truth and justice. As if to give testimony of his intentions, the president-elect invited Dr Sheila Cassidy, a British doctor who had been tortured by the DINA, to the inauguration.[45] The Concertación had accepted both continuity in the economic model and autonomy of the Armed Forces, but it expressed its desire for a rupture with the past through its radical human rights discourse. Thus, the stage was set for a confrontation between a Concertación committed to telling the truth about human rights violations and a defiant General.

Accounting for the Success of Truth and Justice Policies in the Democratic Period

The Chilean transitional process was characterized by some negative and some positive features: the former were favourable to the cause of truth and justice and the latter promised to make their implementation difficult in the democratic period. What were the negative factors?

First, like the Uruguayan case, the transition in Chile was negotiated. Neither side could hope to impose its conditions upon the other entirely. It was, furthermore, a transition which was administered by a military which had not suffered the series of defeats that their Uruguayan counterparts had lived through. The corollary of this was a political climate which emphasized moderation and prudence in all future democratic undertakings.[46] This was the case even for the left for which 'piecemeal reform had become responsible, democracy essential, pragmatism desirable and moderation a virtue'.[47] The above conditions promised to place real limits on both on the ability and willingness of the democratic government to expand the boundaries on what might be perceived to be politically possible.

Secondly, the Concertación had to deal with the 'Pinochet Factor'. General Pinochet, who was still very popular, could convincingly claim that he was leaving power with his 'mission accomplished'. The close identification of the troops with the Commander-in-Chief was compounded by the fact that 'in uniting in one person the double representation of the President of the Republic and the Commander-in-Chief of the Army, it becomes impossible for his subordinates to make distinctions about which capacity of their leader is questioned.'[48] As in Uruguay, therefore, the opposition were confronted with strong military–institutional opposition to the government promotion of justice and truth-telling.

Thirdly, because Pinochet's regime had won the Constitutional plebiscite in 1980, the Concertación faced great legal constraints in its attempts to deal with the human rights issue. Despite the modifications made during the transition, the Constitution still effectively 'turned the Armed Forces into the fourth arm of government'.[49] Thus, unlike Uruguay, implementing human rights policies would require constitutional changes. The 1978 amnesty law protected the military from prosecution, and Article 9 of the Constitution and the Anti-Terrorist Law would have to be reformed to permit political prisoners the benefit of pardons and amnesties.[50]

Fourthly, since the right held the balance of power in the legislature, the implementation of human rights policies would be very difficult. The right's strong 'parliamentary presence assured them that no important legal initiative could be adopted without their approval'.[51] The attitude of the right to human rights varied from party to party, but it was basically willing to defend the regime. The right was united in believing that the crimes covered by the amnesty law should not be investigated. It backed the state-of-war thesis, agreed with the military's view of the nature of the enemy and interpreted the violations as mere excesses, not systemic features of the regime.[52] Moreover, none of the parties favoured a specific policy of global truth-telling, because the military's version of events was essentially acceptable to them.

The opposition were also faced with an essentially hostile judiciary. As noted in Chapter 2, the Supreme Court had consistently refused to interpret the amnesty law as the Concertación intended, so that cases covered by the amnesty could not be investigated. The Court had also almost always recommended that cases involving military officers be transferred to the military justice system. Given that the government's policy was to be based on the prosecution of individuals through the ordinary courts, this conservatism was a formidable obstacle to overcome.

Finally, continued terrorism was also negative for the future of truth and justice. Its existence gave the military much mileage in terms of seemingly legitimating their repressive actions.[53] Terrorism had emerged in 1980 following change in the Communist party's strategy of opposition. Its armed organization, the Frente Patriótico Manuel Rodríguez (FPMR), was joined by a number of smaller groups in its violent campaign to depose the regime. The Frente had called a truce during the 1988 plebiscite, fearing that the regime might call it off using terrorism as an excuse.[54] In January 1990, the Communist party had finally renounced its commitment to the *via armada* or 'armed path'. None the less, the FPMR, now *Autónomo*, and its companions-in-arms, continued to advocate the legitimacy of political violence.[55]

Two of the negative factors outlined above, however, were mediated by positive elements: both the military and the right were in a worse position to resist truth and justice than their counterparts in Uruguay. On the one hand, the Chilean military, despite the protection of the amnesty law, were more vulnerable than their Uruguayan counterparts; long before the onset of the transitional process, the civil justice system had begun to investigate a number of human rights violations cases. Only one military officer had been successfully prosecuted, being imprisoned for 300 days in the Quemados, or Burned Ones, case. None the less, the jurisdiction of the civil courts had been *de facto* accepted by the military.[56] In Chile there were 'cases still pending and there would be no reason to interrupt them under a democratic regime'.[57] The democratic government's human rights policy could therefore be presented as an attempt to expedite an already existing state of affairs. It could not be rejected easily on the grounds that it represented revenge especially designed by the enemies of the Armed Forces.

Moreover, 'it is clear that any attempt to pass a new amnesty, supported by the government and applicable to the crimes which occurred during the second period, would imply an acceptance of responsibility for those crimes, in total contradiction to the official position of not assuming responsibility for them'. Similarly, because the amnesty law was seen by the military and their allies as the turning-point between emergency rule, under which 'excesses' were understandable, and institutionalized authoritarian rule under which rights were constitutionally guaranteed, arguing for impunity after 1979 'would also mean that the process of institutionalization of power had never existed'.[58]

For the same reasons, the right was in a difficult position when it came to arguing for impunity for cases of human rights violations committed after 1979. Although unlike the Concertación the right had a *laissez-faire* attitude to justice, holding that individuals could seek recourse from the courts privately, and that the government should not actively promote trials, they did claim to support the right to justice.[59] The UDI believed that the crimes committed after the amnesty law would have to be punished in the ordinary courts.[60] In June 1986, RN's political commission emphasized the importance of the need to punish violations committed after 1978 in the ordinary courts.[61] Hernán Büchi's electoral platform stated that the 1978 amnesty law should be respected, but that the courts should resolve all pending cases.[62] Finally, it should be noted as a mitigating factor, that the climate of moderation was double-edged; while suggesting the possibility of a stultifying immobilism, it also gave hope of success in the human rights field. The danger of excessive illusions and demands, the difficulties of expectation management in a climate of democratic euphoria of *todo es posible* (anything is possible) had, by the time of the Chilean transition, been demonstrated in the case of Argentina.[63]

Despite the disadvantages outlined above, the Chilean transition was also characterized by a number of advantages not found in the Uruguayan context, which proved to be crucial to the future success of human rights policies. In the first place, unlike Uruguay, the transition was characterized by a dynamic and discourse of renovation; central to that discourse was the issue of human rights. The depth of the crisis prior to military rule and the subsequent deep transformation of the political and economic system brought about by the regime's successful foundational project, led the opposition to create a new democratic project, based not on a return to the symbols of the past but on the universal symbols of human rights. The meta-language of human rights was the perfect realization and representation of this dynamic of renovation.

For the Christian Democrats, Chileans needed 'to offer a new project which will use the lessons of the recent past but which will also have the power of a renovating inspiration as well as the necessary realism to recreate our social fellowship'.[64] The universalization of the discourse of opposition was perhaps of even greater importance for the left. The failure of the socialist project and its contribution to the breakdown of democratic rule, and the experience of repression, led to a process of self-criticism and to the reformulation of political priorities and imperatives. Whereas before 1973 the left had referred to the rights of the working class and had criticized bourgeois democracy, after the coup, in supporting the universalist ideology of human rights, it radically reviewed its position on the validity and legitimacy of political democracy. Such was the internalization of the human rights discourse, that the PPD, which united all renovated socialists, integrated the Universal Declaration of Human Rights into its party platform.[65]

A second positive feature of the transition was that, rather than encouraging party fragmentation and divisions as it did in Uruguay, in Chile it tended to foster the strategic and ideological unification of the opposition. Ironically the longevity and institutionalization of the Chilean regime was a factor which helped to unite the parties during this period. The failure of the strategy of opposition through mobilization almost eliminated inter-party struggles over the means to press for the transition to democracy by 1988, when the parties decided to act according to the regime's rules. Because they did not have to expend their energy fighting over this issue as they did in Uruguay, the opposition had more time to focus on designing policies and building coalition consensus for specific human rights initiatives. Furthermore, as the above account makes clear, the latent conflict between social movements and parties in Uruguay was successfully avoided in Chile. Although some of the social organizations gave the Concertación only qualified support, they were aware of the fact that only this coalition represented an alternative to the regime. The co-operation between the social organizations and the trade union movement with the Concertación meant that the coalition, unlike the Colorados, felt a commitment to represent its demands.

Not only were basic strategic and ideological differences settled before 1988, but the dynamic of the transition after 1988 did not contribute to divisions and competition between the opposition, but rather encouraged unification. Unlike Uruguay's intensely 'political' and élite negotiated transition, Chile's was essentially a legal transition administered by the laws imposed by the Constitution of 1980. Thus, parties had to spend little time focusing on persuading the military to negotiate and exit as they did in Uruguay, since this objective, however restricted the conditions, was already constitutionally ensured in Chile. Unlike Uruguay, where opposition energies were consumed by inter-party competition and negotiations, the opposition in Chile further consolidated its government policies prior to the inauguration of democracy. The Aylwin campaign was said to be 'marked by the curious phenomenon that it . . . was planning for government during the campaign'.[66]

Thirdly, the tone set by Aylwin in his relations with the Armed Forces was very different from that set by Sanguinetti. The latter forged an associative 'caudillesque' alliance with General Medina, and in order to strengthen the hand of the pro-negotiators he exchanged assurances of impunity for reductions in military institutional demands. Aylwin initially attempted to assert both his desire for limited military prerogatives and a radical judicial policy. He called for Pinochet's resignation as a contribution to national reconciliation and supported the derogation of the amnesty law. Failing with this, however, the Concertación abandoned attempts to get rid of the dictator and to restructure relations between the government and military, and modified its commitment to derogate the amnesty law. At the same time it also stressed that its truth and justice commitment would not be abandoned. Unlike Sanguinetti, Aylwin did not exchange a cut in military demands for impunity; he did not present himself as a protective shield for the Armed Forces; he stuck to his moral agenda; and he aimed indirectly to weaken Pinochet by cultivating ties with the commanders of the other branches.

In this, he was undoubtedly helped by existing resentments against the Army by the other branches which surfaced in this period. Unlike Uruguay, where all the branches were 'friendly', in Chile Aylwin was able to take the edge off Pinochet's threats by taking advantage of inter-service rivalries.[67] The Carabineros under General Stange, for example, were quick to forge autonomous contacts with Aylwin without first consulting Pinochet. The Navy resented the Army because of the latter's construction of a US$9 million social club at a time when the other branches were suffering from budgetary cuts. Moreover, the other branches also resented the Army's exclusive access to information about certain financial deals which had been legalized under the auspices of General Pinochet. This was compounded by what was characterized as a generalized suspicion of the 'Rambos' of the 'lower grade officers', the 'the class most unconditionally loyal to General Pinochet'.[68]

Fourthly, unlike Uruguay, where the most conservative, pro-military party won the elections, it was the coalition most committed to truth and justice which succeeded in Chile. Moreover, in contrast with President Sanguinetti, whose apparent overriding consideration was accommodation with the military, President Aylwin was personally committed to truth-telling and justice; accommodation with the military was not in principle to be achieved at the cost of these aims.

The historical timing of the Chilean transition also benefited the opposition. The Concertación had many years to draw conclusions from the experience of other countries' attempts to deal with the legacies of military repression. It had five years to learn from the Uruguayan and Brazilian cases, and seven to learn from the Argentine policies of truth and justice. In choosing an independent commission, and in setting defined time-limits on its truth-telling task, the calculation was that other paths might lead to 'an endless debate with unforeseeable consequences. In this they used the Uruguayan case as an example, where the Congress spent four years debating this issue with sterile results.'[69]

Finally, unlike Uruguay, human rights and the debate over the amnesty law were the focal points of the transition and of the electoral campaign. From 1988 onwards, meetings between the Concertación and the human rights organizations intensified as policy options were debated and formulated.[70] Truth and justice were issues intensely debated in the press, eliciting responses from all quarters.[71] Both were a key part of the Concertación's electoral platform of August 1989. Because of the prominence of the human rights question, the right was forced to take a public stand on the question and to admit the importance of justice.[72] The issue was explicitly taken up by Büchi, who claimed that crimes committed after 1978 would have to be tried if the parties failed agree on a new amnesty law and that the victims of human rights violations would have to be compensated.[73] From denying the very existence of violations and victims, the right was therefore forced to confront the realities of the human rights situation.

In addition to the dynamics of the transition process itself, a number of factors related specifically to the human rights issue also helped the successful promotion of truth and justice in the democratic period. First and most importantly, Chile had developed one of the longest-lived, strongest, and largest human rights movements in Latin America, with deep links to the major opposition parties. Unlike Uruguay, where internal human rights opposition only began towards the end of the military regime, the formation of a human rights movement in Chile coincided with the beginning of state repression and human rights violations: 'Chile is the only country where, right from the beginning a response in defence of human rights was organized which involved innumerable activities and programmes.'[74]

As in Uruguay, the first organizations to emerge were the victims' associations, the Agrupación de Familiares de Detenidos Desaparecidos (AFDD) and Agrupación de Familiares de Ejecutados Políticos (AFEP).[75] However, unlike Uruguay, these organizations were immediately offered institutional support which was crucial for their survival and continued growth. The first pluralist and ecumenical legal defence organization, the Comité Pro Paz (CPP), was formed in October 1973. Under the protection of the Comité Pro Paz the AFDD and the newly formed Agrupación de Familiares de Prisioneros Desaparecidos (AFPD) flourished. The Committee mitigated the impact of the repressive policies of the state and established ties with social and political groups affected by authoritarian rule.[76]

The CPP was replaced by the Vicaría de la Solidaridad or the Vicariate of Solidarity in January 1976 due to regime pressures. The Vicaría counteracted the effects of silence, promoted a network of opposition organizations, and provided a forum for the birth of future human rights organizations.[77]

The Fundación de Ayuda Social de las Iglesias Cristianas (FASIC), famous for its work on psychological re-habilitation programmes, emerged in 1974. The Chilean Servicio de Paz y Justicia (SERPAJ) was set up in 1977. It was, along with the Comisión Chilena de Derechos Humanos (CCDH), created the following year, the organization which did most to advance truth and justice among the opposition parties. Other groups to emerge were the Comisión Nacional Pro Derechos Humanos Juveniles (CNPDHJ) of 1978, an organization which united the youth of a number of different political groups and the Comité de Defensa de los Derechos del Pueblo (COPEDU) of 1980, which was set up by members of the left to represent those accused of terrorist activities. All of these organizations, the associations of victims and their relatives, the AFDD, the AFEP, the Asociación de Familiares de Procesados por la Justicia Militar (AFPJM) and the Asociación de Familiares de Presos Políticos (AFPP), and academic research institutes specializing in human rights, such as the Academia de Humanismo Cristiano (AHC) benefited from the protection provided by the Church.[78]

The Vicaría was unique in the world, and it was central to the consolidation of the most successful human rights movement in the region. Its uniqueness lay in the fact that it was an integral part of the institutional structures of the Catholic Church and in that it provided the protection and focus for all opposition activity up until the early 1980s. Thus, in Chile, unlike Uruguay, the human rights movement replaced party activism as the centre of regime opposition.[79] The parties remained behind the social movement, and the Church had an almost monopolistic presence as an opposition force.[80] The human rights movement was crucial in initiating the dynamics of opposition to military rule. It became the motor driving the opposition's calls for democracy.[81]

Unlike Uruguay, where the parties were always dominant in the business of regime opposition, in Chile the human rights movement succeeded in replacing partisan activities for over ten years. Thus, instead of partisan identities constantly 'trumping' human rights activist identities as they did in Uruguay, in Chile, party members became human rights activists within their own parties, transforming the ideological and programmatic structures of these and incorporating into them the demands for truth and justice. Unlike Uruguay where it was limited to pressuring the parties from a position of relative weakness, in Chile it acquired sufficient autonomous power to lead the opposition. The role of these organizations was 'of extreme importance in Chile where all political activity was declared in recess and where, at the same time, the programmes of the NGO's expanded significantly and were tolerated by the regime, even if with hostility'.[82]

As a result of this, unlike Uruguay, the links between the human rights movement and the opposition bloc were tried and tested, solid, and well developed. Through their work in the human rights movement, many individual party leaders formed a personal commitment to the aims of truth and justice. The links between the opposition parties and the human rights movement, as well as the overlap of partisan and human rights activist identities, became a structural characteristic of the movement itself. The CCDH, for example, was primarily led by key figures of the Christian Democratic party. Many academics working in the Church-sponsored AHC were also members of the parties. The movement, being pluralist in composition and universalist in values, was also crucial in uniting different ideological groups which had been bitterly opposed to one another since the downfall of the Popular Unity government. Partisan enmities were replaced by the solidarity of a common experience in the defence of human rights.[83] Thus:

> Only when one looks back with hindsight at the degree of polarization and political antagonism between the Christian Democrats and the Left in 1970–1973, is it possible to understand the critical role played by these organizations in allowing the joint work of lawyers of political tendencies at such odds at the time . . . this is where a permanent front against the regime was gradually forged, where greater consensus became more possible than in other arenas.[84]

> The relevance of the issue [of human rights] emerged due to the close links in the case of our [country] between the efforts made towards democratization and the struggle to defend human rights, as moral and political obligations were contracted nationally and internationally by those involved in these efforts, regarding the way in which those violations should be dealt with.[85]

Moreover, the intensive defence work undertaken on behalf of the victims of repression permitted the compilation of a critical mass of information which was centralized and available to the public. Data collection for the presentation of cases and the formation of a core of human-rights oriented legal personnel associated with both parties and humanitarian or religious organizations were central to the formation of a strong, well-informed human-rights lobby: 'The act of denouncing turns public, and subject to investigation, the acts denounced . . . the denunciation is always judicial in the first instance and later becomes simply political.'[86] The bulletins produced by the Vicaría and the CCDH became the major source of information on the issue for international organizations and journalists. The Vicaría produced the greatest collection of data on human rights violations in Latin America.[87] Thus, unlike Uruguay, where the democratic Congressional investigating commissions encountered great difficulties in collecting data, the extensive data collected in Chile facilitated the democratic government's truth-telling policy.[88]

The national extension and regional networks of the Chilean movement were also much more developed and longer-lived than those in Uruguay. The Vicaría had offices in all but five of the provinces. In the four years between 1976 and 1980 it offered services to over 700,000 individuals.[89] The FASIC had 128 base committees in the 63 provinces by 1988. Similarly, the CCDH had 60 offices in Santiago and 20 in the provinces in 1984, and by 1988 all 63 provinces were covered.[90] Moreover, the human rights organizations developed highly sophisticated administrative structures, had a high number of personnel specialized in different aspects of human rights issues, and undertook programmes which dealt with a great variety of social, economic, political, and psychological matters.

The co-ordination of activities among these organizations began much earlier and was more fully developed than in Uruguay. The process of co-ordination commenced in 1980. By 1984 co-ordination was formalized and institutionalized with the creation of the Plenario de Derechos Humanos or the Human Rights Plenary. The latter was launched with the campaign Para Que Nunca Más en Chile (Never Again in Chile). Later, from 1984 onwards, the Plenario set up temporary organizations to lead periodic campaigns for truth and justice, such as the campaigns Chile Defiende la Vida (Chile Defends Life) (1984) and those organized by the Comité Por la Vida la Justicia y la Verdad (the Committee for Life, Justice and Truth) (1985).

Four major factors contributed to the impressive development of this movement in Chile. In the first place, despite the higher level of illegal repression resulting in death, civil society was not submitted to such a totalitarian form of social control as was the case in Uruguay. Despite severe censorship and the persecution of journalists, several opposition journals were able to publish information on human-rights related issues from the early 1980s onwards. Even in the official press, 'The legal cases of greatest importance gained a relatively wide-ranging press coverage.'[91] Human rights organizations published reports on their activities and on human rights violations, in such periodicals as the CCDH's monthly bulletins and the Catholic Church's two magazines, *Mensaje* and *Solidaridad*.[92]

Because the ordinary courts remained in operation under authoritarian rule, the opposition was able to engage in the presentation of *recursos de amparo* and *protección* for the victims of repression. This legal opposition acquired 'considerable relevance due to the institutional and human resources invested in it and because of the impact that they managed to have in turning the human rights situation into a problem with national and international visibility.'[93]

Again in contrast to the Uruguayan case, where the Church did not emerge as a 'substitute political actor', in Chile the role of the Catholic Church was central to the development of the human rights movement.[94] The ability of the Church to oppose the regime effectively was much greater because Chile was, unlike Uruguay, a profoundly Catholic country whose Church had historically played a politically prominent role.[95] Thus, 'The Chilean government frequently invoked Christian motivations and its members declared themselves Catholics. Part of the sectors which were closest to the regime were also practising Catholics. This situation made it difficult to prevent the Church from intervening in one way or another in the political and social process.'[96] It also made it very difficult for the regime to dismiss the criticism of the Church. Secondly, unlike Uruguay, the Church chose to actively protect human rights, a fact that has been amply documented.[97] 'The fact that the churches adopted a firm position in defence of human rights created the conditions for the development of the movement.'[98]

Thirdly, much more attention was focused on Chile by the international community. This was a prolongation of interest in its experiment with the 'Peaceful Road to Socialism', and a product of the extreme suddenness and violence of the coup. It was the country in Latin America which received the most attention from the international community in the area of human rights violations.[99] 'The effort to protect human rights in Chile using various international mechanisms was extraordinary and represents a model for human rights organizations all over the world.'[100] Moreover, interest was sustained because of the international links of the parties in opposition and the Church. They provided natural channels for international financial and moral solidarity.[101] The human rights movement in Chile was given a huge amount of financial aid from abroad. Between 1973 and 1974, it received US$16 million from Catholic organizations in Europe and North America. The Comité Pro Paz alone received US$2 million from the World Council of Churches. Between 1976 and 1979, the movement received US$67 million from similar sources. The Vicaría received up to US$8 million of this from different protestant churches.[102] The institutionalizing pretensions of the regime, the pressure of right-wing civilian élites on the military to improve the country's international image, and the success of the human rights organizations in publicizing violations forced the government to concede the United Nations and the Organization of American States regular visits.[103]

The nature of the parties in opposition also favoured the development of a strong human rights movement. The Socialist and Christian Democratic parties which formed the core of the Concertación were either immediately or very soon in direct opposition to military rule. Both had long established and well developed international ties. The Socialist International and international Christian Democratic networks and the experience of exile both increased the commitment of these parties to the struggle for human rights and provided them with moral and financial international partisan solidarity, as this issue was the major area of concern of European democrats and socialists interested in Latin America.[104]

As noted above, the experience of human rights defence work under the Vicaría was critical in transforming the traditional socialist view of rights and thereby strengthening socialist commitment to a liberal democratic concept of human rights. In turn, human rights became a central commitment for the Christian Democrats. With the creation in 1978 of the Grupo de Estudios Constitucionalistas, or the Group of 24, headed by Patricio Aylwin, the party began to formulate a Proyecto Alternativo (Alternative Project), which recognized as its inspiration the humanism of the Universal Declaration of Human Rights.[105] According to this project, a future democratic government was to develop a permanent judicial policy and, through the creation of a Consejo Nacional de Justicia (National Justice Council), to protect and promote human rights.[106] A commission for the study of human rights was set up alongside the project on the initiative of Eduardo Frei. Towards the end of 1978 the party signed the Santiago Compromise which, under the auspices of the Archbishop of Santiago, committed the party to defending human rights. In 1983 the party created the Comisión Nacional de Fiscalización (National Monitoring Commission), which also aimed to defend human rights and monitor partisan activities in the human rights movement. Although the party did not define policies of truth and justice clearly until 1988–9, it committed itself rhetorically from the earliest days of the regime. According to a survey of 148 leaders at a party conference in 1985, the Human Rights Commission was the most highly valued social organization.[107]

As a result of the above factors, the number of formal commitments between the parties and the human rights organizations was much higher than in Uruguay, making it much harder for parties to subsequently renege on them. Although the most elaborate documents came from the organizations, the latter were successful in persuading the Concertación to adopt their demands. The CCDH and the SERPAJ were the organizations which did most to promote party commitment to truth and justice. The Commission initiated this process with Para Que Nunca Más en Chile in November 1983. This was followed by the Compromiso por la Vida, los Derechos Humanos, y la Democracia (Commitment to Life, Human Rights and Democracy) in April 1985, which were signed by all parties with the exception of those on the right. In December the opposition parties, the Asamblea Nacional de la Civilidad (National Civic Assembly) and the Movimiento Juvenil por la Democracia y las Elecciones (Youth Movement for Democracy and Elections) signed the Declaración y Compromiso Nacional Con los Derechos Humanos (Declaration and Commitment to Human Rights). The AHC also promoted a series of seminars with party and human rights leaders on the issues of truth and justice in 1985, which produced a series of documents that formed the basis for policy formation. The SERPAJ sponsored a similar dialogue before the 1988 plebiscite around a document entitled Exigencias Concretas para la Reconciliación en Chile—Verdad y Justicia (Concrete Demands for Reconciliation in Chile—Truth and Justice). This dialogue produced very positive results. Later, the Acuerdo por el NO of February 1988, committed the parties to backing the 'consensus achieved on the issue of human rights and to ensure justice'.[108] Finally, the SERPAJ successfully promoted the creation of a Comisión de Justicia y Derechos Humanos within the Concertación in March 1989.

Despite complaints that the organizations were often ignored by the Concertación in their more radical demands, it was nevertheless the case that those people who worked in the human rights movement and who belonged to the coalition, provided a bridge and a core of commitment to the issue which was not seen in Uruguay.[109] Thus, on the anniversary of the Universal Declaration of Human Rights in 1988 the Concertación recognized the role of the human rights organizations in bringing about a new democratic era and promoting basic rights.[110]

The nature of party commitments to human rights in Chile was also different from that in Uruguay. In the first place, a 'basic, widespread and highly representative consensus on the matter' existed between the democratic parties on the issues of truth and justice.[111] Although they differed by degree, the Christian Democrats, Socialists, and Communists were committed to the punishment of violations and to truth-telling. Secondly, truth-telling and justice were seen to be inextricably tied with the re-establishment of democratic rule. Rather than an amnesty for political prisoners, in Chile truth and justice were the central demands of the human rights movement.[112] In the Mensaje al Pueblo de Chile de la Concertación de Partidos Políticos por la Democracia (Message to the People of Chile from the CPPD) of 2 February 1989 truth and justice along with social justice were defined by the coalition as the three major tasks of the new democracy.

Furthermore, over a number of years party policies became increasingly clear-cut and defined. In contrast with Uruguay, truth-telling was seen as a measure necessary to reveal the political and institutional guilt of the Armed Forces. A clear separation was therefore made between justice and truth-telling: 'If one seeks truth and justice at the same time it is probable that neither of the two will be achieved.' By 1989, the idea of creating an independent commission of notables for global truth-telling had surfaced. Unlike Uruguay, judicial policy was not to be guided by a *laissez-faire* attitude. It was to be actively promoted by the government which was to give 'the ordinary courts the resources and the procedural instruments to determine the fate of the victims and the pertinent responsibilities'.[113]

To this end, a Consejo Nacional de Justicia was contemplated to formulate the government's judicial reform policy.[114] Unlike the truth-telling policy, which would disclose institutional guilt, the pretence of individual guilt was to be maintained in the government's judicial policy, pursued in the ordinary courts. Despite the lower profile of the issue of amnesty for political prisoners, the Concertación also formed a Comisión Para Presos Políticos (Commission for Political Prisoners) in 1989, responding to pressure from the Socialists and prisoners' associations.[115] Military jurisdiction over civilians was to cease, the sentences would be revised, and pending cases speeded up. Pardons would be extended for those who had not committed blood crimes, thus extinguishing penal responsibility.[116] Finally, international human rights norms were to be raised to the rank of constitutional law.

These formulas were arrived at by a process of successive discussions and agreements. The Acuerdo Nacional para la Transición a la Plena Democracia (National Accord for the Transition to Full Democracy) in August 1985, the Bases de Sustentación del Régimen Democrático of September 1986,[117] and the 1987 Declaración y Compromiso Nacional Con los Derechos Humanos all pointed in this direction.[118] It was only in 1989, however, that the Concertación came up with specific policies for truth and justice. These were outlined in the Programa Básico del Gobierno de la Concertación of January 1988, and were developed in early 1989 when the Concertación set up specialized sub-commissions with the participation of human rights and victims organizations and lawyers. The Comisión de Justicia y Derechos Humanos produced a series of working documents published in July 1989 by important figures in the party political and human rights community, which came to form the basis of the democratic government's truth and justice policy. In August 1989 these policies were incorporated into the Concertación's electoral platform.

Unlike Uruguay, there was also a high degree of consensus

between party positions and the human rights movement. The key human rights organizations which had promoted policy commitments within the opposition, the CCDH and the SERPAJ, held views very similar to those of the opposition. The Concertación also received the moral backing of the Church, which placed more emphasis on discovering the truth and on the subsequent possibility of pardon, than on the establishment of penal responsibilities.[119] A number of groups, however, were more radical. The victims' associations for example, were not very convinced by the Concertación's constant emphasis on reconciliation and its lack of determination to abrogate the amnesty law. For the AFDD, justice could not be subjected to 'political contingency'.[120] Similarly, the prisoners' associations were unhappy with the Concertación's decision to review cases, demanding that political prisoners should be immediately released through a general pardon.[121] Nevertheless, in the absence of a viable radical opposition coalition able to compete with the Concertación and give these demands a political representation, these groups were willing to co-operate with the coalition and to offer it their critical support. Moreover, they were forced to recognize that the Concertación was restricted by political and constitutional *amarres*, which made the fulfilment of more radical demands very difficult.

Conclusions: Preparing for Limited Confrontation and Accommodation

On the eve of the inauguration, Pinochet outlined his position once more. When asked what should be done about human rights violations, he stated that he had the solution because he had '80,000 armed men'.[122] He also told the Minister of Defence to mind his own business with regard to military matters and delegated contacts with the President to the vice-commander of the Army, General Lucar.[123] None the less, although Pinochet boasted that 'The courts could call on eight, nine or ten officers, until at some point, impossible to predict, the institutional response would be forthcoming', the other branches were more willing to compromise. Their attitude was more that 'All governments have the right to investigate and judge if necessary the preceding political-administrative authorities . . . he who involves himself in politics has to answer as a politician.'[124]

The government could also take heart from a number of positive signs. Its concern with truth and justice was shared by a majority of the well-informed population. A poll in April 1989 found that 67.5 per cent of those surveyed nationwide felt that human rights violators should be tried.[125] Secondly, the moderate right seemed willing to accommodate the government. In February 1990, the RN and the *Concertación* agreed to co-operate in order to pass the government's legislative package.[126]

Thirdly, if the problem for the implementation of policies of truth and justice in Uruguay had been a lack of inter-party co-operation and pre-transitional coalition-building, in Chile the reverse was true. The Concertación united practically all of the democratic opposition parties. The fact that it included the Socialists, one of the political parties most affected by human rights violations, meant that there were pressures for more radical measures emerging from within the governing coalition itself, and that these pressures had to be somehow reconciled if cohesion was to prevail. The Christian Democrats would have to adhere to principles if they were to maintain the unity of the governing coalition. On the other hand, the inclusion of the Socialists in the coalition meant that the left was also more willing and obliged to accommodate compromise solutions.[127]

Finally, there was no political force further on the left able to compete with the Concertación or in a position to threaten or polarize the political debate under democracy. Apart from the rightwing opposition, there were no parties of strength in the parliament of the left which did not belong in the Concertación.[128] While this promised to push the government to conservatism, it ensured that a polarization would not develop over the human rights issue. Thus, the Chilean party situation in comparison with the fragmentation characteristic of the Uruguayan case, was better for facilitating policy consensus and implementation. As the *Concertación* prepared to take power, it was faced with four major dangers: Pinochetista resistance, right-wing legislative filibustering, internal coalition splits, and radical and armed opposition: it would have to neutralize these dangers if it was to be able to carry out its truth and justice policies successfully.

PART III

Truth and Justice under Successor Democratic Regimes

The past cannot be reconstructed. Although we cannot bring the dead back to life nor restore jobs to those who lost them, we can try to paliate and repair the damage and avoid or diminish its consequences.

President Aylwin, 1993

My government was characterized more by what it avoided than by what it did.

President Sanguinetti, 1990

5

The Long and Tortuous Path to Military Amnesty and the Referendum in Uruguay, 1985–1989

Introduction

On his inauguration on 1 March 1985 President Sanguinetti presented his human rights package. The release of all political prisoners was the centrepiece of his Proyecto de Pacificación Nacional (PPN), or National Pacification Project; it was to be the 'first step' on the road to democratic restoration.[1]

All political prisoners who had not been accused of *crímenes de sangre* or blood crimes would be amnestied after a review of their sentences. The rest would have their sentences revised and reduced if the charges against them were found to be legally acceptable.[2] As the President made his speech, 338 political prisoners were still in gaol, nine of whom were democratic military officers. By 10 March their liberation was underway, and five days later all of them had been liberated.[3]

The project also provided for the creation of a Comisión Nacional de Repatriación or a National Repatriation Commission to facilitate the social re-incorporation of returning exiles. It was set up in April 1985, successfully providing aid to 16,000 returning exiles, offering jobs, medical insurance, and housing and financing work projects.[4] A commitment was made to restore jobs to public employees who had been fired under military rule for political reasons. In November 1985, the Ley de Reposición de Destituidos (Law for the Reintegration of the Exonerated) was passed. It promoted the rehabilitation of 10,500 public employees, and extended retirement benefits to 6,000 people.[5] The project also derogated the LSE, limiting the jurisdiction of the military justice system to its pre-authoritarian state. Finally, it committed the government to pursuing the ratification of the American Convention on Human Rights.

In April 1985, President Sanguinetti sent Senators Alberto Zumarán from the Blanco Party, and Luis Hierro Gambardella of the Colorado party to the United Nations Human Rights Commission. Uruguay was removed from the human rights blacklist and both representatives explained that the new democratic government would investigate and prosecute the human rights violations committed by the military.[6] This was confirmed by the President at home on a number of occasions.[7] In accordance with the above, with the multi-party commitment to truth and justice within the CONAPRO in October 1984 and public expectations, the law which amnestied political prisoners expressly excluded 'police or military officers responsible for inhuman, cruel and degrading treatment and for the detainment of people subsequently disappeared.'[8]

In April the first cases of human rights violations were presented to the courts by the human rights organizations.[9] By December 1986, 734 human rights violations were being investigated in the courts, including cases of violation of the Constitution against Junta members and ex-president Bordaberry.[10] Despite this apparently auspicious beginning, a bitter political and judicial battle over human rights prosecutions had developed by mid-1985. The Supreme Military Tribunal claimed jurisdiction over all human rights cases in the courts and the judicial process was stalemated for months. The military social clubs and retired generals issued defiantly deliberative statements accusing their accusers of subversion. Early in 1985, the government entered into a conflict with the opposition in parliament, first supporting the military judiciary's claims and later pressing for a military amnesty.

Despite the Blanco Party's initial opposition to an amnesty for the military, at the end of December 1986, only two days before thirteen military officers accused of involvement in disappearances and other violations were due to appear in court, the party presented the Chamber of Deputies with the Ley de Caducidad de la Pretensión Punitiva del Estado.[11] According to the law's first article, it was recognized that 'as a consequence of the logic of the events stemming from the agreement between the political parties and the Armed Forces signed in August 1984, and in order to complete the transition to full constitutional order, the State relinquishes the exercise of penal actions with respect to crimes committed until March 1, 1985, by military and police officials whether for political reasons or in fulfilment of their functions and in obeying orders from superiors during the *de facto* period.'[12]

On 20 December the law was passed in the Chamber of Deputies by 60 out of 97 votes. The following day it was passed in the

Senate by 22 out of 31 votes. In both cases, the Colorado party had voted in favour of the law, with the exception of the representative of the Corriente Independiente Batllista (CBI) in the Chamber of Deputies. The FA opposed it unanimously in both houses. The Blanco Party was divided. In the Chamber of Deputies, thirteen deputies voted against it.[13] In the Senate, Por la Pátria led by Ferreira Aldunate voted in favour, with the exception of two senators. Senator Carlos Julio Pereyra of the Movimiento Nacional de Rocha (MNR), on the other hand, voted against.[14] The political élite was bitterly divided over the law. The debate in the Chamber of Deputies, for example, had culminated in fist-fights. According to one observer, the debate 'could have ended in a gunfight, the tension was unbearable and I was told that some people were armed'.[15]

What had led the greater part of the traditional parties to shift from an initial commitment to truth and justice to a vote for a military amnesty? This chapter will examine the contorted 'logic of events' which produced this outcome. The account which follows is perforce schematic: The path to amnesty in Uruguay was tortuous, complex, difficult to trace and fraught with ambiguities and contradictions which were difficult to unravel. To simplify the story, the following will be divided into two parts. The first will examine the issue of political prisoners. The second will trace the political class's and society's attempts to come to terms with truth and justice.

The Release of the Political Prisoners: The Emblem of Democratic Restoration (March 1985)

In Uruguay, the release of the regime's political prisoners was synonymous with democratic restoration. All parties were in favour of it, and 68 per cent of Montevideans believed that liberation was a necessary measure.[16] Eight days after the inauguration of the President, the Senate approved the LPN by 28 votes out of 30.[17] The law amnestied political prisoners gaoled between 1 January 1964 and 1 March 1985. It excluded homicide cases, although Article 9 gave the courts 20 days to review these cases. If the courts determined that these sentences lacked legal validity, these were to end immediately. Valid sentences were to be reduced. The following day, the Chamber of Deputies approved the project by 86 of 91 votes. Only Deputy Pintos on the right of the Colorado party attacked the amnesty proposals for expressly excluding police and military officers.[18] The FA voted only against Article 9, which accorded different legal treatment to those accused of homicide. The overwhelming majority vote and the subsequent speed with which the political prisoners were released, however, concealed the intense partisan battles which surrounded the passage of the pacification law. These conflicts presaged the problems which were to plague the resolution of the human rights issue in the following three years.

In Uruguay, democracy had been inaugurated by the legislature on 15 February 1985, two weeks before President Sanguinetti was handed the presidential sash. In order to prevent the legislative pre-emption of the executive, the parties had agreed in late 1984 not to introduce any substantive bills in parliament until 1 March.[19] None the less, during the latter's first session, the FA violated this agreement, presenting a bill in the Senate to amnesty political prisoners. The Blancos followed suit five days later.[20] Despite the Colorado's refusal to reveal the content of the president's project for discussion before Sanguinetti's inauguration and their decision to oppose further debates, the Blancos and the Frente, holding a majority, voted to create a multi-party Comisión Especial Para el Estudio de la Amnistía or a Special Commission for the Study of Amnesty to study the opposition proposals.[21] Conspicuously, the Commission was mandated to end its deliberations two days before Sanguinetti's inauguration. The day before it was due to expire, it approved a unified Blanco–Frente project.[22]

Despite this attempt to speed things up, the opposition were unable to vote on their bill before the inauguration of the President, as the Colorado legislators refused to take a vote in protest. The bitter and intense debate had to be interrupted to prepare the Legislative Palace for the presidential ceremony.[23] It was with partisan tempers already running high that Sanguinetti appealed for calm in his inaugural speech. He called on the legislature to demonstrate a 'spirit of understanding' to prevent dissension from reaching 'the point of compromising or debilitating institutions', and asked the opposition to restrain itself 'to that delicate and necessary degree'.[24] His call for conciliatory politics was not heeded. On 4 March the executive sent its project to parliament for debate. It was blocked by the opposition. The Colorado legislators attempted to prevent the approval of the FA–Blanco project with a vote to postpone the debate, but the opposition's majority enabled them to block the discussion of the executive's project, to approve the joint Frente–Blanco project in the Chamber of Deputies by 55 out of 94 votes, and to relegate the presidential bill to the Constitution, Codes, General Legislation, and Administration Commission.[25]

The Colorado party and the President were incensed. Whilst the former threatened the opposition with the Senate's rejection of their project,[26] the latter condemned the attempt 'to impose circumstantial majorities'. Sanguinetti was angered that his project had not even been debated, despite the government's 'conciliatory attitude'. He claimed that although the executive was 'profoundly respectful of the pronouncements of the parliament', the latter would have to be 'respectful of the conduct of the Executive'.[27] In order to break the stalemate, the President sponsored a meeting between the party leaders. It was agreed that the Commission would study both the joint Blanco–Frente bill recently approved by the deputies and the presidential proposal in order to arrive at a consensus solution. The latter came up with a draft proposal which combined the opposition's demand for speedy releases and the government's resistance to a blanket amnesty. Despite the fact that the Frente's and Blanco Party's representatives in the Commission had agreed on this consensus solution, the parties' representatives in the parliament argued that their bill, already approved by the Chamber of Deputies, rather than the Commission's consensus draft should be voted on. The Colorados, on the other hand, claimed that the consensus project which had emerged out of the negotiations in the Commission was the last word on the subject and that it should therefore take precedence over the opposition's joint project. The Colorados prevailed. The Ley de Pacificación Nacional was passed on 8 March after a long and bitter debate lasting until 4 a.m.[28]

Why was it that, despite the fact that there had been a general consensus on the need to liberate the prisoners and that the only opposition to liberation came from a minority faction of the Colorado party, the resolution of the political prisoners issue was so fraught? In part, it resulted from genuine and legitimate ideological differences, the Colorados opposing a blanket amnesty covering homicide cases, the opposition favouring a total amnesty. But the conflict was essentially partisan: the crux of the matter was that each party wanted to make a point about the role it played in the transitional period in general, and in the Club Naval pact in particular. The Frente, especially its radical sectors, wanted to show that, unlike their strategic Colorado pact partners, they were true representatives of the interests of the political prisoners and generally of all regime victims, participation in the pact notwithstanding. The Blancos, on the other hand, claimed the same for themselves, accusing the Frente of political inconsistency for participating in compromises with the Colorados and the military at the Club Naval.[29] In turn the Colorados were angered over the opposition's apparent attempt to pre-empt the President's first legislative gesture in the restoration of democracy. For them, the behaviour of the opposition was not evidence of its concern with the well-being of the prisoners but a political move to 'trump' the ruling party and the executive.[30] Thus, the events which culminated in an amnesty for the prisoners, rather than contributing to inter-party unity and to cordial relations between the Colorado executive and the opposition-dominated legislature, exacerbated underlying tensions and prepared the ground for future confrontation. It was on this note that the parties embarked on the long road to amnesty.

The Long and Winding Road to Amnesty

Jurisdictional Conflict, Government Stalling, and a Joint Opposition Human Rights Proposal

In August 1985, five months after the first human rights cases had been taken to the courts, the Supreme Military Tribunal interposed a jurisdictional claim against the civil judiciary. The civil courts refused to comply, continued their investigations, and at the end of August they called for the arrest of three military officers accused of human rights violations.[31] Despite the refusal of the courts to hand over jurisdiction to the military, the Supreme Military Tribunal's claim held up judicial action for months.[32] The government's response to this conflict revealed that the promotion of justice was not on its agenda. First, it supported the jurisdiction of the military courts. In April 1985, President Sanguinetti asserted that the military courts should have jurisdiction over human rights violations.[33] Then the government attempted to postpone the arbitration of the conflict by supporting the continued presence of two military-appointed judges in the Supreme Court, by vetoing the opposition's majority vote against the judges in May, and finally by delaying the confirmation of these judges when they were effectively approved by the Senate in November.[34]

In the face of this judicial impasse and the apparent unwillingness of the government to intervene in favour of the ordinary courts, the leaders of two opposition *sub-lemas* united to present a bill to make justice politically feasible. The draft proposal presented in October 1985 by Senator Batalla, leader of the moderate FA PGP-*lista* 99 and Senator Zumarán of the Ferreira's PLP *lema*, recognized that the only chance for successful prosecution was to impose time limits on the resolution of cases and to find suitable criteria to limit the number of cases. It therefore advocated that only cases presented to the date of the project's eventual approval be processed. Furthermore, with an eye on the future, the concept of due obedience was to be limited and a public prosecutor created. Finally, the bill advocated the inclusion of crimes against humanity as a criminal category in the Uruguayan penal code.[35]

The project, however, was never even considered, owing to the intransigence of the government, of the Frente's radical sectors, and the ambiguity of the Blanco Party. The government simply refused to study the project and made it clear that the President would veto it if it were passed in the legislature.[36] Although Seregni and the moderate sectors of the Frente supported it, the radical sectors rejected it as insufficient.[37] The first compromise project therefore failed partly because 'some wanted nothing and others wanted everything'.[38]

Added to the problem of intransigence was the ambiguity of the Blanco Party and Ferreira Aldunate in particular. In April 1985 Ferreira had claimed that 'we cannot settle all accounts and I am not even sure that it would be a good idea to do so'.[39] More revealingly, he had stated that all Uruguayans knew 'that there would be no legal action here against those who violated human rights'. He claimed that although impunity had not been pacted, it had been implicit 'in the terms which inspired the exit which my party did not participate in'.[40]

The ambiguity of Ferreira's position was compounded by his increasing rapprochement with Sanguinetti. In late June 1985 the president had invited Ferreira to a secret meeting with himself and General Medina at the President's farm at San Juan de Anchorena.[41] Sanguinetti's aim was to persuade Ferreira that he would have to overcome the uncompromising stance which had led to his party's exclusion from the Club Naval and its displacement by the Frente from its traditionally prominent place in the bipartisan system. The Blancos should settle their differences with both the military and their traditional Colorado partners, and distance themselves from their Convergencia partners if they hoped to regain their past influence and true place in the bi-partisan system, historically a hallmark of Uruguayan politics.[42] After the Anchorena meeting Ferreira had cancelled a trip to Buenos Aires where he was to testify in the cases of Michelini and Gutierrez Ruíz. He had also reiterated the notion that those who did not accept the logic imposed by the Club Naval pact were either 'the dummies, those who pretend to be dummies, and those which both pretend and really are dummies.'[43]

As a result of this, divisions emerged within the ranks of the Blanco Party, as the leaders of other *lemas* criticized the secrecy of the meetings and wondered where their national leaders' military and human rights policy was heading.[44] Furthermore and predictably, these statements and the secrecy of the talks aroused the anger and suspicion of the Frente. The coalition could not be sure whether the Blanco leader was their ally or enemy. Not only had the content of discussions not been revealed, but the event was only discovered to have taken place almost two months later. Compelled to defend the FA's participation in the pact and its support for justice, Seregni argued that if other parties had pacted impunity, it had not been within the walls of the Club Naval.[45] He referred to the CONAPRO agreement of October 1984 as 'a commitment made in the struggle', which obliged the parties to press for justice, and he reminded people of Medina's first statement permitting the ordinary courts to prosecute the military.[46] Referring to Anchorena, Seregni claimed that justice was not negotiable: 'These things are not meant to be negotiated but determined. And as far as I am concerned they are already determined.'[47] The Frente also felt that the traditional parties were conspiring to exclude it from power, as they gave it no representation in the Electoral Court and the Tribunal de Cuentas.[48]

Open Confrontation with the Judiciary and the First Colorado Amnesty Project

In May 1986, with the judicial and political impasse still unresolved, and with press and legislative accusations mounting, the government sponsored a round of meetings with the party leaders in an attempt to arrive at a political consensus.[49] The initiatives which emerged out of these discussions were again doomed to failure.

First, Ferreira suggested that a General Assembly be convened to allow the parties to engage in an *operación sinceramiento* ('operation sincerity'). The Blanco leader wanted to have a public discussion as to whether or not impunity had been pacted at the Club Naval.[50] As it then became known, General Medina had claimed at Anchorena that after the Club Naval pact Sanguinetti had promised him that trials would not occur, an assurance which the general had transmitted to the Armed Forces in a tour of the country's garrisons in 1984. Moreover, the general had said that if anyone in the military was forced to appear in court, he would resign.[51] The Blanco leader therefore wanted everyone to 'confess' to the real state of affairs, dispel or confirm rumours, and thus to build an honest human rights policy.

The General Assembly, however, was postponed indefinitely; instead, party leaders engaged in another round of reserved meetings in June 1986.[52] Talks continued throughout July, but no consensus was reached.[53] On the one hand, the government refused to allow the human rights issue to be a part of the Acuerdo Nacional, an agreement made between the parties in June to facilitate the passage of essential legislation. Instead, it proposed that the parties make a second Club Naval pact with the military to put a *punto final* to the conflict. The government argued that such a pact was necessary to avoid confrontations which would threaten civil–military relations, and that the primary responsibility of the politicians was to maintain institutional stability, leaving the past 'to historians'.[54] The other parties, however, were both unconvinced by these arguments and unwilling to make deals with the military in such an overt manner.[55]

Seregni and Ferreira then contemplated the possibility of applying an amnesty after the investigation of the violations, but it was subsequently abandoned.[56] Solutions failed firstly because all parties were awaiting the outcome of the Supreme Court's arbitration. Secondly, Seregni, always in fear of losing authority over the radical sectors in his party, was at pains to reassure them that 'nothing was being negotiated' and that talks did not involve a capitulation *vis-à-vis* long-held commitments to justice.[57] Thirdly, the Blanco leadership was ambiguous about whether to remain with its Convergencia partners or whether to ally with the other traditional party. Furthermore, it was as yet unwilling to pay the political price for abandoning its commitment to justice. It therefore alternated between an outright rejection of an amnesty and possible acceptance of the latter following proper investigations.[58] Finally and most importantly, the President consistently opposed proposals for limited justice, insisting that he would not 'negotiate with or make scapegoats of a few names'.[59]

The effectiveness of the negotiations was also undermined by tensions generated by increasingly overt governmental attempts to prevent the courts from acting on the human rights cases. In April 1986, for example, the Ministry of Defence caused a furore by sending secret information compiled by one of the parliamentary human rights investigating commissions to the military instead of ordinary courts.[60]

In June 1986, when the Supreme Court finally arbitrated in favour of the civil justice system—now examining over 40 disputed cases involving 180 military and police officers—Sanguinetti accused it of partiality and claimed that it was not in a position to arbitrate on the issue of human rights violations.[61] In doing so, the executive explicitly challenged the legitimacy and independence of the judiciary. Finally, in October, the government refused to comply with Argentine requests for the extradition of a number of military officers who had engaged in repressive activities in Buenos Aires.[62]

Furthermore, the animosity of the government and the Blancos towards the Frente escalated as the coalition's radical sectors stepped up their human rights agitation inside and outside the legislature. In one of many incidents, Senator Araújo of the Frente, the most outspoken human rights advocate in the legislature and much disliked by the opposition, faced accusations of complicity with the military in a letter published in the national press, until it was discovered that the letter had been concocted by the security services and that some of his critics and government representatives had been aware of this at the time.[63]

The June meetings had also led to the formation of a multiparty Commission of Jurists to design a consensus project.[64] This initiative, however, also failed. First, the Colorado representative in the commission presented a draft bill which gave the military jurisdiction over homicide cases, with the right of appeal to the Supreme Court. All other cases were to be closed by an amnesty.[65] The other commissioners rejected the project and voted against an amnesty as unconstitutional.[66] Failing to reach a juridical consensus without prior political agreement, the jurists asked the party leaders to meet with them to arrive at a politically negotiated solution.[67] Before this could be arranged, however, the Colorado party presented an amnesty proposal to parliament in August 1986. The new Ley de Pacificación Nacional proposed an amnesty for military and police officers directly or indirectly involved in the war against subversion between 1 January 1962 and 1 March 1985, covering authors, co-authors, accomplices, and those covering up the crimes. It recommended the closure of all cases currently in the courts.

President Sanguinetti adopted the arguments of the military to justify this law. He claimed that there was no evidence linking the Armed Forces to human rights violations, that violations had been no more than excesses and that there had indeed been a state of internal war. He accused critics of being part of the subversive threat, which sought to reawaken the conflict with the military. He often referred to a supposed terrorist threat.[68] In his view, for example, the human rights organizations were 'taking sides with the subversives'.[69] He equated a military amnesty with the amnesty for political prisoners saying that if the military had committed excesses 'the terrorists were also responsible for grave crimes, and they were none the less amnesties. It is normal to amnesty the military as well.'[70]

The President met with Seregni and Ferreira in an unsuccessful attempt to gain their support for the project.[71] Tensions increased as sectors of the Frente, led by Senator Araújo, demonstrated in front of the Centro Militar, eliciting a harsh reaction from the commanders. In late September the project was unanimously rejected by the opposition in the Senate by 16 votes out of 29.[72]

Explaining the Government's Attitude: The Voice of the Deliberating Soldier

Why had the government shifted from its public commitment to allow individuals to take their cases to the ordinary courts to supporting military jurisdiction over human rights violations and finally to advocating an amnesty? The explanation for these rapid changes lay mainly in the government's relations with the military.

Between March and October 1985, the government's biggest challenge appeared to be its vain attempts to arrest the process of deliberation within the ranks, led by the Army's hardline-dominated Centro Militar and its ideological mouthpiece, *El Soldado*.[73] The military clubs were on the whole supportive of human rights violators. In April 1985, for example, a majority of the Navy Club membership had rejected a motion to expel Admiral Márquez, one of the most infamous leaders of the dictatorship, from the club for corruption and human rights violations.[74] In July 1985, six army officers had challenged Senator Jose Araújo to a duel for his denunciations of human rights violators in parliament.[75] In September 1985, General Paulós, whose election list explicitly rejected any attempts to take the military to court and included several of the worst known human rights violators, was elected president of the Centro Militar with 71 per cent of the vote.[76]

In November the military clubs made their institutional position on justice explicit in a public statement issued in the name of the Centro Militar, the Club Militar Artigas, and the Centro de Oficiales Retirados. They declared their solidarity with two retired generals who had been accused of violating the constitution and claimed that the military tribunals were the only bodies competent to review crimes committed by active duty military officers.[77]

The government's response to this situation was two-fold. On the one hand, it refused to accept military activities which challenged the authority of the civilian executive and which were unrelated to the human rights issue. Thus, Generals Julio César Bonelli, José María Siqueira, Alonso Feola, and Washington Varela, Director of the SIFA, were dismissed for questioning the authority of the executive.[78] The government also supported a cutback in military institutional prerogatives. In April 1985 it supported the derogation of the Ley Orgánica Militar, which reformed the military's mission from national security to national defence and partially democratized promotions.[79] On the other hand, the President accepted and even condoned military contestation on the issue of human rights. He demonstrated, for example, that human rights violations would not affect promotions. In January 1986, Colonel Nelson Marabotto, a doctor who had been involved in the torture of prisoners, was promoted by the executive to the directorship of the Hospital Militar. In March 1986, Colonel Cordero, who had been accused of disappearances and was under an Argentine extradition order, was promoted. Sanguinetti also praised the decision of the Military Court to absolve ex-Commander-in-Chief of the Navy, Vice-Admiral Jose Imizcoz, accused of human rights violations by navy deserter, Daniel Rey Piuma.[80]

This policy was based on two premisses. In the first place, Sanguinetti was apparently committed to the promise he had made to Medina in 1984 that he would protect the military from prosecution. Secondly, it appeared that the president feared General Medina would be unable to contain the aggressive insubordination of the hard-line which had increased alarmingly as accusations against military officers proliferated in the press, parliament, and the courts.

Medina undoubtedly faced problems in his attempt to calm the stormy waters in the military clubs. In August 1985, for example, a Colonel of the Centro Militar had proposed a motion to collectively condemn attacks on the armed forces, rejecting 'all pronouncements which led to the moral condemnation of the Armed Forces', and demanding the burial of the past.[81] When Medina had the Colonel arrested, *El Soldado* attacked the 'modern inquisitors' who claimed that the military had no right to deliberate, and stated that 'institutions with dignity will not be cornered'. To this it added that Generals Massera and Videla of Argentina were the 'victims of marxist vengeance', and that the attempts to judge the military in Uruguay were also manifestations of a revenge by the 'Internationals'.[82] Medina attempted to counteract the impact of this publication by launching a new magazine, *El Ejército*. It aimed to represent the official voice of the Armed Forces but it did not silence the deliberating *Soldado*.[83]

Moreover, the activities of the security services continued largely uncontrolled. In March 1985, for example, *Opinar* had published a document prepared by military intelligence which described the parliamentary session in which the amnesty for political prisoners had been debated. It accused the political wing of the Tupamaros of planning the formation of a national liberation army like the Sandinistas. The following day Medina met with Sànguinetti, and the Command was asked to issue a statement asserting that the document did not reflect the official opinion of the Forces.[84]

The bottom line was that the hard-line expected Medina to deliver, a demand he felt bound to respond to:

> General Medina had come out of the Club Naval and had told the commanders that there would be no trials. His word was at stake. This was no small matter because if General Medina's word lost credibility this could have serious consequences . . . General Gregorio Álvarez had allowed the elections to take place against his better judgement and was not at all pleased with the pacted 'exit'; the loss of Medina's credibility would mean strengthening of the sectors within the army which thought like General Álvarez. These people would have said: 'The traitor (Medina) handed over power to the civilians and now, to top it all, we have to go to gaol' . . . 'we did not want to strengthen the pro-coup sector of the army which was a minority' . . . there were many indications that Medina and various generals wanted democracy to survive, they thought that the period of the dictatorship had harmed the Armed Forces and they wanted to reinsert themselves peacefully and gradually into the life of the nation. There were many signs, on the other hand, that minority sectors did not want this, and they were looking for an opportunity to gain supporters within the Armed Forces.[85]

General Medina may have feared that he might lose his grip over the military. But his will to exert control over these elements was doubtless reduced because he was himself opposed to trials. He defended the military's record in the war against subversion, commending the 'high spirit manifested in carrying out its duty'. He claimed that all accusations made against the military were 'insidious propaganda' promoted by subversives.[86] He argued that the general tenor of the human rights was unbalanced and the armed forces 'intimately and repeatedly asked themselves if there was complete equanimity in the consideration of these issues which had such an effect on the moral climate within the institution.'[87]

Thus, even though General Medina forbade the Centro Militar's officers from challenging Senator Araújo to a duel, he criticized the Senator, questioned the veracity of the accusations, and claimed that these attacks were 'attacks by the same enemies that the army once fought'. He then sent an internal circular to the clubs, warning them that although 'it was a grave error to suppose that the battle was over', officers should stay calm because the leadership assumed full responsibility for the violations and that 'if any one of the charges were ever proven, they would be the concern of the military alone'.[88]

As was revealed only after the amnesty law was finally passed, the problem for Medina was that the Command was threatened by its inferiors. Many officers demanded protection in return for not implicating the hierarchy in corruption and violations. According to Ferreira, when one of the most notorious military officers, Gavazzo, who was accused of disappearing Uruguayans in Argentina, had personally requested institutional protection from Medina, the latter had at first refused. The general had told Gavazzo that the disappearances which he was being accused of were not the institutional responsibility of the military. He subsequently changed his mind.[89]

Whatever their commitment to prevent trials, the president and Medina had to find a specific formula to protect the military. The president had initially supported military jurisdiction, given the military's refusal to appear before civil magistrates. On 12 September 1985, for example, Lieutenant Gavazzo publicly declared that he would never appear before a civil judge to be tried for 'acts of service'.[90]

This policy, however, became inadequate as the judiciary refused to abdicate from jurisdiction over these cases. Yet, amazingly enough, the president could not propose an amnesty because of opposition to such a policy from within the military itself. In July 1986, a group of retired generals, mostly men accused of human rights violations, issued a statement claiming that an amnesty would destroy the 'honour and military principles', since in their view, no crime had been committed. A week before the first Colorado amnesty project was presented, sixteen retired generals had issued another declaration in which they again declared their solidarity with those accused of violations, and rejected the possibility of an amnesty.[91]

General Medina intervened with more success after this last

declaration. He met with three of the most vociferous retired generals, who told him that either all were guilty or none. He persuaded the generals to claim responsibility for all actions undertaken in the battle against subversion, and persuaded the army club to indefinitely postpone the proposed assembly to defend the honour of the armed forces.[92] The road to amnesty was now cleared, but the government and Medina still faced a last Blanco challenge.

The Blancos' Last Stand

In late September the Blancos presented a project akin to the Zumarán–Batalla initiative, which attempted to ensure limited justice. The Proyecto de Ley de Defensa de la Democracia (Bill for the Defence of Democracy) aimed to condemn morally 'those who in the recent past destroyed the *Lex Magna* or supported those who did', and to strengthen the laws 'which seek to preserve the Constitution'. It provided for the punishment of human rights violators and for the introduction of a number of laws to penalize future attempts to overturn the constitutional order. Its solution for the current human rights problem was to limit prosecutions to the crimes of 'homicide, aggravated crimes, violations . . . the disappearance of people', to exclude the crimes committed between 1 March 1967 and 1 November 1967, and to prosecute only those cases presented to the courts by 22 September 1986. Finally it clarified and limited the amount of time that the courts could take to investigate and resolve these cases.[93]

In early October, the bill was rejected in the Senate by both the Colorados and the Frente in a vote of 11 to 30.[94] On the one hand, the Colorado party was by then totally committed to an amnesty.[95] On the other, the Frente had again initially accepted the proposal in principle, and responded with a document outlining a number of reforms.[96] These proposals had in turn been well received by the Blancos.[97] As with the Zumarán-Batalla project, however, it was rejected by the radical sectors. On the day of the vote, the PIT–CNT led a protest of 10,000 outside the legislative palace.[98]

Finally, the military had refused to accept the Blanco proposal. On 1 October 1986, the ever-alert sixteen retired generals had issued a statement through the Centro Militar. Ominously, this declaration was made in the name of all military social clubs and, unlike the first declarations, was signed by a number of officers in active service. It condemned the attacks on the institution, 'the intensification of defamatory techniques, the incitements to violence, and the types of social agitation that . . . were preludes to subversive acts'. This time they explicitly demanded an amnesty like the Colorado proposal rejected by the Senate two months before which they had previously claimed to be unacceptable. Furthermore, they stated that they would only accept a solution to this problem from the executive, thus invalidating the legislature as a legitimate branch of government.[99]

The Blancos were angered with the Frente and the Colorados, blaming the Communists and the Pachequistas for the failure of the project. But again their ambiguity had partially been to blame. They had done little to consult with the Frente in designing the bill, and had expended much energy courting the Colorado party, a move bound to alienate the left.[100]

The rejection of the Blanco project led to a complete breakdown of inter-party relations, culminating in the failure of the legislature to pass the 1987 government budget in mid-November, and with the government threatening to dissolve parliament.[101] It was only after this crisis that the Blanco Party shifted allegiances on the issue of justice for human rights violators.

The Re-Constitution of the Traditional Bi-Partisan Alliance: The Blanco Impunity Law, November 1986–December 1986

The military statement rejecting the Blanco project was, as usual, followed by meetings between the President, General Medina, and the Commanders. This time the outcome proved more successful, leading to the first remotely apologetic statement by the armed institution.[102] On 20 November the generals of the high command regretted the possible 'loss of points of reference' in the anti-subversive war, and assumed full responsibility for the 'acts committed by members of the Armed Forces'. They explained that the lower ranks could not be held responsible because this would 'seriously damage the morale which sustains the principle of authority, the guarantor of subordination, discipline and integrity of the military institution'. The Commanders claimed that the Armed Forces felt 'excluded from the national reconciliation'. They explained that 'the decision to reach an agreement [at the Club Naval] had been the result of a long process of mental and spiritual evolution towards institutionalization'. As a result, they hoped that the civilians would make their contribution and leave behind a 'past, marked by disagreements and violence'. After it, General Medina declared that the institution would defend all those who had carried out orders in the war against terrorism, although it would not support anyone who had engaged in economic fraud.[103]

Now that the military were willing to accept an amnesty and had made an inadequate apology, the president needed to persuade one of the parties to vote with it to occasion an amnesty. Sanguinetti called on the parties to respond to the high spirit of the military's declaration by making 'gesture of generosity to put an end to revisionism'.

He found no welcoming echo in the Frentista camp. Seregni said he would not make 'acuerdos chanchos' (dirty deals).[104] He was 'open to dialogue' but he thought his coalition would not arrive at an agreement with the other parties 'because it will not admit the consagration of impunity for human rights violations'.[105] He continued to insist that civil jurisdiction over human rights violations had been decided at the Club Naval and that prosecutions should follow.[106]

The president therefore renewed his earlier efforts to win over the Blanco leader. Ferreira, however, who had not been convinced by the government's previous arguments in favour of an amnesty, did not share Sanguinetti's views regarding the war against subversion, nor did he agree with the President's arguments that an amnesty for the military would be the moral and political equivalent of the March 1985 amnesty for political prisoners. The government had to come up with better arguments if it was to convince the Blanco leader to change his party's policy. Sanguinetti thus developed a new line of argument: the transition to democracy was officially announced as incomplete.[107]

It was now admitted that the government's main problem was its fragile relations with the Armed Forces resulting from the conflict over human rights. For the first time, it was publicly admitted that the military had adopted an institutional policy to ignore court orders.[108] The crux of the argument was that Uruguay was facing a potential institutional crisis. If he, Sanguinetti, were to call on the military to comply with court summons and the latter were to refuse to do so, his authority as Commander-in-Chief of the Armed Forces and as President of the Nation would be irremediably shattered.

Although Ferreira seemed increasingly willing to sacrifice justice in the name of 'governability', he was also wary of paying the political price attached to a betrayal of the party's human rights platform. He was willing to help the Colorados on the condition that they accepted that if an institutional crisis was at hand it was because impunity had been part of the logic of the Club Naval pact. If impunity was a condition for democratic stability, it was a condition which the Colorados and the Frente had determined through their choice of transition. As such, impunity could not be the political responsibility of the Blancos who had refused to participate in the pact. The pacting parties could not expect the Blanco's to fix the problems and pay the political price for that which they had laid the ground for at the Club Naval.[109] Thus, in the words of Zumarán, if 'the National Party was willing to defend institutions with a great effort' it would do so if it was very clear that 'impunity had been pacted two years earlier at the Club Naval'.[110]

Although the Blancos made constant references to the Club Naval, their increasing willingness to support an amnesty was probably reinforced by a series of secret meetings which took place in October 1986 between Blanco Senator Zumarán, Sanguinetti, and the Commanders-in-Chief. According to Zumarán, General Medina had told him that if anyone was forced to go to court he would lose his authority over the Armed Forces. This was reinforced when, in mid-December, General Medina told party leaders that if the issue was not resolved by 22 December the day before a number of officers were due to appear in court, he would make the fact of institutional resistance to trials public. He would personally announce that he was in possession of the court citations for the accused officers. Furthermore, the military would bring a claim of unconstitutionality against the amnesty for political prisoners.

The Club Naval was again the ghost which haunted the human rights summit sponsored by the president between the UC leader, Ciganda, Seregni, Ferreira Aldunate, General Medina, and himself at the Estevez Palace on 1 December 1986.[111] Everyone claimed that although the issue of justice had not been explicitly dealt with, there had been an 'understanding' and it had been 'deliberately sidestepped'.[112] Interpretations differed, however, as to the implications of that deliberate omission. General Medina claimed that although nothing had been made explicit, both the Colorados and the military had assumed that there would be no prosecutions. This was confirmed by Sanguinetti, who claimed that there had been 'no secret or tacit clause which ensured an amnesty, but there was no doubt that the logic of the facts led one to believe that if one agreed to an institutional "exit", it meant that the pacting parties would not claim responsibilities.'[113]

The Frente was outraged: it rejected the Club Naval 'argument' as untrue, the declaration of the Commanders in Chief as insufficient, a negotiated amnesty as unconstitutional, and insisted on the application of the 'legislation in force for the judgement of crimes against humanity' and government support for the continued action of the courts.[114] It saw the attack on the pact as a manipulation of the issue. For the Frente, this interpretation of events was unacceptable. To have accepted this would have meant admitting to an incredible hypocrisy and political and strategic inconsistency: either the method they had chosen to ensure the transition to democracy was consistent with demands for justice, in which case they were being maligned, or the pact was inconsistent with these demands, in which case their continued support for justice was nothing more than political pyrotechnics. By accepting nothing but total justice, they were wanting to have their cake and eat it too. On the one hand, they had participated in the pact in order to ensure political respectability for themselves, in the process of which they had sacrificed both the unity of the opposition front and Ferreira's presidential chances. On the other hand, they continued to claim to be the vanguard of the struggle against impunity which rightly belonged to the only party which had refused to participate in the pact.

The battle over the pact's implications was waged between Seregni and Ferreira Aldunate on 4 December in a televised debate. The Blanco leader accused the Frente of political irresponsibility, of demanding justice regardless of the political realities and consequences.[115] In order to demonstrate the political inconsistency of the Frente and its unwillingness to pay the price for impunity, Ferreira claimed that Seregni had proposed that either the Blanco or Colorado party should advocate a two-year moratorium on the human rights issue, and that in exchange for this, he would ensure that his party would only half-heartedly oppose his own proposal. By claiming this, Ferreira seemed to indicate that Seregni recognized the political difficulties involved and yet was unwilling to take political responsibility for the problems stemming from the struggle over justice.[116]

Although Seregni was unable to clearly refute this accusation, he did make a spirited and convincing defence of the pact: contrary to assuming that impunity had been guaranteed, all the participants had acted as if justice would in fact be done and the Club Naval talks had almost broken down over the issue of military justice because none of the parties had been willing to see its role expanded. The Frente accused the Blanco Party of using the Club Naval as a red herring to cover up the fact that they had already secretly agreed to support the government's plans to ensure impunity. The coalition claimed that Ferreira had already changed his mind at Anchorena in June 1985, and that the summit meetings and the televised debate had been a set-up designed by the two traditional parties to destroy the left by making it pay the price for impunity, to 'cover up impunity'.[117] After this interview relations between the Frente and the Blancos broke down completely, as Ferreira accused the Frente of being controlled by the communists, and the communists insulted Ferreira in their daily, *La Hora*.

Although the Frente refused to back down, its attitude was not sufficiently constructive. It provided neither an alternative to the Colorado's amnesty nor to projects of partial justice which the Blancos had proposed. Seregni claimed that the Frente had not presented its own project because its jurists had decided that the country's 'juridical order is in perfect condition to ensure the judgement of the crimes against human rights'.[118] However, his claim that 'if there is contempt of court we will put constitutional mechanisms into action' was at this stage of the game manifestly insufficient.[119]

On 18 December the FA presented its first concrete legislative proposal to deal with the issue of justice for human rights violators. The project was a strange animal. Its apparent aim was to produce a public and administrative rather than a judicial solution for the military accused of human rights violations. It proposed that the Supreme Court inform the General Assembly of the names of the military and police officers who had refused to comply with court summonses; that the Court order the publication of their names and the causes of their refusal to comply in the *Diario Oficial* and in the national papers; and that, if following these measures the accused did not then obey the summonses within a given period, they be deprived of their military or police status, thus forsaking retirement and other corporate benefits.[120]

It was unclear whether the final measure was intended to facilitate the future prosecution of these officers by depriving them of their institutional links. Whatever the intent, the project died a premature death. The Colorado party announced the presentation of its second amnesty on the same day. This draft bill was rejected by the opposition in the Chamber of Deputies, while the FA-sponsored protest took place outside the Congress.[121]

The following day, on 19 December, the Blanco Party presented the Ley de Caducidad de la Pretension Punitiva del Estado to the lower house.[122] Reminiscent of Ferreira's speech in 1972 when voting for the Ley de Seguridad del Estado, the party's leader claimed that the Blancos would vote 'with pain and we take responsibility'.[123]

For him it was to be the 'moment of greatest suffering' in his political life.[124]

Again debates centred on the ever-present pact. The Colorado deputies declared that at the Club Naval the military had said they would not accept trials.[125] This claim, however, was rejected with some indignation by Colorado Vice-President Tarigo, who had been present at the talks. The latter assured everyone that the Colorados had explicitly mentioned that the human rights issue would be solved according to the law. This revelation exacerbated already existing divisions within the Blanco Party. Many Blancos had decided to vote for the law precisely because they had been persuaded that an institutional crisis was at hand because impunity had in fact been pacted at the Club Naval. Thus, after Tarigo's speech, two Ferreirista Senators refused to vote for the law.[126] Moreover, many in the party complained that a majority of the party's members had not known about the writing of the project, and that they had never been informed about the meetings between their party leaders and the military in October.[127]

The following day, the Colorado and Blanco senators approved the expulsion of the human rights senator, Jose Araújo, from the Senate. Ostensibly based on the argument that the senator had encouraged a mass demonstration outside the parliament on the day of the vote and was thus unfit to be a national representative, the move was seen by the FA as an exercise in expiation of guilt by scapegoating.[128] On the same day, Lieutenant Gavazzo finally appeared in court, only to be sent home again untried and unsentenced.[129] Thus ended the first episode of the human rights battle. The ball was now in civil society's court.

Civil Society Responds: The Nunca Más *Report and the Referendum Campaign*

The failure to promote truth-telling and justice 'from above' led to two major initiatives to redress this outcome 'from below'. One consisted of a truth-telling exercise, the other of an attempt to derogate the amnesty law. The truth-telling project began in March 1986 in response to the failure of the parliamentary investigating commissions to offer a social, official, and public truth about military repression. In April 1985, the FA and the Blanco Party had set up two investigating commissions in the legislature which aimed to provide the necessary information to the courts about the disappeared and the assassination of two famous legislators. In November 1985, the Comisión Investigadora Sobre la Situación de

Personas Desaparecidas y Hechos que la Motivaron concluded that the Uruguayan military had definitely been involved in the disappearances under investigation. Its findings were handed over to the ordinary courts.[130] In October 1987, the Comisión Investigadora Sobre los Secuestros y Asesinatos de los Ex-Legisladores Zelmar Michelini y Héctor Gutiérrez Ruíz concluded that the military regime had been guilty of crimes against humanity, including genocide.[131] In November, after recommending that its findings be sent to the courts, the former were handed over to the Executive branch for review.

Despite the efforts of the commissions, they failed to produce a national truth. The results of the reports were never officially announced. Their limited coverage elicited no official explanation or response from the previous government and military authorities. The commissions had lacked the necessary investigating faculties. The FA had presented a project to the Chamber of Deputies to give the commissions the power to oblige people to testify. Although the measure had been passed in the Chamber of Deputies with the support of the Blanco Party, it never reached the Senate. The Colorados opposed it on the grounds that it invaded the jurisdiction of the judicial system.[132]

Neither of the commissions had been able to find conclusive proof of an institutional decision-making process leading to these crimes. Although the co-ordination of repressive actions between the Argentine and Uruguayan armed forces and the institutional responsibility of the Uruguayan military had been 'proven' by the testimonies of a number of people, the commission on the disappeared had, in its final statement, changed at the last minute under political pressure, claiming that it could not 'conclude that these irregularities were imputable to organic decisions'.[133] Finally, the President himself had disqualified the findings of the commissions, stating that 'None of these investigations concluded with the clarification of the authorship of the crimes and nor did they produce credible conclusions about them . . . there were no conclusive testimonies in any case; and the responsibilities cannot be established.'[134]

The human rights organizations had made numerous unsuccessful attempts to press for truth and justice. Their attempt to gain the support of legislators for a bill to ensure justice, however, had been ignored and the Colorados had threatened to veto it.[135] Along with the Commission of Jurists, the Colegio de Abogados, the directorate of the national university had rejected the Colorado amnesty as unconstitutional.[136] They had also rejected the

Blanco project as insufficient.[137] In April 1985 they had set up the Asamblea Por la Verdad y la Justicia (Assembly for Peace and Justice) which had organized marches and protests and a hunger strike with no visible impact on the party political debate. The television channels had consistently refused to give them publicity space.[138]

The organizations had initially co-operated extensively with the investigating commissions, but had eventually come to criticize their performance. None of the accused had been called on to testify, and the reports had concluded that there was no proof of organic decision-making within the Armed Forces despite a wealth of testimony to the contrary.[139] In the face of these frustrations, SERPAJ and members of progressive church-related or Christian organizations, under the auspices of SERPAJ's leader, Luis Pérez Aguirre, launched the so-called *Nunca Más* project. They worked in co-operation with lawyers and doctors and the public opinion poll organization, Equipos Consultores.[140] In the complete absence of any official records and the paucity of non-governmental organization documentation, the data was gathered by an extensive and scientific random survey of 311 ex-political prisoners, and was complemented by SERPAJ's documentation, information from several international and exile organizations, and by direct testimony.[141] The *Nunca Más* team was financed by funds from the United Nations Fund for the Victims of Torture, and from a number of international organizations such as the United Church of Canada, Pan for the World of West Germany, Diakonia-Ecumenical Action of Sweden, and the MacArthur Foundation through a request made by Americas Watch.[142]

The report, written by members of the SERPAJ, examined the breakdown of democracy and the nature of military rule. It studied the system of prolonged imprisonment and systematic torture and the cases of disappearances. The lack of governmental support, the paucity of human and financial resources, and the lengthy survey meant that the report took three years to complete. It was released on 9 March 1989.[143] The launching of the report, however, did not constitute a ceremonial event on the elected government's agenda, so it appeared with no fanfare. Its release was also completely overshadowed by the plebiscite to overturn the amnesty law, which took place only a month later. Thus, the report never became the focus of national attention, partly because of the lack of national press coverage and partly because it had been undertaken by organizations which, merits aside, were not politically prominent or powerful. None of the parties nor the military were forced to respond to it. None the less, the report was a best-seller. In 1992, it had gone through three printings and there were 5,000 copies in circulation.[144] In producing the report, these groups reaffirmed their status as 'truth-tellers', isolated from the formal political arena, but speaking in the name of the politically unrepresented victims whose aspirations for truth and justice had been betrayed by the political class.

The second major initiative emanating from civil society was against impunity. According to the Uruguayan constitution, referenda can be carried out on the stringent condition that 25 per cent of registered voters sign to support the initiative within a year of a contested law's promulgation.[145] On 12 January 1987 the wives of three famous assassinated legislators informed the Electoral Court of their decision to promote such a referendum to derogate the Ley de Caducidad. The initiative represented the first attempt in the history of the country to use this constitutional right to overturn a national law.

The Comisión Nacional Pro-Referendum (National Pro-Referendum Commission), composed of fifty notables, among them the novelist Mario Benedetti, aimed to 'call the people above banners and political parties to permit them to pronounce themselves'. It claimed to represent the 'indignant citizen'.[146] The campaign was immediately supported by a whole array of social and political organizations, and by the parties and *lemas* which had opposed the amnesty law in parliament.[147]

Although the campaign was clearly not meant as a partisan initiative, most of the organizers were members of the parties which had opposed the amnesty in parliament. Twenty-five out of the fifty members of the Commission were Frentistas, and Frente supporters, for example, were told that the work of collecting signatures was a party duty.[148]

The campaign generated an intense political debate and faced much resistance. Jurists were called upon by different parties to declare the juridical validity or invalidity of the initiative.[149] The government and the Blanco faction which had supported the law claimed that the effect of derogation would be retroactive and therefore illegal. The organizers were constantly equated with subversives; the door-to-door campaign was denounced as totalitarian. The opposition threatened that the derogation of this law might lead to the derogation of the amnesty law for political prisoners.[150]

The President himself stated that 'This signature is for rancour and revenge. We send out a warning to all citizens to all those who in good faith may feel tempted to do so, that what they will be doing is simply taking the country back to a period it has already overcome.'[151] He stated that 'it would be a great victory for the [former subversives], and everyone, government and opposition will have acquired a gigantic political problem'.[152] Finally he argued that it was 'as morally debatable to amnesty the Tupamaros and other subversives. By amnestying everybody there is no discrimination.'[153] In a speech on 18 July 1988 celebrating the 155th anniversary of the Constitution of 1833, Sanguinetti made nineteen references to law and order and twenty one to radicalism, reminding 'the violent ones' (there was no violence occurring at the time) 'that the first gunshot will never come from the Armed Forces on parade here . . . but there will be no hesitations in defending the Constitution or ensuring peace in the face of a threat'.[154]

The military also campaigned aggressively against the referendum, and although the statements they made violated Article 77 of the Constitution, the President did not penalize deliberations. When asked how the armed forces would react to an unfavourable outcome, General Medina declared that 'it [was] difficult to know' and that 'time would tell', adding that in Uruguay there had been 5,000 prisoners when there could have been 5,000 disappeared.[155] In October 1988, Medina stated on television that only the mentally ill supported the vote, thus suggesting that almost one-third of the Uruguayan population was insane.[156] Finally, in March 1989, the army carried out an operation in one of the provinces supposedly in preparation for the 're-emergence of subversion' and Medina warned that the vote would 'provoke very bitter and unfortunate moments' and a 'strong confrontation'.[157]

The campaigners also faced a dirty tricks campaign by the Electoral Court, which had no Frente representatives. On 17 December 634,703 signatures were handed over to the Electoral Court for verification and review.[158] The court arbitrarily disqualified 20,000 signatures in January 1988 changing the rules of the game a month into the verification process. In June 1988 it claimed the 'non-existence' of 30,000 electoral lists. In August General Medina ordered the imprisonment of two officers who had signed the referendum petition. The arrest of Captain Silbermann for signing the petition produced great fear, as people realized that the military had been given access to the list of signatories.[159] On 13 September 1988 Medina sent a list of 25,000 names of military personnel to the Electoral Court with Sanguinetti's permission to check if any of them had signed the petition.[160] The court even invalidated Seregni's and Carlos Julio Pereyra's signatures. Finally, in December the Court gave citizens two days in which to personally ratify the 36,000 signatures still in dispute. Only the huge efforts of the campaigners and popular support made this venture possible.[161] In October 1987, 45 per cent of Montevideans felt that the Electoral Court's behaviour was doubtful, and 19 per cent thought it was engaged in outright fraud.[162]

On 16 April 1989 the Ley de Caducidad was ratified by a narrow national majority of 53 per cent.[163] In Montevideo, the result was reversed, with those opposed to the law winning with 53 per cent of the vote. In Uruguay, it was a popular referendum which brought the political battle over human rights to an end. It was a result fraught with the ambiguities which had characterized the whole process of coming to terms with the legacy of repression. On the one hand, the results expressed society's disapproval of the inept and ambivalent way in which the political class had dealt with the issue, and their desire for justice; through the campaign, society 'called the political system to account for its inability to act and its divorce from its social base.'[164]

On the other hand, the vote indicated that Uruguayans were inclined, as the Colorados had been, to take the safer path. The campaign and the vote expressed the coexistence of two incompatible logics: the former, the *lógica ética* (ethical logic) and the latter, the *lógica estatal* (state logic).[165] The former called for derogation, the adherence to principle, and risk-taking; the latter marginally for security and the abdication of principle in favour of pragmatism.

Conclusions

At the end of 1986, Blanco leader Zumarán accused Seregni of having exchanged his release and the acceptance of negotiations with Ferreira's proscription for impunity. Moreover, he claimed that the Communist party had decided to vote against the Blanco project of September 1985 so that the Blanco Party would be forced to opt for an amnesty, paying the price for a political volte-face as the Frente would put them through the 'meat-grinding machine'.[166] Days later, however, Colorado Senator Jorge Batlle claimed that he and Alberto Zumarán had agreed to an amnesty in October 1986. The events which had followed had merely been 'a complex act consisting first in a military declaration and then a law which would sustain our point of view'.[167]

At the beginning of January 1987, President Sanguinetti claimed in the national press that the threat of military rebellion had only been a rhetorical artifice.[168] In early 1987, General Medina stated that the military had resisted trials, not because of the pact but because subsequent politicization of the issue had led the high command to conclude that the ordinary courts were not in a position to try military officers.[169] He thanked the traditional parties and the President in particular for their support. On his retirement, Medina again thanked the traditional parties for their support and expressed his satisfaction at seeing his mission accomplished: the armed forces had been seen through the transition intact.[170] In 1989, the Executive approved the promotion of 54 officers, eleven of whom were proven to have violated human rights and to have been involved in operations in Argentina.[171] In that year, Army Commander-in-Chief de Nava, Medina's replacement, was accused of involvement in torture.[172]

Thus ended Uruguay's attempt to come to terms with the legacies of state repression. At the level of formal politics, it had produced a conflict characterized by 'factious fighting, zero sum games, merely defensive strategies, the recourse to a system of mutual tolls on the part of collective actors more preoccupied with protecting their corporative interests.'[173] In response to this, at the level of 'informal politics' it had produced the idealism of the *Nunca Más* report and of the referendum campaign. In the end, however, the logic which had produced the amnesty law at the formal political level, and the logic which had led to the ratification of the law at the social level had apparently coincided; the resigned consensus expressed in the vote, seemed to be that democracy could only survive in the absence of justice. In Sanguinetti's words, the amnesty was the price to pay for democracy.[174] If the referendum was a vote of assessment of the transition and its outcome in the field of human rights, the majority had voted, if not for the Colorados, then at least against testing the limits of military loyalty to democratic civilian supremacy. Four years later it seems that Chileans were faced with the same choice: their response will be the subject of the next chapter.

6

Negotiating Truth, Justice, and Pardons under the Concertación Governments of Aylwin 1990–1993 and Frei 1993—

Introduction

On 12 March 1990, in his inaugural speech in Santiago's National Stadium, President Aylwin announced that the key tasks of his government would be to deal with past human rights violations and to pay the 'social debt' accumulated by the economic policies of the Pinochet regime. The overriding theme of his presidency would be reconciliation. Aylwin claimed that he would attempt to combine morality with prudence and that full knowledge of the truth would be his primary goal.[1]

A year and a half later, on 7 August 1991, the president announced that the transition was over and that the theme of national reconciliation was to be replaced by that of efficiency. It was recognized that 'authoritarian enclaves' still persisted. None the less, the statement indicated that Aylwin felt his administration had succeeded in both managing the hardest issue of the transition and achieving reconciliation among Chileans: he had dealt with the legacies of military repression while ensuring the continued subordination of the armed forces to democratic institutionality.[2]

The President's verdict seemed to correspond with the facts. The Concertación's government platform had targeted four areas in the field of human rights violations: truth, justice, political prisoners, and reparations for the victims of repression. In April 1990 the President had formed the Commission for Truth and Reconciliation, which was charged with telling a 'global truth' about human rights violations under the Pinochet regime, with investigating all individual cases brought to its attention which had resulted in death, and finally with recommending measures of reparation for the victims of repression and measures of prevention so that similar human rights violations would never again occur in Chile. Nine months later, in a solemn ceremony at the Presidential palace, Aylwin had publicly announced the contents of the Commission's report and apologized to the victims of repression on behalf of the state. The government had thus managed 'to give solemnity to an act of revelation of things which many Chileans suspected, knew or believed for some time, but which had not been presented to them in the form of a truth, acceptable, desirable and final'.[3]

Moreover, 'the Chilean government had not treated the Rettig Commission as a one-off solution'.[4] Between March 1990 and December 1992, the government had passed legislation which aimed to comply with the recommendations for reparation and prevention made by the Rettig Commission. The Reparations Law passed in January 1992 targeted 7,000 people for reparations. It gave a monthly 'salary' of US$380 to each family affected by disappearances or deaths resulting from human rights violations, and it extended health and educational benefits to these families.[5]

The government had created an Oficina Nacional de Retorno to help returning exiles.[6] In June 1992, it reached an agreement with the Comando de Exonerados and legislation was sent to parliament to compensate 55,000 former public and private sector employees dismissed for political reasons.[7] In August 1993, the Ley de Exonerados (Law of the Exonerated) was finally passed. It extended provisional benefits to 58,000 ex-public sector employees fired between 11 September 1973 and 10 March 1990, as well as their families.[8]

The government had also managed to pass laws which had led to the liberation of almost all the political prisoners of the Pinochet regime. Finally, it had attempted to reform the judiciary and had encouraged the prosecution of human rights violations in the courts. Despite the resistance of the Supreme Court, by June 1993 there were an estimated 200 cases of violations being investigated by the courts.

By early 1993, as President Aylwin's term neared its end, the population's attitude to the human rights issue was described thus: 'after three years and a few high points around the issue, [people] read about the reopening of human rights cases with a certain degree of normality'.[9] Reconciliation seemed to have been achieved. Despite a number of concessions to the right and although the military had publicly demonstrated its discontent with the handling of the human rights issue on a number of key occasions, the government had apparently largely succeeded in implementing its human rights policies without provoking a serious military backlash.

On 28 May 1993, however, as President Aylwin promoted the achievements of his government in an international tour, the country was shaken by an unannounced and massive show of force by black beret troops throughout the centre of Santiago. The aggressive display of military might was a warning to the government of the Army's growing dissatisfaction over the increasing number of human rights cases in the courts. The Army was worried that the investigations threatened the guarantees provided by amnesty law, and that the prosecution of men, at the time of the crimes lowly captains and colonels but now high-ranking officers in command of garrisons, would provoke rebellions of support and loyalty among the troops.[10]

Aylwin still claimed that 'the government would not give up on its aim to do justice as far as possible' and that this was 'a permanent position which [he would] maintain . . . until the last day of [his] government'.[11] He also admitted, however, already nearing the end of his term, that he might have been overly optimistic in his earlier political assessment and that the transition to democracy in Chile was still not complete. A similar admission made by President Sanguinetti in November 1986 had signalled the turning-point which had led to the passage of an amnesty law for the military in Uruguay.

Three years after Aylwin's assessment of the incomplete transition, similar analyses of the Chilean political situation are being made under the successor Concertación government headed by Christian Democratic President Frei.[12] The human rights issue continues to be the main source of tension in civil–military relations as well as the key source of divisions within the ranks of the Concertación.

Unlike Uruguay, where the problem was resolved before the Sanguinetti government was replaced by a successor democratic government under the Blanco Presidency of La Calle, in Chile the Concertación has failed to bring this chapter to a close. The search for the truth is still incomplete, and justice has been done only symbolically. Since Aylwin's admission that the transition was incomplete, several efforts have been made to limit the pursuit of justice in order to eliminate the single most important point of tension with the military. To date, none of these attempts have succeeded. Are Chileans finally faced with the same choice that Uruguayans had to confront in 1989? Can they stick to principle and risk the stability of process of democratization or will they have to sacrifice a greater truth and real justice in order to proceed with democratic consolidation?

This chapter examines Chile's attempts to come to terms with the legacy of military repression. The first part analyses the Concertación's truth-telling policy under Aylwin; the second its attempts to liberate the political prisoners of the Pinochet regime; the third part looks at the measures of reparation for the victims of repression and the government's attempts to pursue the judicial prosecution of human rights violations in the ordinary courts; the fourth and final part assesses the evolution of the human rights issue under the successor Frei administration.

Truth-Telling in Chile: The Jewel in the Concertación*'s Human Rights Crown*

The *Concertación*'s political programme had promised that the government would undertake to establish 'the truth of the cases of human rights violations which occurred after the 11th of September of 1973.'[13] In contrast to President Sanguinetti, Aylwin was personally committed to truth-telling. He claimed to take personal responsibility for the demands of 'the moral conscience of the nation demanded that I established the truth . . . however painful that might be.'[14] It was for Aylwin 'the great theme of the transition.'[15]

On 25 April 1990, the National Commission for Truth and Reconciliation was created by Supreme Executive Decree no. 355, which Aylwin is said to have drafted personally.[16] Thus, in contrast to Uruguay, the investigation of the facts of repression was undertaken not by parliament, but by a presidentially appointed, executive decreed, independent blue-ribbon commission of notables.[17] The Commission was to produce a 'global truth', giving a complete account of the causes and circumstances of the violations which had occurred under military rule. It was to produce an 'individual truth' by establishing on a case-by-case basis what had happened to the victims of repression resulting in death only. It was to recommend measures of reparation to help to restore the dignity of the victims. Finally, it was to propose measures for the future consolidation of a culture of human rights which would prevent the repetition of similar violations.

The overall aim of truth-telling was to contribute to a process of national reconciliation. The suffering of the victims would be recognized by society as a whole, and acknowledgement would become the first step on the path to justice and moral and material reparation. Thus, unlike Uruguay, where calls for truth and justice were portrayed by the executive as demands for 'revisionism' by a radicalized minority, in Chile they were presented as a national conciliatory duty of both state and society.

In keeping with the government's desire to make this a national enterprise, a consensus policy was adopted. First, a point was made to ensure the pluralist and non-partisan character of the Commission. For Aylwin 'one of the points of greatest interest for the government was that the Commission have a pluralist character and that the sectors which had supported the former regime should not be excluded.'[18]

The right, initially very hostile to the initiative, nicknamed it the Commission of Resentment and Revenge.[19] The UDI refused to participate, as did RN members Ricardo Rivadeneira and Fransisco Bulnes, who were personally invited by the President to join the Commission.[20] None the less a number of important conservatives agreed to participate, so that the Commission eventually comprised a group of people of 'recognized prestige and moral authority' whose 'members have different ways of explaining life'.[21] One of its members, Gonzalo Vial, Minister of Education in 1979, claimed that he was 'frankly right wing and a Catholic' and that for this reason it was impossible for him to 'refuse to participate in the search for solutions and answers to the cry of the victims of political violence.'[22] The fact that the commission was presidentially appointed, that carefully selected individuals from the right could be appointed, thus removing truth-telling from obstructive manœuvres in the legislature, contrasted starkly with the Uruguayan situation, where the Frente and Blanco members of the investigating commissions were constantly obstructed by Colorado representatives.

The human rights violations to be investigated were to include terrorist acts resulting in death. This latter concession to the right contradicted traditional human rights theory, which claims human rights violations are by definition only committed by states. It was a sign that seeking the truth would be pursued within the larger goal of reconciliation and consensus-building. For practical and political reasons, the scope of investigations was also dramatically limited, excluding torture and other human rights violations not resulting in death.

The government also determined that the names of those found guilty of violations should not be made public and that the commission would not have the power to subpoena individuals to give testimony. This was part of the government's policy ensuring that the Commission would in no way infringe on the jurisdiction of the judicial system. Thus, unlike Uruguay, where truth-telling and judicial prosecution had never been separated in policy terms, thus eventually contributing to the failure of the parliamentary investigating commissions, the Chilean government was at pains to separate the aims of the Commission from the judicial activities of the courts. The Commission was to be the vehicle for a political and moral, but not a judicial justice. Although the Commission's findings were ultimately of crucial importance for the judicial investigations which ensued, the government made a point of separating the work of the Commission from the eventual activities of the court, stressing that it would not invade the jurisdiction of the judiciary.[23]

Furthermore, the report was to include an analysis of the Popular Unity period, in response to the right's claim that the UP and even Frei's agrarian reform had been responsible for initiating the spiral of political violence.[24] Finally, the Commission was also limited by a well-defined and relatively brief nine-month time period. Investigations of explosive facts were not prolonged indefinitely as they were in Uruguay, where the commissions, lacking power and backing, constantly requested time extensions. The time limit served to reassure the human rights organizations that the government was serious in its commitment to tackle human rights violations. It allowed for the immediate treatment of the issue, limiting the impact of potential conflict to the first year of democratic rule.[25] It also gave the government a period of grace before the inevitable debate over the contents and recommendations of the final report exploded. Chile had learned the Uruguayan lesson. According to the president 'the worst that could have happened would have been to delay the problem as in other countries'.[26] These compromises made in the name of a democracy of consensus represented the government's view that the stability of democracy was in itself part of its struggle for human rights. Unlike the Uruguayan government, it linked rather than counterpoised the instrumental aim of ensuring democratic stability with the moral aim of recognizing the importance of basic human values.[27]

The Commission's work was impressive: its sixty staff members studied the documentation gathered by the human rights organizations, and between July and September all the provincial capitals were visited by members of the Commission to receive over 4,000 testimonies in the Regional Municipalities, the Provincial Governments, and in Santiago. 'We interviewed each person who wanted to present their case and we did so travelling around the country from the North to the South.' Information was requested from national public institutions, such as the Civil and Electoral

Register, the Regional Ministerial Secretariats for Justice, the National Archive, the Controlaria General, the Gendarmería, the military, and numerous ministries and embassies. 'Approximately two thousand *oficios* were dispatched by the Commission, and responses were received in approximately eighty per cent of the cases.'[28]

Testimony was also gathered from foreigners and nationals in exile by members of the Commission who travelled abroad.[29] Unlike Uruguay, where information collected by human rights organizations was very slim, the bulk of the Commission's material came from the records of these groups. The support of the Church through the Vicaría was of critical importance. Its enormous archives were opened to the Commission. In its introduction, the report stated that it had received 'without exception, the collaboration of all the humanitarian organizations which had gathered data about these facts'.[30]

In contrast to the Uruguayan case, state sponsorship gave the truth-telling enterprise credibility, legitimacy, and material viability. Also unlike Uruguay, where press leaks had debilitated the parliamentary investigating commissions, the discretion with which the members of the Commission worked boosted its legitimacy and respectability. In the words of one commissioner, they were careful not to allow the leaking of 'even a single document'.[31] Decree no. 355 obliged public institutions to give 'all the collaboration that is asked of them, to place at its disposal all the documents which it may need and to facilitate access to the places it deems necessary to visit'.[32] State support eased the task of compiling data, provided the Commission with adequate physical locations, an army of dedicated staff, the ready availability of experts, travel grants, computer systems, and gave the Commission the necessary credibility to encourage otherwise fearful witnesses to go forward and testify.

Despite government backing, however, the Commission encountered great difficulties in obtaining material from the military authorities because the Commission had no power to subpoena witnesses and thus legally oblige people to declare before it. Although most enquiries received a reply, only a small number were of any use in the investigations. In the majority of cases, the Commission was informed either that the documentation had been legally destroyed or that the information was protected by military secrecy laws.

Predictably, reactions to the existence of the Commission ran the gamut from total support to aggressive hostility. *Fortuna*, however, combined with skillful political management to largely neutralize the voice of reaction. *Fortuna* made its appearance in the macabre form of a clandestine mass grave discovered at Pisagua in June 1990. The public horror and outrage provoked by this finding proved that a truth-telling mission was truly necessary and not just an example of state-sponsored vengeance against the outgoing regime.[33]

It also dealt the right a severe blow. Some of its leading figures were asked about the role they had played in the Pisagua events.[34] RN's youth sector called for the 'decontamination' of the party's leadership at a conference in Viña del Mar.[35] The right was forced to condemn Pisagua and calls were made for a complete investigation of the deaths.[36] As a result of the discovery, the Commission 'ceased to be an object of debate' becoming 'the minimum organization that could have been established'.[37] Thus, in February 1991, both the Chamber of Deputies and the Senate declared their unanimous support of the Commission.

Before the launching of the report, the right attempted a policy of damage limitation, which parts of the Concertación were willing to accept. In February 1991 Renovación drafted a Propuesta por la Paz in the Senate Commission on Human Rights, advocating the expansion of the amnesty law and the non-publication of the names of human rights violators for 25 years, with subsequent publication subject to a plebescite, claiming that 'there were victims from all sectors' and that nobody was 'free of responsibility'.[38] This proposal failed because it was not supported by the PPD, and was countered by a Socialist proposal to create an Asamblea de la Civilidad Por los Derechos Humanos.[39] The latter aimed to locate the disappeared, to counter-act the arguments of equality of moral and political responsibility emanating from the right, and to propose measures for moral reparation to the victims of repression, asserting 'the legitimacy of the motivations which gave rise to their conduct.'[40]

The Rettig report was launched nine months after the Pisagua incident on 4 March 1991 and the following day it was made available to the public in the form of serialized papers.[41] In contrast to the Uruguayan *Nunca Más* Report, it emerged with great fanfare and presidential ceremony. It symbolized the official admission by the Chilean state that the lies of the past had to be put to rest for the sake of reconciliation.

Aylwin was careful to reduce the potential conflict surrounding the report. He allowed a month to pass between the time the report was handed to him and the public announcement of its contents.

The effect was to permit a period of grace for tempers to cool before the debate re-emerged.[42] Determined that the report should be accepted as the 'common truth', the president received the 'widest spectrum of people, he spoke and listened to everyone' in the week before the official announcement.[43] When Aylwin did make his Rettig speech, he did so 'almost as if he were reading a judicial report, making the verdict known but not making any value judgements'.[44]

The President launched the report in a solemn ceremony which was broadcast nationally on television. The report established that 2,115 people had been the victims of human rights violations resulting in death, while 641 people had died as a result of terrorist actions. It had been unable to resolve 641 cases conclusively, had rejected 508 which fell outside its jurisdiction, and had left 449 cases aside for insufficient information.[45] Aylwin acknowledged that the truth had been hidden, apologized on behalf of the state to the victims of repression, and asked for their forgiveness for the unrecognized suffering they had undergone. The report had established that the Armed Forces had been institutionally responsible for the deaths. The President therefore appealed to 'the Armed Forces of Order, and all those that participated in the excesses committed, to make gestures of recognition of the pain caused and to cooperate to diminish it'. He also criticized the performance of the courts during the regime, and encouraged them to pursue the cases researched by the Commission with added zeal, claiming that the amnesty law, in his opinion, did not impede investigations.

The recommendations of the Rettig Commission for reparation were also addressed. The report had stated that reparations were absolutely necessary and that the state should take responsibility for making them possible. It suggested undertaking cultural and symbolic measures of reparation, as well as awarding material benefits, such as health provisions, pension benefits, educational grants, and cancelling debts contracted by the victims' families. Finally, it recommended a law which would declare the presumed death of the disappeared in order to regularize their legal status.[46]

The President announced the creation of pensions plans for the families of the victims and of an Institute of Public Defence. Finally, the report had an extensive section on preventive measures. It recommended the reform of legislation, of the judiciary, and of the Armed Forces, so that legislation pertaining to all three would comply with international human rights standards.[47] Blaming violations on 'the insuffiency of a national culture of respect for human rights', it advocated the promotion of the latter through educational and cultural measures. It called on the government to create a Defensor del Pueblo to look for the disappeared, to resolve the cases left pending by the Commission, and to generally advance and protect human rights. It also recommended the centralization of all information on human rights violations to facilitate future research, called for the extension of legal and social aid to the victims of repression and finally suggested that terrorism be classified as a human rights violation.

In response to these proposals, the President called on the Supreme Court to expedite all pending cases as quickly as possible, recommending the intervention of the Public Ministry when necessary for the resolution of the latter. He asked the Armed Forces to help the courts locate the detained disappeared. The creation of a Chilean Ombudsman was announced, whose task it would be to undertake the reform of the judicial system as put forward by the Commission. These measures were announced in the name of 'so that this never happens again in Chile'.[48]

Given the conservative political climate in Chile, the launching of the report was almost anti-climatic. The crowds which gathered outside the Presidential palace in Chile were sparse. The few calls by the radical left and victims' associations for a massive popular show of strength went largely unheeded. According to one observer, there was 'a profound sense of relief. Many are going on holiday. The door of La Moneda, the placard of the families stating *Chile Jamás Aceptará la Impunidad* is semi destroyed. The families of the disappeared are gone. Only a lone youth holds a poster in his hands stating *Dónde Están?*'.[49]

The support of the human rights organizations and the Church was almost complete.[50] The victims' organizations, however, 'supported the general policy but they were skeptical'.[51] They hoped that the report would be a first step on the path to justice so that the constant emphasis on reconciliation made them suspicious: 'This permament effort to impose a state of reconciliation almost by decree, has turned into a form of political manipulation which seeks to hide the truth behind the supposed warm fellowship among us all.'[52] They were critical of the report for two reasons. First, they thought it suffered from 'narrowness of vision . . . not including the wide gamut of human rights violations'.[53] Secondly, they thought the names of those involved in torture and other crimes should be made public.[54] Thus, the AFEP threatened it would do just that if the government failed to do so.[55] It described the report as 'biased and partial', and its leader, Hugo Cárcamo, thought it was a 'product of a negotiation with the right and military sectors'.[56]

Although with reservations, Aylwin gained these groups' support not only because they recognized his commitment, but also because they realized the political limits imposed on the government. As one victim claimed: 'I was very moved, I am very pleased with what he has done, because I always thought that he has to carry a hot potato which does not belong to him.'[57] Similarly,

> 'We the families decided to throw our lot in with the Commission although many of the relatives did not understand the importance of this . . . Aylwin did not commit himself to justice, his commitment was with the truth. Aylwin also put the issue of reconciliation forward as well as reparations for human rights violations. It is a question of political will versus political reality. I'm not going to complain too much.'[58]

The victims' groups also calculated that 'as one participates the possibilities widen to press for the demands which are being left aside'.[59] Added to this basic faith in the government, it was often felt that the interest of the extra-parliamentary Left in the human rights issue 'is more of a political manipulation . . . than the search for the truth'.[60] When the Communist party paper, *El Siglo*, published a list of the names of human rights violators, it was condemned not only by the government and the right, but also by the majority of human rights organizations.[61] Thus, unlike Uruguay, where more radical demands found effective political representation in the Frente Amplio, in Chile there was no party aside from the Communist Party willing and able successfully to mobilize to press for more wide-ranging measures. The Communist party's promise that it would promote a general strike if the whole truth and justice were not achieved came to nothing.[62]

The report forced the right to admit that the crimes described were inexcusable whatever the context.[63] The horror over the crimes investigated by the conservative members of the commission helped to force the right to accept the findings of the Commission. According to Sergio Diez, an ex-minister of the military regime, 'nobody in Chile realized the magnitude of the violations of human rights'.[64] Similarly, conservative commissioner Ricardo Martín claimed that 'I don't think I ever would have imagined what I now know.'[65]

Unable to deny the facts, both right-wing parties were obliged to resort to a criticism of the report's historical interpretations. Both claimed that it was 'an inadequate document' since it did not highlight the 'internal war deliberately waged by the UP'.[66] The UDI, for example, taking a 'free ride as an opposition force taking on the banners of the previous regime',[67] felt that 'the Rettig report is not the whole truth, it is not the balanced truth, it is not the deeply sought truth'.[68] According to its leader, Senator Jaime Guzmán, 'we are witnessing a process of historical falsification which must be counteracted'.[69]

The Concertación's greatest challenge, however, was confronting the military. General Pinochet's first act of defiance had taken place on the day of the President's inauguration. He had refused to attend the ceremony, instead touring the country's northern garrisons and warning troops in Chuquicamata that the armed forces were coming under attack from the President.[70] More seriously, there were numerous cases of political espionage, attacks, robberies and threats to politicians during the first three years of democratic government. It was, 'despite the many formal and verbal denials . . . it is a known secret that Army units still carry out internal intelligence tasks which are focused on the political parties in particular'.[71]

The government confronted the military essentially by forfeiting any attempts at internal institutional reform and by concentrating instead on attempting to impose presidential and civilian authority over Pinochet. In order to do so it abandoned (and did not permit) any attempt to make Pinochet himself accountable for human rights violations. It was recognized that 'As one confronts Pinochet, what one really achieves is to strengthen him and thus to enter into conflict with the institution.'[72] Through regular meetings between Aylwin and the General, the government constantly reassured Pinochet, and through him the Army, that it had no intention of challenging military prerogatives, of threatening institutional integrity and General Pinochet's position as Commander-in-Chief, and finally of derogating the amnesty law. Calls made by members of the Concertación for the derogation of the law and Pinochet's resignation were explicitly and publicly rebutted by government officials and by the President himself.

On the other hand, however, the President repeatedly reminded Pinochet that he was constitutionally subordinate to civilian authority.[73] Unlike Sanguinetti, Aylwin always presented his meetings with the Commander-in-Chief not as private fora for negotiation, but as proper institutionalized arenas for communication. Attempting to assert his authority and to show who was the boss, the president often refused to comply with Pinochet's demands for immediate audiences, refusing such requests only to call meetings himself later. The government was at pains to make relations as formal and 'normal' as possible, to minimize any hints of special treatment. Similarly, and very much unlike Sanguinetti, it minimized the significance of any acts of public military defiance and although it 'negotiated' with Pinochet, the President was always quick to remind the General that any extra-constitutional activities only led him to violate his own and the country's laws. In Uruguay relations between the military and the government were personalized and privatized in a politics of 'informal gentlemen's agreements'. In Chile, on the other hand, it was a point of pride for both the General and the President to present themselves as faithfully fulfiling formal and constitutional requisites. The government also made discreet efforts to isolate Pinochet, reducing his importance as the privileged channel for communication between the civilian and military worlds. It did so by cultivating direct and positive ties with the other branch commanders, taking advantage of existing latent and overt enmities against the Army inherited from the Pinochet regime.[74]

The attitude outlined above was exemplified in the handling of the first moment of civil–military tension which arose with the discovery of the Pisagua graves. Pinochet was declared morally responsible for the crimes, there were calls for his resignation and for either the derogation of or for a positive law of interpretation of the 1978 amnesty, such that crimes against humanity would be excluded from it.[75] The right came to the military's defence, blaming the UP for initiating the violence and claiming that the government was politically manipulating the issue. Both parties ardently defended Pinochet and the amnesty law which was seen to be the 'pillar of political peace'.[76] In response, the Army released its first, already familiar, ideological defence of the regime and its repressive policy.[77] More importantly, the attacks on Pinochet fostered the solidarity of the other branches.[78]

In the face of this resistance, Aylwin adopted his dual policy. On the one hand, the government publicly renewed its commitment to justice, presenting an accusation for illegal inhumation and encouraging the courts to investigate the Pisagua case.[79] On the other hand, however, it chose not to challenge the doctrinal position of the Army and not to support the demands for Pinochet's resignation. Aylwin assured the military that 'beyond the problems which may originate in relation to the theme which is being debated these days, there is . . . on the part of the government, the disposition to respect the constitutional regime of the armed forces, according to constitutional and legal norms in the country, and there is a climate of increasing overcoming of mutual distrust and fear.'[80] Finally, the government removed itself from the debate, allowing the parties and the human rights organizations to challenge the military's ideological defence of their repressive policies.[81]

The Commission presented Aylwin with his first major test of strength *vis-à-vis* Pinochet. Unlike Uruguay, however, where the government consulted military commanders privately on human rights initiatives, the Aylwin government deliberately presented the Commission as an indisputable *fait accompli*. According to the Minister of Defence, it was not right that 'the military chiefs issue a formal response, because they were not being asked to do so but rather were being informed of a government initiative. Similarly, the President refused General Pinochet's demand for an immediate audience five times after the latter had been informed of the formation of the Commission and had accordingly suspended his holidays and demanded an audience on 24 April 1990.

In the face of this intransigence, Pinochet called a meeting of the Army high command which issued a statement repudiating the Commission and calling for a Security Council meeting and a joint Armed Forces statement pending the approval of the other branches.[82] Both attempts failed, however, as the other branches preferred not to enter into a confrontation with the executive. General Matthei, for example, declared that the decision to form the commission was 'a political decision which is the competence of the president and is abided by, one hundred per cent, by all institutions. This is not a matter for debate. We wish all the success in the task it has been given.'[83]

At the beginning of May, the president finally met with General Pinochet. He rejected the General's claims that the Commission was unconstitutional and that its members were partial.[84] Failing to persuade the President to back down and unable to gain the backing of the other branches, Pinochet resorted to Lone Ranger tactics. The day after his meeting with Aylwin he refused to attend a meeting arranged between the President and the four commanders of the Armed Forces.[85] On 24 May Vice-Commander, General Lucar met with Rettig and declared the Commission unconstitutional.[86] The Army was forced to back down, however, when the branches demonstrated their willingness to co-operate with the Commision in their meeting with Rettig. Finally, on 25 May Rettig met with General Ballestrino, Pinochet's representative on the Comite Asesor, and forced the latter to accept the Commission's continued existence.[87]

The military's responses to the Commission's report, officially received by Aylwin at a Security Council meeting on 27 March, were a disappointment. None of the branches apologized, all of them blamed the Popular Unity government, all confirmed the existence of a state of war dismissed by the report, and all reaffirmed their commitment to the principles which had guided the coup and the regime. The tone of the responses varied. The Airforce and Carabineros were the least aggressive. Although General Matthei claimed to share 'the ideals which had inspired the military pronouncement of September 11, 1973', he supported the President's truth-telling initiative.[88] The Carabineros also affirmed their support. General Stange, who had led a process of internal purges before the inauguration of the new government, was criticized by the ranks for being too conciliatory. The 'pre-judgement' of members of the collectivity was rejected.[89]

Navy and Army responses were much harsher. The Navy claimed that the facts in the report were mere opinions and violently opposed the preventive and reparation measures which, in its view, threatened state security. The recommendations which referred to the need to inculcate a respect for human rights within the ranks was found to be 'offensive'.[90] Predictably, the Army's response was the most intransigent. It issued two different statements, the second presented by General Pinochet to an audience at the Military School. Both statements made a direct link between terrorist violence and the report. The historical and juridical validity of the report was dismissed and the members of the Commission were accused of partiality, politicization, and of harbouring hatred towards the Armed Forces. The Army asserted that it saw absolutely no reason to apologize since there had been a war and force was used legitimately. It refused to be held responsible for unproven facts, and emphasized that the branch would never accept being 'placed in front of the nation on the accused's stand for having guaranteed the freedom and sovereignty of the Nation at the insistence of the citizenry'. The report was seen to constitute an attack on the honour of the Armed Forces, and all forms of reparation for the victims of repression were rejected.[91] If the military's responses did not contribute to reconciliation by their lack of repentance, they were at least unable to disprove a single fact in the report.[92] The official nature of the report forced the military to publicly confront their crimes and complicity, unlike Uruguay, where the military had been able to completely ignore the *Nunca Más* report.

If *fortuna* had come to the Concertación's rescue in June 1990 with the discovery of the mass grave, it did it a disservice on 1 April 1991, when leading UDI Senator Jaime Guzmán was assassinated. The crime placed terrorism at the centre of political debate, seemingly validating claims that repression under military rule had been necessary due to the ruthless nature of the enemy.

It provided the right with the opportunity to shift from a defensive to an offensive position. Andres Allamand of the *Renovación* said it was time for the government 'start wearing the trousers' and the UDI added that the murder revealed the government's erroneous priorities and 'ineptitude'.[93] The reversal of *fortuna* effectively announced the end of state involvement in truth-telling and its, disengagement from the intense ideological-historical debate which the parties conducted thereafter.

Releasing the Political Prisoners: Hostages to the Conflict over Justice

The path which led to the release of the political prisoners in Chile was as long and fraught as the Uruguayan road to military amnesty. Unlike Uruguay, it took one year and 11 months for the government to pass laws to reform the regime's security laws, thereby permitting a partial solution to the problem of the political prisoners. It took over three years to achieve the release of the bulk of the political prisoners of the Pinochet regime.

The government faced four major and interrelated obstacles in its attempt to resolve this issue: terrorism, right wing resistance, the nature of the *Concertación*'s political prisoner policy, and the slowness of judicial proceedings. Public concern with continued terrorism reduced sympathy for the plight of the political prisoners. When asked in 1989 which issues concerned them most, a majority rated terrorism after human rights violations.[94] When asked a year later whether they believed the government was dealing effectively with terrorism, 45 per cent of all men and 40.6 per cent of all women thought so, while a higher percentage, 48.3 and 49.6 per cent respectively, thought the government was using a *mano blanda* or 'soft-handed' policy.[95] When asked in June 1990 what they thought most notable about the first 60 days of the democratic government, 33.8 per cent pointed to the level of robberies and armed violence. Only 13.3 per cent mentioned the Rettig Commission.[96] By July 1991, only 38.1 per cent thought the government was handling terrorism effectively and 57.6 per cent were negative. Similarly, when asked what the government's priority should be, 16.3 per cent agreed that political violence was the most pressing problem, whereas the human rights issue was seen as paramount by only 3.4 per cent.[97] At the end of 1991, only 3.7 per cent of the population believed that liberating the political prisoners was necessary for democracy to flourish in Chile.[98]

Throughout the first three years of government, right-wing politicians, generals, army officers, policemen, and carabineros were assassinated; Supreme Court ministers were attacked and followed; and banks were robbed mostly by the FPMR-A, but also by the Mapu-Lautaro, the Fuerzas Populares Rebeldes Lautaro (FPRL), the Movimiento Juvenil Lautaro (MJL) and the splinter, Movimiento de Izquierda Revolucionaria–Comisión Política (MIR–CP).[99] The timing of some terrorist acts seemed designed to make things harder for the government. Only ten days after the inauguration of the Aylwin presidency, attempts were made on the lives of Generals Leigh and Ruíz.[100] Just hours before Aylwin's Rettig speech, an army doctor accused of torture and his wife were assassinated. The Guzmán murder also seemed timed to help the military and the right as it had the effect of cutting the human rights debate short.[101]

The government's opponents used continued terrorism to attack the state's political prisoner policy, as well as its attempted judicial and security law reform.[102] Linking past and present terrorism, the right tried to show that although left-wing terrorists had claimed to combat the dictatorship, they had not ceased to use terror with the arrival of democracy.[103] In their view, these prisoners were mere delinquents who did not deserve special treatment. Furthermore, terrorism pushed *Renovación* to the right, as it was reluctant to be labelled 'soft' on terror by the UDI. The attempted murder of Generals Ruiz and Leigh in March 1990 effectively diminished the RN's will to negotiate with the government.[104] The impact of terrorism was such that in May 1990 even three Concertación senators broke ranks and voted with the right against the proposed reduction of penalties for political crimes.[105]

More importantly, however, the right was willing to use political prisoners as leverage in its attempt to put a stop to the prosecution of human rights violations, a condition which the Concertación and the government would not accept and which therefore slowed down negotiations. Since liberating the prisoners required constitutional and legislative reform, the right was in a good position to block the government's objectives. In March 1990 there were 417 political prisoners and approximately 1,300 people awaiting trial for politically motivated crimes. The government's ability to resolve this situation was circumscribed by both constitutional and anti-terrorist legislation. Article 9 of the Constitution made most terrorists ineligible for pardon, and only those with sentences were eligible, so that only 50 of the 417 political prisoners stood a chance of being released without legislative reform. Furthermore, by virtue of existing anti-terrorist legislation, almost 80 per cent of these cases were under military jurisdiction.[106]

Since the Chilean 'public conscience' would not accept the equal treatment of prisoners of conscience and prisoners who had murdered, the Concertación programme, unlike Uruguay's Blanco and Frente parties, proposed different formulas for each case. A blanket amnesty was out of the question even for the Concertación. Not only was there no 'real possibility to pass a law, even had the government wanted to', but since 'a distinction was made between political crimes and blood crimes, the possibility of simply liberating them was never contemplated; rather, the idea was to submit them to a new trial'.[107] The path chosen by the government of liberating prisoners combined specific transitory legislation to resolve the immediate question of the political prisoners with an attempt to permanently reform the anti-terrorist and security legislation so that national law would comply with international humanitarian standards. Thus, progress was slow because the fate of the political prisoners became inextricably tied to the government's attempts at judicial and security law reform both of which were resisted by the right.

The process of liberation evolved at a snail's pace even after the legislative reforms had been passed because of the slowness of the judicial proceedings. Many of the prisoners had either never been sentenced, had more than one sentence pending, or had to be re-tried and re-sentenced before release could be contemplated. The courts were either overloaded and/or unsympathetic to the prisoners. In addition, a number of jurisdictional battles developed between the military courts and the civil courts over a number of these cases.[108]

A few days after taking office, Aylwin pardoned 47 political prisoners, thereby signalling his commitment to pursuing releases. It was a symbolic measure. All but nineteen of those pardoned were already on some form of parole. On 11 March 1990, Aylwin presented the legislature with the Leyes Cumplido, named after the Minister of Justice who had designed them. The three laws aimed to abolish the death penalty, to modify the Anti-Terrorist Law no. 1.834, and to reform a number of laws, such as the Arms Control Law, the State Security Law, the Code of Military Justice, and the Penal Code to better guarantee individual rights. The reforms which were directly aimed at the political prisoners were contained in eleven transitory articles. These proposed to place politically motivated crimes under the jurisdiction of the civil justice system, to increase the possibilities of bail and early release benefits, to reduce prison sentences, to introduce norms ensuring procedural guarantees, to redefine terrorist crimes, and finally to guarantee fair trials for prisoners previously tried by military courts.[109]

These laws were intensely debated in parliament between March and December 1990. During this period the right tried twice to use the government's desire to liberate the prisoners as leverage to reduce penalties for, or even amnesty, human rights violators. In April 1990, Renovación proposed the formation of a National Project for Reconciliation which would counteract the supposed partiality of the Cumplido Laws. It claimed that it was necessary to 'deal with the situations as a whole', that a solution to the problem of the so-called political prisoners had to be linked to a solution for those accused of human rights violations.[110]

The UDI supported this initiative but was much more forthright with its demands. It requested that the President's prerogative to pardon be limited. In its view, these crimes should either be dealt with as the Concertación proposed to deal with human rights violations committed after 1978, or else a new reciprocal amnesty law should be passed.[111] The CPPD and the RN commissioned jurists to outline reforms to the Cumplido Laws which would satisfy both parties, but the initiative collapsed due to irreconcilable differences. After two subsequent failures to legislate, a second 'global solution' was suggested in May 1990, the Acuerdo Marco Político Acordado Por Miembros de la Comisión Constitución, Legislación y Justicia Para Ser Sometido a Consideración del Gobierno y de los Partidos Políticos.[112] It advocated an overall reduction in penalties and the exemption from criminal prosecution of crimes which, after reductions, had minimal sentences attached.[113] The aim of the initiative was to create 'an agreement which will permit an effective national reconciliation with the greatest possible backing of the Legislature, as well as seeking the truth and the application of justice in cases of human rights violations'.[114]

This initiative was extremely important for a number of reasons. In the first place, in a reversal of the usual state of affairs, it was the first human rights related initiative to emerge from the legislature and to be presented to the executive for consideration. Secondly, the accord was symbolic of the politics of consensus between the ruling coalition and the moderate right. The accord was voted for unanimously by all members of the Commission. Thirdly, this was the first time that all parties agreed on the human rights issue. After weeks of debate, however, the Acuerdo Marco was abandoned. Public opinion was still unwilling to accept an overt reduction of penalties for human rights violations and a 'hidden amnesty' for crimes such as torture. As the Socialist deputy, Jaime Estevez, put it, the population was unprepared for a reconciliation 'by decree'.[115] The political moment was not ripe to equate human rights violations with the crimes committed by the enemies of the Pinochet regime. The human rights organizations, the political prisoners, and the President himself would not contemplate liberation at the expense of impunity for human rights violators at a time when the Rettig Commission was just beginning its work.[116] Finally, the discovery of bodies at Pisagua and elsewhere put paid to the whole effort, forcing CPPD members previously in favour of the Accord to oppose it.[117]

In December 1990, the Cumplido Laws returned to the Chamber of Deputies; they were unrecognizable. The Senate had not only radically altered them, but essentially rejected the eleven transitory provisions pertaining to political prisoners.[118] The deadlock was finally broken after further negotiations between the Concertación and Renovación. The latter agreed to support a reform of Article 9 of the Constitution to widen the scope for the concession of pardons, amnesties, and provisional freedom and to introduce a transitory provision enabling the President to pardon political prisoners convicted before 11 March 1990 under the Anti-Terrorist and Arms Control Laws.[119] The parties finally agreed to speed up the passage of the Cumplido Laws as they had emerged from the Senate. The pardons law was made by agreement with the moderate right on the basis that the President take full political responsibility for the consequences of conceding pardons.[120] Thus, in January 1991, the modified version of Article 9 was made law.[121] In return, the Cumplido Laws were passed by the Senate in February 1991, with all the modifications imposed by the right.[122]

In January 1991, the President pardoned 63 political prisoners.[123] Yet in March, 181 prisoners still remained in gaol, partly because the President exerted his presidential right to pardon very cautiously and usually on the condition that those benefiting sign a document renouncing the use of violence, and partly because of slow judicial proceedings. The prisoners were therefore released in dribs and drabs. In June 1991, with 133 prisoners still in gaol, and in response to hunger strikes and gaol occupations,[124] the government presented a new bill to Congress in late June 1991. It proposed to speed up procedures by allowing the ministers of the courts of appeal to dedicate themselves exclusively to the resolution of these cases, and by setting a time limit for the courts to sentence the prisoners. If the time limit was not respected, prisoners would be allowed provisional freedom. Finally, it recommended the formation of a Comisión de Fé dependent on the Ministry of Justice, the aim of which was to permit closer co-operation between the government and the prisoner lawyer associations.[125] After another hunger strike lasting 43 days, the legislation was finally passed.[126]

Releases continued to proceed very slowly none the less. At the end of September there were 90 political prisoners, by the end of December there were 61. On 9 January 1992 there were still 60 prisoners awaiting release.[127] At the end of September 1993 only those who attempted to assassinate Pinochet in 1981 were still in gaol. The saga of the political prisoners only finally came to its natural end during the Frei administration. On 15 March 1994, six of the last nine prisoners had their sentences commuted to exile. At the time of writing, the three that remain still await sentencing and so are not yet eligible for pardon, but Frei has said that he will review each case once sentencing is concluded.[128]

Reparations and Symbolic Justice by Individual Prosecution

According to the Rettig report, reparations were 'a necessary task in which the government will consciously and deliberately intervene'.[129] Attempting to encourage the active participation of the victims in the formulation of its recommendations, the AFDD had received a letter from Raul Rettig in August 1990, requesting its suggestions for the measures it deemed necessary. Three types of reparation measures were envisaged: moral or cultural-symbolic, material, and judicial. On 30 April 1990, at the Second National Meeting of Human Rights Organizations in the National Stadium (where thousands had been held and tortured in the first days of the coup), the *caídos* were homaged.[130] Throughout 1990 and 1991 numerous symbolic events of this nature, many of them sponsored by the government, took place. Other examples included the funeral of Salvador Allende, attended by the President and the political élite in September 1990, the Informe Especial on the disappeared transmitted on national television in October 1990, and the CCDH's government-sponsored campaign, Para Creer en Chile (Believe in Chile), which aimed to divulge the contents of the Rettig report and to carry out educational projects based on its findings.[131] At the end of 1990, the Fundación Memorial de Detenidos Desaparecidos y Detenidos Ejecutados was created. Under the direction of the Sub-Secretary of the Ministry of the Interior, Belisario

Velasco, and the leaders of the AFDD and AFDE, it was charged with building monuments and memorials for the disappeared. This foundation promoted the construction of a Memorial for the Disappeared and the Executed for Political Reasons in the Santiago Cemetery. Consisting of a plaque with the names of 4,000 disappeared, it was inaugurated in August 1993 by President Aylwin.[132] The most important symbolic reparation, however, was the truth-telling process itself, which allowed people to give testimony for the first time, and which led to the recognition of their suffering by the state.[133]

The implementation of material reparations was initiated three days after the public launching of the report, when the newly created Comisión Inter-Ministerial de Subsecretarios Sobre Medidas de Reparación met for the first time. In March 1991 it sent a Proyecto de Reparación to Congress. It determined that the 140 families accounted for in the Rettig report should receive pensions, scholarships, and free health services, and that military service should be optional for male family members.[134]

The project, however, was rejected by the victims' associations. The families were upset that they had not been consulted during the elaboration of the project, and they disagreed with a number of provisions. It was felt that the pensions were insufficient and that the proposed distribution of the awards among family members excluded the mothers. The AFDD was also critical of the failure of the Corporación de Derecho Público (Public Law Corporation) to establish the disappeared peoples' whereabouts. Furthermore, it was incensed with the Commission's attempt to declare the 'presumed death' of the disappeared. The latter policy proposal had serious implications for future prosecution. Juridically, as long as the disappeared were still officially alive the statute of limitations on the crime of disappearance would not expire. The AFDD accused the government of having 'a certain interest in disengaging from the problem' of the disappeared.[135]

The negotiations between April and June 1991 led to the breakdown of relations between the AFDD and members of the Commission. None the less, it soon emerged that despite the difficulties, enough political will existed to overcome these differences. In July 1991 Aylwin met with the AFDD leaders, deciding that he would take personal charge of the issue. The President also accepted almost all the changes proposed by the families, although he left it up to Congress to rule on the clause concerning the presumed death of the disappeared.[136] According to the leader of the AFDD, Aylwin had dealt with the issue 'quickly, with understanding and effectively'.[137] In January 1992, the President signed the Ley de Reparaciones. By September, over 80 per cent of eligible families had accepted the US$400 awarded them by the Commission.[138]

The final area of reparation concerned justice. For the Chilean government, the promotion of justice for human rights violations was tied to a general commitment to improve the state of the judiciary. As with the political prisoners, the attempt to address a past issue was connected with attempts to improve conditions for the future. With respect to the former, the coalition's programme had pledged to repeal all laws which prevented investigations. It had also proposed a system for reducing the sentences of human rights violators prepared to co-operate with the courts. It had promised, furthermore, to collect the necessary information on the violations to send them to the courts. Finally, it proposed to extend the statute of limitations for a year on crimes which had not been investigated under military rule, as well as to repeal the amnesty law.[139]

On 8 February 1992, in order to tackle the issue of human rights violations and in accordance with a provision in the reparations law, the National Corporation for Reparation and Reconciliation was created.[140] Believing that it was the 'inalienable right of the relatives of the victims and of Chilean society' to locate their dead, the Corporation was given 90 days in which to locate the detained or disappeared, to investigate the cases that the Rettig Commission had been unable to conclude, to promote measures for the moral reparation of the victims, and to publish its findings within the year.

With regard to the reform of the judiciary, the Concertación's government programme had promised to promote legislation to 'guarantee the authentic independence of the judicial power, providing it with broad and sufficient powers to make it into a true guarantor of human rights and public liberties'.[141] In January 1991 the executive launched its judicial reform campaign, submitting its proposals to the Supreme Court, the Bar Association, and the university law faculties. The reforms included the creation of a Consejo Nacional de Justicia, composed of members of the legislature, the executive, the Bar Association, and the judiciary, which would plan, administer, and budget for the judiciary. Furthermore, it was to select five candidates, previously chosen by the Supreme Court, from which the President would select new Court appointees. This body aimed to enable the Court to concentrate on jurisprudence rather than administrative tasks. It proposed the creation of a national judicial school, the formation of a judicial police, and a network of local courts to provide a free and rapid service for the resolution of local conflicts. The reforms also recommended the creation of a Defensor del Pueblo or Ombudsman as added protection from state abuse. Finally it suggested that the size and composition of the Supreme Court be changed to include jurists and lawyers outside the regular career judiciary. The Court was to be divided into specialized branches with special emphasis on constitutional jurisprudence and hearing the annulment of appeals, the *recursos de casación*.[142]

Both policy measures, however, encountered numerous difficulties. In the first place, its judicial reforms met with resistance from the right and the Supreme Court. On 30 March 1990 the President announced his plans for judicial reform at the Annual Chilean Magistrates Convention. Only a month earlier, the President of the Supreme Court had stated that the judiciary was badly in need of reform. None the less, these reforms were rejected both by the Supreme Court and by the parties of the right. The President of the Court, attacking the activities of numerous protesters outside his building, accused the government of fomenting violence with its campaign against the judiciary.[143] In April 1991, the two bills for Organic Constitutional Laws, aiming to implement the reform proposals were sent to Congress after consultation with the Supreme Court and a number of legal institutions. They were again opposed by the RN, the UDI, and the Supreme Court.[144]

The Court's response to the Rettig report on 16 May was also an attack on the government's reform pretensions. The government was accused of promoting a climate of hatred. In an obvious attempt to intimidate the government, the Court sent a copy of its statement to the National Security Council, indicating that the government's proposals were threatening national security.[145] In April 1992 both organic constitutional laws on judicial reform suffered defeat in the Chamber of Deputies. In February 1992 the government attempted a Pinochet-style solution, passing a law which gave ministers over 70 years of age the option to retire and receive a bonus of US$54,000. Of the nine eligible, however, only one accepted.

The government's 'justice for human rights violations' policy met with similar obstacles. From the outset, Aylwin had emphasized that justice would only be pursued 'en la medida de lo posible'.[146] The government's justice policy was to be based on a rejection of special tribunals for collective or institutional trials. Justice was to proceed in the ordinary courts, and only individuals could be tried. The ability and the willingness of the judiciary to take positive steps to solve cases of human rights violations was therefore critical. It was one of the government's greatest hopes that, having abandoned its initial commitment to derogating the amnesty law, the Supreme Court would interpret the law favourably. In his Rettig speech, the president expressed the hope that the courts would 'do their duty and undertake an exhaustive investigation, for which the amnesty law in force [should not be] an obstacle'.[147] He hoped, in other words, that the Court would determine impunity only after the discovery of facts of the crime. The philosophy behind this was, firstly, that pardon could only be granted if the subject of pardon was known, and, secondly, that by permitting investigations, the bodies of the disappeared would be located. This interpretation was extremely crucial in light of the fact that most of the 2,279 cases which the Rettig Commission had investigated were covered by this law.[148]

The government's was a vain hope. The response of the Supreme Court to a new interpretation of the amnesty law in August 1990 was unequivocal. It unanimously determined that the application of the amnesty law to the cases of the detained and disappeared was constitutional, and it expressed the opinion that the amnesty law precluded investigation of the facts surrounding these cases, thus contradicting Aylwin's wish that the truth be known, the bodies of the victims found, and the causes of death established.[149] It was a verdict fully backed by the right.[150] A plea for a review was unanimously rejected. The government could do little but declare that 'despite the sentence, the government will continue with the investigations of human rights violations'.[151]

The Court not only opposed the humanitarian interpretation of the amnesty law, but also insisted on giving the military courts jurisdiction over the cases involving the recent discovery of mass graves.[152] Both the Pisagua case in 1990 and the Chihuio case in January 1991, around which a jurisdictional battle had developed, were decided in favour of the military courts. Despite the appeal of the civil judges, the Court upheld its decision. The Calama case was the only one in which the Court adopted a positive verdict. It decided to allow the case to be reopened in April 1991, ordering the military court to investigate the matter. A week later it reversed its decision on a technicality, following an appeal by the Military Public Ministry.[153]

In another case of May 1991, the Supreme Court dismissed charges against a CNI officer implicated in the 1986 murder of four communists and Miristas, even though they had been previously confirmed by the San Miguel Court of Appeals. The Court also challenged the jurisdiction of the Executive. In July 1990, it exonerated 16 policemen who had been dismissed by the government after being found guilty of corruption during the purges undertaken by the Police. The Court questioned the government's faculty to fire police on such charges.[154]

Despite the government's frustration, it opposed any attempts to overturn the amnesty law, as well as court investigations which sought to judge not only individuals who had committed crimes, but those responsible for planning them. According to Aylwin, 'my desire is that everyone be tried for all cases . . . but . . . justice should be done to the degree it is possible. It is probable that without the amnesty law the proliferation of cases would have created a climate that might have been harmful to reconciliation. But, without a doubt, the law has been an obstacle to justice.'[155]

These, then, were the practical limits apparently imposed by 'lo posible'. Thus, the government opposed the attempt by six socialist deputies in June 1990 to pass a law which would enforce the government's interpretation of the amnesty law.[156] Similarly, when the Congress unanimously approved the American Convention of Human Rights, giving international law constitutional ranking in August 1990, the government did not support its retroactive application as advocated by some socialist members of the Concertación.[157] In June 1992, when the court investigating the *degollados* case tried to establish the guilt of those who had organized and cooperated in the crime, Minister Correa declared the latter had not been 'committed by individuals and individuals will have to answer for their actions'. Demands for General Stange's resignation were rejected.[158] Finally, the government reduced the political impact of court investigations by covering controversial cases with press bans.[159]

The battle between the Concertación and the Supreme Court culminated in a constitutional accusation brought against three of the Court's ministers and the Military Prosecutor General, General (retd.) Fernando Torres, by the Chamber of Deputies in December 1992.[160] The ministers in question were accused of 'gross abandonment of duties', for transferring a case of disappearance to the military courts, despite an earlier verdict to the contrary. The Supreme Court, claiming that its independence was under threat, demanded that President Aylwin convene the NSC.[161] On 20 January, with the support of Renovación, the Senate approved the impeachment of Minister Hernán Cereceda with one vote over the required minimum. The others were exonerated.[162] The only response of the Court's President was to claim that the accusation had 'put the country at serious risk of an institutional imbalance.'[163]

The Corporation for Reparation and Reconciliation also met with numerous difficulties. Its fact-finding mission failed because the military refused to co-operate. By March 1993, the Corporation had received 1,800 denunciations, but, failing to locate the disappeared, it requested and was subsequently granted a 60-day extension by the Senate. It was mandated to end its work in October 1993.[164] Moreover, the Corporation had no control over further investigation of cases by the judiciary. Once in the courts, the amnesty law and the jurisprudence of the Supreme Court made the successful resolution of these cases extremely difficult. In January 1993, the Corporation delivered a report to the President: 850 of the cases reviewed by the Corporation were classified as human rights violations. The Corporation has therefore at least contributed to the truth-telling aspect of the human rights issue, by adding to the cases acknowledged by the Rettig report.

Despite these failures, conflicts, and setbacks, human rights violations were investigated by the courts, many of which were only too happy to comply with the government's interpretation of the amnesty law. By June 1993 there were over 200 cases in the courts, all at different stages of resolution. It is impossible to outline the progression of all these cases, not least because the necessary information is not yet available to the public. It is useful, however, to provide a brief overview of a few representative cases which did receive coverage.

Although exceptional, the Letelier case, for example, was reactivated by the democratic government after the Ministry of Foreign Affairs' investigation into the forging of passports. Due to a provision in one of the Cumplido laws stating that crimes which affect inter-state relations be placed under the jurisdiction of the ordinary courts, the Supreme Court, despite much resistance, was eventually forced, by a vote of nine to seven, to appoint Judge Bañados to investigate the case in July 1990. In August 1991, only days before the statute of limitations on the crime was due to expire, and following the presentation of a criminal accusation against General Contreras and Colonel Espinoza on behalf of the victim's family, the case was reopened.[165] In September the two men were arrested on charges of falsification of passports and homicide.[166]

There was also some development in cases not covered by the amnesty law. The *degollados* case, for example, was re-opened in March 1990.[167] In April 1991, 21 carabineros were detained, including General César Mendoza, director of the institution at the time of the crime. When the Supreme Court refused to grant Mendoza his request for *habeas corpus*, the Carabineros, who up until then had been denying any involvement in the crime and giving their institutional and financial backing to all the accused, withdrew and condemned the terrible crime. In May 1991, five of the accused were charged with murder and sentenced.[168]

Another case which met with success is that of murdered trade union leader, Tucapel Jiménez, and the related case of the murder of a worker, Juan Alegría. Reopened in July 1990, the case led to the arrest and prosecution of three retired members of the army intelligence service and of the CNI. In May 1992 the ex-Chief of the CNI, General Alvaro Corbalán and an associate, the so-called 'Dr Destiny', the latter on bail for his involvement in the Cutufa financial fraud, were arrested and charged.[169]

The worst crisis between the government and General Pinochet had occurred in mid-December 1990, when investigations into financial corruption revealed that Pinochet had been involved in fraudulent multi-million dollar contracts with the Army and international arms traders. The evidence pointed to Pinochet's involvement in extending loans to his son from the reserves of the Banco del Estado for US$971 million and it indicated irregularities in his daughter's and son-in-law's business in the Instituto de Seguros del Estado, the State Insurance Institute, or the so-called Cutufa, which managed most Army retirement and pension benefits.[170]

Although the possibility of a constitutional accusation against Pinochet had been discarded and although the President assured the military that the Commander-in-Chief would not be attacked, the investigations were initially pursued.[171] By January 1990, however, the case had been abruptly dropped; Pinochet had put the Army on state of alert in mid-December after Defence Minister Rojas had called for the General's resignation.[172] Pinochet had not been isolated: the Army had reaffirmed institutional loyalty to its Commander-in-Chief, 'whatever the defamatory circumstances and characteristics which seek to damage his person'.[173]

The alarming conclusions of the investigating committee had, as a result of this corporate display of solidarity, been dispatched to the Controlaria instead of the courts. The so-called Pinocheques case thus produced the first 'danger consensus' of the transition; in the words of one commentator they had been the first cheques 'in the history of Chile that provoked an *acuartelamiento*, various rounds of negotiations, much confidential to-ing and fro-ing and a torrent of threats against individuals and against the transition'.[174]

Unlike the Uruguayan government, which had emphasized the dangers of military deliberation, the Concertación government had attempted to minimize the significance of the Army's rebellion.[175] None the less, although the President tried to present the abandonment of the case as an action of mercy towards the Commander-in-Chief, it was clear that the Pinocheques had provided a clear indication of the limits imposed on the search for both judicial truth and justice.[176]

Three years later, the Pinocheques case returned like a nightmare, producing another confrontation between the Aylwin government and the military over the human rights issue.[177] The Boinazo of May 1993, a public military show of strength through which the Army expressed its anger over continued human rights investigations, violating their interpretation of the amnesty law, and expressing Pinochet's anger over the reactivation of the Pinocheques case, had faced the government with a stark choice: to stick to its agenda of truth and justice and risk the possibility of worsening relations with the military command or worse, rebellions of solidarity and resistance within the lower ranks *à la* Rico and Seineldin in Argentina, or to give up its pursuit of justice in this case.

Although the government had succeeded in linking the instrumental aim of preserving democratic stability with the moral or ethical aim of pursuing a positive human rights agenda in the truth-telling period, it was eventually faced with a conflict between the two objectives in its attempts to pursue justice. If the 'Aylwin Doctrine', which established that the truth was a necessary and indispensable pre-condition for democratic consolidation, had kept the Concertación united in the face of military and right-wing resistance, the emergence of an apparent conflict between stability and principle over the implementation of justice threatened to divide the coalition roughly between the Socialist wing, which had suffered most from repression and was most closely linked to the victims' associations, and the Christian Democrats, who, with some exceptions, were more willing to find a political solution to the human rights issue.

The conflict between justice and democratic consolidation or stability resulted from differing responses to military intransigence embodied in the Boinazo of 28 May 1993 (this word refers to a military show of strength). It was a product, too, of different perceptions of what and how much it was admissible to sacrifice in the name of regime stability. After the Boinazo, the President met General Pinochet. Unlike Uruguay, where military manifestations of force and open deliberation were either tolerated or bolstered by

Presidential rhetoric, Aylwin condemned the army's movements and reminded Pinochet that his actions bordered on the unconstitutional. Pinochet, on the other hand, was careful to portray the event as being within the limits of legality.[178] Following the meeting, a Commission was formed composed of Military Prosecutor General, Fernando Torres Silva and Jorge Burgos, the lawyer of the Ministry of the Interior, to determine how many cases were in the courts, as the military claimed that there were over 1,000 cases in the courts and the government maintained that there were only 230.[179]

A number of solutions were proposed by party leaders. The possibility of a new amnesty law, already rejected by the military in 1990, was discarded by all sides.[180] The President of the Senate, Christian Democrat Gabriel Valdéz, suggested that a three-month limit be placed on the resolution of all the cases, that the churches should anonymously receive information on the whereabouts of the disappeared, that the cases covered by the amnesty law be abandoned, and that only a few key cases—such as the Letelier assassination, the *degollados*, and the Tucapel Jiménez case—be prosecuted. This proposal was well received by the right, but the President, the Minister of Justice Cumplido, the PPD, the PS, and parts of the Christian Democratic party rejected it on the grounds that justice could not be sacrificed for expediency, and that applying the amnesty law without prior investigations would subvert the government's total commitment to truth.[181]

On 29 June the government announced that it would not promote the old interpretation of the amnesty law and that a possible solution was to nominate extra judges to accelerate the resolution of the cases.[182] On 12 July the President met with General Pinochet again. Aylwin informed him that the government was willing to seek formulas to close the pending cases if the military contributed by informing the courts of the whereabouts of the disappeared; 'the President was ready to gamble all his political capital and personal prestige in the resolution of this issue, but only in so far as the army responded in the same spirit'. The following day the President met with representatives of human rights groups and again stated that he was committed to pursuing justice.[183]

In the last week of July, the President declared that no fixed time limits would be placed on the resolution of cases, that an amnesty was inadmissible on moral, political, and legal grounds, that the government would not pass a law declaring the presumed death of the disappeared, and that any solution to the problem would have to be jurisdictional and not legislative; the resolution of the cases would be left to the discretion of the judiciary.[184] In that week the President held four meetings with the Generals of each of the branches of the Armed Forces and another two private meetings with Pinochet to make this position clear to the military.

Unlike President Sanguinetti, therefore, Aylwin both made it clear that the end of prosecutions could only be arranged if the military admitted to the crimes by informing the courts of the whereabouts of the disappeared, and that the opinions of the victims' relatives were important and valid. The solution finally presented by Aylwin, however, provoked the first serious split within the ranks of the Concertación. On 3 August the President announced that he would send a project to the parliament, which, responding to the military's main preoccupations would: expedite the cases by putting Ministros en Visita, or Visiting Judges in charge of cases. These would be able to nominate Ministros Suplentes or Suplementary Judges to speed up cases in the Courts of Appeals and to guarantee the secrecy of proceedings and penalize the violation of secrecy to protect the identity of military personnel called to declare. The President declared that the viability of this solution depended upon the co-operation of the military in informing the courts of what they knew about the disappeared.[185]

Despite the military's public refusal to apologize on the grounds that there was nothing to be forgiven, on 5 August the project was sent to the Chamber of Deputies with a request for its urgent consideration. This request was based on fears that lower-ranking army rebellions could arise over the pending prosecution of twenty active service officers.[186] Following the President's statement that improvements were acceptable, Ministers Cumplido and Boeniger met with the leaders of the Concertación parties to hammer out an accord which would satisfy the left. The PS and the PPD succeeded in changing the project in the Comisión de Constitución, Legislación y Justicia so that the facts of the cases would not remain secret, that the investigating judge would be obliged to produce a report describing the whole case which could be made public, that cases which had been temporarily dismissed could be re-opened, and finally that the Ministros en Visita should be able to review cases currently in the military courts.[187]

These changes were unsurprisingly rejected by the right. Less predictably, however, they were subsequently rejected by the PS and the PPD. After consultations with lawyers representing the families of the disappeared and pressured by the extra-parliamentary left, both parties changed their attitude to these reforms: they claimed that the law made it possible for the Ministros en Visita to be members of the military judiciary and that the severity of demands for secrecy were such that they violated the basic premise of the Aylwin Doctrine of total commitment to truth. The PS then proposed to the Christian Democrats that the law should stipulate that Ministros en Visita had to be civilians and that the identity of military personnel should only remain secret if they provided information which would definitively resolve the cases. Both suggestions were rejected by the PDC.

With the backing of the UDI and RN, and despite the opposition of the Socialists, the Christian Democrats succeeded in approving their proposal to vote on the law urgently. Thus, on 18 August the law was voted on in the Chamber of Deputies. Most of the articles were approved by joint DC–RN–UDI votes with the exception of the third article on secrecy which was rejected both by the left and the right, although for different reasons.[188]

Following this débâcle, and at the same time that Michael Townley revealed the already known but never the less sensational facts surrounding the Letelier murder, a working group was formed to overcome the differences within the Concertación over the law.[189] An initial request by the Socialists for the President to withdraw the project was rejected. The aim was then to reform the project and to take it to a vote whereby the political cost would be shifted to the right if the latter rejected the revised version. Again these negotiations failed. In the first place, although the issue of secrecy had been resolved, the socialists refused to accept that military judges might be appointed to investigate these cases. To prevent such an occurrence, however, would have required undertaking the impossible and undesirable task—only months from the end of Aylwin's mandate and in the face of right-wing opposition—of reforming existing legislation and constitutional law. Secondly, the risk that the right-wing dominated Senate would approve the original version of the bill and thus provoke a Presidential veto was deemed undesirable. Thirdly, the Christian Democrats were not united behind the project, particularly since their support for it had damaged their pro-human rights image in contrast with the principled attitude of the Socialists. Fourthly, after a final meeting with Pinochet, the General had told Aylwin that he preferred no law to a law modified by the Socialists. Finally, after a party conference, the PS decided to reject continued negotiations and announced that it would not support the motion for legislating 'in general'.[190]

In the face of these obstacles, the Concertación parties united and opted to request that the President withdraw the bill definitively.

Thus, at the beginning of September, Aylwin announced that the law was to be withdrawn and that no legislative solution would be sought for the human rights problem. The courts would proceed as before, and justice would remain in the hands of the judiciary. In his view, the military should not be worried since the normal functioning of the judiciary should not 'cause confusion within any institution'.[191] The Concertación was back to square one, to a judicial and not a legislative solution.

The Boinazo did have an effect on the trend in the courts to apply the Aylwin Doctrine. In early 1993, several cases were encouraging, and the civilian courts were able to clear up the crimes and responsibility of DINA agents in the 1976 murder and disappearance of Spanish civil servant, Carmelo Soria, of Alfonso Chanfreau, a student leader, and two brothers in 1974. This was due to the application of the Aylwin doctrine, the testimony of former DINA agents, and the changed climate resulting from the impeachment of a Supreme Court judge for transferring the Chanfreau case to a military court.

By the second half of 1993, however, following the Boinazo, the trend was reversed as military courts claimed and won jurisdiction over many cases, including those cited above. In most cases, the Supreme Court confirmed the application of the amnesty on appeal, following the closure of cases by the military courts. The Supreme Court ratified a decision to prosecute two retired members of the DINA from the Mulchen Brigade for the 1976 death of the Spaniard Carmelo Soria by torture. It rejected the defence's appeal to the 1978 amnesty law on the grounds that international legal commitments did not permit an amnesty.[192]

President Aylwin thus ended his term faced with opposition to his human rights agenda from within his own coalition. For the first time, too, differences between the left and centre-right of the Concertación became threatening to coalition unity. Ironically, considering that the coalition was created in opposition to dictatorial rule, the conflict was over the issue of human rights violations.[193]

The Frei Administration and the Continuing Struggle for Justice, 1993–1996

In December 1993, the Concertación led by Frei won the elections with 58 per cent of the vote. Despite Frei's overwhelming majority, the political balance of forces remained much the same as it had under the Aylwin government.[194] When campaigning, Frei had backed Aylwin's 'courage and valiance' and had promised to act to pursue justice.[195] Official government statements once he had taken power, however, indicated that the human rights issue would not be a major concern of the new Concertación government.

Despite these statements, the first crisis faced by the Frei Presidency was related to the issue of human rights violations. In March 1994, 16 former police agents were convicted in the Degollados case. They were also all ordered to pay compensation adding up to millions of dollars to the relatives of the victims.[196] Among those charged was General Stange, with the prosecuting civilian judge recommending the Chief of the Police be prosecuted by a military court for obstruction of justice. Despite Frei's call for his resignation, Stange refused to leave his post. This act of (legally permissible) defiance proved the merely nominal control that the civilian authorities continue to have over the military.

The investigating judge finally determined that Stange would not be prosecuted, a decision backed up by the Supreme Court and the Court Martial. In October 1995, however, General Stange announced his voluntary retirement as chief of the Carabineros. With his departure, Pinochet becomes the last remaining Commander to have been appointed during the dictatorship.[197] The *Degollados* case represented a breakthrough, as up to that date only three people had been convicted of human rights violations, all of them still free. 'The verdict . . . breached a wall of impunity which held intact for more than 20 years. Despite the long delays, a Chilean court had at last handed down a sentence commensurate with the gravity of a human rights crime. For the first time, a scrupulous judicial investigation had proved that state officials had conspired to commit acts of terrorism.'[198]

The other judicial case which has come to a conclusion under the Frei administration is the Letelier case. Its resolution may have produced what may prove to be the last of the civil–military crises over the human rights issue. At the end of May 1995, the Supreme Court found General Manuel Contreras and Colonel Espinoza guilty of planning the Letelier assassination and sentenced them to seven and six years' imprisonment respectively.[199] Espinoza finally declared that he would accept the six-year imprisonment he had been sentenced to. General Manuel Contreras, on the other hand, said he would refuse to fulfil his sentence, accusing the CIA of the assassination, denying his involvement, and claiming that his prosecution was organized by the same 'marxist rabble' that he had fought to save the country from.[200] The government stated that it would take Contreras to gaol even if force were necessary. In a further measure to prevent any backlash from the military, it was decided that both Contreras and Espinoza would be gaoled in a specially constructed prison.[201]

The military was initially silent, dispatching envoys to Contreras's farm in the South of the country, whose apparent purpose was to advise Contreras not to resist.[202] Moreover, worries about shows of support for Contreras by fellow military officers led the high command to send 80 paratroopers to his farm to keep him in isolation.[203] This was followed by a declaration by General Pinochet that military acceptance of the imprisonment of both Contreras and Espinoza was guaranteed.[204] The subsequent Defence Minister's meeting with the Army's high command was positive.[205] Manuel Contreras was finally gaoled in October 1995. He, Espinoza, and the four ex-carabineros and the one civilian convicted for the *Degollados* case are the only inmates of the special prison contructed for the military.[206]

The Letelier case seems to have marked a new watershed in the human rights saga, much as the *Boinazo* had done earlier on. It seems to have led to a reversal of the cautiously positive attitude of the courts. The judiciary seems to have heeded the calls for an end to investigations and the application of the so-called Aylwin doctrine. Since May 1995, 25 cases were dismissed by the Supreme Court with automatic application of the amnesty law, a speeding up which has occurred since the sentencing of Contreras.[207]

The resolution of the Letelier case has also led to a renewed effort on the part of the right and the military to terminate the human rights episode. In response to increasing pressures for a legislated solution to the issue, in May 1995 a bill was put before Congress by the government which would allow the courts to suspend all trials in which penal liability has either been prescribed or extinguished by previous legislation. It produced a repetition of the Socialist outcry which followed the Aylwin Law and had to be dropped.[208] In September 1995 Frei proposed a package of three laws linking the human rights issue with the reform of the constitution and the Organic Law of the Armed Forces. At the end of October 1995, after months of negotiations with the RN, key constitutional reforms were agreed to. The designated senators will disappear, the Congress' powers of oversight will be increased, and the National Security Council as well as the Constitutional Tribunal will be restructured. The Law of the Armed Forces was excluded from the negotiations, as the RN refused to contemplate its reform. Finally, the Frei bill regarding the human rights trials was rejected and a bill by RN's Senator Miguel Otero was put forward.

Unlike the previous bill, the new one proposes that cases already in the military courts remain there. All cases still pending, currently 600 of the latter exist affecting 1,000 people, will be under the care of special judges. Unlike Frei's bill, which stated that cases would remain open until the fate of the disappeared was established, the new bill, while emphasizing the determination of the whereabouts of the disappeared and establishing mechanisms to encourage those who wish to volunteer information, states that the special judges will be empowered to close cases if no new information is forthcoming.[209] In December the Senate Constitutional Commission approved the bill despite the objection of the Socialists and the UDI.

This latest development has led to splits and conflicts both within the right and the Concertación. The Socialists are opposed to the proposal and have threatened that passage of the bill may force them to leave the Concertación.[210] The PPD and the DC, as well as the Partido Radical Socialdemocrata (PRSD), on the other hand, are in favour.[211] The right is divided on the one hand between the UDI and the RN old guard in opposition to both the human rights bill and the constitutional reforms, and the 'youth patrol' of the RN led by Allamand and Espina on the other.[212]

Conclusion

Whatever the outcome of the human rights question in Chile, what is clear is that the judicial coming to terms with the legacies of authoritarian rule is not a closed chapter. There are still some 600 cases in the courts. The human rights organizations, such as the FASIC and the AFDD, are unwilling to accept the recent reversal of the Aylwin doctrine, and plan to campaign for the impeachment of the Supreme Court panel. The Letelier case which was televised live has reawoken public interest such that it probably cannot be said today, as in late 1993, that people read about the reopening of human rights cases 'with a certain normality'.

It is likely that the left of the Concertación will, together with the families of the victims, keep pressing for justice. If the Concertación is to remain united, a coalition president will not be allowed easily to abidicate from such a committment if he is to keep the Socialists in tow. The need to keep the parties of the

Concertación united may therefore ensure that wholesale abdication will not occur. Moreover, even if domestic judicial solutions are exhausted, there is always the possibility of recurring to international courts.[213]

What is unclear is whether the truth will ever be known. President Aylwin had created a Corporación de Reparación y Reconciliación only a month after the release of the Rettig Report. It was mandated to work on the cases that the Rettig Commission had been unable to determine beyond doubt as legitimate cases of human rights violations, work on new cases presented to it, and locate the disappeared and other dead. The Corporation inherited 989 cases from the Commission. Given the endless number of new cases it kept receiving thereafter, its life was prolonged on a number of occasions by the Congress. By January 1994, the Corporation was working on 2,119 cases, 55 per cent of them new, but it had only arrived at conclusions with regard to 793 of those cases. As far as the search for the bodies of the disappeared was concerned, in January 1994 the Corporation was still searching for 1,553 of the dead. The Congress extended the life of the Corporation for another 24 to 36 months to allow it to continue with the search.[214] Like the Commission, the Corporation has no powers to subpoena witnesses. Thus, the greatest single obstacle to both the determination of cases and the location of the dead has been the silence of the Armed Forces. As the imprisoned Espinoza has said, Chile is still a country of 'corpses and memories'.[215]

None the less, unlike Uruguay, the question in Chile is finally not whether truth and justice are compatible with stability and military subordination, but rather how much truth and justice are compatible with these aims. Rather than facing an apparent choice between all (and a democratic institutional crisis) or nothing (and a stable democracy existing in an ethical vacuum), Chileans face a choice between symbolic truth and justice and attempting both symbolic and 'real' truth and justice. However far from the ideal, this is a qualitatively different state of affairs from the Uruguayan case. The following chapter will assess comparatively the Uruguayan and Chilean efforts to deal with the repressive legacies of the past.

PART IV

Assessing Truth and Justice in Uruguay and Chile: The Road to Democratic Consolidation?

No real democratization can take place unless we take respons-ibility for fear.

Norberto Lechner, *Some People Die of Fear*, 1992.

The deconstruction of cultures of fear is a long, fragile, and incomplete process. For those who embark on such a journey there are no magic formulas nor a clearly charted course. The appropriate mixture of political skill, constraining and enab-ling conditions, and sheer luck can be ascertained only after the failure or success of the enterprise.

Juan Corradi, *Societies Without Fear*, 1992.

7

Assessing Truth and Justice Policies in Uruguay and Chile

Introduction

This book has demonstrated that the ability or willingness of the government and of the political élites to implement policies of truth and justice is inextricably tied to the national legacies of military rule, the political nature of the transitional processes, and finally to the political conditions operating under the democratic successor regimes. This final chapter will assess comparatively Uruguay's and Chile's attempts to come to terms with the legacy of human rights violations under democratic rule. It will examine the political and institutional factors which shaped the different paths taken by the Sanguinetti and Aylwin governments in the pursuit of truth and justice.

The aim of this analysis is to demonstrate the intensely political nature of the human rights issue and to show how each country's attempt to deal with its past was influenced by peculiar national characteristics which make each case unique and irreproducible—not least because the quality of presidential leadership seems to be of key importance in the resolution of this issue. The second part of the chapter will evaluate the success or failure of each country's policies in the light of an 'ideal', asking how far the Uruguayan and Chilean political classes were able to approximate 'ideal' truth and justice policies.

Comparing Uruguay's Coming to Terms with el Conjunto de Ficciones Perezosas[1] *and Chile's Partial Truth and Symbolic Justice*

When assessing the reasons for the different levels of success in Uruguay's and Chile's efforts to come to terms with the legacy of repression, key differences shaping the processes come to light. First, in Uruguay the human rights issue as a whole had a 'low moral profile'. Its 'nature as a conciliatory arrangement without commitment or risks explicitly taken on board' did not bode well because, as one observer pointed out, 'the defect of all excessively sensible moral arrangments is that nobody feels too worried about denying them.'[2] Commitments were for the most part fleeting and contingent.[3] In Chile, on the other hand, human rights had a high 'moral' profile. Truth and reconciliation were the names of the game. Confronting the legacy of human rights violations was the centre-piece of the the path towards that goal.

Secondly, the way in which the political parties envisaged the implementation of truth and justice policies also differed. In Chile, a clear distinction was made between truth and justice. Truth-telling was both autonomous from justice as a policy and the centre-piece of the government's human rights policy. Thus conflicts were contained and separated by time and it was ensured that, were justice to fail entirely, the realities of military repression would still be unmasked publicly. Moreover, because the truth-telling commission was set up immediately, and was limited in scope and time, it did not result in sensationalist press leaks, and its results were proclaimed only a year after it had been formed. Justice was also limited by Aylwin's warning that it would never be total, that it would be done only 'as far as possible', that responsibilities could only be established individually and that the amnesty law would not be derogated. Unlike the *laissez-faire* attitude of all parties in Uruguay, however, the government participated actively in the promotion of justice. It promoted a positive interpretation of the amnesty law, set up a corporation to investigate cases and to find the disappeared, and resisted attempts to reduce penalties for violations in exchange for a quick release of the political prisoners.

In Uruguay, on the other hand, no distinction was made between truth-telling *per se* and judicial prosecution. The results of the legislative investigating commissions were destined for the courts, they did not explicitly aim to form the basis for an official, publicly announced national truth. Thus, truth as a policy objective in and of itself never acquired autonomous life. The subsequent failure of judicial prosecution thus condemned the revelation of the truth to a similiar failure. Furthermore, all parties adopted a *laissez-faire* attitude to judicial prosecution. Despite the obvious difficulties associated with this position, the opposition continued, for the most part, to sustain it, acting on the unrealistic assumption that the judiciary would be able to proceed without governmental backing and that the military would indeed obey court summonses, despite the government's advocation of military jurisdiction and an amnesty and despite the fact that the judiciary lacked an adequate working budget as well as political clout.[4]

The lack of a pre-designed and clear-cut prosecutions policy meant that no limits were imposed on the extension of the accusations and on the time the courts could take to resolve these cases. Cases included Junta members and lower-ranking officers, as well as accusations ranging from violations of the right to life committed by individuals, and violations of the constitution committed by the Junta, pro-military civilian ministers and officials, and the military as an institution. Thus the political class had no control over the judicial process and over the potential political damage it might bring about. It was reduced to reacting to events on an *ad hoc* basis rather than being in a position to shape them. They limited rather than expanded political opportunities. As time passed, the difficulties of finding an adequate solution increased. As Ferreira had warned, justice would be 'impossible to attempt if the first year is wasted'.[5] 'The problem should have been re-dimensioned' from the start, determining the who, when, and how of judicial action.[6]

Another key difference between Uruguay and Chile was the power of the human rights movement and the Church and their relations with the parties. In Uruguay there were no state-autonomous institutions such as the Church, or powerful human rights organizations capable of successfully challenging party inconsistencies. The human rights organizations were too weak to press for a different outcome. The Catholic Church, despite its rhetorical support for both truth and justice in the democratic period, had no hold over the political class, particularly over the Colorado party which has a history of anti-clericalism as well as a masonic tradition.[7] Furthermore, the alliance between the parties and the human rights movement had never been consolidated.

In Chile, on the other hand, the bonds forged between the Concertación parties and the human rights movement and the Church, meant that these powerful groups were, for the most part, supportive of the government's truth and justice policy. Because they believed in the government's commitment to resolve this issue, polarization did not occur as it did in Uruguay. According to one study, whatever the disenchantment, it was not enough to 'lead to attitudes of anomie . . . essentially because of a basic trust in the government which remained unbroken despite disenchantment'.

Moreover, 'the demand for an alternative policy [did] not lead to a maximalism which de-legitimiz[ed] the policies; rather, it radicalized the promise of the policy within a logic of political realism which espous[ed] the guidelines adopted by the government'.[8]

Another reason for the support of the human rights groups for the government was that, unlike Uruguay where the credible party political spectrum was wider and more diverse, in Chile there was no credible left to turn to. Had the human rights organizations wanted to challenge the government, there was no political force on the left outside the Concertación which would be able to channel their demands effectively in the formal political arena. In Chile, the mobilizing left strategy had been defeated early on as an oppositional strategy. In Uruguay the debate as to which method had done most to defeat the military was still very much alive, and the left had led great mobilizations which had served as catalysts to push the transition ahead. Thus, in Chile the Communist Party threat to mobilize in the face of a lack of government commitment to justice sounded hollow. As became apparent with the opposition of the Frente Amplio, both in the legislature and later in the referendum campaign, this was not the case in Uruguay. In Chile, the left was either preaching moderation within the bounds of the Concertación, losing all political influence in the case of the Communist party, or was even more isolated from public sympathy, fighting in the ranks of the armed groups. In the climate of moderation, it is interesting to note that even the Communist party was opposed to institutional trials and to the state prosecution of members of the Armed Forces.[9]

This lack of 'alternatives' and concomitant unity of the opposition in Chile bring us to what may be one of the most important differences between the two cases. Unlike the partisan divisions present in Uruguay, the political parties in Chile remained for the most part united throughout the period due to the nature of the Concertación. The latter included those elements in the Socialist parties which were both committed to justice but willing to negotiate and work within the restricted legal framework. These parties were thus allies of the President in his efforts to find a solution. They both legitimized the President in the eyes of the more leftist population and provided the necessary impetus for the President to act on his convictions. Thus, unlike Uruguay, where the transition ultimately led to the breakdown of the pro-human-rights élite settlement between the Blanco Party and the FA, and subsequently between it and the Colorado party, the Chilean transition consolidated the unity of the opposition, strengthening the élite settlement reached between the moderate and the radical opposition in the five years leading up to the transitional elections in 1989. The Concertación in the legislature therefore backed the executive's initiatives. A case in point is Andres Aylwin, brother of the president, a member of the Comisión de Presos Políticos de la Concertación and the President of the Comisión de Constitución, Legislación y Justicia of the Chamber of Deputies, who played a crucial role as a liason between the government, the legislature, and the political prisoners' organizations in the attempts to liberate the political prisoners, preventing a breakdown in the often tense relations between the different players.[10]

In Uruguay, on the other hand, truth and justice became the victims of partisan politics. First, 'al no lograrse consenso partidario' ('not having achieved consensus among the parties') previous to the inauguration of democratic rule, and with the failure of the *pre-pacto para la gobernabilidad* (pre-pact for governability) within the CONAPRO, each party felt it had its 'its hands free' to follow its own individual course.[11] Then as 'each one wanted to save their little banner',[12] the search for solutions degenerated into a competition in which, as one observer noted, there abounded 'mutual reproaches, speeches of self-exoneration of any guilt, competitions to exhibit perfect intentions, thundering condemnations of the moral prophets waiting for an opportunity to show their beautiful souls condemned to live in an impure world, submitted to the logic of power.'[13]

A key factor contributing to opposition disunity was the shift in the Blanco Party's alliances. As noted in Chapter 1, the 'electoral law tended to punish parties of principle and reward alliances of convenience'.[14] The Frente–Colorado élite settlement of 1984 was one such alliance arguably achieved at the cost of principle. It was an alliance which was both historically and ideologically unnatural. The alternation of the historical pattern of traditional party alliance did not sit well with either of the transitional partners.[15] As the Frente demanded justice and the Colorados an amnesty, what had always been a marriage of convenience, quickly degenerated into outright hostility. The Colorado party, in need of an ally, sought the revival of the historical Blanco–Colorado power-sharing arrangement.

Similarly, the alliance between the Frente and the Blancos forged in exile did not sit well with Ferreira. The experience of exile and close ties with the left had radicalized the Blanco leader, leading him to identify more closely with the mobilizing social organizations and the left. This Blanco radicalism brought them closer to the Frente. This alliance soon crumbled. Not only was it fragile due to the Blancos' perception that the Frente had betrayed them in agreeing to participate in the pact instead of encouraging a mobilizing defeat of the military, but also because Ferreira Aldunate soon came under pressure from the Colorado party to re-establish the traditional bi-partisan model of government. The Blanco leader, already resentful of the Frente's betrayal in 1984, and with an eye on a future presidential bid, succumbed only too readily to Sanguinetti's siren call.

This second élite settlement made in the name of 'governability' was achieved at the cost of justice. As one observer noted, 'the governability thesis has no clear or precise origin. But its management can be discerned through the accumulation of political common ground which the National Party, led by its president Wilson Ferreira Aldunate and supported by the dissident Carlos Julio Pereyra, discovered that it had with the Colorado Party or, more precisely, with Sanguinetti.'[16] Despite the unquestionably unfavourable conditions implicit in the mode of transition, the traditional parties' decision to centre the human rights debate around the Club Naval Pact was less a faithful reflection of its real determining impact on the human rights issue than an expression of their unwillingness to pay the price for a policy-shift in the case of the Blanco Party, or to admit anything less than total impunity in the case of the Colorado government.

Government resistance and opposition disunity were exacerbated by the fact that the logic of extremes predominated, undermining the initiatives undertaken by the moderate sectors of the Frente and the Blanco Party. The attempt to implement a policy which would permit the realization of minimal objectives was co-opted by the extremes who wanted either all or nothing. As Ferreira liked to point out, it was the fault of the CO–CO:[17] Editorials in *El Día* by the 'anonymous' Marco Aurelio and inflammatory statements by different Colorado leaders represented one side of the CO(lorado) equation, while Senator Jose Araújo, who had called for a demonstration outside the Centro Militar in August 1985, became the symbol of CO(mmunist) intransigence. The aggressive propagandistic tone adopted by the Colorados and the minority radical sectors of the Frente, the latter unable or unwilling to offer any concrete policy alternatives, therefore exacerbated tensions. In the words of Seregni, the left's problem was that it had not overcome its tendency to act as an intransigent opposition and that 'a purely denunciatory attitude' tended to predominate.[18] In a sense, this attitude reflected the left's attachment to a wishful vision of the transition as a product of popular mobilization rather than one resulting from a negotiated pact between élites.[19]

The intense partisan nature of the human rights affair was aggravated by the bitter and sensationalized way the whole issue was treated in a country where, more than anywhere else in the Southern Cone, 'the daily press has been divided along party political lines'.[20] This general climate affected the parties in the democratic opposition most committed to truth and justice. They were divided and were unable or unwilling to produce a coherent consensus policy within the legislature which would adequately face the challenge of executive indifference. Moreover, the opposition parties were also internally divided. This, too, weakened their ability to press for justice. Pursuing contradictory human rights strategies, they expended much energy in internal conflicts. Seregni and his Frente allies were check-mated by the coalition's radical minority. The Blanco Party was paralysed by the ambiguity of Ferreira's position both on the human rights issue and on the question of political alliances. These conflicts culminated in the definitive split of the Frente in 1988, and led to the defeat of the progressive sectors of the Blanco Party and their replacement by the conservative LaCalle *lema* in the 1989 elections.[21]

The problems presented by the Uruguayan situation might have been remedied had the government come to power equipped with a moral commitment to represent the victims of repression in some way. The opposite, however, was true. The president chose not to lead a collective and national effort at truth-telling and to design a politically viable judicial policy. Efforts to arrive at a knowledge of the past were privatized or occurred at the level of civil society. The importance of a policy of global truth-telling autonomous from judicial prosecution was not admitted. There was no sense that the plight of the victims of repression was a collective social problem and responsibility. In Sanguinetti's own words, 'My government was characterized more by what it avoided than by what it did.'[22]

The government party and the executive were essentially in favour of an amnesty and opposed to truth-telling. The government initially dealt with the issue 'using the passage of time, with silences and supports which favoured the armed corporation'. It accepted 'the delays and, what is more, it attempted to resolve the problem in this way'.[23] Thus, the 'accusations made were unable to incriminate effectively the corporation and tended to become increasingly personalized, reduced to an ever smaller nucleus of people'.[24] Furthermore, challenging the Supreme Court, and pressing for an amnesty, Sanguinetti 'opened the way for the military not to go to the courts and then . . . he asked the opposition to lend him their support so that his authority would not be damaged'.[25]

Lack of executive commitment was exacerbated by the fact that 'the military issue became a sort of sub-theme of the human rights issue'. The Colorados adopted a 'a policy of shock absorption', using the Senate Defence Commission, the only commission in which the governing party reserved for itself an absolute majority, to neutralize any activity 'other than the activity of neutralization itself'.[26] Accommodation overrode all other commitments. The government's motto could well have been 'para que no me desobedezcas no te mando'.[27]

Moreover, by advocating the jurisdiction of the military courts and later an amnesty, the executive eliminated all chances of a military acceptance of partial justice. As Ferreira put it, 'you can't be more realistic than the king'. It would have been naïve to expect 'that an army go to court when its Supreme Chief wants to amnesty it'.[28] According to Medina himself, if the President was asking for an amnesty, the army could expect nothing less.[29] Thus, the government's attitude to justice had the effect of increasing rather than reducing institutional resistance to trials by raising military expectations. The implementation of justice became increasingly dangerous as deliberation was allowed to continue unchecked.

The peculiar dualism of both General Medina's and Sanguinetti's public presentation of the military issue contributed to legitimizing the hard-line. While both attempted to stamp out deliberation when it was unrelated to the human rights issue, they used the arguments of the hard-line and threatened opponents with the wrath of the armed forces when dealing with human rights violations. As Minister of Defence, Medina used hard-line resistance as evidence that any attempts to impose justice would lead to a breakdown of military discipline with dire, albeit unspecified, results. As Commander-in-Chief he tolerated the worst manifestations of deliberation and stood as a buffer between the military institution and the 'revanchists'.[30] Similarly, Sanguinetti 'convinced the national community that he was limited by military power; the effort therefore consisted of defending national institutions'.[31] On the other hand, however, he contributed to strengthening the legitimacy of those deliberations by adopting the same language they used. Although Sanguinetti and Medina presented themselves as the voice of moderation, alone in the struggle to bring about peace in the face of unreasonable demands by two lunatic fringes, the hard-line and the 'revanchists', they in fact contributed to polarizing the management of the issue.

The key to a positive military policy lies in the ability of the government to isolate the hard-line and strengthen the elements within the military who are willing to tolerate the punishment of some abuses in the name of better civil–military relations and to build a more a positive public image of the Armed Forces. By demanding protection for the whole institution, Sanguinetti legitimized the arguments of the hard-line and put all the military into the same guilty bag, all in need of protection from the 'threat of justice'. The honour of the Armed Forces was thus equated with the worst crimes.[32] Furthermore, democratic stability was allowed to be defined according to the arguments of the hard-line.[33]

One of the main reasons for Sanguinetti's closeness with the military was that the Colorado Party had come to power to the detriment of its main democratic contender, and in an unnatural alliance with the left which soon soured, as the Colorados made clear their more natural inclination towards the traditional Blanco Party and the military. In the absence of a possible alliance between the two traditional parties on the issue, the Colorados 'depended' on the military to counterbalance their weakness in the legislature.[34]

Another difference between the Uruguayan and Chilean stories is the manner in which the negotiations were conducted to resolve the human rights dilemma. In Uruguay, the parties never engaged properly in an open debate in which 'the participants jointly sought a shared set of general criteria' and therefore never 'risked their legitimacy as political actors'.[35] The arenas in which tactical decisions were made by party leaders were essentially hidden from public scrutiny. Moreover, public party positions more often than not did not mirror private intentions. There was a constant gap between public statements reaffirming leadership commitments to truth and justice, which tended to deny the difficulties involved in attempting to implement such policies, and the logic of the secret meetings, which tended to reveal a lack of traditional party commitment and to admit to the difficulties involved. The opposite was true in Chile.

Moreover, in Uruguay nobody admitted to the problems caused by the internal situation of the armed institution. Sanguinetti only conceded this in November 1986. Thus, not only was the debate essentially 'dishonest', but leaders were also ultimately not accountable to the public and party constituencies. This exacerbated inter- and intra-party tensions, increased mutual suspicions, and reinforced animosities inherited from the transitional period. It provoked confusion and tensions within party ranks and it produced contradictory assessments of the implications of secret talks. The style of negotiation adopted also strengthened the hand of the military. By engaging in reserved meetings with military commanders and by-passing official channels of communication, the traditional parties legitimized the military's right to deliberate and participate in determining the content of human rights policies and legitimized them as 'invisible partners in power'.[36] Asking the military what they thought best inevitably decreased the Blanco and the Colorado's ability to then impose solutions to which the military had already expressed their opposition in a 'friendly' private environment. It was Colorado and Blanco leaders who were primarily responsible for this, as the FA was largely excluded from these 'cosy chats'. In Ramirez's view, the relationship between Sanguinetti and the Armed Forces created a kind of 'associative democracy'. There was an 'association with the Armed Forces in the exercise of power, whose limits were diffuse but through which the Armed Forces doubtlessly' . . . acted as Sanguinetti's 'reserve power', as a 'dissuasive factor' *par excellence*.[37] Similarly, both traditional parties adopted a 'caudillesque' style, preferring reserved élite accommodation to open political debate and consensus-building, and both increasingly willing to exclude the Frente from these decision-making arenas. 'Governability', the watchword that described the relationship between Ferreira and Sanguinetti, was 'like a gentlemen's agreement. It is not written nor is it consulted'.[38]

In Chile the style of negotiations adopted by the government and the parties contributed to a greater clarity. Unlike Uruguay, where as a result of the style of transition Sanguinetti seemed to be more loyal towards General Medina than towards the human rights opposition, the emphasis seemed to be on the importance of good personal relations between the ruling party and the military, de-emphasizing the 'popular' character of the transition and leading to a quick reversal of the initial 'popular' commitment to a human rights policy, in Chile, the government attempted to be as transparent as possible in its dealings both with the military and with the right during the transition and beyond. Discussions were not privatized, and the private meetings between the President and General Pinochet were conducted and presented in an 'official' and 'constitutional' language and tone.

The tone and thrust of the Chilean government's military policy was also the reverse of the Uruguayan. Whereas in Uruguay the

Colorado government presented itself as the protective wall which sheltered the military from the demands for justice and truth emanating from society and the legislature, in Chile the government presented itself as the mediator between the Armed Forces and the right and the more radical left and human rights groups. Its human rights policies were presented as the minimum that could be done without a backlash from the victims and the left. Aylwin's determination both to command and mediate, to give in when necessary, but to stick to fundamental principles, was critical in shaping the responses of the Armed Forces, and in forcing Pinochet to tone down his aggressive opposition. Rather than being reduced to respond to manifestations of military resistance on an *ad hoc* basis, the government forced the military to respond to its initiatives.

When reactions were hostile, Aylwin assured the military that he would always protect institutional integrity but also reminded them that they were at all times subordinate to his authority. The government was willing to 'pay the political cost of moderation . . . in order to avoid the emergence of a crisis' and Aylwin 'ceded in part from his position to protect fundamental objectives with the idea that persisting in minor conflicts endangered greater achievements.'[39]

None the less, it is possible to say that Pinochet's intransigence largely failed to have the intended impact, partly because of the government's refusal to stand down and partly due to the unwillingness of the other branches to follow suit. The goverment helped to reinforce this division by encouraging constant exchanges with the different branches of the Armed Forces and cultivating ties between the Church and the military. Thus, in contrast to Uruguay, in Chile, the executive and the Concertación remained committed to its electoral platform throughout. Unlike Sanguinetti who abandoned his initial commitment to truth and justice, President Aylwin was adamant that without such policies democracy would not be properly consolidated. Reflecting this conviction is the fact that almost all of the executive's first legislative projects were human rights related.[40]

In addition to the above, unlike the second élite settlement which occurred under democratic rule in Uruguay between the Blanco and Colorado parties on the basis of impunity for human rights violations, the partial élite settlement between the moderate right and the Concertación in Chile, while implying the negotiation of solutions, was not based on an outright abandonment of truth and justice. The release of the political prisoners was possible, for example, essentially because of the 'politics of consensus' which produced a legislative accord between the Concertación and Renovación Nacional, but it was not achieved at the expense of truth and justice. It must be said that the success of the 'democracy of agreements' was partially possible due to the RN's willingness to pursue a pragmatic rather than a UDI-style ideological path. Had its choice been different it is unlikely that the political prisoners could have been released given the need for constitutional reform.[41]

All of the above shows the Chilean case in a very positive light when compared with Uruguay. There are, however, a number of negative aspects attached to Chile's policy which reflect the less democratic nature of the process. One of the reasons for the discretion with which the Commission was able to work and perhaps why the human rights issue as a whole was more easily dealt with in Chile is that in Chile the media, unlike the combative and partisan press of Uruguay, was generally seen to be very tame, to have lost its 'critical capacity'.[42]

Another of the reasons why the Commission was not subjected to the same challenges as its Uruguayan counterparts was because the policy was administered entirely by the executive and was therefore not subject to a parliamentary debate. The battle for truth and justice was waged between an executive and a president committed to dealing with the legacies of state repression and a powerful legislative right. The room for manœuvre in Chile was thus restricted in the legislature, whereas in Uruguay it had been the pro-human rights opposition which had dominated a General Assembly where the right was politically insignificant. Although 15 per cent of all the bills sent to the Congress and the Senate in the first two years of government were human-rights related, only five out of the executive's fifteen human rights projects were approved. Most of them, particularly the Cumplido Laws, suffered substantial modifications. Unlike Uruguay, where the legislature emerged as the human rights vanguard, almost all legislative proposals on human rights emerged from the executive in Chile. Presidential initiative ruled supreme; there was an almost total absence of parliamentary motions pertaining to the human rights issue.[43] From the start it was accepted that 'it would be the President who would lead the orchestra'.[44] Thus, the whole debate was contained, as the executive, taking the initiative, pre-empted the mobilized human rights organizations and the left from taking a leading role in the battle.

As opposed to the Chilean case, where the battle-lines were

drawn between the executive and the military, particularly Pinochet, in Uruguay the battle-line was drawn between the opposition in parliament supported by the human rights organizations and the military, with the executive increasingly siding with the military institution. It is ironic that presidential control over the process of transition and human rights policy was one of the factors which helped Aylwin carry out his truth and justice mandate, whereas it was a mobilized left that contributed to the failure of a human rights policy in Uruguay. In Uruguay the scope of the debate was widened because the opponents were on the extremes of the human rights spectrum. The left was not incorporated into the governing coalition, but was in fact in direct and increasingly hostile opposition to it precisely over the issue of human rights and amnesty.

Finally, while it is true that the separation of the truth policy from the policy of prosecutions allowed the Commission to work in relative peace, this is also one of the reasons why the truth is still not known in Chile. The Commission was given no teeth to legally force the military to bear witness before it. This weakness becomes particularly clear when one contrasts Chile's policy with the current development of the South African truth and justice policy.

Uruguay's Unofficial Truth and Absent Justice and Chile's Partial Truth and Symmbolic Justice in the Light of an 'Ideal' Human Rights Policy

Comparing Truth-Telling

In Uruguay, knowledge of human rights violations was widespread. According to a poll taken in June 1986, 85 per cent of Montevideans believed that the military had committed human rights violations.[45] In the absence of an official truth-telling, however, there was no acknowledgement. The *Nunca Más* report went some way to remedying this situation, but it was no substitute for an official government recognition of the truth. There were no measures to restore the dignity of the victims, nor were the military forced to either admit their errors or at least to be publicly confronted with the inconsistencies of their defence. Furthermore, the executive in Uruguay did not force the military to distance their world-view from their human rights resistance strategy. To the contrary, their world-view was actually endorsed by the President. Violations were thus deemed 'excesses' despite the fact that institutional responsibility was assumed for violations. The military never had to admit to the institutional nature of the violations and pay a political price for that admission. Similarly, they were allowed to deny institutional responsiblity for the disappearances and refuse to allow those who would then logically be renegade officers acting in defiance of institutional policy to be put on trial for disappearing individuals. They were allowed to get away with assuming institutional responsibility for a mere loss of *puntos de referencia* and on the condition that 'they would not be called to account.'[46] Essentially, they were allowed to have their national security cake and eat it too. In 1991, General Iván Paulós, still the Director of the Centro Militar, was able to claim that Uruguay was once more under the threat of international communism, and that one should worry about the 'exaltation of democracy, as a supreme good to be protected, above nationality.'[47] Similarly, General Medina himself was able to state without shame that torture had not been a mistake and that he himself had ordered the torture of prisoners.[48]

In Chile, knowledge of human rights violations was also widespread. Only 9.4 to 14 per cent believed that the Pinochet regime had not violated human rights.[49] Unlike Uruguay, however, the global acknowledgement of human rights violations also became reality. Although the government did make consessions to the right in its truth-telling policy, unlike Uruguay where the conclusions of the investigation commission on the disappeared were negotiated to the point where they denied the evidence presented in its own report, the truth of the Rettig report was essentially non-negotiable.[50] The 'blame' for violations was not diffused but placed squarely on the military and the DINA in particular. Institutional rather than individual responsibility for the crimes was clearly stated. After the launching of the Rettig report, there was no 'political party or an opinion group in the country which denied such facts; and there was no politician, not even on the right most loyal to the military, that did not claim that at the time they had tried to do something to stop the excesses, either against the DINA, or against illicit methods.'[51]

The report was known by the great majority of the population. In April 1992, 79.1 per cent claimed to know it directly or to have heard about it. Only 20.3 per cent claimed they did not know what it was.[52] In July 1993, a report based on interviews with people representing all sides of the human rights spectrum concluded that 'los derechos humanos parecen haberse constituido efectivamente en una cultura política de carácter universalista' and that there existed 'una comunicación no bloqueada, abierta, en proceso de elaboración colectiva—espacio virtual de elaboración del trauma y de constitución de un "nosotros" que excede a las afiliaciones sociales e ideológicas de origen'.[53] Moreover, unlike Uruguay, the ideological justification–explanation proffered by the military was publicly and categorically rejected by the democratic authorities and the truth and suffering of the victims was officially recognized by the state. The truth-telling policy therefore opened a political space for military admissions of guilt or remorse. In June 1991, as he retired from his position as Commander of the Air Force, General Matthei stated: 'Yo no hice nada . . . siempre pense que no fuí lo suficientemente valeroso que debí haber sido.'[54]

Justice Compared

As far as justice in Uruguay is concerned, no human rights violators have been successfully prosecuted. Moreover, the Ley de Caducidad has been widely regarded as unconstitutional and as contradicting international human rights legislation. Throughout 1989 the government consistently misapplied the provisions of its own amnesty law. The first article obliged the courts to hand each case over to the executive within thirty days for the latter to determine whether the law was applicable.[55] The government ordered cases to be closed which the military courts determined as lacking evidence of involvement of military personnel, and which were therefore not covered by the law. The provision which stated that the accusers should receive notification of the results of executive deliberation was also not fulfiled. Although the command was not covered by the law, none of these were ever brought to trial.[56] Finally, although crimes of corruption were excluded from the amnesty and although the military command itself had declared that these cases could be prosecuted, the government systematically applied it to these cases.[57]

The Uruguayan human rights organizations made a last stand against impunity in co-operation with international human rights organizations. IELSUR and America's Watch filed eight cases of multiple victims to the Inter-American Commission of Human Rights. All the cases involved the violation of non-derogable rights such as the right to life and physical integrity. They claimed that the law deprived citizens of the right to judicial recourse and remedy. In September 1991, the Inter-American Commission prepared a report which concluded that the amnesty violated a number of provisions of the American Declaration of the Rights and Duties of

Man and recommended the payment of just compensation to the victims by the state. Although this was a historical achievement, representing the first instance that any inter-governmental organization had directly addressed the question of the compatibility between a national amnesty law and a state's obligations contracted by a ratified human rights treaty, justice has not been done in Uruguay.[58]

The Uruguayan goverment did make some efforts to offer reparations to the victims of repression in its policies concerning returning exiles and affecting individuals dismissed from employment for political reasons. With the creation of the Comisión de Re-encuentro and the law on the *destituidos*, the state took on the responsiblity of re-integrating returning exiles, and re-incorporating people dismissed by the military from public administration. To date, however, no surveys exist which permit an assessment of the success of these policies.

In Chile, justice has and will continue to be elusive and numerous obstacles remain. The Concertación was both unable and unwilling to attempt to derogate the amnesty law. No military officer guilty of disappearances or other crimes prior to 1978 will therefore be prosecuted for human rights violations. Prosecutions have been limited to cases of disappearances or assassinations carried out after 1978. There will be no prosecutions of violations not resulting in death. Many cases currently in the courts will most likely be transferred to the military courts, where the Supreme Court's interpretation of the amnesty will be applied and the cases closed.[59] Thus, in April 1992, only 17.9 per cent of people felt that both truth and justice had been achieved, 53.3 per cent felt that the truth had been achieved and that justice had not, and 16.2 per cent believed that neither had been achieved.[60] As far as reparations are concerned, since the latter were based on the victims defined by the Rettig Commission, the fact that the report only included those victims who died means that the majority of those affected by repression not resulting in death are not represented in the material compensation.

The Political Prisoners

The liberation of the political prisoners was the only successful officially sponsored human rights policy in Uruguay. Only 15 days after the inauguration of the President all of the political prisoners of the regime had been liberated. This success reflected an overwhelming national consensus on the injustice of these imprisonments.

In contrast with Uruguay, 'Few things in the Chilean transition were as difficult as the political agreement around the *Leyes Cumplido* and the effect that these had on the resolution of the basic issue of human rights violations, the political prisoners and terrorism.'[61] The absence of widespread public enthusiasm and right-wing resistance makes it important to underline the political will which led to the resolution of this issue. Both Aylwin and the Minister of Justice, Francisco Cumplido, 'one of the most active ministers' of the government and the author of three of the first four projects sent to Congress, were determined that 'in Chile there should be no political prisoners left'.[62] Intended as criticism, but indicative of this commitment, were the words of an editorial in *El Mercurio*:

> It is paradoxical that that first law which emerged from the Concertación programme should be the one seeking to benefit the political prisoners, 450 people who were not a part of the alliance which took President Aylwin to power because they had adopted another path: not that of the vote but that of violence.[63]

Comparing Levels of Legitimacy

The popular legitimacy of the paths adopted in each case also differs greatly. In Uruguay there was a great gap between public desires and government performance and public perceptions indicated that the government had 'chickened out' and that it was the military and not the government that 'was wearing the trousers.' In June 1986, when asked whether punishment of the military should be avoided because this could lead to another *golpe*, only 8 per cent thought that they should not be punished; 78 per cent still believed that justice should proceed. Already however, 40 per cent thought they would never be punished. Only 10 per cent thought they would be punished that year and 27 per cent thought that it would happen after a long time.[64] Similarly, public opinion was also opposed to the Colorado's attempt to transfer human rights cases to the military courts. In June 1986, 73 per cent were in favour of the ordinary courts and only 6 per cent in favour of the military courts.[65] Although most Montevideans wanted to see justice done, only 40 per cent of them believed that the military would never be punished, 58 per cent thought that the government preferred to forget the whole matter. Finally, when asked whether they were in favour of an amnesty for the military, only 9 per cent said they were, whereas 66 per cent were opposed. Again in October 1986, 82 per cent of Montevideans thought that human rights violations should be punished and 81 per cent believed that the violations should be investigated.[66]

Distrust of the democratic parties was also apparent. The ambiguity with which the parties had dealt with the issue was reflected in public opinion. Among Blanco supporters, 58 per cent believed the problems with justice stemmed from the Club Naval. The percentages for the Colorados and the Frente were 31 and 40 per cent respectively. Overall, 39 per cent believed the pact was the source of the problems and 42 per cent that it was not. When asked whether the Club Naval Pact had implied impunity, 62 per cent of those interviewed who identified themselves as Colorados disagreed with the party's assessment of the pact; only 50 per cent of Frentista interviewees believed in the version proferred by their party, and only 46 per cent of Blanco supporters believed in the version supported by that party.[67] Public opinion was overwhelmingly opposed to the amnesty law. A Gallup poll of December 1986, showed that 68.1 per cent would not have voted for the amnesty law had they been legislators.[68] In January 1987, 74 per cent of Montevideans were opposed to the law and only 5 per cent thought that the law provided a definitive solution to the institutional crisis over the human rights issue. Moreover, 55 per cent believed that the military had been strengthened by the law, 51 per cent thought the legislature had been weakened, and 53 per cent felt that the democratic system as a whole had suffered a blow. When asked how they assessed the political solution offered by political parties to the issue, only 22 per cent were satisfied with the conduct of the Blanco Party. The Frente Amplio, who had voted against it, had the highest rate of approval with 89 per cent, and the Colorados were supported by 43 per cent.[69]

The greatest opinion poll in Uruguay was the referendum campaign itself. Montevideo, where the most well informed and educated members of the population live, voted in favour of derogating the amnesty law. Moreover, in many cases it is calculated that the votes in favour of the law were less an expression of a lack of concern over human rights than a recognition that the political situation had progressed beyond the point where justice could safely proceed. As a mitigating factor it must be taken into account that these results often reflect an ethical rather than a political assessment. Thus, in September 1986, 51 per cent of people believed that the military would never comply with court summonses. Similarly, 26 per cent of Montevideans thought that the military had the power to co-govern and 44 per cent believed that they had the power to determine events in specific matters.[70] It is ironic that in

Uruguay, the failure of the government to deal effectively with the legacies of military repression led to one of the most impressive exercises in democratic political participation. Uruguayan citizens have to take credit for their attempts to demand truth and justice through a referendum campaign which faced very harsh odds.

In Chile, on the other hand, whatever the failings of Aylwin's human rights policy, his actions were well regarded by public opinion. Belief in the President was high. Unlike Uruguay, he was seen to be wearing the trousers. His decision to represent 'the conscience of society' and to combine 'prudence with justice' was largely supported by the population.[71] According to a poll of April 1992, 55.9 per cent of people felt that the government inspired confidence.[72] Even the government's fiercest critics admitted that if more had not been done it was because of the enormous power of the military and the right and due to the legal *amarres* inherited from the Pinochet regime. Volodia Teitelboim, the leader of the Communist party, stated that Aylwin was a good and serious leader but that he had been limited by the fact that the 'country was tied, hand and foot.'[73] Similarly, the government's good will and efforts were recognized by one of the most radical human rights organizations, the AFEP: 'We have sustained a permanent relationship with the government and parliament and have jointly discussed the problem of justice'.[74] Aylwin's moral authority was also bolstered by international recognition of his efforts.[75]

A majority were also in favour of the government's truth-telling policy. When asked if they thought the Rettig Commission would contribute to reconciliation, 70.9 per cent believed it would, and only 23.1 per cent believed that it would cause more divisions.[76] When asked whether the President's Rettig speech had been positive, 91 per cent agreed.[77] None the less, the public was also aware of the insufficiencies of the truth. When asked if the Rettig report told the whole truth, 69 per cent believed it did not and only 25 per cent thought it did.[78] The government's prosecutions policy was also backed. In March 1987, when asked which was the sentence that best expressed their attitude to human rights violations, 9.6 per cent of Santiaguinos were in favour of not touching the past and forgetting what had occured, 51.3 per cent wanted the courts to investigate the violations and pardon the offenders, and 70.1 per cent wanted investigations followed by punishment.[79] In 1989, 67.5 per cent believed that human rights violations should be judged, 64.3 per cent thought they should be judged by the ordinary courts, and only 13.3 per cent believed trials should be conducted by a special tribunal. Only 22.9 per cent thought violators should be amnestied and 9.5 per cent that the military should be judged by military courts.[80] By March 1991, 80 per cent believed that the courts should undertake investigations and only 15 per cent disagreed.[81] However, in Chile, few believed that justice was needed for real democracy to exist in the country and the percentage declined as time went on. At the end of 1991, 26.1 per cent felt that justice was necessary, yet at the end of 1992, this figure had declined to 24.5 per cent.[82]

The government's attempts to reform the judiciary were also seemingly supported. In 1987, only 15.8 per cent thought that investigations should be in the hands of the existing judiciary, 69.3 per cent believed that they should be carried out by a reformed judicial power.[83] In 1992, only 14.2 per cent felt that the judiciary was operating acceptably, and 50.3 per cent felt that justice always favoured the powerful.[84] In 1992, 47.8 per cent felt that there would be no justice and truth in the cases already in the courts. Only 29.2 per cent believed that both truth and justice would be done by the courts.[85] The recent imprisonment of key offenders may change this level of scepticism. The sentencing of Contreras and Espinoza met with 65.8 per cent approval.[86] The balance of opinion on the sufficiency of measures of reparation was less positive. It was almost equally divided between negative and positive assessments: 42 per cent believed they were sufficient, and 46 per cent that they were not.[87]

Concluding Remarks

When assessing the Uruguayan and Chilean policies in the light of an ideal type, both fall short. Uruguay's attempts to come to terms with the legacies of repression failed to meet the legal and moral standards outlined in the introduction: by failing to comply with an international human rights standard; by not leading to a national, officially promoted acknowledgement of the truth and of the suffering of the victims of repression; by largely failing to offer material and moral measures of reparation for the victims; and finally, by not resulting in justice. In Chile, truth-telling was lacking in that the whole truth was not explored. The report did not include a case-by-case account from the victims of torture, or of other violations not resulting in death. More importantly, lacking the power to subpoena witnesses, the Commission and the Corporation were and continue to be unsuccessful in locating the disappeared. The question '*¿Dónde Están?*' is therefore still being asked.[88] Moreover, only very few people have actually been prosecuted and imprisoned for human rights violations.

The most positive feature of the Uruguayan case was the speedy and virtually uncontested release of the political prisoners; the greatest achievements in Chile were the official recognition of the truth of repression and the concomitant rejection of the military's ideological justification, the unmasking of the 'national security lie', the state's acknowledgement of the suffering of the victims and finally, its taking responsiblity for the compensation of those victims.

The definition of a successful human rights policy adopted in this book, however, makes it difficult to completely separate an assessment of an ideal from an assessment which takes political conditions into consideration; as noted in the introduction, one of the requirements of successful human rights policies in the transition to democracy is that such policies strengthen democratic institutions.

In each case political élites assessed differently where the dividing-line lay between strengthening democracy and weakening it. At the heart of this differing assessment are the following related questions: how far is it possible to consolidate a democracy in the absence of truth and justice? Are truth and justice for human rights violations the concern of the minority of those affected, in which case they are of little relevance to the grand scheme of democratic consolidation, or are they the necessary starting points through which a whole society assumes responsibility for its past actions and reconstitutes its democratic political myths and identity? Are truth and justice the means by which the 'logic of the democrats' begins to undermine the 'logic of the authoritarians' by strengthening the judiciary in a positive way to safeguard individual rights in the face of encroachment by the state and through which the democratic credentials and inclinations of the military are strengthened by destroying the national security logic which led to human rights violations in the first place? If one agrees with the former, as was the case of Uruguay's government, ignoring the human rights question in order to maintain stable relations with the military was right and proper. If one favours the latter, as the Chilean government did, ignoring the legacies of repression becomes as dangerous and undesirable as not doing so. The question of the link between democratic consolidation and policies of accountability will be the subject of the conclusions.

Conclusions

This book has illustrated, through the analysis of the Uruguayan and Chilean experiences, that the politics of truth and justice are intricately tied up with and shaped by the legacy of repressive rule, the dynamics of the politics of transition and of the balance of power under the new democratic governments peculiar to each country. It has also shown how the issue is central to the politics of transition for ethical and symbolic as well as practical and political reasons. Politically it is the most explosive transitional issue, and even its hasty burial because of fears of polarization and instability testify to the political importance of the problem.

At a practical level, only official acknowledgement can resolve pending legal questions which pose great problems for survivors and the families of victims. In Brazil, for example, relatives of the disappeared were unable to receive indemnity and collect life insurance in the absence of official recognition of the death of their relatives in the 1960s and 1970s. Only in 1995 was it finally announced that President Cardoso would officially acknowledge that the registered 152 disappeared are dead.[1]

At an ethical level, although politics are not ethics implemented, and although absolute moral standards are not the stuff of working government, without ideals and principles it is hard to generate democratic consensus, let alone the social endorsement for programmes of structural change and social reform without involving principles and ideals that appeal to the underlying values and aspirations of the citizenry. Admittedly, it can be argued that ideals 'smack of *hybris*, [and] are always excessive' but this is 'as it should be, since ideals are designed to overcome resistances . . . and the more the ideal is maximized, the greater, possibly, its efficacy.'[2] Demands for truth and justice may appear excessive when placed against the limitations imposed by reality, but they are not for that reason merely peripheral; on the contrary, they are central issues, products of inherited political expectations about what governments should and should not do to the people they preside over.

Dealing with legacies of state repression improves the ethical content of democratic politics. It may begin to unite a divided society. It permits a proper mourning for the dead and is therefore a first step in a process of healing. It may begin to mark a crucial break with the past. It permits the beginning of the process of the 'deconstruction of cultures of fear' without which democratization cannot occur. The principles governing calls for truth and justice are the ethical foundations upon which a healthy democratic politics can flourish since 'democracy is more than just tolerance; it involves recognizing the other as a co-participant in the creation of a common future'.[3]

This book has also demonstrated, on the basis of the cases examined, that truth-telling is not only desirable, but also that some kind of such policy has proved both necessary and feasible in a wide range of contemporary regime transitions. On the other hand, it is also shown that justice is not always possible. One can argue on a case-by-case basis that limitations on prosecutions are more self-imposed than 'structural', more political than institutional. Yet it is difficult to assess conclusively the 'correctness' of decisions not to prosecute in such uncertain circumstances and to know whether different choices would have produced better outcomes. Zalaquett, for example, argues that the Alfonsín administration attempted to go too far and subsequently lost political authority; others feel, on the other hand, that with more vision and courage, backtracking might not have been necessary.[4] Garretón, for example, throws a generally less positive light on the Chilean process than that presented in this book.

Whatever the correct view, clearly there is a tension between the conditions necessary to ensure accountability and those which govern periods of transition. This is because these democracies are not consolidated and therefore are not be able to practise the politics of a consolidated democracy. Among other things, the politics of consolidated democracies include the capacity to call the powerful to account. Indeed, perhaps this is the yardstick by which to measure consolidation. When the military are loyal enough to the democratic ideal to permit their members to be judged; when the judiciary is capable, through a necessary combination of autonomy and adherence to a culture of defence of civil and political rights, to pursue justice for individuals who are victims of state abuse, consolidation is clear. On the other hand, 'a consolidated democracy cannot be said to exist where there are groups or sectors that systematically enjoy immunity from the requirements of law'.[5]

Instead of practising the politics of consolidated democracy, what these countries have to engage in are the politics of democratic consolidation. Thus the analysis of the nature of civil–military relations in Uruguay given in *Búsqueda*:

> In a completely democratic regime, the military institution is firmly subordinated . . . through the President of the Republic who is constitutionally its Commander-in-Chief. In a completely democratic regime it is inconceivable that politicians of the party in power or the opposition should formally or informally exchange notes on their political positions and opinions and ask the military to do the same before a delegation of the Armed Forces—unless this occurs within a clearly determined constitutional framework.[6]

Is the pursuit of accountability for past abuses part of the politics of consolidation? Is it necessary for the consolidation of democracy? Although it is not easy to make clear-cut separations, the final argument put forward in this book is that the pursuit of accountability for past abuses is more a characteristic of the politics of transition than of consolidation and furthermore that it may not even be necessary for consolidation. It is part of the politics of transition because dealing with the legacies of state repression is a backward-looking, short-lived, and one-off policy issue. While it remains on the political agenda, it is politically explosive. Once it is resolved, be it positively or negatively, it largely disappears from the political map.

This is not to say that it does not remain relevant after the transition and 'leak into' the politics of democratization. It clearly lives on as part of a society's self-image and historical identity and can continue to be a source of conflict in the judicial system and of latent or overt painful and deep-seated social animosities. In Argentina, for example, although officially resolved, the human rights issue was re-kindled by the confession of two officers in October 1994 to the murder of two French nuns and by another officer in March 1995, who testified in gory detail about the dumping of over 1,000 drugged prisoners in the Mar de Plata with the collusion of the Church.[7] Even the old animosities of the Spanish Civil War are easily reopened, as recently demonstrated by the polemic raised by the decision of a Partido Popular representative to celebrate the pro-Franco poets of the Generation of 27.[8]

The resolution of the issue in the formal political arena, however, can and does make it marginal in terms of day-to-day politics. It is an issue which is qualitatively different from economic policy or government–labour relations which are ongoing sources of governmental concern. The nature of labour and entrepreneurial interests, political actors with the power to represent themselves continuously and effectively in the face of government inertia or hostility, makes them constituencies ignored only at a high political cost. The same can be said of the military which, by 'force of arms', can assert itself in the political sphere. By contrast, once democracy or simply a different regime is installed, the issue of past human rights violations is of immediate political importance only as long as it is a threat to the government. Precisely because they are a thing of the past, because the new regime is therefore not 'directly' politically responsible for these abuses, past human rights violations, once 'resolved' at the political level, become part of the policies which make up any given transition.

What of its impact on consolidation? If consolidation is the desired end, the means towards it is to strike at the cause of its absence, not the symptom. The inability to prosecute is more a symptom of the absence of consolidation than it is a cause. The ability to prosecute would indicate that the cause has been tackled and that democracy is already well on the way to consolidation. The cause is the distortion of key institutions which permit abuse and impunity; the means must be the thorough reform of the judiciary and of the forces of repression. Attempting to deal with the symptom may be a first step towards tackling the cause but, in and of itself, is neither sufficient nor precludes the desirable result of consolidating a democracy, whatever our 'democratic common sense' tells us. Chile, for example, went further than Uruguay in its politics of accountability, yet democratic consolidation is arguably further away than it is in Uruguay, where a greater level of democracy was demonstrated with the referendum campaign. In Chile, on the other hand, the legislature has often complained of the overweening power of the executive, and members of the Concertación have protested that the coalition often seemed to be a mere executor of government policy.[9] As Garretón has pointed out, social actors in Chile have been either inhibited or self-inhibited.[10]

What is clearly the case is that if a government does not undertake a proper reform of the institutions which made abuse and impunity possible, the democracy it presides over will be lame and incomplete. The reform of these institutions must be both legal and procedural as well as ideological. It is only with a fully functioning and independent judiciary whose members are imbued with the principles of human rights that accountability can be ensured. Similarly, it is only with a tamed military whose mission has been radically reformulated that one can prevent rebellion in the face of abuse, as well as further abuses.[11]

Neither Uruguay or Chile have fared well with such institutional reforms. As far as the judiciary is concerned, it is clear from the human rights saga in Uruguay that the judiciary is institutionally and politically much weaker than it is in Chile, even if it has demonstrated a greater democratic ethos. The Supreme Court was unable to resist the pressure placed upon it by the Colorado administration in the jurisdictional battle between the ordinary courts and the Supreme Military Tribunal. In Chile, on the other hand, the Supreme Court has demonstrated the great power that the judiciary has in the political process and its relative autonomy *vis-à-vis* the executive branch. Democratic empowerment will require a 'changing of the guard' as well as institutional reform to diminish the overly wide jurisdiction of the military courts.

Military reform has also presented problems in both countries. The Uruguayan government met with more success than the Chilean, principally because the military did not succeeded in passing an authoritarian constitution legally placing them 'above' the political system. The system of promotion was placed under civilian control and the mission of the Armed Forces was modified. Despite these reforms, however, signs of continued fear and military autonomy emerge with regularity. In June 1993, President La calle cancelled a trip to Europe in order to deal with a military crisis caused by the kidnapping of a DINA agent implicating both the Chilean and the Uruguayan military. The head of the Servicio de Información del Ejército, however, was reassigned and not dismissed. The caution recommended on all sides of the political spectrum to deal with this 'crisis' demonstrated how the military continue to exercise a 'threatening' power over elected civilian authorities.[12]

In Chile, the military reforms met with success in some areas. The government managed to reduce the Army's participation in the anti-terrorist campaign, with the Carabineros placed at the forefront of the campaign under the jurisdiction of the Ministry of the Interior. It refused to re-activate the DINA as Pinochet demanded, creating instead a new information agency within the Carabineros, the Dirección de Inteligencia de Policia de Carabineros (DIPOLCAR). It also rejected the Army's interpretation of terrorism as a manifestation of continued international communist aggression.[13] The reform of the police force also met with some success.[14]

More fundamentally, however, both the Aylwin and Frei governments were unable to challenge institutional autonomy and prerogatives. The Aylwin government attempted to reform the Organic

Constitutional Law of the Armed Forces which ensured the immobility of the Commanders in Chief but it was essentially forced to back down.[15] Frei's attempts to put this reform on the agenda have also failed. Moreover, in contrast to the military in Uruguay as well as Argentina, where severe budget cuts have obviously weakened military power, the Chilean defence budget continues to be one of the highest in Latin America.[16] The military has succeeded in retaining the law ensuring a 'defence' tax which consists of 10 per cent of the state copper company's yearly revenues. They have also retained pension rights which far exceed those of any other social group or corporation and the army's conscript base of 25,000 with an almost equal amount of officers, is one of the highest in the Southern Cone.[17]

As noted above, there is a clear link that can be made between consolidation and this kind of institutional reform. The politics of backward-looking truth and justice may, and for the moral and practical reasons outlined above, should, be a part of this process, but they are not strictly necessary either to ensure its success or to advance with democratic consolidation. None the less, as noted in the introduction, it is best not to assess the politics of *Nunca Más* too narrowly, according to an instrumental logic. These policies are necessary and desirable above and beyond their contribution to consolidation. This is why the clear-cut 'exchange' advocated by the Sanguinetti administration in Uruguay between military subordination and impunity is so unsatisfactory.

The need for institutional reform is apparent in Latin America as a whole, where more complete democratization 'is hindered by constitutional guarantees of regimes of exception and expanded missions for the armed forces, buttressed by statutes and national security laws enacted both during and since military rule by military jurisdiction over civilians as well as by lingering fears of a military response should civilian governments be deemed to have acted "imprudently" in matters of concern to the armed forces'.[18] In Peru, for example, Fujimori's *auto-golpe* of April 1992 was undertaken under pressure from a military concerned with Congressional opposition to an amnesty.[19]

The authoritarian ethos can be found alive and kicking everywhere. When the Brazilian Minister of Justice attempted to prosecute military officers who had killed three people during the violent suppression of a strike at the Volta Redonda steel plant in 1988, the Minister of the Army both prevented prosecution and decorated the soldiers involved.[20] In May 1995, the Minister of Defence in El Salvador justified the dirty war in defence of the 'institutionality' of the state.[21] In July 1995, General Bussi, a retired general involved in the Argentine dirty war in Tucumán was actually democratically elected in the provincial elections heading the Defensa Provincial Bandera Blanca party he founded in 1987.[22] Even in Spain, some of those involved in the dirty war against the ETA have justified the use of torture and kidnapping on the grounds that they were acting for the greater good, an argument which duplicated those espoused by the generals of the dirty wars in Latin America.[23]

Moreover, threats to physical integrity through disappearance, torture, and extrajudicial executions are grave problems under elected civilian government in Colombia, Peru, Guatemala, El Salvador, and Brazil, among many other countries. In Brazil, more than 1,000 peasants and rural trade union leaders have been murdered since the arrival of democracy. In only 30 cases have the criminals been condemned.[24] In Colombia, 1,542 members of leading trade unions have been killed since 1986. No one has been called to account.[25] Continued impunity may even threaten to bring the military back to centre stage. In El Salvador, the new National Police Force (PNC) continues to violate rights, overwhelmed by a crime-wave related to poverty, drugs, and former death squad activity. In February 1995, President Calderón Sol ordered the military to provide the PNC with support.[26] Brazil also resorted to a similar measure in 1994, using the military to control crimes in Rio de Janeiro.

Lack of accountability breeds 'paralegal' violence fed by 'unregulated social spaces' emerging from wide-spread poverty, drug-trafficking, money-laundering, mineral prospecting, and public works profiteering.[27] Under elected civilian rule today, threats to physical integrity predominantly affect not middle-class individuals involved in left-wing political activity, but marginals and/or criminals excluded from true citizenship:

> The death squads and the street children that are their victims are perhaps the best example of this new category of people who live on the fringes of state and society. They represent a blurring of the frontiers between the legitimate and the illegitimate. In spite of their living in between the limits of society, we should not ignore their growing centrality in terms of the sheer number and social relevance of these people who both physically and symbolically occupy the centre of many Latin American cities.[28]

Following on from the above, it is clear that there are two separate issues to be dealt with whose common denominator is impunity.

On the one hand, there is the question of backward-looking justice, an issue which is classically associated with periods of regime transition and the subject of this book. Another is the question of 'contemporaneous' justice and impunity, which is a subject of ongoing and fundamental concern to the process of democratization.[29] Although separable, the problems of past and contemporaneous abuse overlap. It has been argued that truth and justice for past abuses are not in and of themselves necessary for the consolidation of democracy; none the less, the principles which lead governments to do something about the issue are those which inform the decisions of democratic rulers who want to make all individuals democratic citizens (people who feel they have rights and therefore accept duties).[30] Unless contemporaneous abuse is dealt with, the problem of accountability for past abuse will keep reappearing and the consolidation of democracy will grow increasingly distant. The link between past and contemporaneous impunity is graphically illustrated by the former (unpunished) participants in dirty wars crossing the boundary into criminal activity. Such is the case of the Polibanda in Argentina, a group of former 'dirty war' police officers who engaged in kidnappings and other forms of organized crime in 1991 and 1992.[31] The absence of enforceable rights makes for weak duties or democratic principles. With judicial systems unable or politicians unwilling to deal with insecurity and violent crime, illegal violence often carries the seal of approval of middle class populations who feel under siege: Brazilian opinion polls show that a great number of people are in favour of assassinations of criminals carried out by the police.[32]

It is worrying that democratic governments seem less willing to admit to contemporaneous police abuse and use of torture than to the same phenomena under military rule. President Aylwin, for example, the Latin American champion of truth-telling, reacted very defensively when the military killed and wounded a number of people in Santiago in October 1993 after opening fire on a bus in pursuit of terrorist suspects. He has also rejected Amnesty International reports of torture under his rule.[33] President Menem's response to the confessions made by Scilingo, for example, was more accepting of the logic justifying the 'dirty war' than the reaction of the new Commander-in-Chief of the Army. Menem praised the role of the military in the dirty war, removed the offending Captain from active duty, and promoted another involved in human rights violations;[34] Commander-in-Chief Balza, on the other hand, became the first active duty general in Latin America to reject the justifications of illegal repression. He had the moral and political courage to state that the military should assume their share of guilt, that it was a crime to contravene the Constitution, to give and carry out immoral orders and to seek to achieve a just end by unjust immoral means.[35] Similarly, having got rid of communist domination, some democratically elected governments in Eastern Europe are now only too happy to ignore the persecution of Roma (gypsy) people.[36]

The violations of the rights of 'people who nobody likes' pose a central problem not only for new democracies but also in many long-established democracies. Accountability should not, according to democratic principle, be a privilege only of middle class political dissidents. A positive step towards recognizing this problem was taken in Brazil in February 1995, when the Foreign Ministry sent to the United Nations a report drawn up in conjunction with a human rights group and the University of São Paulo. For the first time the Brazil officially recognized that approximately 30 per cent of Rio de Janeiro police agents participate in extermination groups.[37] There is a danger, however, that truth-telling or admission of violations by the state, become an 'easy substitute' for real action. Admission by the Brazilian state was accompanied by assurances that the military would not be called to account. Colombia's President has recently apologized on behalf of the State to the relatives of the disappeared; on the other hand, however, he vetoed a Disappearance Law in July 1994 proposed by Congress and human rights organizations which would have placed the crime under civilian jurisdiction.[38]

Accountability is an issue which needs to be dealt with by all democracies, including the most developed. In Spain, the recent scandal over the discovery that para-military Grupos Anti-Terroristas de Liberación GAL (Anti-Terrorist Liberation Groups) which kidnapped, tortured and disappeared real and presumed members of the ETA, were part of a police and military co-ordinated anti-terrorism campaign designed by top government ministers with the possible knowledge of the president himself, shows that dirty wars are not solely the speciality of military authoritarian regimes. As one observer has noted, this case 'has led to the extraordinary situation for a Western European nation that a judge has raised the "hypothetical" case that a prime-minister in office—and acting European President—might be charged with "promoting an armed group or terrorist organization".'[39]

Recent revelations that US government bodies participated directly in the Salvadorean, Honduran, and Guatemalan human rights disasters suggests that lack of accountability strikes at the very heart of the greatest 'exporter' of democratic values.[40] Spain's 'dirty war' revelations, systematic police abuse accompanying the growth of anti-immigrant and racist violence in Europe, as well as the American example cited above, demonstrate that these are not merely 'third world' issues. Furthermore, national action against impunity needs to be bolstered by measures adopted at the regional as well as international levels. Impunity cannot be combated unless the more powerful countries participate in the international system in such a way as to strengthen existing legal mechanisms to counter impunity. Yet they are often the first to balk at subordination to international human rights law. As one observer has noted, Washington's 'traditional unwillingness to subject itself to international human rights mechanisms' is partially informed by 'the desire to avoid prosecution of American pilots or soldiers.'[41] Another example of internationally sanctioned impunity is the Governor's Island Agreement brokered to allow Aristide to return to Haiti whilst simultaneously ensuring that the military rulers would not be called to account for human rights violations.[42] Well-connected international campaigns can create the conditions for a successful prosecution of human rights violators as demonstrated by the Contreras and Harbury cases, as well as by the dismissal of Captain Astíz from the Argentine Navy following French diplomatic pressure.[43]

The myth of the 'end of history' and of a brave new world of global democratization has collapsed after the initial euphoria produced by the fall of the Berlin Wall and in the face of evidence of the rise of nationalisms in Europe and elsewhere; the war in the former-Yugoslavia and the inability of the European Union and its democratic allies to put a stop to the genocide being committed on its doorstep; the evidence of the rise of human rights violations in the democratic and non-democratic world. All of this clearly demonstrates that the utopias that 'designed societies in which rights arising from equalities and liberties were guaranteed' are in crisis and need to be reformulated urgently everywhere.[44] Despite the overwhelming emphasis on the political aspects of democratization, the social dimension of the process of democratic deepening needs to be addressed if one is to come to terms with violations of basic rights and the lack of widespread consolidated citizenship stemming from social inequality and extreme poverty. Having recaptured the importance of the formal dimension of democratic procedure, and in the face of evidence that there is no automatic link between the formal establishment of democracy and more profound social democratization, it is necessary to re-think and discover the crucial links between the two dimensions.

Negligence in dealing with the repressive actions of a preceding non-democratic government may not disqualify a regime's formal democratic credentials, but if a regime is to maintain and legitimize its democratic credentials the state must not only cease to violate but also begin to create the necessary conditions so that the basic human rights of all members of society are safeguarded. This book concludes with the assertion that this is the task at hand.

Notes

Introduction

1. Linz (1988), pp. 1 and 5.
2. Rial (1986a), p. 46.
3. Schmitter (1980).
4. Nunca Mais (1985). See also Barahona de Brito (1991); Dassin (1986); Weschler (1990).
5. In El Salvador by the UN Mission ONUSAL. In Guatemala by the UN-sponsored MINUGUA and in Namibia by the Red Cross.
6. In Brazil, individuals from the Catholic Church were aided by the World Council of Churches (Geneva). In Rwanda by Africa Watch (USA), Federation Internationale des Droits de l'Homme (France), Union Inter-Africaine des Droits de l'Homme et des Peuples (Burkina Faso), and the Centre Internationale des Droits de la Personne et du Développement Démocratique (Canada). In Honduras, Americas Watch (USA) and the Centre for Justice and International Law (US) co-operated with national NGOs and the National Commissioner for Human Rights.
7. Hayner (1994). For other studies of truth commissions see Carver (1990); Benomar (1993); Cassell (1993); Ensalaco (1994); Pasqualucci (1994).
8. Please refer to the first chapter for description of and relevant bibliography for these cases.
9. Hertz (1978), p. 560.
10. Typical references are O'Donnell, Schmitter, and Whitehead (1986a), pp. 131–33; (1986b), pp. 28–32; (1986c), pp. 28–9; Whitehead (1989), p. 83–4; Hakim and Lowenthal (1990), p. 28; Linz and Stepan (1989), p. 48; Linz *et al.* (1989), pp. 373–7; Gillespie (1986a), p. 195; (1992), pp. 194–5 and 198–201.
11. See, for example, *General*: Benomar (1993); Cassell Jr. (1993); Claude (1983); De Zurilla (1981); Egeland (1982); Garretón (1994); Garro (1990); Hampson (1995); Hertz (1978), (1982); Kaplan (1980); Kritz (1994); Medina Quiroga (1988); Méndez and Vivanco (1990); Orentlicher (1991); Pasqualucci (1994); Paust *et al.* (1990); Pion-Berlin (1994); Rickard (1981); Roht-Arriaza (1990), (1995); Sikkink (1991); Tobin *et al.* (1990); Wilde *et al.* (1990); Zalaquett (1988), (1992). *On Uruguay*: Araújo (1989); Burt (1988), (1989); Cassinelli Muñoz

(1987); IELSUR (1984); López Goldaracena (1986); Perelli (1987d); Pérez Aguirre (1986), (1987); Rial (1986a); Tribunal Permanente de los Pueblos (1990); *On Chile*: Aylwin (1995); Brett (1992); Correa (1992); Detzner (1989), (1991); Ensalaco (1994); Frühling (1985a), (1986b), (1987); López Dawson (1986); Mera (1986); Mera *et al.* (1989); Orellana and Frühling (1991); Sánchez (1990); J. E. Vargas (1990a); M. C. Vargas (1990b); Wiessbrodt and Fraser (1992); Zalaquett (1989), (1995). *On Argentina*: Acuña and Smulovitz (1991); Asociación Americana de Juristas (1988); Crawford (1990); Garro and Dahl (1987); Groisman (1985); Jelin (1994); Malamud-Goti (1989); Mignone (1992); Mignone *et al.* (1984); Nino (1985), (1991); Osiel (1987); Rogers (1990); Weissbrodt and Bartolomei (1991). For other countries and list of reports by international human rights organizations see the References.

12. State Crimes Conference, Aspen Institute, Maryland (1988); 'Truth and Justice, the Delicate Balance', Budapest, Hungary (1990); 'Reconciliation in Times of Transition', San Salvador, El Salvador (1991); 'Justice in Times of Transition', Salzburg, Austria (1992); 'Dealing with the Past', Capetown, South Africa (1994); 'South Africa Conference on Truth and Reconciliation', Capetown, South Africa (1995). An example of a project is the Project for Justice in Times of Transition of the Foundation for a Civil Society sponsored by the Soros Foundation (1993). Numerous national conferences have also focused on the subject.
13. Books include Hertz (1982), which covers Germany, Italy, Austria, Japan, Portugal, and Greece and is the first such comparative analysis; Weschler (1990) compares the *Nunca Más* reports in Brazil and Uruguay; Carver (1990), Benomar (1993), Cassell (1993), Ensalaco (1994), Hayner (1994), and Pasqualucci (1994) examine a number of truth commissions comparatively. Rosenberg (1995) compares the Eastern European cases. Frühling (1985b) and (1991b) and Frühling *et al.* (1989) examine comparatively the role of human rights organizations in transitions. Zalaquett (1988) discusses Argentina and Uruguay. Excellent single-country analyses of the Argentine case, which examine types of transitions and their impact on legacy policies, include: Nino (1985), (1991), Acuña and Smulovitz (1991), and Smulovitz (1995). Most comparative assessments have been undertaken at the aforementioned international conferences.
14. See Zalaquett (1995), pp. 51–2; Du Toit (1995), p. 131.
15. Truth-telling is usually undertaken in the wake of extreme ideological polarization in which two radically opposed ideological views of events exist. Only a partial common ground will therefore be established by official truth-telling. Comment by Whitehead, 13 Aug. 1995.
16. Dworkin (1995), pp. 43–6.
17. Comments made by Laurence Whitehead at the 'Conference on a Comparative Analysis of Transitions in Chile and South Africa', Capetown, Nov. 1995.

18. For the legal and political dilemmas and ironies of this problem see: Malamud-Goti (1989), pp. 72–3. While individual prosecution is a farce in some senses, collective or institutional prosecution can be unjust in that innocent individuals are not afforded an individual defence.
19. As noted by Zalaquett, punishment cannot be revenge and it is better to be limited than to undermine the rule of law: Zalaquett (1988), p. 42, and Zalaquett (1994), p. 104.
20. Zalaquett (1988), p. 54. Exceptions are the Truth Commissions of Rwanda and El Salvador, which were undertaken by outside groups or organizations, of South Africa, where amnesty is ensured, and in the Chad.
21. Corradi (1992), p. 287.
22. Burton (1994), p. 120.
23. Du Toit (1994), p. 132.
24. The title *Nunca Más*, adopted by a series of truth-telling reports in Latin America, is an implicit reference to deterrence.
25. Zalaquett (1988), p. 27. For the strong view of state duty to prosecute see: Orentlicher (1991); Roht-Arriaza (1990). For the weaker view see: Zalaquett (1988); Nino (1991).
26. Neier argues that justice should not be subject to majority consensus, as it has a retributionist value and moreover responds to the needs of minorities: Neier (1994b), pp. 99–102.
27. Corradi (1992), pp. 285–6.
28. Perelli (1993), p. 154.
29. Neier (1994a), p. 2, quoting Michael Ignatieff. See also: Corradi (1992), pp. 285–6. On the battle over history see: Index on Censorship (1995); Michnik (1994), pp. 15–18.
30. Krog (1995), pp. 112–19. For the damaging effects of repression and impunity refer to the following chapter.
31. Rosenberg (1994a), p. 66.
32. Zalaquett (1994) p. 15.
33. On the importance of official truth-telling see: Aylwin (1995), pp. 38–43; Zalaquett (1995), pp. 44–55. Some would argue that there is a right to truth established by international law: La Rue (1995), pp. 73–81.
34. As Michnik states 'history shows that which is presented as a demand for justice can become a tool in the battle for power.' Michnik (1994), p. 17.
35. Sachs (1994), p. 127. See also p. 126 on difficulties of suddenly seeing a government as 'ours' after years of seeing it as 'the enemy'.
36. Zalaquett (1994), p. 15.
37. As noted above, the names of the perpetrators of human rights violations, an indispensable part of the truth, are often left out of truth-telling reports to avoid trial by publicity, with criminal charges being brought against individuals without formal charges. For Argentina see: Zalaquett (1988), p. 54.

38. Zalaquett (1994), p. 13.
39. This scheme is largely based on the Human Rights Watch (1989) policy document.
40. See: Garretón (1994) and Loveman (1994) for issues of military reform.
41. Brandon Hamber quoted in 'Firing Up the Truth Machine'. *Mail and Guardian*, 28 July–3 Aug. 1995, p. 8.
42. Lipset and Rokkan (1967), p. 37.

Chapter 1

1. Bettleheim quoted in Perelli (1992), p. 221; Politzer (1985), p. 11.
2. Corradi (1992), p. 281.
3. Garretón (1992), p. 17; O'Donnell (1989), pp. 66–7.
4. Arriagada (1986a), p. 70.
5. Martins (1986), p. 72.
6. For an analysis of the links between regime types and human rights violations see: Linz (1988).
7. Dahl (1971), pp. 15–16. For the subversive impact of human rights defence see: Frühling (1986a), p. 21.
8. Ibid., pp. 18–19 and 31.
9. Linz and Stepan (1989), p. 47.
10. Weinstein (1988), p. 22. See also: Taylor (1952), pp. 312–13; (1960), p. 23.
11. Taylor (1960), p. 57. On apoliticism and isolation from civilian life see: Barros-Lémez (1987), pp. 35 and 57.
12. It was seen to be the model country: Vanger (1980), p. vii.
13. Taylor (1960), p. 69.
14. Valenzuela (1978); Lipset and Rokkan (1967).
15. After Canada, the United Kingdom, the United States, and Switzerland: Agor (1971), p. 5.
16. Nunn (1976), pp. 221 and 236.
17. Brett (1992), p. 213.
18. Maran (1989), p. 37.
19. For traditional constitutional military prerogatives see: Loveman (1993b). For the NSD justifying human rights violations see the following chapter. For tensions produced by human rights violations for authoritarian regimes see: Garretón (1982). For the crucial role of the Church as moral opposition see: Comblin (1979b); Lowden (1996).
20. Macridis (1982), p. 169–76.
21. For the transitions see: Hertz (1982). For the trials and de-Nazification see: Appleman (1954); Conot (1983); Hertz (1982); Hertz (1988); Brackman (1987).
22. Hertz (1982), p. 20.
23. For juridical problems faced by the Tribunal see: Woetzel (1960), p. 92 ff.

24. 'Bosnia in Light of the Holocaust: War Crime Tribunals', Madeleine K. Albright, US Permanent Representative to the United Nations, *US Department of State Dispatch*, 18 Apr. 1994, vol 5., no. 16, pp. 209–12. For war crimes see: HW (1991c); (1992c); (1993d). For problems facing the Tribunal see: HW (1993a); (1994). For a successful international prosecution of a Paraguayan torturer in US courts see Claude (1983), pp. 275–301; Rickard (1981).
25. See: 'Goldstone Hands Down Genocide Indictments', *Mail and Guardian*, 15–21 Dec. 1995, p. 13.
26. Costa Pinto (1994), pp. 1 and 25.
27. OAS-IACHR (1981), p. 93. Although a Commission for the Protection and Promotion of Human Rights was set up to review these cases, it did not carry out a satisfactory task. AI (1986). For violations see: OAS-IACHR (1981); AW (1989e).
28. For an excellent account of dealing with the past in Eastern Europe see Rosenberg (1995).
29. HW (1992a), p. 4. 'Lustration' is derived from the Latin for purification and described StB loyalty checks under Communist rule. Savage purges had taken place with the fall of the Third Reich in 1945 and again in 1948 with the Communist takeover. An estimated 200,000 people out of a total population of 15 million were put in gaol, camps, or used as slave labour: Schwarzenberg (1994), p. 81. For a similar process in Albania see: 'Albania Plans Law to Purge Ex-Communists', *Financial Times*, 25 Oct. 1995.
30. For a description of the political situation and splits see: HW (1993b) and Petrova (1994), pp. 75–80. The Law for Temporary Introduction of Additional Requirements for Members of the Executive Bodies of the Scientific Organizations and the Higher Certifying Commission of December 1992 was upheld by the Supreme Court: HW (1993b), p. 5.
31. Osiatynski (1994), pp. 62–3.
32. Rosenberg (1994b), p. 96.
33. Steven Engelberg, 'The Velvet Revolution Gets Tough', *New York Times Magazine*, 31 May 1992, pp. 30–54. Also: AW (1992c).
34. Two bills for tracing the names of informants failed to be passed: Osiatynski (1994), p. 62. For Bulgaria see: Petrova (1994), p. 78. For the Czech Republic see: Schwarzenberg (1994), p. 8. For Poland see: Michnik (1994), p. 17. For Germany, where truth-telling consisted of gaining access to the files kept by secret police, see: Gauck (1994), p. 71.
35. In Czechoslovakia around 3,000 judges were fired and in 1992 a third of these posts were still vacant. Bulgaria's Supreme Administrative Court does not exist due to lack of resources and staff. Rosenberg (1994b), p. 95. The costs of these initiatives can also be very high. For the high cost of processing Stasi files in Germany see: Gauck (1994), p. 72.
36. Rosenberg (1994b), p. 96.

37. On the Commission see: Benomar (1993).
38. Rosenberg (1994b), p. 97. In May 1995, the German Constitutional Court determined that German citizens could not be prosecuted for spying for the former Communist East German State. The decision led to the annulment of over 6,300 cases against former East Germans including the Markus Wolf case. German Unification also poses the problem of judging former East Germans under a legal system of what is effectively a new country. See: 'Germany Abandons Trials for Many Ex-East German Spies', *Financial Times*, 24 May 1995; 'Impossible Justice After the Cold War', *El País*, 25 May 1995. The decision not to prosecute former premier Honnecker (leader and planner) also makes it difficult to justify the prosecution of common soldiers who followed orders in shooting individuals attempting to escape over the Berlin Wall on orders.
39. HW (1990).
40. For Hungary see: Sajo (1994), p. 65.
41. For Bulgaria see: HW (1993b). At the end of 1994 between 50 and 60 people were being investigated for past human rights violations in Bulgaria: ibid., pp. 17–18. These trials are still ongoing: HRW (1995a), p. 200. For Romania see: HW (1990). In March 1994, all former members of the Romanian CP involved in the December 1989 massacre were pardoned by law: see: HRW (1995a).
42. Sajo (1994), p. 64. Poland has no statute of limitations and is prosecuting torturers of the early Stalinist period of the late 1940s and early 1950s see: Rosenberg (1994b), p. 94.
43. See: AW (1992b); AW (1993b); 'García Meza: Del Exílio a la Cárcel', *El País*, 16 Mar. 1995, p. 72.
44. Gunther (1992), p. 77. The central issue was the release of political prisoners: ibid., pp. 47–8. According to Salas Larrazabal, 271,444 people were killed during the Civil War, but 47% of these were not killed in action but under the repression that followed. Salas Larrazabal is quoted in Rodrigo (1992), pp. 8 and 9.
45. Sanders (1981a), pp. 186–7 and pp. 192–5; Skidmore (1988), pp. 218–19 and p. 269; Dassin (1986); Weschler (1990); Barahona de Brito (1991).
46. ICJ (1991b).
47. The main issue at stake was the fate of detainees held by both sides. In June 1991 the government asked the Red Cross to investigate the cases of people who went missing during the armed struggle: Africa Watch (1992a).
48. See: ICJ (1972); AI (1983b); (1989); Carver (1990).
49. HRW (1995a), pp. xxii and 16–21.
50. Hayner (1994), p. 635.
51. AW (1991d) and AW (1994a). The Central American Peace Plan had previously led to the release of many political prisoners. In November 1979, 985 people held for security-related crimes were pardoned; in March 1988, 100 prisoners selected by the Contras on the occasion

of a partial cease-fire were released; 1,800 former National Guardsmen were pardoned in April 1989. A remaining 30 were finally released in early 1990. See: AW (1989e), pp. 15–17. In September 1993, Chamorro declared an end to amnesties for crimes committed by rearmed groups. A Comisión de Verificación y Apoyo or the Tripartite Commission composed of the OAS, the Church, and the Foreign and Interior Ministries of Nicaragua was set up to oversee demobilization and the human rights situation of demobilized fighters and their families. After the war it also began to investigate the continued murder of disarmed Contras by presumed Sandinistas. AW (1994a).

52. Hayner (1994), pp. 653–4.
53. See: HRW (1995b), pp. 80–96; AI (1995).
54. HRW (1995), pp. 1–17. See also: 'Ruanda Quiere Importar 600 Jueces', *El País*, 16 Mar. 1995.
55. See: Hayner (1994), p. 630.
56. AW (1993a), p. 4. The report ordered a ten-year ban from public office and a life ban from public security positions for all those named. It recommended the immediate suspension of the whole of the Supreme Court for its responsibility in impunity, a full investigation into armed squad activity, and the reform of the Armed Forces and the Judiciary. The Ad Hoc Commission surprisingly called for the dismissal or transfer of 103 officers, including the Minister and Vice-Minister of Defence. 'El Salvador: The Truth Comes Out', *International Herald Tribune*, 23 Mar. 1995. See also: AW (1991b); IJC (1991a); Veverka (1992); UN (1993); Buergenthal (1994); Tappatá de Valdez (1995). For the problem of violations on both sides of civil conflict in El Salvador: AW (1989b); (1990b).
57. The amnesty law passed 47–9, with 13 abstentions. See: 'La Depuración en del Ejército en Aras de la Paz Fue Exagerada, Cristiani', *El País*, 24 Apr. 1995; 'UN Leave with Praise and Warning', *Caribbean and Central America Report*, RC-95-04, 18 May 1995, p. 2. The assassination of six Jesuit priests in 1989 led to the trial of nine officers but the jury acquitted seven of them, despite detailed confession. See: AW (1991b); ICJ (1991a); Stahler-Sholk (1994).
58. 'Counting the Toll of State Terrorism', *Latin America Weekly Report*, 8 June 1995, p. 249.
59. AW (1994b), p. 4.
60. See: HRW (1994).
61. AW (1990c), p. 1. See also: AW (1989d) and Méndez and Vivanco (1990). The Court has since made a similar ruling on two other cases but to date the government has still not paid compensation.
62. Walter and Williams (1993), pp. 39–88; 'Blocks Remain on Path to El Salvador Peace', *Financial Times*, 3 Apr. 1995. For advantages and disadvantages of internationally led solutions see: Hayner (1994), pp. 642–3.
63. See: HRW (1995a), p. xxii. MINUGUA issued a report on the human

rights situation in 1995, which also implicated the CIA and thus set off a demand for a parallel investigation in the US. See: AW (1995) and 'Could CIA Exposé Affect Peace Talks', *Latin American Weekly Report*, 11 May 1995, p. 197; AW (1995).

64. IRELA (1995).
65. See: 'Potential Witnesses are Murdered', *Latin American Weekly Report*, 9 Nov. 1995, p. 515; 'New Twist in Human Rights Trials', *Latin American Weekly Report*, 14 Dec. 1995; 'Row Over Amnesty for the Military', *Latin American Weekly Report*, 21 Dec. 1995, p. 579; 'Honduras, Prosecutors Take on the Military', *International Herald Tribune*, 18 Oct. 1995.
66. AW (1995), p. 106. For Honduras: 'Honduras, Prosecutors Take on the Military', *International Herald Tribune*, 18 Oct. 1995.
67. See: CONADEP (1984); Mignone *et al.* (1984); Groisman (1985); Nino (1985), (1991); AW (1987b); AI (1987); Garro and Dahl (1987); Osiel (1987); Asociación Americana de Juristas (1988); Malamud-Goti (1989); Zalaquett (1988); Crawford (1990); AW (1991f); AI (1991a); Acuña and Smulovitz (1991); Barahona de Brito (1991); Weissbrodt and Bartolomei (1991); Méndez (1994a); Jelin (1994); Smulovitz (1995).
68. AI (1975b). Psomiades (1982), pp. 262–5.
69. Schlemmer (1995), p. 1.
70. Despite attempts by the dissident *militante* faction or *Movimiento Institucionalista Colorado* (MIC) to arrange for the return and amnesty of General Stroessner, President Carlos Wasmosy, leading a minority faction in the Colorado Party, has declared that if he returns he must face charges: 'Return of Stroessner', *Southern Cone Report*, RS-95-03, 20 Apr. 1995, p. 3. Since the trial noted above, only two members of the military have been indicted in human rights trials. One served his sentence at home and charges against the other were dropped. At the end of 1989 there were 54 cases of human rights violations in the courts; by April 1992, only 17 were still ongoing: AW (1992c).
71. The new government also still has to deal with continued violence and lawlessness on a large scale, resulting from the rivalry between the ANC and the Inkatha Freedom Party (IFP). On continued violence: HRW (1995b), pp. 45–66. See also: Omar (1995); Boraine and Levy (1995); Boraine *et al.* (1994); 'Mandela to Probe Apartheid Crimes', *International Herald Tribune*, 19 Aug. 1994.
72. 'Much to Learn form South Africa's Miracle', *International Herald Tribune*, 30 Apr. 1994.
73. 'Reconciliation: Mandela Finds a Sound Model in Chile', *International Herald Tribune*, 13 Aug. 1994; 'South Africa: Truth Commission', *Oxford Analytica Daily Brief*, 4 July 1995.
74. 'How the Commission Will Work', *Mail and Guardian*, 28 July–3 Aug. 1995, p. 8.
75. 'Avoiding the Inevitable', *Mail and Guardian*, 5–11 Jan. 1996, p. 4.

76. 'PW Could Face Prison', *Mail and Guardian*, 24–30 Nov. 1995, p. 4.
77. This has already started happening as security force operatives, fearing that other colleagues will speak to the commission, have already testified before the Goldstone Commission set up to investigate political violence or gone to the press to 'bolster their appeals for pardon', *Mail and Guardian*, 28 July–3 Aug. 1995, p. 9.
78. 'South Africa to Charge 11', *International Herald Tribune*, 30 Oct. 1995; 'South Africa Charges Ex-Defence Chief', *International Herald Tribune*, 3 Nov. 1995; 'Caprivi Camp at the Heart of Evidence Against Generals', *Mail and Guardian*, 24–30 Nov. 1995, pp. 10–11.
79. 'President Tames the Afrikaner Tiger', *Mail and Guardian*, 24–30 Nov. 1995, p. 5.
80. The studies referred to are: O'Donnell *et al.* (1986c), p. 3 and Linz *et al.* (1990), p. xiii.
81. Danopolous (1992), p. 50 quoting Cronin (1989). For the importance of leadership see: Linz *et al.* (1989), p. 11. Implicit in: Boeker (1990); Linz and Stepan (1989).
82. The only comparable system is the Swiss: Lijphart (1977), pp. 212–16. It was founded by president José Batlle y Ordoñez, who was critical of the political and philosophical foundation of modern Uruguay. It has been said that Uruguay is only 'the lengthened shadow' of this man: Fitzgibbon (1954), p. 122. For the formative impact of Batllismo see: Vanger (1963); (1980); Barrán y Nahúm (1979), pp. 213–68; Finch (1990), pp. 4–10; Perelli (1985); Panizza (1990), pp. 37–53.
83. On system see: Pérez (1971); Caetano (1983a), p. 59.
84. Parties represented a cross-section of all groups and classes: Real de Azúa (1971), p. 66.
85. González (1984), p. 3.
86. The system prevented the emergence and participation of smaller or extra-system parties: Gillespie (1985). Repression was exerted not through violence but through electoral engineering: Rial (1984c), pp. 105–9. After the Terra dictatorship, electoral legislation ensured that the dominant parties controlled the party names or *lemas*: Caetano and Rilla (1985), pp. 35–6.
87. Angel (1990); Angell and Carstairs (1987) for the impact of exile, and Angell and Pollack (1990) for the reformed party system since 1989.
88. Linz *et al.* (1989), p. 11.
89. Skidmore (1988), p. 269; Sanders (1981a), p. 161.
90. Real de Azúa (1984). A close translation would be 'a shock-absorbing society'.
91. Taylor (1960).
92. Uruguay was ruled by a Collegial executive between 1918–1933 and 1952–66, by a President and the Council of Government, a nine-man executive whose objective was to allow for bi-partisan power-sharing. On the collegiate executive see: Vanger (1980), p. 162; Lindahl

(1962), pp. 26–7, 34–5. The 1934 Constitution gave the two parties achieving most votes 15 out of the 30 seats in the Senate. Taylor (1960), p. 20; Finch (1990), pp. 10–17. Shared patronage of the state enterprises was inaugurated with the famous Pacto del Chinchulín in 1933 under the Presidency of Terra: Weinstein (1988), p. 31; Caetano (1983b), p. 59. For co-participation see: Fonseca (1951).

93. For the politics of pacts and accommodation see: Vanger (1963), pp. 13–14; Taylor (1960), p. 8; Weinstein (1988), p. 73.
94. Real de Azúa (1964), pp. 21–5. A close translation would be a 'country of proximities', where everyone knows everyone else. As Azúa points out, defeat was always less bitter because of the possibility of participation: Real de Azúa (1971). 'It was not unusual for antagonists in legislative sessions to nod amiably to each other a short time later at *El Aguila*, Montevideo's leading downtown noon restaurant, or chat quietly at a social gathering under a neutral roof.': Taylor (1960), p. 45.
95. Taylor (1960), p. 44.
96. For an interesting discussion of the foundational myths informing political behaviour in Uruguay see: Rial (1993).
97. O'Donnell and Schmitter (1986c), pp. 51–2. Also: Huntington (1991), p. 13 and Lowden (1996).
98. Taylor (1960), p. 57; González and Gillespie (1989), p. 211.
99. For the historical role of the Catholic Church in Chile see: Smith (1982). For the critical role of the Church under authoritarian rule see: Lowden (1996).
100. For Argentina see: Malamud-Goti (1989), p. 74.
101. For the difficulties of establishing such limiting criteria and of the political difficulties inherent in avoiding such limitations see: Malamud-Goti (1989), pp. 71–88; Corradi (1992), pp. 287–8.

Chapter 2

1. For military interpretation of crisis and threat see: Comando General del Ejército Uruguayo (1976), (1978a), (1978b); and Pinochet (1991).
2. Vicaría de la Solidaridad (1993), p. 21. For estimates of death from repression in the Southern Cone see Table I in the appendix. For a new technique on disappearances see: Veil (1986).
3. Linz (1978), pp. 14–49.
4. Stepan (1971), p. 123.
5. See Rouquié (1987b), pp. 73–5; Stepan (1971), pp. 123–87; Stepan (1976). For US backing in repressive techniques see: Langguth (1978), pp. 124–42, 200 and 251.
6. Uruguayan Coronel Laitano, *El Día*, 15 Apr. 1980.
7. Interview with Chilean General Horacio Toro in Marras (1989), p. 137.

8. For analyses of breakdown in Uruguay: Gillespie (1984); Bruschera (1986); Vasconcellos (1987); Finch (1990), pp. 225–45 and pp. 247 ff; Weinstein (1975); (1988) pp. 40–7; (1993); Handelman (1981b); Gitli *et al.* (1987); Del Huerto Amarillo (1986); Kaufman (1979); Zubillaga and Pérez (1988).
9. Kaufmann (1993), p. 22; For Tupamaro guerrillas see: Panizza (1990), pp. 163–72; Mercader (1969); Gillio (1970) and (1971); Arocena (1989).
10. On Frente Amplio see: Aguirre Bayley (1985).
11. On escape see: Fernández Huidobro (1990).
12. For anti-subversive battle see: Caula and Silva (1986); Panizza (1990).
13. For the judiciary see: Cortiñas (1982).
14. For the militarization of state see: Del Huerto Amarillo (1981); (1986); Caetano and Rilla (1989); Kaufman (1979). For report on torture see: DSCSROU (1968), (1970), (1970b).
15. Garretón (1986a), p. 97; Remmer and Merkx (1982), pp. 3–40.
16. For conflict with judiciary see: Frühling (1988), pp. 23–8. For institutional-juridical strains see: Cumplido and Balbontin (1978); Echevarría and Frei (1974). For an account of the UP years and crisis see: Faúndez (1988). For the role of the Christian Democrats see: Fleet (1985).
17. Remmer (1989), p. 117; Valenzuela (1978). For the role of the media in polarizing and contributing to the climate of hysteria see: Dooner (1989a).
18. Decree Law I, 11 Sept. 1973.
19. Weiss Fagen (1992), p. 49.
20. SERPAJ (1989), p. 78.
21. ICJ (1983), p. 341.
22. Institutional Act I; II with the COSENA and the newly created *Consejo de la Nación* or Council of the Nation integrated by the 25-member *Consejo del Estado* or Council of the State and the 28 generals; III; IV; VII respectively: SERPAJ (1989), pp. 35–95.
23. CNVR (1991), p. 58.
24. Decree Law no. 128: OAS (1985), p. 10.
25. For Pinochet's successful politics of hegemony see: Arriagada (1985); Valenzuela (1991).
26. CNVR (1991), pp. 66–7.
27. IACHR (1985), p. 12.
28. In the 140 years between 1833 and 1973, the country had been subjected to states of emergency for a total of 12 years and six months: Vicaría de la Solidaridad (1993), p. 4.
29. CNVR (1991), pp. 63–4.
30. Frühling (1982), pp. 49–50.
31. ICJ (1974a), p. 7; Zabel *et al.* (1987).
32. Frühling (1982), pp. 28–31.
33. For a judge's critique of the Judiciary see: García Villegas (1990a).
34. Decree Law 788, Diario Oficial, Santiago, 4 Dec. 1974.
35. CNVR (1991), p. 58.

36. IACHR (1985), p. 14.
37. Frühling (1982), p. 52; see also 1981a.
38. This connection was not only *de facto* but *de jure*, according to the secret laws which governed DINA operations: AW (1983), p. 19.
39. CNVR (1991), p. 452.
40. UNECOSOC (1975), p. 51.
41. For accounts of the repression see: Aguiar (1988); Espínola *et al.* (1986); Baumgartner (1986); Díaz and Wettstein (1989); Dinamarca (1989); Gil (1990); Iribarne (1990); MFDD (1984), (1985), (1986); Martínez Moreno (1988); Michelini (1975); Rial (1992); SERPAJ (1982), (1989); Sosnowski and Popkin (1993); Tarigo Scheck (1985); Víctor (1981); Galeano (1983); Lee Gardo (1987). Reports from international humanitarian organizations are listed in the References.
42. *Le Monde*, Paris, 21–2 Aug. 1977.
43. SERPAJ (1989), p. 4.
44. For the University under the regime see: Maggiolo (1988).
45. Weinstein (1988), p. 51.
46. SERPAJ (1989), p. 119.
47. Rial (1992), p. 95. For the psychological impact see: Vignar and Maren (1989); Aguiar (1988); Díaz and Wettstein (1989); Gil (1990); Perelli and Rial (1986). General: Stover and Nightingale (1985). For the impact of fear as a system of repression see: Lechner (1992).
48. SERPAJ (1989), p. 119.
49. Ibid., pp. 130–6.
50. Testimony of Hugo García Rivas, ex-member of the Armed Forces: ibid., p. 143. See also: Rey Piuma and García Rivas (1984).
51. Daniel Rey Piuma, ex-member of the Navy: SERPAJ (1989), p. 147.
52. Martirena (1988) and Bloche (1987).
53. During the second half of 1976 and in 1977 members of the smaller guerrilla groups, the Por la Victoria del Pueblo (PVP) and the Grupos de Acción Unificadora (GAU) comprised most of those detained and processed: SERPAJ (1989), pp. 31 and 115.
54. Ibid., pp. 234–8.
55. Ibid., p. 116. For the military justice system see: Artucio (1982); Martínez Moreno (1986a, 1986b), (1988).
56. SERPAJ (1989), pp. 120–2.
57. 70% of those processed by the military courts were held in military establishments. The remaining 30% were held in other military establishments. The great majority were held in one of two prisons, Libertad and Punta de Rieles: ibid. pp. 195–200.
58. Ramírez (1989), p. 54.
59. Lee Gardo (1987), p. 25.
60. MFDD (1986) and SERPAJ (1989), pp. 255–99.
61. Ibid., pp. 286–98.
62. Trobo (1986).
63. Anderson (1993), p. 230.
64. Dinges and Landau (1980), pp. 237–9.

65. DSCRROU (1985g).
66. These are proven cases. The number is probably much higher: see: CCDH (1990a), p. 14. For overall accounts of repression see: Ahumada *et al.* (1989); Constable and Valenzuela (1991), ch. 4; Cavallo *et al.* (1987); CNVR (1991); Vicaría de la Solidaridad (1990), (1993); Rojas (1988). Reports from international humanitarian organizations are listed in the References.
67. For secret detention camps see: Rojas (1989); Valdez (1975); Gómez (1990).
68. Ahumada *et al.* (1989), p. 45; UNECOSOC (1975), p. 50.
69. Bitar (1987).
70. For the mass grave at Pisagua see: García Villegas (1990b). For the mass grave in the Hornos de Lonquen see: Pacheco (1980).
71. Ahumada *et al.* (1989), p. 389. For other accounts of this period see: Timmerman (1979); Hauser (1978); Politzer (1985); Verdugo (1989), (1990); Witker (1977); Castillo (1986).
72. UNECOSOC (1975), p. 43.
73. CNVR (1991), pp. 462–74.
74. Ibid., pp. 451–74.
75. Ahumada *et al.* (1989), pp. 271–347.
76. Dinges and Landau (1980); Branch and Propper (1982). For the assassination of constitutionalist General Prats see: Ahumada *et al.* (1989), pp. 65–89.
77. AW (1983), p. 131.
78. CNVR (1991), pp. 623–4.
79. One of these was the murder of Tucapel Jiménez, leader of the newly emerging trade union movement: Sésnic (1985); Signorelli-Wilson (1986).
80. AW (1983), p. 133.
81. For the famous *Quemados* Case (the case of the Burnt Ones) in this period, which led to the first successful prosecution of Carabineros officers, see: Verdugo (1986).
82. Monckeberg *et al.* (1986).
83. CNVR (1991), p. 885. For the persecution of members of the UP government and the MIR see: Cavallo *et al.* (1988), pp. 39–49.
84. Barros Lémez (1987), p. 122; in English they mean 'the tourniquet method' and the 'hammer method'.
85. For the issue of threat perception see: Remmer and Merkx (1982); Perelli (1987b).
86. SERPAJ (1989), p. 114.
87. 'Tough hand'.
88. Garretón (1986a), p. 99. For the testimony of General Nicanor Díaz Estrada of the Airforce see Marras (1988), p. 111.
89. 'Los Cesantes de la Democracia', *Hoy*, no. 670, 20–7 May 1990, pp. 24–5.
90. Stepan (1988), p. 23.

91. SERPAJ (1989), p. 112.
92. Rama (1987), p. 173.
93. Stepan (1971), p. 21.
94. Ibid., p. 168.
95. Regino Burgueño (1980), pp. 9, 97, 99, and 120.
96. Maran (1989). See also: Crahan (1982); Arriagada (1986a), pp. 44–7 and pp. 48–52. For the influence of French ideology in Uruguay see: Rial (1986a), p. 47 and in Argentina see: Anderson (1993), p. 133. Particularly popular were the novels of Larteguy (1979), (1961) and operations expert Trinquier (1975). For ideology generally see: Crahan (1982). On Chile see: Arriagada (1979), (1980), (1986a); Comblin (1979a). On Uruguay see: Castagnola and Mieres (1989); Perelli (1987a); Perelli (1987b). On manuals of operation following this ideology in Uruguay see: Bolentini (1977); Regino Burgueño (1980) and in Chile see: Cortes Rencoret (1976).
97. Rouquié (1987b), p. 74.
98. Rial (1986a), pp. 26 and 36; Perelli (1987a).
99. CNVR (1991), p. 42.
100. Arriagada (1985), p. 55; Vasconcellos (1987), p. 60. For the personal testimony of Leigh see: Varas (1987).
101. Arriagada (1986a), p. 124.
102. Comando General del Ejército Uruguayo (1976).
103. Cortes Rencoret (1976), p. 23.
104. Rovira (1981), pp. 1–13.
105. General Pinochet, Speech at the Third Anniversary of the Government, 11 Sept. 1977: Arriagada (1986a), p. 176.
106. Lechner (1992), p. 30.
107. General Pinochet in *Apsi*, 8 Nov. 1988.
108. 'Ante el Nuevo Año', *El Soldado*, no. 99, Nov.–Dec. 1984. When the belief exists that one participates in historical mission, all acts become justified: Arendt (1985), p. 105.
109. Frühling (1982), p. 51.
110. Linz (1968), p. 218. Similar 'themes répétitifs' such as 'un complot contre la nacion', the presence of a 'conspiracion qui menacent la sustance vitale du peuple' and the existence of 'l'énemi caché', accompanied the Terror in France, and permitted repression to be presented as 'un acte de legitime défense ou de vengeance contre les "scélerats" que trament des crimes abominables s'ils ne les ont pas déjà commis': Backzo (1989), p. 42.
111. Arendt (1968), p. 427.
112. Linz (1968), p. 219.
113. Weiss Fagen (1992), p. 44.
114. Monckberg *et al.*, (1986), p. 53. Terror was used to 'keep the masses perfectly obedient': Arendt (1973): p. 6.
115. Sartori (1987), pp. 41–2.
116. General Esteban Cristi of Uruguay, *El País*, 18 Aug. 1977.

117. Definition given at the XIV Conference of American Armies, Washington DC, Nov. 1981, in *El Soldado*, Dec. 1981.
118. *Análisis*, Santiago, 7 Mar. 1988.
119. Teniente Coronel Teófilo Gómez Vera, 'La Academia Superior de Seguridad', *El Mercurio*, 19 Dec. 1976.
120. Arriagada (1986a), p. 174.
121. Lechner (1992), p. 27.
122. Regino Burgueño (1980), p. 96.
123. Argentine Teniente Coronel Durand in Frontalini and Caiati (1984), p. 17.
124. Arriagada (1986a), pp. 195–6. For the same logic in Algeria see: Maran (1989), p. 79. For the mirror image effect of these kinds of ideologies see: Girardet (1986), pp. 10–17.
125. Rouquié (1987*a*) p. 110.
126. Rial (1992), p. 102.
127. Linz states this about the difference between the two totalitarianisms: Linz (1968), p. 236; Sartori (1987), p. 201.
128. For backward-looking utopias see: Frank (1966), p. xii.
129. Lechner (1992), p. 29.
130. For loyalty to republican state see: Frühling (1982), pp. 35–58 and Rouquié (1987b), pp. 98–116.
131. These rights were enshrined in Article 19 of the Constitution.
132. See: Ahumada *et al.* (1989), vol. ii, p. 280–2. For the secret laws governing the DINA see: Garretón (1985); on the secrecy of operations see: Rey Piuma and Rivas (1984), p. 110 and DSCRROU (1985g).
133. Duhalde (1983), p. 79; 'Desaparecidos Detenidos: Las "Exhaustivas" Investigaciones Oficiales', *Apsi*, 12–18 Oct. 1987, pp. 19–23.
134. Monckberg *et al.* (1986), p. 136.
135. General Pinochet in *La Tercera*, 1 Apr. 1982. Frühling and Sanchez (1988), p. 18.
136. SERPAJ (1989), pp. 297–8.
137. In Chile, the secrecy of documentation was assured by Decree Laws 18.667, 18.771, and 18.845 all in 1989: CNVR (1991), p. 19. In Uruguay, as the military left power, they ordered the burning of documents from Ministry of Defence in November 1984: 'Facultan al Ministro de Defensa a Destruir Documentos Sin Interés' *Búsqueda*, 3 Mar. 1985.
138. Linz (1968), p. 218.
139. For a definition of authoritarianism see: Linz (1964), p. 255.
140. For Bordaberry's thought on a corporatist system see: Bordaberry (1980).
141. Ahumada *et al.* (1989), vol. ii, p. 277.
142. Rial (1992), p. 98.
143. For repressive structures in Argentina see: Moyano (1991); Duhalde (1983); CONADEP (1984); Anderson (1993); Miranda (1988); Simpson (1985); Simpson and Bennett (1985); Seoane and Ruíz (1986); Timmerman (1981); Guest (1990). For the ideology see: Frontalini and

Caiati (1984); Pion-Berlin (1989); Arriagada (1980); Miguens (1986); Camps (1983). For lower level in Brazil see: Nunca Mais (1986).

144. Pereira (1986), p. 54.
145. Schull (1992), p. 737. See also: Goldfarb (1989), p. xiii.
146. The so-called *caravana de la muerte* (Caravan of Death), a group of officers which toured the country in late 1973 carrying out executions in many cases without the knowledge of local commanding generals was certainly part of Pinochet's 'coup inside the army': Verdugo (1989), pp. 234–5.
147. Article 192-G of the 1974 Decree Law 14.157: Rial (1986a), p. 28. The first prisoners of the *Junta* were soldiers and officers of all ranks for imputed communist leanings: Hugo García Rivas, ex-SIE officer, confession in Norway 6 June 1983. Rey Piuma and García Rivas (1984), p. 77. The personally ambitious were retired from the armed forces: see the case of General Chiappe Posse in Gillespie (1986a), p. 197.
148. Marras (1988), pp. 27–9 and 32–3; Ahumada (1989), pp. 40–8; Dinges and Landau (1980), pp. 314–16.
149. Monckberg *et al.* (1986), pp. 57–8; Varas (1979), p. 78.
150. Ahumada *et al.* (1989), vol. ii, pp. 302–3. A similar rivalry developed later between the CNI and the DICOMCAR: Monckberg *et al.* (1986), p. 234.
151. Ramírez (1988), p. 65.
152. These men were involved in the disappearances. For Brazil see: Stepan (1988), p. 28; for Uruguay see: Ramírez (1988), p. 68.
153. Before Medina's promotion, he had been Chief of the Third Army Division in the province of Fray Bentos where Roslik was tortured to death. See: 'El Caso Roslik', *Las Bases*, 17 Feb. 1985; 'El Pase a Retiro de Medina Cierra el Ciclo del Comandante de la Transición', *Búsqueda*, 29 Jan. 1987.
154. The same occurred in Algeria. 'Through the discourse of the agents of the state it became clear that those responsible for torture at both policy and implementation levels, were aware of the taboo and sought to support the violations through recourse to prevailing ideology': Maran (1989), pp. 191 and 82–6.
155. 'Violación de los Derechos Humanos Producto de la Lucha. Borad: A Las Fuerzas Armadas no les Será Difícil Integrarse a la Vida Democrática', *Búsqueda*, 31 Oct. 1984.
156. *Análisis*, no. 135, 25–31 Mar. 1986; CNVR (1991), p. 27.
157. *El Soldado*, no. 94, Jan.–Feb. 1984, in Perelli (1987a), p. 40.
158. *Hoy*, 7 Oct. 1985.
159. Speech by General Abdón Raimúndez, Chief of Fourth Army Division of Uruguay in 'Rechazo Tutela en Derechos Humanos', *El País*, 24 Feb. 1978.
160. Almirante José Toribio Merino, referring to the International Parliamentary Assembly of 1986: Magnon (1987).
161. Magnon (1987), p. 167.

162. 'Bolentini: Hay Presos Porque se Respetaron los Derechos Humanos', *Búsqueda*, 12 Oct. 1983.
163. Arriagada (1986a), pp. 53, 64–5.
164. Response to the accusation made in the Uruguayan Parliament regarding the death in military custody of Luis Carlos Batalla on 21 May 1972, by the *Frente Amplio* and the Blanco Party. 'A Través de la Justicia Militar las FF. AA Buscaron en el Club Naval Poner una Valla al Revisionismo', *Búsqueda*, 13 Apr. 1989.
165. *El Soldado*, Sept.–Oct. 1985.
166. General Medina in *Búsqueda*, 23 May 1985.
167. Rovira (1981), p. 27. See also: 'La Conferencia de Álvarez', *La Opinión*, 21 Sept. 1982.
168. Constable and Valenzuela (1991), p. 79, and Correa and Subercaseaux (1989), p. 141.
169. Pinochet (1991), pp. 199–201.
170. *La Democracia*, 2 Oct. 1987.
171. 'Civiles y Militares', *Hoy*, no. 613, 17–23 Apr. 1989.
172. Rovira (1981), p. 25.
173. General Hugo Molina, Actas del Diálogo del Parque Hotel, IV, p. 10.
174. General Pinochet in *Hoy*, 23 Feb. 1988.
175. Teniente General Vadora of Uruguay, *Notícias*, Buenos Aires, 21 Oct. 1976.
176. Speech by Coronel Caraballo in *El Día*, 20 June 1984, and 'Teniente General Medina: Si Se Dan Las Mismas Causales Que Se Dieron en 1973, No Vamos a Tener Más Remedio Que Darlo', *Búsqueda*, 14 Feb. 1985.
177. Pinochet speech on 16th Anniversary as Army Commander: WOLA (1989), p. 15.
178. For such a threat in Chile see: Verdugo (1989), pp. 276–7. For Uruguay see Carrió (1987), p. 5.
179. Verdugo (1989), pp. 248 and 200.
180. Orden del Comando General del Ejército, signed by Commander-in-Chief, General Gregorio Alvarez, 3 July 1978, *La Democracia*, 3 July 1978.
181. Correa and Subercaseaux (1989), p. 141
182. Handelman (1981a), pp. 3–6. For economic policy see: Astori (1989); González and Notaro (1980).
183. For a lack of support relative to Chile from entrepreneurs and society as a whole see: Handelman (1979). For the military legitimacy crisis see: Handelman (1986).
184. For the neo-liberal revolution see: Foxley (1986); Vergara (1986).
185. Garretón (1986a). For a comparison of differing levels of success in institutionalization and legitimacy in Uruguay and Chile see: González (1983b).
186. Aguero (1990), p. 20.
187. Danopolous (1992), p. 66, quoting Rustow (1970). For an analysis of military resistance to justice see: McSherry (1992).

Chapter 3

1. 'A Dishonest Way Out'. See: Pareja (1987).
2. González (1985a), p. 102.
3. González (1983b), pp. 104–9, (1991), p. 54. Also: Handelman (1986).
4. Handelman (1981).
5. The Frente's imprisoned leader, Líber Seregni and the coalition's Christian Democrat *sub-lema*, had advocated a blank vote for the internal elections. The Communist *sub-lema* on the other hand, had recommended that Frente supporters vote for Ferreira in exchange for the Blancos' continued support for the de-proscription of the Frente. The blank vote represented only 7.6% of the total votes cast: Pérez (1985). For Seregni's orders that supporters vote blank see: Aguirre Bayley (1985), pp. 56–7. For an analysis of primaries see: Gillespie (1985), (1986b); Handelman (1981a); Mieres (1983).
6. 'La Formula de Álvarez Sería de Llevar la Transición Más Allá del 85', *Aquí*, 26 Apr. 1983. The talks were directed by the hardline President Álvarez, through representative General César Rapela: 'El Acuerdo del Club Naval Sigue Sonando', *Alternativa Socialista*, 23 Feb. 1989.
7. Rial (1990), p. 24.
8. Gillespie (1990), p. 182.
9. 'Convención Colorada: Una Marcha y Muchas Críticas', *Aquí*, 19 July 1983; 'El Golpe Bueno', *Búsqueda*, 26 July 1983.
10. The Ferreira sector of the Blanco Party and the Communist and Socialist factions of the Frente had formed a coalition in exile called the Convergencia Democrática. The Colorados feared its transformation into a national coalition.
11. Rial (1990).
12. For this fear see Seregni interview: Barros Lémez (1987), p. 128.
13. Del Huerto Amarillo (1987), p. 22.
14. 'Golpe de Estado Secreto', *Primera Plana*, 3 Aug. 1983; 'Mito y Realidad: Reflexión Necesaria', *La Democracia*, 30 Jan. 1987.
15. See: 'Anunció Rapela que las Fuerzas Armadas Están Dispuestas a Hacer Concesiones a los Partidos', *Búsqueda*, 3 Nov. 1983.
16. On role played by Medina see: Del Huerto Amarillo (1988b).
17. 'WFA Regresó Ayer y de Inmediato Fue Detenido', *El Día*, 17 June 1984.
18. For the conflicts between the Frente and the Blanco Party see: 'Aspectos de la Asamblea General del 9–10 de Julio: Aportes Para la Historia de un Pasado no Tán Lejano', *Búsqueda* 25 July 1985.
19. De Sierra (1985), pp. 149–60; Pérez (1985), pp. 129–47.
20. Gillespie (1992), p. 191.
21. For this justification see Seregni's speech on 10 Aug. 1984 at a mass meeting at the Municipal Square of Montevideo: Aguirre Bayley (1985), p. 66.
22. 'Avanzar Con Realismo', *Hoy,* Santiago, 27 June–3 July 1984.

23. Editorial by Blanco Senator, Juan Martin Posadas in: *La Democracia*, 14 Nov. 1986. The pact was rejected by the party directorate by 13 votes out of 15: 'Texto Completo de la Carta de Ferreira', *Tiempo de Cambio*, 20 Aug. 1984. For a very funny and bitter Blanco criticism of the pact see: Jotaeme, 'El Pactito Feo: Una Historia Para Niños', *La Democracia*, 10 Aug. 1984.
24. Charles Gillespie (1992), p. 196.
25. On the fiction of the military's explanation for non-interference in the Ferreira case see: interview with Young, leader of the Christian Democrat *sub-lema*: 'Para Abrir la Noche', Radio CX30, 4 Aug. 1984.
26. For an analysis of the electoral results see: Mieres (1988); Rial (1984b).
27. 'A Través de la Justicia Militar las FF. AA. Buscaron en el Club Naval Poner una Valla al Revisionismo', *Búsqueda*, 13 Apr. 1989. See also: 'Militares Analizan el Futuro de la Transición' *Aquí*, 3 May 1983.
28. *Actas del Parque Hotel*, Montevideo, p. 13.
29. Del Huerto Amarillo (1987), p. 23.
30. *Actas del Parque Hotel*, Acta 7.
31. Television interview on Telemundo 12, 20 Mar. 1987. 'La Democracia Está Bién Asentada Afirmó Medina', *El Día*, 21 Mar. 1987.
32. 'El Acuerdo Sigue Sonando', *Alternativa Socialista*, 23 Feb. 1989.
33. Seregni interviewed in: 'A Través de la Justicia Militar las FF.AA Buscaron en la Club Naval Poner Una Valla al Revisionismo', *Búsqueda*, 13 Apr. 1989.
34. Ibid.
35. Ibid.
36. Ibid.
37. 'Medina Tenía el Mandato de la JOG de Plantear la Amnistía Pero no lo Hizo', *Alternativa Socialista*, 23 Feb. 1989.
38. 'No se Admitirá Ninguna Forma de Revanchismo Dijo Medina', *El Día*, 4 Aug. 1984.
39. 'Medina: El Ejército Sale Con Honor, Como Era Nuestra Esperanza', *Búsqueda*, 4 Aug. 1984.
40. 'Medina Dijo Que Fue Superada Inquietud en Militares Sobre el Acuerdo del Club Naval', *Búsqueda*, 22 Aug. 1984.
41. See: 'Sanguinetti y los Derechos Humanos', *El Día*, 15–21 Dec. 1984; 'Sanguinetti: La Justicia Civil Juzgará a Militares Que Hayan Violado Derechos Humanos', *Búsqueda*, 7–13 Feb. 1985.
42. This is, for example, the opinion of Del Huerto Amarillo, who argues that although the pact produced no juridical guarantees, political guarantees were given: Del Huerto Amarillo (1987), pp. 21–32.
43. 'El Acuerdo del Club Naval Sigue Sonando', *Alternativa Socialista*, 23 Feb. 1989. For Medina's loyalty to Sanguinetti by his own admission: Boeker (1990), p. 79.
44. *Búsqueda*, 4 Aug. 1984.
45. Gillespie (1990), p. 184.

46. 'IDI: Una Voz Frentista Contra el Pacto', *La Democracia*, 10 Aug. 1984.
47. In favour: Lista 90-Socialist Party; Lista 99-Por el Gobierno del Pueblo; Lista 808-Christian Democratic Party; Communist party; Movimiento Socialista; Movimiento Popular Frente Amplista. Against: Izquierda Democrática Independiente, including the groups, Democracia Avanzada, Progreso y Cultura, Unión Popular, Grupos de Acción Unificadora (GAU), Agrupación Batllista Pregón, Patria Grande, Nucleos de Base Frenteamplistas, Movimiento Acción Nacionalista. Abstentions: Frente de Izquierda de Liberación (FIDEL). See: *Nuevo Tiempo*, 4 Aug. 1984.
48. Líber Seregni, *Boletín del Centro de Prensa del Frente Amplio Para Uso Interno*, mimeo, 11 July 1984.
49. 'Líber Seregni: Hacer Una Campaña Electoral Contra el Acuerdo es Algo Cercano a la Irresponsabilidad', *Boletín del Centro de Prensa Para Uso Interno del Frente Amplio*, 8 Aug. 1984.
50. Only the minority *lema*, the Corriente Batllista Independiente, voted against it in the Colorado Convention, due to its opposition to the continued proscription of Ferreira.
51. Vice president Tarigo in the Senate on the occasion of the debate on the Ley de Caducidad, Dec. 1986.
52. *Aprobado por la Mesa Ejecutiva de la CONAPRO en el Día 26 Octubre 1984: Grupo Derechos Libertades y Garantias. Tema: Esclarecimiento de las Violaciones a los Derechos Humanos*, mimeo. See also: 'Investigarán los Casos de Desaparecidos', *El Día*, 5 Feb. 1985.
53. 'Concertación o Búsqueda Durante Dos Años del Entendimiento Entre la Oposición al Gobierno Militar', *Búsqueda*, 14 Feb. 1985. For the weakness of CONAPRO and the *Concertación de Partidos* see: Weinstein (1988), p. 86; Rial (1985c).
54. 'Sanguinetti: Ejerceré el Mando del las FF.AA Sin Sentimientos de Revanchas', *El Día*, 2 Mar. 1985.
55. For pacted reforms and ruptures see: Linz (1990).
56. Rial (1990), p. 12.
57. SERPAJ (1989), p. 106.
58. Weinstein (1988), p. 126.
59. Rial (1986b), p. 260. For an interesting analysis of Uruguayan political culture and its fossilization see: Rial (1993) pp. 59–82.
60. Meaning 'a yesterday improved for tomorrow': see: Rial (1984a), p. 27.
61. Meaning 'a realistic way out'.
62. Equipos Consultores, *Informe Mensual*, no. 3, Dec. 1984.
63. Weinstein (1993), pp. 90–1 and Kaufmann (1993), pp. 34–7.
64. Gillespie (1990), pp. 22 and 184.
65. Rial (1984a).
66. González (1985a), p. 118.
67. De Riz (1985), p. 133.
68. 'La Confusión Engendra la Confusión', *La Razón*, 23 Oct. 1986.
69. For a comparative analysis of Uruguayan transition see: De Riz

(1986); González (1983b), (1985b). For a general analysis see: Gillespie (1982), (1985), (1986a), (1990); González (1985a); Rial (1983), (1984a), (1984b), (1984c), (1985b), (1990).

70. SERPAJ document, no title, June 1983.
71. For an account of the role played by human rights organizations see: Pinto (1988); IELSUR (1984).
72. Michelini (1975).
73. For Ferreira's activities and thought in exile see: Ferreira Aldunate (1986).
74. See: Handelman (1981a).
75. See: 'Discurso Pronunciado Por Juan Raul Ferreira, Presidente de la Convergencia Democratica Uruguaya (CDU) en el Acto Efectuado el 25 de Mayo de 1981, Ciudad de Mexico, en el Primer Aniversario de la Creacion de CDU'.
76. SERPAJ (1989), pp. 374–5.
77. For different forms of cultural and other resistance see: Masliah (1993), pp. 108–19; Rosencof (1993), pp. 120–32; Legaspi de Arismendi and Rico (1989); Artucio (1982); Yanez (1993).
78. In 1983 a number of groups emerged linked to religious organizations such as the Federación de Religiosos del Uruguay (FRU) and the Justicia y Paz InterFransiscanos-Paz y Bién.
79. SERPAJ (1989), pp. 168–73.
80. 'Crean Comisión de Derechos Humanos', *Aquí*, 30 Aug. 1983; 'No Estamos Animados por la Denuncia o el Escándalo Sino Empeñados en Lograr la Reparación de los Derechos Lesionados', *Búsqueda*, 22 Sept. 1983.
81. Del Huerto Amarillo and Serrentino (1986), p. 18.
82. Ibid., p. 21.
83. Ibid., p. 22.
84. Ibid., pp. 22–3.
85. Delgado (1988), p. 12.
86. Ibid.
87. Faraone and Fox (1988), p. 153; SERPAJ (1989), pp. 356–61. Between 1967 and 1984, for example, 44% of the print media was definitively closed down: Gabay (1988), p. 61.
88. Ibid., p. 377.
89. This paper was directed by Luis Pérez Aguirre, the founder of SERPAJ in Uruguay.
90. 'La Amnistía es un Derecho Irrenunciable', document presented MYFPJM in 'Un Año Sin Respuesta', *Cinco Dias*, 26 Mar. 1984.
91. 'Difunden Nómina de Personas Desaparecidas en Uruguay', *Búsqueda*, 23 Nov. 1983.
92. SERPAJ (1989), p. 105.
93. See, for example: Lowden (1996).
94. Del Huerto Amarillo and Serrentino (1986), p. 5.
95. 'Educar Para los Derechos Humanos', *Revista CIAS*, Buenos Aires, no. 338, Nov. 1984.

96. Sikkink (1991); Schoultz (1981). For an account of the position of Uruguay *vis-à-vis* the international community see: SERPAJ (1989), pp. 379–90.
97. Shoultz (1981), p. 295.
98. ICJ (1976).
99. Weinstein (1993), p. 89.
100. The Red Cross was subsequently banned from visiting the country because its 1979 report on prison conditions was leaked: Guest (1990), p. 491.
101. Nevertheless, the OAS published six annual reports on the situation of human rights in Uruguay between 1978 and 1984. For a description of international support for democratization in Uruguay see: Luján (1993), pp. 277–312.
102. Tribunal Permanente de los Pueblos (1990), p. 68.
103. According to Gillespie, based on numerous interviews with party political leaders, none reported many links with the human rights organizations. Moreover, exile contacts were infrequent among the traditional parties. Finally, links with the Church were minimal: Gillespie (1990), pp. 64 and 65.
104. SERPAJ (1983), internal document, no title, p. 11. For the position of its leader see: Pérez Aguirre (1986) and (1991).
105. Tribunal Permanente de los Pueblos (1990), p. 68.
106. SERPAJ (1983).
107. For party commitments to the above see: 'Lo Que Va de Ayer a Hoy: La Amnistía y el Partido Colorado', *Alternativa Socialista*, 28 Aug. 1986.
108. Del Huerto Amarillo and Serrentino (1986), p. 25.
109. 'Paro Cívico y Protesta Nacional', *Aquí*, 20 June 1984; 'La Proclama del Pueblo', *La Democracia*, 6 Apr. 1984; 'Marcha Por Amnistía: Unas 4.000 Personas Manifestaron por 18 de Julio', *Convicción*, 1 Mar. 1984; 'ASCEEP se Expidió Sobre Amnistía', *La Democracia*, 6 Apr. 1984; 'Comisiones Obreras Reclaman Amnistía Amplia y Sin Restricciones', *Cinco Días*, 9 Apr. 1984; 'Plenario Intersindical de Trabajadores-Manifiesto del 1 Mayo 1984', *Cinco Días*, 23 Mar. 1984; 'Mons. Partelli: Hay Clamor General Por Amnistía', *Cinco Días*, 23 Mar. 1984.
110. 'Sanguinetti Convocó a una Concertación Nacional', *Aquí*, 10 Apr. 1984.
111. SERPAJ (1989), pp. 103–4.
112. 'Dr Gonzalo Aguirre (MNR): Cualquiera Puede Atribuirse el Voto en Blanco', *Búsqueda*, 22 Sept. 1982.
113. 'Derechos Humanos: Seregni, Marchesano, Ferreira', *El Popular*, 5 Dec. 1986.
114. Gillespie (1992), p. 195.
115. Delgado (1988), p. 27.
116. 'Informe de la Convención del Partido Colorado: Julio Maria Sanguinetti', *Correo del Viernes*, 13 Apr. 1984.

117. *Por Un Uruguay Para Todos: Programa de Gobierno y Carta Orgánica del Partido Colorado* (Montevideo: Fundación José Battle y Ordoñez, 1984). Amnesty was incorporated into the party's Programme of Principles by a great majority, but only due to the efforts of the more radical minority *sub-lema*, the Corriente Batllista Independiente. The *Unión Cívica* had a similar position, not favouring an amnesty for those who had committed blood crimes: *Unión Cívica: Programa de Principios y Plan de Gobierno 1984–1989* (Montevideo, 1984, mimeo).
118. See: *Declaración de Principios Aprobada por la Concertación del Partido Nacional el 17, Diciembre, 1983* (Mimeo, Montevideo).
119. *Bases Programáticas de la Unidad: Líneas Fundamentales de Acción de Medidas de Emergencia* (Montevideo: mimeo, 1984). For the UC same as above.
120. See: 'Bases Programaticas de la Unidad: Lineas Fundamentales de Acción y Medidas de Emergencia', *La Hora*, no date, 1984; 'Proyecto de Amnistía Aprobado por el Frente Amplio', *La Hora*, 29 Jan. 1985. For a comparative analysis of party platforms see: Perelli (1984).
121. Rial (1986b), p. 37.
122. 'Tiene Que Haber una Gran Capacidad de Perdón', *Tribuna Saltena*, 20 Mar. 1984; 'Sanguinetti: Justicia Civil Juzgará Militares Que Hayan Violado Derechos Humanos', *Búsqueda*, 7–13 Feb. 1985; 'Sanguinetti Precisó Como se Juzgarán las Denuncias Contra Miembros de las FF.AA', *Búsqueda*, 21 Mar. 1985.
123. 'Tiene Que Haber una Gran Capacidad de Perdón', *Tribuna Saltena*, 20 Mar. 1984.
124. Speech at the Colorado Party Convention on the 9 Apr. 1983: 'Sanguinetti: Cumpliremos Con Brum Cuando Regresemos a las Instituciones Democráticas', *El País*, 10 Apr. 1983.
125. 'Sanguinetti: Las Voces del Temor', *La Semana*, 14 Jan. 1984.
126. 'Sanguinetti: Revancha No, Justicia Siempre', Statement made on 7 Apr. 1984 in 'No Se Puede Edificar la Casa Sobre Una Ciénaga', *Brecha*, 19 Sept. 1986.
127. 'Sanguinetti: El Gobierno no Juzga; Juzgan los Jueces', *El Día*, 3 Nov. 1984.
128. 'Sanguinetti: Si Hay Espíritu de Revancha Habrá Golpe de Estado Otra vez en Nuestro País', *La Mañana*, 30 Oct. 1984.
129. 'Antes Aún de Recuperarla, Pensemos en Cuidar la Democracia Que Vendrá', *Opinar*, 27 Sept. 1984.
130. 'Zumarán: Es Fundamental la Destitución de la Miembros de la Suprema Corte', *El País*, 27 Jan. 1985.
131. Meaning 'a discourse of forgetfulness'.
132. 'En Aras de Entendimiento: Líder Blanco Proscripto: No Interesa Cobrar Viejas Cuentas', *Búsqueda*, 14 Mar. 1984; 'Zumarán: La Verdadera Reconciliación Nacional Se Logrará Sin Saldar Cuentas', *El Día*, 25 July 1981.
133. 'A Un Año de la Declaración del Partido Nacional: Superar las Heridas y Forjar la Reconciliación', *Búsqueda*, 18 Dec. 1984.

134. Gillespie (1990), p. 198.
135. 'Botinelli: No Impulsar Revisionismo Sino Garantizar Justicia Independiente', *El Día*, 30 Sept. 1984.
136. 'Seregni: Amnistía y Militares: Si Alguien Dió Orden de Torturar y Otro la Ejecutó Ambos Son Culpables', *Búsqueda*, 27 Dec. 1984.
137. 'Texto Completo de la Conferencia de Prensa de Seregni', *Aquí*, 27 Mar. 1984.
138. *Búsqueda*, 27 Dec. 1984.
139. SERPAJ (1983).
140. 'Pide SERPAJ Que El Futuro Gobierno Investigue y Juzgue Delitos de Lesa Humanidad Originados Por el Terrorismo de Estado', *Búsqueda*, 24 Oct. 1984.
141. General Washington Varela on 18 May 1984, Army Day, ibid. Other examples: 'Al Recordar a Raimúndez: Las Fuerzas Armadas Reiteraron Que no Permitirán Revanchismos', *Búsqueda*, 25 Apr. 1984; 'Revisionismo: El Presidente Reiteró la Posición Oficial Establecida en 1978', *Búsqueda*, 22 Sept. 1982; 'No Se Permitirá Ninguna Forma de Revanchismo, Dijo Medina', *El Día*, 4 Aug. 1984.
142. 'La Conferencia de Alvarez', *Opción*, 21 Sept. 1982. After making his initial statement, Alvarez asked a Commander-in-Chief 'What did you think?' The response was 'It wasn't your best moment.' 'A Través de la Justicia Militar las FF.AA Buscaron an la Club Naval Poner una Valla al Revisionismo', *Búsqueda*, 13 Apr. 1989.
143. 'Cuando se Reclama la Amnistía y el Indulto Están Pidiendo la Liberación de los Delincuentes Asesinos Tupamaros y sus Secuaces, que Mataron, Torturaron, Secuestraron y Vejaron?', *El País*, 14 Dec. 1983; *Dirección Nacional de Relaciones Públicas a Los Dirigentes de los Partidos Políticos*' *El País*, 14 Dec. 1983. 'Rapela Se Reiteró Contrario a Una Amnistía Irrestricta', *La Mañana*, 14 Nov. 1984; 'Invidio Advirtió Sobre Intención de Aprobar Una Amnistía General e Irrestricta', *El País*, 2 Dec. 1984.
144. On Military Honour Tribunals see: *Búsqueda*, 4 Feb. 1988.
145. Pareja (1987): 'The misfortunes of being excessively sensible.'
146. Blanco senator Juan Martín Posadas, in *La Democracia*, 14 Nov. 1986.
147. Gillespie (1986b), pp. 215–44. The Frente contained within it 13 groups, with the most radical ones having approximately half of the internal coalition votes: Aguirre Bayley (1985), p. 69.
148. Gillespie argues that the social movements were used as surrogates for real coalition cohesion on the left: Gillespie (1990), p. 66. The Colorados and the Blancos were more internally homogeneous. Sanguinetti won 31.2% of the Colorado vote, with the pro-regime faction under Pacheco Areco winning 23%. The Wilsonistas in the Blanco Party gained 83% of the party's vote.
149. Mieres (1988), pp. 72–4.
150. For first result see: Equipos Consultores, *Serie Estudios de Opinión Pública, Informe Mensual*, no. 6, July 1985. For latter results see:

Equipos Consultores, *Serie de Estudios de Opinión Pública, Informe Mensual*, June 1986.

151. 'No Hubo Pactos Secretos', *Aquí*, 4 Aug. 1984.

Chapter 4

1. Meaning 'a constitutional way out'.
2. For the plebiscite see: Garretón (1988); ICLASAOCP (1989).
3. Garretón (1990), p. 4.
4. For difficulties in uniting the opposition see: Garretón (1991), pp. 211–51.
5. For the trade union movement and the protests see: Barrera and Valenzuela (1986), pp. 230–69.
6. For the renovation of the socialists see: Arrate (1987); Loveman (1993a).
7. Alianza: the PR, PL, PSD, PDC, PR, UPS, and PS-Briones/Nuñez. The radical left was organized within the Unión Popular Democrática, including the PS-A, PCCh, and the MIR and the Bloque Socialista, which existed up to 1985 uniting the PAS, IC, MAPU-Obrero, and CS.
8. This organization included all the parties of the Alianza and the IC, PN, and UN. In 1986 it was joined by the Socialist groups and the MAPU.
9. For the evolution of party political opposition and difficulties of unity see: Valenzuela and Valenzuela (1986b) pp. 184–229; Garretón (1987), (1989b), (1991), pp. 214–24. For the left see: Loveman (1993a), pp. 30–6.
10. For the unifying and mobilizing impact that the 1980 constitutional plebiscite had on the opposition see: Garretón (1991) and Constable and Valenzuela (1991), p. 305.
11. Garretón (1991), p. 226.
12. See *Acuerdo Político por el NO*, Santiago, 2 Feb. 1988, signed by the PDC, PS-A, MAPU-Obrero, MAPU, PR, IC, PSD, PS-N, PDN, PH, PR, UPS, and the UDL. Despite an initial decision to boycott the plebiscite, the Communists also finally opted to support the NO vote along with a faction of the Movimiento de Izquierda Revolucionaria.
13. Maira (1991), p. 15. The co-operation between the parties and the social movement had been inaugurated during the protests with the Asamblea de la Civilidad, in which the Christian Democrats were the dominant party. With the *Demanda de Chile* produced by the Assembly, the social movement accepted its role as supportive of the united opposition. The Assembly included the trade unions under the CNT, a number of social and professional organizations and the constitutional study group of the Christian Democrats, the Grupo de Estudios Constitucionales: see: Garretón (1987).
14. The latter united the PCCH, PAIS, and PRS.

15. ICLASAOCP (1989), p. 12.
16. Maira (1991), p. 17.
17. Cavarozzi (1992), p. 224. The right, which had dissolved itself under military rule, was reconstituted into two main parties with the beginning of the transition process. These were the more moderate Renovación Nacional and the more ideological and radical Unión Democrática Independiente.
18. Garretón (1990), p. 4.
19. 'Quién Apuntaló el Ejército', *Hoy*, no. 613, 17–23 Apr. 1989, pp. 3–5.
20. AW (1989a), p. 52. For analysis of the constitutional reforms see: José Antonio Viera Gallo, 'El Acuerdo Constitucional', *Revista Mensaje*, no. 300, July 1989.
21. 'Cómo Desatará Aylwin las Leyes de Amarre', *Hoy*, no. 651, 8–14 Jan. 1990, pp. 10–12.
22. The nine appointees are two former Supreme Court judges, one former Comptroller General, four former commanders from each of the services, one university rector, and one former Minister of State. Pinochet also attempted to isolate the parliament geographically by separating it from the Presidency in the Palacio de la Moneda and building a new home for it in Valparaíso at the incredible cost of US$95 million: AW (1988b), p. 45.
23. *El Mercurio*, 24 Sept. 1989.
24. Correa and Subercaseaux (1989), p. 141.
25. See: 'Cambios en el Alto Mando', *Hoy*, no. 634, 11–17 Sept. 1989, p. 12. 'Generales Para la Democracia', *Hoy*, no. 639, 16–22 Oct. 1989, pp. 10–13, and 'La Hora de los Leales', *Hoy*, no. 639, 16–22 Oct. 1989, pp. 12–13.
26. 'Pinochet a "Gente" (Italia): Me Iré al Cielo', *Hoy*, no. 625, 10–16 July 1989, pp. 3–6.
27. Decree Laws 18.667, 18.771, and 18.845 of 1989: CNVR (1991), p. 19.
28. Brett (1992), p. 33.
29. 'Las Exigencia de Pinochet', *Hoy*, no. 632, 28 Aug. to 3 Sept. 1989, pp. 8–10. For the opposition of General Pinochet to the Armed Forces Law proposed by the CPPD see: 'La Vieja Estrategia del "Tejo Pasado"', *Hoy*, no. 650, 1–7 Jan. 1990, pp. 8–10.
30. 'Un Estado Militar Dentro del Estado Democrático', *La Epoca*, 22 Oct. 1989 and 'Antonio Varas: Hay Que Evitar Que las Fuerzas Armadas Sean Manoseadas', *Hoy*, no. 689, 1–7 Oct. 1990, pp. 18–20.
31. *Propuesta de Derechos Humanos: Documento Conclusiones de la Comisión de Justicia y Derechos Humanos de la CPPD* (Santiago: mimeo, 5 July 1989).
32. See, for example: 'Cardenal Silva Henríquez Critica La Ley Sobre Amnistía', *El Mercurio*, 23 Aug. 1989; 'Jose Antonio Viera Gallo: Concertación Insistirá en Derogar Ley de Amnistía', *El Mercurio*, 26 Aug. 1989.
33. 'RN: La Ley de Amnistía No Puede Negociarse Porque Pone en

Jaque Todo el Ordenamiento Jurídico del País', *El Mercurio*, 26 Aug. 1989. Even the more moderate Airforce Commander, General Matthei reacted against it: 'Un Rocket Contra la Concertación', *El Mercurio*, 30 July 1989; 'Chile General Tells Opposition Not to Tamper With Authority', *New York Times*, 1 Aug. 1989.

34. *El Mercurio*, 4 Aug. 1989.
35. Brett (1992), p. 23.
36. Meaning 'there will be no clean slate'. See: 'En Materia de Derechos Humanos: Zaldívar Dijo Que No Habrá Borrón y Cuenta Nueva', *El Mercurio*, 4 Aug. 1989.
37. Ahumada *et al.* (1989). For the role of the Church in supporting reconciliation and democracy see: Dooner (1989b).
38. There was another coalition represented by a maverick business man Errazuriz, the Alianza Liberal Socialista Chilena.
39. For analysis of elections see: Angell and Pollack (1990).
40. Within the *Concertación* it was the Christian Democrats who gained the greatest number of seats: they got 39 deputies and 13 senators. The Partido Por la Democracia gained 17 and 6 respectively.
41. CCDH (1990), p. 17. The opposition protested to the Constitutional Tribunal, but the law was ratified by that body in a divided vote.
42. 'Los Cesantes de la Democracia', *Hoy*, no. 670, 21–7, May 1990, pp. 24–5; 'La CNI se Camufla', *Apsi*, 23 Oct. 1989, pp. 16–19.
43. 'Los Asesores del General Pinochet', *Hoy*, no. 679, 23–9 July 1990, pp. 10–113; 'Que Va a Ser de los Hombres de Pinochet', *Hoy*, no. 657, 19–25 Feb. 1990, pp. 5–7.
44. 'President Aylwin and General Pinochet Heading for Inevitable Showdown', *Southern Cone Report*, RS-90-02, 15 Mar. 1990, p. 1.
45. *Chile Update*, Bulletin of the Chile Committee for Human Rights, Jan. 1990, p. 2.
46. For Aylwin's personal emphasis on moderation see interview in Boeker (1990), p. 45.
47. Loveman (1993a), p. 36.
48. 'Civiles y Militares', *Hoy*, no. 613, 17–23 Apr. 1989, p. 6.
49. Loveman (1991), p. 65.
50. CCDH (1990), p. 18.
51. Thus, according to Andrés Allamand of the RN: 'Quien Gane Gobernará Con Nuestras Ideas', in 'El Quiebre Que No Fue', *Hoy*, no. 661, 19–25 Mar. 1990, pp. 15–17.
52. For Avanzada Nacional see: 'Entrevista a Pablo Rodríguez de Elizabeth Subercaseaux', *Apsi*, no. 185, 11–24 Aug. 1986, p. 9. For the UDI see: Politzer (1985), p. 205. For RN and all of right see: Viera-Gallo and Rodríguez (1988).
53. For a list of the victims of terrorism on the military side see: 'La Otra Represión', *Análisis*, no. 224, 25 Apr.–1 May 1988, pp. 33–6.
54. WOLA (1988), p. 9.
55. 'Rebellion Via the Polls Says Teitelboim', *Latin American Weekly Report*, 1 June 1989, pp. 4–5.

56. For the indictment of Officer Fernández Dittus in the *Quemados* case in 1987 see: 'Caso Jóvenes Quemados: Hasta Cuándo Mentirás Fernández Dittus?', *Análisis*, no. 184, 20–6, July 1987. For the *Degollados* case: 'Investigación Del Triple Asesinato los Acusa: Servicios Secretos al Banquillo', *Cauce*, no. 33, 30 July–5 Aug. 1989, pp. 12–15.
57. *La Epoca*, 25 Apr. 1989.
58. Frühling and Sanchez (1988), pp. 36–7.
59. The only exception was the politically insignificant radical right, represented by the Avanzada Nacional: 'De Cara al País: Entrevista con los Máximos Dirigentes del Partido Avanzada Nacional', *Canal* 13: 4 Apr. 1988.
60. See: Interview with Andrés Chadwick in Politzer (1985), esp. p. 215.
61. Declaración de Principios de Renovación Nacional, *El Mercurio*, 3 May 1987.
62. It also suggested that a new amnesty law should be passed but only if all the parties were in agreement: 'Las Promesas', *Hoy*, no. 638, 9–15 Oct. 1989, pp. 3–7.
63. For difficulties of the Argentine case see: Acuña and Smulovitz (1991).
64. *Un Planteamiento Para Un Futuro Proyecto Alternativo: Segundo Seminario Nacional de Profesionales, Técnicos e Intelectuales en Homenaje al Ex-Presidente Eduardo Frei*, ii (Santiago, Jan. 1984), p. 9. For the importance attached to human rights by Christian Democrat leader, Gabriel Valdez see: Boeker (1990), p. 32.
65. See: 'Propuesta del Partido Socialista de Chile de un Pacto por los Derechos Humanos' (Departamento Nacional de Derechos Humanos: mimeo, no date).
66. WOLA (1989), p. 7.
67. For rivalries see: Arriagada (1986b), p. 131.
68. For all of above see: 'Adónde Apuntan los Cañones: Reacomodo Castrense Se Efectua en Medio de Tensiones', *Hoy*, no. 652, 15–21 Jan. 1990, p. 11.
69. 'Un Camino Pedregoso', *El Mercurio*, 29 Apr. 1990. The Academia de Humanismo Cristiano, for example, held seminars in 1985 on the issues of truth and justice, examining the cases of Argentina and Brazil. See: Orellana and Frühling (1991), p. 60.
70. See, for example, academic papers by members or supporters of the *Concertación*: Roberto Garreton, 'Amnistía y Prescripción', *Comisión Justicia y Derechos Humanos de la CPPD* (Santiago: mimeo, Nov. 1989); Detzner (1989); Mera (1986); Mera *et al.* (1989).
71. See, for example: 'Qué Pasará Con Lo Que Pasó', *Apsi*, no. 276, 31 Oct.–6 Nov. 1988, pp. 23–5; 'Se Pide Justicia Para los Afectados Por 15 Años de Represión', *Cauce*, no. 174, 5–11 Sept. 1988, pp. 20–1.
72. For examples of this recognition by Buchi see: 'Una Sorprendente Carta Abierta', *La Epoca*, 16 Nov. 1989; 'Reconocimiento Tardío', *El Mercurio*, 2 Dec. 1989.
73. 'Büchi en Campaña Electoral: Indemnizaremos a las Víctimas de

Violaciones a los Derechos Humanos', *Análisis* no. 297, 18–24 Sept. 1989, p. 10

74. Frühling (1985b), p. 3. For an analysis of human rights movement in Chile see: Frühling (1980), (1982), (1985a), (1985b), (1984), (1987), (1988), (1991a), (1991b); Orellana and Frühling (1991); Orellana (1991); Osorio Vargas (1985); Hutchinson Quay (1991); González (1990); Ahumada *et al.* (1989).
75. See: Orellana (1991), p. 12.
76. Frühling (1985b), p. 5.
77. For an account of the role and activities of the Vicaría see: Ahumada *et al.* (1989); Cavallo *et al.* (1988) esp. chs. 10, 13, 25, 39, and 42; Frühling (1985b); González (1990). For the umbrella function of Church see: Garretón (1986b), p. 214; Smith (1986), pp. 277–81.
78. For a full list of all the human rights organizations in Chile see: Orellana (1991), p. 12.
79. Garretón (1986b), p. 166.
80. Ibid., pp. 166 and 170.
81. Garretón (1991), p. 266.
82. Frühling (1991b), p. 52.
83. For this effect see: Frühling (1986b), pp. 18–19.
84. Frühling (1981b), p. 33.
85. Frühling and Sanchez (1988), p. 1.
86. Frühling (1981b), pp. 72 and 84. Between 1978 and 1984, for example, the Vicaría presented 4,034 *recursos de amparo*: Frühling (1991b), p. 39. For the importance of legal defence as opposition see: Frühling (1986b), p. 21; Detzner (1989); Frühling (1980); González (1991); Garretón (1986); Mera *et al.* (1989).
87. Orellana (1991), pp. 9–68.
88. CNVR (1991), p. 5.
89. Smith (1986), p. 289.
90. Orellana and Frühling (1991), p. 42.
91. Frühling (1981b), p. 3.
92. Frühling *et al.* (1989), pp. 129–79. *Solidaridad*, the Vicariate's bi-weekly bulletin, had a circulation of 33,000 in 1979. See: Smith (1986), p. 289.
93. Frühling (1981b), p. 2; Frühling (1984).
94. Garretón (1986b), p. 168.
95. For this role see: Smith (1986), p. 270.
96. Frühling (1981b), p. 64. For the moral power of discourses in competition see: Meneses (1989).
97. See: Smith (1986), (1990); Aldunate *et al.* (1984); Correa and Viera-Gallo (1985).
98. Orellana (1991), p. 14.
99. See: Detzner (1991), pp. 85–109.
100. Ibid., p. 96. See: Detzner (1991); M. C. Vargas (1990); J. E. Vargas (1990). For an interesting account of the biggest and most expensive Amnesty International Concert in Latin America (for Chile, of course)

in 1988 see: Tina Rosenberg, 'Amnesty Hour', New Republic, 17 Dec. 1990, pp. 12–14.

101. Angell (1990).
102. Smith (1986), pp. 282–3, 289, and 290–1.
103. For the different measures taken by the international community to deter regime violations, and the establishment of regular missions see: Detzner (1991), pp. 89–94. See also: Muñoz (1986), pp. 304–22.
104. For the impact of exile see: Angell and Carstairs (1987).
105 *Un Planteamiento Para el Futuro Proyecto Alternativo*, ii (Santiago, Jan. 1984), p. 10.
106. Ibid., pp. 60–2.
107. 'Cómo es un Cristiano Demócrata', *Hoy*, no. 417, 15–21 July 1985, p. 8. For the human rights ideology of the Christian Democrats see: Viera-Gallo and Rodríguez (1987).
108. See: *Acuerdo Por el NO*, 2 Feb. 1988 in CCDH (1988). Similarly, the *Carta Abierta a los Chilenos y Chilenas* of 9 June 1988 of the *Acuerdo Social por el NO*, committed the social organizations to truth and justice. See: CCDH (1989).
109. For a critique of the gap between party identities and human rights activist identities see: Vargas (1985).
110. 'Mensaje de la CPPD con Motivo de los 40 Anos de la Declaración Universal de Derechos Humanos', Santiago, 13 Dec. 1988.
111. Frühling and Sanchez (1988), p. 38.
112. The Asociación Nacional de Familiares de Presos Políticos, the Grupo de Procesados por Leyes Especiales, the Coordinadora Nacional de Presos Políticos, and the Abogados de Presos Políticos were the organizations mainly concerned with this issue of amnesty for political prisoners. See: *La Época*, 18, May 1988; *La Época*, 21 May 1988.
113. *Propuesta de Derechos Humanos: Documento de Conclusiones de la Comisión de Justicia y Derechos Humanos de la CPPD* (Santiago: mimeo, 5 July 1989).
114. 'Las Promesas', *Hoy*, no. 638, 9–15 Oct. 1989, pp. 3–7.
115. See: 'Concertación: Comisión Para Presos Políticos', *La Nación*, 21 Oct. 1989.
116. 'Programa Político Institucional de la Concertación', *La Epoca*, 16 Feb. 1989.
117. Both were signed by all parties which subscribed to the Human Rights Commision's 'Declaración' of December 1987.
118. CCDH (1987).
119. 'Reconciliación en la Verdad: Declaración del Episcopado', Asamblea Plena Extraordinaria, June 1985 (mimeo). 'Los Desafios de la Reconciliación', Conferencia Episcopal de Chile, 1987 (mimeo).
120. 'Agrupación de Familiares de Detenidos Desaparecidos a los Partidos Políticos', *La Epoca*, 22 May 1988. 'Carta al Pueblo de Chile', AFDD, 27 Jan. 1988.
121. 'Libertad Para los Presos Políticos: AAPP', *La Época*, 26 Mar. 1989; 'Indulto General Para Presos Políticos: AAPP', *La Época*, 18 Sept. 1988.

122. 'La Dificultad de Hacer Justicia', *Hoy*, no. 665, 16–22 Apr. 1990, pp. 3–7.
123. See: 'President Aylwin and General Pinochet Heading for Inevitable Showdown', *Southern Cone Report*, RS-90-02, 15 Mar. 1990, p. 1.
124. 'Los Corcoveos del Ejército: Alto Mando Borró Acuerdo Gobierno Oposición En Torno a Ley de Fuerzas Armadas por Temor a Represalias', *Hoy*, no. 653, 22–8 Jan. 1990, pp. 7–8.
125. Survey of the Centro de Estudios de la Realidad Contemporanea, Apr. 1989.
126. 'Pasando y Pasando', *Hoy*, no. 657, 19–25 Feb. 1990, pp. 8–11; 'Que Trama RN', *Hoy*, no. 656, 12–18 Feb. 1990, pp. 3–6.
127. For the preoccupation of the socialists with the potential of the right to attack the *Concertación* and their goal of sticking together and increasing the fluidity of relations between the executive, the parliament, and the Commissions and Ministries see: 'Concertación: La Comezón de los Socialistas', *Hoy*, no. 668, 7–13 May 1990, pp. 21–2.
128. The left coalition, PAIS, had only gained one seat in the lower house.

Chapter 5

1. 'Transcribimos Algunos Fragmentos del Discurso del Presidente', *Las Bases*, 3 Mar. 1985.
2. The rest of their sentences were to be based on each year of prior imprisonment counting as three.
3. 'Hoy Comienza la Liberación de Presos Políticos Por la Amnistía', *La Hora*, 10 Mar. 1985; 'Fueron Liberados Raúl Sendic y Todos Los Presos Políticos', *La Hora*, 15 Mar. 1985.
4. Presidencia de la República (1990), p. 2.
5. Law 15.783. This process was fraught with problems. The government delayed the formation of the Special Commission to study the situation of the *destituidos* and subsequently attempted to change the law it had passed.
6. AW (1989c), p. 12.
7. 'Sanguinetti: Justicia Civil Juzgará a Militares que Hayan Violado Derechos Humanos', *Búsqueda*, 7–13 Feb. 1985; 'Sanguinetti Precisó Como se Juzgarán las Denuncias Contra Miembros de las Fuerzas Armadas', *Búsqueda*, 21 Mar. 1985.
8. For the text of the law see: 'Amnistía Amplia y Generosa, Salvo Homicídio Intencional', *La Mañana*, 5 Mar. 1985.
9. 'Se Formalizan Primeras Acusaciones Contra Ex-Miembros del Regimen Anterior', *Búsqueda*, 11–17 Apr. 1985; Presentarán 24 Denuncias Acerca de la Desaparición de Personas en Uruguay. Araújo Anunció que Denunciará el Martes Próximo 23 Presuntos Delitos de Ex-Gobernantes Militares', *Búsqueda*, 11–17 Apr. 1985.
10. See: 'Diputado Lorenzo Presentó Denuncia Judicial Contra Bor-

daberry y Junta Militar', *Búsqueda*, 27 June 1985; 'Denuncian Ante Suprema Corte a Aparício Méndez y Alvarez.' *Búsqueda*, 10 Oct. 1985.

11. Rough translation: Law for the Annulment of the State's Punitive Capacity. See: 'Nueve Militares Citados a Declarar Esta Tarde', *La Hora*, 9 Dec. 1986 and 'Otros Cuatro Oficiales Citados Para Hoy', *La Hora*, 18 Dec. 1986.
12. *Diario Oficial, Documentos*, 325 (22295) 1981 (Montevideo, 31 Dec. 1986).
13. Four from Por la Patria, eight from the Movimiento Nacional de Rocha and deputy Carlos Pita.
14. DSCRROU (1986a), (1986c). For the Caducidad discussion and vote see pp. 169–261; (1986d) see the Article by Article votes on pp. 134–45. Opposing Blanco senators were Carlos Julio Pereyra, leader of the Movimiento Nacional de Rocha, and Juan Martín Posadas and Uruguay Tourné of Por la Patria. The Blancos did not impose a party whip on the vote, asking members to vote with their conscience. They knew they could not count on the undivided support of the party's representatives.
15. Interview with Deputy Martín Sturla in *Búsqueda*, 22 Aug. 1988. See also: 'Blanco y Colorados Pactaron Consagración de la Impunidad', La *Hora*, 20 Dec. 1986.
16. Equipos Consultores, *Série Estudios de Opinión Pública, Informe Mensual*, 5 May 1985. Only 16% were dissatisfied with their release.
17. DSCSROU (1985d), pp. 255–7. For the line by line votes see: pp. 261–94; 'La Ley Aprobada por el Parlamento que Permite la Libertad de los Presos Políticos', *La Hora*, 9 Mar. 1985.
18. DSCRROU (1985e), pp. 237–50, (1985f). 'Por 86 en 91 Se Aprobó; En Contra la UCB, Salvo Gestido', *La Mañana*, 9 Mar. 1985. The UCB, to which Pintos belonged, presented an alternative project See: *Proyecto de Ley Con Exposición de Motivos Presentado Por los Señores Senadores . . . Referente a Amnistía Respecto de los Delitos Revistos en la Ley de Seguridad del Estado y del Orden Interno, Ley 14.068, 10, Julio, 1975*: DSCSROU, Repartido no. 5, 5 Mar. 1985, Sesión 8 Mar. 1985, p. 306.
19. Cámara de Representantes, Sesion of 28 Feb. 1985, p. 154. For denial of this agreement by the Blancos see: ibid., pp. 167–9.
20. DSCSROU (1985a), FA project, pp. 9–17, (1985b) Blanco project, pp. 43–7 and pp. 47–51. See: *Ley de Amnistía General: Proyecto de Ley Con Exposición de Motivos Presentado Por los Señores Senadores . . .* DSCSROU, Carpeta 35, Repartido 8, 15 Feb. 1985. For Blanco: *Amnistía General y Irrestricta: Proyecto de Ley Con Exposición de Motivos Presentado por los Señores Senadores . . .* DSCSROU, Carpeta 46, Repartido 7, 20 Feb. 1985.
21. The special Commission included nineteen deputies, six Colorados, six Blancos, six Frentistas, and one Unión Cívica representative.

'Sesiona Hoy Comisión Especial Para Estudiar Tema de Amnistía', *El Día*, 21 Feb. 1985. The Colorado's refusal to discuss the presidential project put the Colorado CBI in a difficult position. It had wanted to vote for a Colorado project but did not want to obstruct legislative efforts to get all the prisoners released: 'La CBI Votará el Proyecto Unificado de Blancos y FA', *La Mañana*, 28 Feb. 1985.

22. 'Amnistía: Blancos y Frente Unifican Proyecto Para que Sea General e Irrestricta', *El País*, 27 Feb. 1985.
23. 'Anistía: Cuarto Intermedio Hasta el Lunes en la Cámara de Diputados'; 'Amnistía: Prolongada Sesión con Fuertes Debates', *El Día*, 1 Mar. 1985.
24. 'Transcribimos Algunos Fragmentos del Discurso del Presidente', *Las Bases*, 3 Mar. 1985.
25. DSCSROU (1985d), (1985f), pp. 197–231. The FA, PLP, MNR, UC, CBI (2), and CNH (2) voted in favour. The Colorado UR, LC, and UCB *lemas* voted against. See also 'Cuarto Intermedio Hasta Mañana, Pero Hay Posibilidades Que se Trate Hoy', *El Día*, 5 Mar. 1985.
26. 'Diputados Aprobó Proyecto de Ley de Amnistía y Pasó a Senado: El de Comisión y el del Poder Ejecutivo', *La Mañana*, 6 Mar. 1985.
27. 'Dr. Sanguinetti: Nos Duele Que El País Ni Siquiera Ha Considerado Nuestro Proyecto de Pacificación', *La Mañana*, 7 Mar. 1985.
28. For the full debate see: DSCSROU, Tomo 287, 7a Sesion Ordinaria, 7–8 Mar. 1985. The project voted on was denominated *Proyecto Sustitutivo de la Comisión Especial*. It stated that it expressed the will of the executive, not just of the legislative.
29. Ibid., p. 237.
30. 'Mayoría Aprobó Pedir Libertad de Todos los Presos Políticos', *El Día*, 16 Feb. 1985.
31. 'Juez Civil Ordenó la Captura de Gavazzo, Cordero y Maurente', *La Hora*, 29 Aug. 1985.
32. 'Justicia Militar Interpuso Recurso de Reposición Contra Primeros Fallos de la Corte', *Búsqueda*, 27 Sept. 1986; 'La Causa Contra el Ex-Jefe Naval en Virtual Impasse y es Iminente una Contienda de Competencia', *Búsqueda*, 22 Aug. 1985; 'Juez Rechazó Pedido de Declinar Competencia.' *Búsqueda*, 25 Aug. 1985; 'Magistrados Civiles Rehusaron Declinar Competencia Ante la Justicia Militar', *Búsqueda*, 5 Sept. 1985; 'Suprema Corte Deberá Definir Competencia de la Causa Que Involucra a José Gavazzo', *Búsqueda*, 10–16 Oct. 1985.
33. Pérez Aguirre (1987), p. 18.
34. 'No Hay Venias Para los Conjueces Castrenses. Contienda de Competencia: Suprema Corte no Fallará Antes de Febrero', *Búsqueda*, 21 Nov. 1985; 'Senado Aprobó Venia de Borad y Pagola Para Integrar Suprema Corte', *Búsqueda*, 5 Dec. 1985; 'No Comunicó Aún Venias de Borad y Pagola: Contienda de Competencia Sigue Trabada Por Culpa del Gobierno', *La Democracia*, 20 Dec. 1985.
35. 'Texto de Proyecto Zumarán-Batalla: Delitos de Lesa Humanidad', *La Democracia*, 15 Nov. 1985.

36. 'Ejecutivo Vetaría Una Eventual Ley: Derechos Humanos, El Gobierno No Aceptó Tratar Proyecto Zumarán-Batalla', *Búsqueda*, 4 Apr. 1986.
37. 'El PIT-CNT y la FEUU Lo Rechazaron Sin Conocerlo. Proyecto Zumarán-Batalla Sobre Derechos Humanos: El Líder de la Lista 99 Responsabilizó al Frente Amplio Por Hacerlo Inviable', *Búsqueda*, 9 Oct. 1986.
38. Quijano (1987a), p. 63.
39. 'Los Sindicatos Actúan Siempre Con Intemperancia Pero no Debe Perdirse Siempre Moderación a los Mismos', *Búsqueda*, 25 Apr. 1985.
40. 'Ferreira: Vamos a Hablar Con Sinceridad: No Hay Ningun Uruguayo Que No Sepa Que Aquí no Habrá Acciones Legales Contra Quienes Violaron los Derechos Humanos', *Búsqueda*, 6 June 1985. See also: 'Ferreira Aldunate: Creo en la Estabilidad del Poder Civil', *El País*, Madrid, 27 May 1985; 'Ferreira: No Se Enjuiciará a Quienes Hayan Violado los Derechos Humanos', *El Día*, 3 June 1985.
41. 'Partido Nacional en Procura de Acortar Distanciamientos', *Búsqueda*, 15 Aug. 1985; 'Entrevistas Con Militares', *La Mañana*, 17 Aug. 1985.
42. For a similar assessment see: Gillespie (1990), pp. 18–20.
43. 'Ferreira Aldunate: Corremos Riesgo Ante Una Política de Opinión Pública Porque Los Polarizados Son los Que No Corren Riesgo Alguno', *Búsqueda*, 29 Aug. 1985.
44. 'Juan Martin Posadas: Fue Un Encuentro Con Estilo del COSENA', *La Mañana*, 11 Aug. 1985. For his defence see: 'Zumarán Calificó de Positiva la Reunión Con Militares en San Juan', *La Mañana*, 10 Aug. 1985.
45. 'Seregni: Un Compromiso Que Asumimos Y Que Deberá Cumplirse', *Brecha*, 30 May 1986.
46. 'Seregni: Tenga la Seguridad de que se Hará Justicia', *Brecha*, 18 Oct. 1985; 'Líber Seregni Recordó Que El Jefe del Ejército Admitió Que los Militares Pueden Comparecer Ante Jueces Civiles', *Búsqueda*, 30 Apr. 1986.
47. 'La Estratégia del Frente Amplio', *Las Bases*, 1 Aug. 1985.
48. On 6 June the Frente abandoned the General Assembly because it was not consulted on the constitution of the Electoral Court and the Tribunal de Cuentas: Barros Lémez (1987), p. 193.
49. 'Legisladores del Gobierno y de la Oposición Manejan la Posibilidad de una Solución Negociada Sobre el Tema de los Derechos Humanos', *Búsqueda*, 22 May 1986.
50. 'Todos Los Partidos Acordaron Discutir Derechos Humanos en Asamblea General', *El País*, 23 May 1986; 'Derechos Humanos: Un Tema a Definir por la Asamblea General', *Brecha*, 23 May 1986.
51. 'Pueden Anticipar las Sustituciones del Comandante en Jefe y Del Ministro de Defensa', *Alternativa Socialista*, 19 Oct. 1986.
52. 'Ferreira Se Reunió Con Sanguinetti: Hoy lo Hace Con Seregni. Contactos al Más Alto Nivel Por Solución Negociada al Tema de los Derechos Humanos', *Búsqueda*, 12–17 June 1986.
53. 'Ferreira y Ciganda Ayer: La Semana Próxima Otra Cúpula', *La*

Mañana, 12 July 1986. For a reserved meeting between Ciganda, Seregni, and Ferreira see: 'Se Avanzó en el Tratamiento del Tema Derechos Humanos', *La Mañana*, 29 July 1986.

54. 'Presidente Sanguinetti: El Objectivo del Gobierno es Mantener la Estabilidad Institucional', *Búsqueda*, 27 June 1986.
55. 'Senadores de los 3 Lemas Pronunciaron en Contra de un Nuevo Acuerdo con la FFAA Por la Cuestión de Derechos Humanos', *Búsqueda*, 7 Aug. 1986.
56. 'Seregni y Ferreira: Amnistía a Militares Trás la Aclaración de los Sucesos', *Búsqueda*, 19 June 1986. There were rumours of numerous proposals, such as a plebiscite and a bill which would amnesty all crimes except the assassinations of Michelini and Gutierrez Ruíz. See: 'Para Seregni Es Inaceptable el Concepto de Una Amnistía Previa', *La Mañana*, 22 Aug. 1986; 'No Hay Paz Sin El Império de la Justicia', *La Hora*, 27 July 1986.
57. 'Seregni: Esclarecimiento y Justicia', *Las Bases*, 13 July 1986.
58. 'Acuerdo Entre Ferreira y Ciganda: No Es Viable Una Amnistía', *La Democracia*, 12 July 1986; 'Zumarán: Conocer la Verdad Antes de Hablar de Amnistía', *El País*, 22 May 1986; 'El Planteo de Una Amnistía Recíproca Antes del Dictamen Judicial es Absurdo y Descabellado', *Búsqueda*, 29 May 1986.
59. 'El Presidente No Esta Dispuesto a Negociar Sobre Algunos Nombres', *Búsqueda*, 22 May 1986.
60. 'Asesinatos Michelini-Gutiérrez Ruíz: El Gobierno Quiere Otra Vez Que Asuma la Justicia Militar', *Brecha*, 18 Apr. 1986. A motion in the Legislature to call on the Minister to justify his actions was defeated; only the Frente Amplio's 22 legislators voted for it, unable to count on the solidarity of the Blancos.
61. Number of cases: AW (1989c), pp. 13–14. On the conflict see: 'Contienda: Fallo en Favor de la Justicia Civil. La Suprema Corte Sostiene Que la Justicia Militar no Integra el Poder Judicial', *Búsqueda*, 31 June 1986. The SC decision was reconfirmed in November following an appeal by the SMT. 'Existe una Justicia Para Todos', *Búsqueda*, 27 Nov. 1986; 'Justicia Independiente? Tajante Rechazo a Expresiones de Sanguinetti', *Aquí*, 24 June 1986; 'El Poder Judicial Defiende Sus Fueros Y Refuta a Legisladores Colorados', *Brecha*, 7 Feb. 1986. *Conjueces* attacks: 'Conjuez Borad Reclamó a Ministros de la Corte de No Ser Equilibristas Que Usan a la Democracia Como Pértiga', *Búsqueda*, 27 Nov. 1986.
62. 'Juez Argentino Decretó Prisión y Solicitó Extradición de 4 Oficiales Uruguayos', *Búsqueda*, 2 Oct. 1986; 'Hoy la Embajada Argentina Presenta Pedido de Extradición en Cancilleria', *La Hora*, 27 Oct. 1987; 'Extradición: Rechazo Por Vicios Formales', *Alternativa Socialista*, 20 Nov. 1986.
63. 'Carta de Araújo a Paulós', *El Día*, 13 May 1986; 'Plena Solidaridad del Frente Amplio Con el Senador Araújo', *Aquí*, 13 May 1986; 'El Triste Papel de Tarigo y Zumarán', *La Hora*, 16 May 1985.

64. 'Derechos Humanos: Los Diferentes Caminos Analizados Por los Juristas', *Brecha*, 8 Aug. 1986; 'Seregni Confirmó Formación de Grupo de Expertos para Analizar el Problema', *La Hora*, 30 July 1986.
65. *Ante Proyecto Considerado por Comisión de Juristas*, June 1986, copy of original document.
66. 'Proyecto de Amnistía Que Llegó a Los Juristas: Lo Califican de Aberración Jurídica', *Aquí*, 5 Aug. 1986; 'Juristas Por Consenso Descartan Amnistía', *El País*, 5 Aug. 1986.
67. 'Derechos Humanos: Grupo de Juristas Concluyó Labor', *La Mañana*, 4 Aug. 1986; 'Se Gestiona Reunión Conjunta de los 4 Juristas Con Cúpula Política', *El País*, 6 Aug. 1986.
68. On war context theory see: 'Sanguinetti: Renunciamos a un Gran Juicio: No Hubo Voluntad de Extermínio. No se Encuentran Evidencias', *Brecha*, 21 May 1985. On the guerrilla threat campaign in government papers see: 'El "Rebrote Guerrillero": Telenovela en Episodios', *Brecha*, 26 July 1986; 'Sanguinetti Aseguró Que Hay Quienes Buscan el Enfrentamiento de Civiles Con Militares', *Búsqueda*, 5 June 1986.
69. Del Huerto Amarillo and Rial (1988), p. 41.
70. 'Un Entretien Avec Le Président Sanguinetti', *Le Monde*, Paris, 13–14 Nov. 1985; 'Sanguinetti: Proyecto de Pacificación el Complementario de Amnistía Que Se Aprobó Para Subversivos el Año Pasado', *El País*, 29 Aug. 1986.
71. 'Sanguinetti Realizará Hoy Una Reunión Con Wilson Ferreira', *La Mañana*, 17 Aug. 1986; 'Declaraciones de Seregni Luego de Su Reunión Con Sanguinetti', *La Hora*, 22 Aug. 1986; 'Frente Amplio: El FA Fundamentó Su Rechazo al Proyecto del Poder Ejecutivo', *La Hora*, 29 Sept. 1986; 'Wilson Ferreira Aldunate: El Proyecto es el Mayor Agravio a las Fuerzas Armadas', *La Hora*, 13 Sept. 1986.
72. 'Senado Rechazó Por 16 Votos en 29 Proyecto de Impunidad Colorado', *La Hora*, 29 Aug. 1986; 'Comisión Especial del Senado Rechazó Amnistía Colorada', *La Hora*, 20 Sept. 1986.
73. Examples: 'El Soldado Publicó Nómina de Crímenes y Secuestros Realizados Por Subversivos e Identidad de sus Autores', *Búsqueda*, 22 May 1986; 'General Iván Paulós: Soportando en Éste Día de Evocación y Reflexión', *Búsqueda*, 18 Apr. 1986.
74. Márquez admitted to the use of torture but this was not, in his judgement, something to get too worried about: 'Dos Ex-Jerarcas de la Dictadura: Exaltaron Uso de la Fuerza Represiva', *El Popular*, 25 Apr. 1986; 'Increíbles Declaraciones del Vice-Almirante Márquez', *La Hora*, 12 Apr. 1986; 'Vice-Almirante Márquez: "Puse un Destello de Luz en el Oscurantismo"', *Búsqueda*, 24 Apr. 1986. In the Club's elections in September 1985 'liberal' Franzini got 38%, 'procesista' Flangini got 37%, and the 'pro-transition' Fernández got 24% of the vote. The latter two defended human rights violators: Rial (1986a), p. 72.
75. 'Cuatro Militares Desean Batirse a Duelo con Araújo', *Búsqueda*, 11 July 1985.

76. 'Acusados a las Urnas', *La Democracia*, 20 Sept. 1985. 'Centro Militar: General Paulós Candidato del Comando', *Últimas Noticias*, 29 Aug. 1985. On General Paulós defended the accused frequently and unapologetically see: 'Paulós Comprometió Todo el Apoyo del Club Militar Para Oficiales Que Cumplieron Con Su Deber y Son Acusados Ahora de Haber Violado a los Derechos Humanos', *Búsqueda*, 12 Aug. 1985; 'Gral. Iván Paulós "No Hay Guerras a Medias: La Guerra es la Guerra"', *Búsqueda*, 3 Oct. 1985.
77. The Military Centre, the Artigas Military Club, and the Centre of Retired Officers. See: 'Clubes Naval y de la Fuerza Aérea no Acompañaron: Tres Instituciones Castrenses se Quejaron por "Ataques Contra la Familia Militar"', *Búsqueda*, 28 Nov. 1985. Only the Navy Club's liberal sector stated that it found the declaration to be out of place: Rial (1986a), p. 75.
78. Bonelli had wanted to resign in protest against the promotion of Colonel (R) Arturo Silva, expelled from the military in 1977 for political reasons, to the General Directorship of the Ministry of Defence. Siqueira resigned in May 1985, for disagreeing with the re-instatement of Generals Licandro and Seregni, also expelled for political reasons. General Feola was relieved of his post on 16 Oct. 1985, for releasing a press statement contrasting law military pay rates with high Congressional salaries. Varela was dismissed from the SIFA for political espionage. For first two see: 'Outspoken General Gets the Sack', *Southern Cone Report*, 15 Nov. 1985, p. 5; 'Pleito Interno', *La Democracia*, 23 Oct. 1985. For latter two see: 'El Pase a Retiro de Medina Cierra el Ciclo del Comandante de la Transición', *Búsqueda*, 29 Jan. 1987.
79. Zagorsky (1992), p. 89.
80. On the promotion see: Navarrete (1989). For the other see: Pérez Aguirre (1987), p. 18.
81. 'El Asado de los Militares', *La Hora*, 28 July 1986; 'Cúpula del Ejército Ratificó el Apoyo a la Constitución y Leyes', *El Popular*, 13 July 1986; 'Todos Somos Responsables o Ninguno es Responsable', *Búsqueda*, 31 Sept. 1986. The Generals who signed the declaration were all responsible for the battle against subversion during the military regime: 'Promovieron Asamblea en Defensa de Honor Militar', *Búsqueda*, 4 Aug. 1986.
82. According to the editorial, the pretext for mounting the Argentine 'trial was the defence of human rights, the same banner raised by James Carter to facilitate Communist expansionism.' See: 'A las Instituciones Con Dignidad No Se Las Acorrala', *El Soldado*, no. 108, 10 Aug. 1986.
83. *Búsqueda*, 7 Nov. 1986.
84. 'Dos Documentos que Darán Que Hablar: Boletín del Comando del Ejército', *Opinar*, 28 Mar. 1985; 'Frentistas Rechazan Contenido de Documento del SIE y Reclaman Una Investigación Pública', *Búsqueda*, 11 Apr. 1985. For other incidents see: 'Diputados Consideró

Insuficientes Explicaciones de Manini Pero Este Recibió Respaldo del Ejecutivo', *Búsqueda*, 1 Nov. 1985 and 'La Justicia Ordinaria Citó a 46 Civiles Para Declarar Sobre Denuncias Contra Inteligencia', *Búsqueda*, 3 Nov. 1985.

85. Quijano (1987a), pp. 61–7. See also: 'Hacia Aceptación del Desacato Como Resultado de la Impotencia', *Brecha*, 21 Nov. 1986; 'El Peligroso Desgaste de Medina ante una Salida que no Aparece', *La Mañana*, 8 Oct. 1986.
86. 'Medina: La Democracia no Llegó Por Presión: Jefe del Ejército Habló en Acto del Día de Esa Fuerza', *El País*, 19 May 1985.
87. 'Medina: El Ejército Esta en Plena Tarea de Re-Inserción', *El Popular*, 19 May 1986; 'Medina: Esperamos Confiados Fallo de la Justicia', *Búsqueda*, 22 May 1986. He argued in favour of reciprocity stating that 'If there are prisoners who were responsible for nine or ten deaths and who are being freed, I don't see why the members of the Armed Forces should be judged for having committed this or that excess': 'Tte. General Medina: Si Se Dan las Mismas Causales Que Se Dieron en 1973, no Vamos a Tener Más Remedio que Darlo [el golpe]', *Búsqueda*, 14 Feb. 1985.
88. 'Medina Negó Tribunales de Honor, Criticó a Jose Germán Araújo, y Dijo que Hay que "Dilucidar la Veracidad" de las Denuncias', *Búsqueda*, 17 July 1985. 'Texto de la Respuesta del Comandante en Jefe', *Búsqueda*, 17 July 1985. For Medina's continued 'national security' outlook see: Boeker (1990), p. 83.
89. Arocena and Quijano (1987b) and Gillespie (1990), p. 221.
90. 'Tte. Cnel. Jose Nino Gavazzo: De Ninguna Manera Concurriré Ante un Juez Civil Para Que Se Me Juzgue Por Mis Actos De Servicio', *Búsqueda*, 12 Sept. 1985; 'Inician Acción Penal Por Incumplimiento de Orden Judicial Para Que Seis Policías Fueran Conducidos a Declarar por el Juez de 6o Turno', *Búsqueda*, 12 June 1986; 'General Ballestrino No Compareció a Citación de Justicia Ordinaria', *Búsqueda*, 2 Oct. 1986.
91. 'Chiape Pose: Fuerzas Armadas Cumplieron Con Su Deber: Una Amnistía Conduciría a Quebrar El Honor y Principios Militares', *El País*, 4 July 1986; 'Militares Se Oponen a Aprobación de la Ley de Amnistía', *El País*, 4 July 1986; 'Reunión de Generales Con Diputados Colorados: Reservas Ante Una Amnistía', *Búsqueda*, 17 July 1986.
92. See: 'Reuniones Cuestionadas y Protestas Populares Aumentaron Inquietud en los Militares', *Búsqueda*, 14 Aug. 1986; for the military response to public protests see: 'Centro Militar a Sus Asociados', *La Manana*, 15 Aug. 1986; for retired generals' declaration see: 'Generales en Retiro Asumen Responsabilidad', *El País*, 20 Aug. 1986; 'Jefes del Ejército Ratifican Su Reponsabilidad por los Cuestionamientos de las Acciones Anti Subversivas', *Búsqueda*, 21 Aug. 1986. For the postponement of the assembly see: 'Directivos de Centro Militar Pidieron Aplazar Llamado a Asamblea de Socios', *Búsqueda*, 28 Aug. 1986.

93. *Proyecto de Ley de la Defensa de la Democracia*, 23 Sept. 1986, copy of original. Also: 'Proyecto Nacional Se Presentó en la Cámara de Senadores', *La Mañana*, 23 Sept. 1986; 'Proyecto Blanco: Más Cerca de la Impunidad o Más Cerca de la Justicia?', *Brecha*, 26 Sept. 1986; 'Sanguinetti Faces Clash with Supreme Court and Congress', *Latin America Weekly Report*, 27 Nov. 1986, p. 1.
94. For the debate in the Senate see: 'Colorados y Frentistas Procuran Hacer Prevalecer Sus Posiciones: El Senado Rechazó la Amnistía Colorada Pero Aprobó en General el Proyecto Blanco para Juzgar los Delitos Considerados Graves', *Búsqueda*, 7 Oct. 1986; 'Senado Rechazó Proyecto Blanco-11-30', *La Hora*, 8 Oct. 1986.
95. The Colorados rejected it despite the Blanco leader's attempts to persuade the government party to vote with it in another series of reserved meetings between the leadership. For the renewed negotiations see: 'La Cúpula Política Podría Destrabar Tema Pacificación', *La Mañana*, 2 Oct. 1986; 'Se Intensifican los Contactos Entre Partidos Tradicionales', *La Mañana*, 6 Oct. 1986. For the Colorados support only for an amnesty see: 'CPN Señala Sus Discrepancias Con el Proyecto Blanco', *La Hora*, 28 Sept. 1986.
96. *Observaciones del Frente Amplio al Proyecto del Partido Nacional*, mimeo, 27 Sept. 1986.
97. 'Ciganda y Seregni Señalaron Puntos de Acuerdo y Apoyarían Proyecto Blanco', *El País*, 23 Sept. 1986; 'Texto Integro del Documento Frentista Sobre Proyecto Blanco', *La Hora*, 28 Sept. 1986; 'Dr Williman: Propuestas de Frente Amplio Sensatas y Viables', *La Hora*, 30 Sept. 1986.
98. 'Informe de Seregni al Plenario', *Las Bases*, 12 Oct. 1986.
99. 'Una Provocación Más?', *La Mañana*, 5 Oct. 1986 and 'En Nombre de Quién Hablan los 16 Generales?', *Alternativa Socialista*, 9 Oct. 1986.
100. For an account of their anger see: 'Zumarán: La Historia Juzgará a los Que Actuaron o No Con Sensatez', *El Popular*, 5 Oct. 1986.
101. 'El Partido Colorado Amenaza Con Disolver las Cámaras: Justicia o Crisis Institucional', *Juventud*, 19 Oct. 1986. 'Coinciden Juristas en Cuanto a Legalidad de Disolución de Cámaras', *La Mañana*, 10 Nov. 1986. For political debate over this see: 'La Opción es un Gobierno de Coalición o Que la Gente Vote: Senador Dr. Luis LaCalle', *La Mañana*, 9 Nov. 1986.
102. 'Reunión Considerada Normal la de Sanguinetti y Militares', *La Mañana*, 10 Oct. 1986.
103. 'Acuerdo En Rendición de Cuentas y Cumbre Por Derechos Humanos', *Búsqueda*, 27 Nov. 1986; 'Apoyo Militar al Afianzamiento de la Democracia', *El Día*, 2 Dec. 1986; 'Documento FF. AA: Se Sienten Marginadas de la Reconciliación y la Pacificación', *Búsqueda*, 4 Dec. 1986; 'FF.AA Repudian Acciones Ilícitas', *El Día*, 24 Nov. 1986.
104. 'Seregni: El Frente Amplio No Hace Acuerdos Chanchos', *Búsqueda*, 18 Dec. 1986.

105. 'Seregni Expuso Posición Ante Conyuntura: Líder Frente Amplista Dispuesto al Diálogo', *La Mañana*, 22 Nov. 1986.
106. 'Seregni: La Jurisdicción Civil Se Estableció Con Claridad en el Club Naval', *El Día*, 2 Dec. 1986.
107. For the support of Ferreira for this interpretation see: Wilson Ferreira Aldunate, editorial in *La Democracia*, 21 Nov. 1986. For Seregni's rejection of it see: *La Hora*, 23 Nov. 1986.
108. 'Colorados Reconocen que los Militares no Concurrirán a Declarar Ante Justicia', *El País*, 19 Dec. 1986.
109. 'Ferreira Dijo Que Bregará para Que el Costo Político de una Solución al Tema Derechos Humanos Lo Paguen Sanguinetti y Seregni', *Búsqueda*, 20 Nov. 1986.
110. See speech by Zumarán in *El Pais*, 18 Dec. 1986.
111. 'Cúpula Político Militar Centro Discusión en Acuerdo de 84', *Búsqueda*, 4 Dec. 1986; 'Derechos Humanos: Gravita en la Polémica el Reconocimiento de un Presunto Acuerdo Implícito en el Club Naval', *Búsqueda*, 4 Dec. 1986; 'Ferreira: Cerrar la Cuentas del Pasado', *El Día*, 29 Sept. 1986.
112. 'Derechos Humanos: Seregni, Marchesano, Ferreira', *El Popular*, 5 Dec. 1986.
113. *Búsqueda*, 18 Dec. 1986.
114. 'Completo Plan Político del Frente Amplio', *Las Bases*, 23 Nov. 1986.
115. 'Ferreira: Deber y Responsabilidad de Evitar Desacato Militar: En Canal 10, Marchesano, Seregni y Wilson Ferreira', *Búsqueda*, 4 Dec. 1986.
116. Another version of events suggests that it was the Blancos who suggested a postponement of the issue with a second pact between all the parties. Seregni had said he could not support it because he did not have the backing of the Frente's Plenario, and the Blancos had asked that if he could not support it, he should at least ensure that the Frente would not *tirar piedras* at it.
117. 'Gonzalo Carambula: Nos Atacan Para Encubrir la Impunidad', *La Hora*, 5 Dec. 1986; 'El Momento Político en Materia de Violaciones de los Derechos Humanos Ocurridos Durante la Dictadura', *Brecha*, 17 Dec. 1986.
118. 'El Proyecto No Trae Pacificación Sino División a los Uruguayos', *La Hora*, 30 Aug. 1986.
119. *Brecha*, 12 Nov. 1986. Also: 'Frente Amplio Resolución de la Mesa Política: Acatar la Constitución La Ley y Los Fallos de la Suprema Corte', *La Hora*, 2 Dec. 1986. At one point there was a suggestion from the Frente that the president go on a hunger strike to force the military to abdicate: see 'Carta Abierta al General Seregni', 28 Nov. 1986, for an internal Frente critique of the coalition and its leader's position.
120. DSCSROU (1986b), pp. 1–17. 'Korzeniak Explica el Proyecto Presentado al Frente Amplio', *Alternativa Socialista*, 18 Dec. 1986. See also 'Juristas del Frente Amplio Prepararon un Anteproyecto

Sobre el Revisionismo Que Declara Competente a la Corte Suprema', *Búsqueda*, 28 Aug. 1986.

121. DSCSROU (1986b), pp. 1–17. 'El FA Convoca a Concentrarse a las 16 Horas en el Parlamento', *La Hora*, 18 Dec. 1986.
122. 'El Partido Nacional Presentó Proyecto para la Pacificación', *La Mañana*, 20 Dec. 1986.
123. 'Wilson Ferreira: Votamos Con Dolor y Asumimos Responsabilidad', *El Día*, 31 Dec. 1986.
124. 'Wilson Ferreira: Ley Salvó Integridad de Instituciones', *El Popular*, 4 Jan. 1987.
125. 'Militares Dijeron En Club Naval Que No Habría Juicios: Declaración de Colorados en el Senado lo Reconocieron', *El País*, 19 Dec. 1986.
126. 'Uruguay Tourné: Luego de Conocer Hechos Creo Que en el Planteo de la Ley de Caducidad me Pasaron la Pelota Por Arriba del Moño', *Búsqueda*, 31 Aug. 1989.
127. The law was actually written by Senator Sturla of the MNR faction of the Blanco Party, who voted against the law: 'Sturla y Sus Confesiones: Yo Redacté a la Ley de Caducidad', *Alternativa Socialista*, 29 Sept. 1989.
128. DSCSROU (1986e), 'Hechos Acaecidos en la Noche del Domingo 21 de Diciembre en las Adyacencias del Palacio Legislativo', pp. 149–217. The result of the vote was 25 : 30.
129. For a detailed account of the 'Gavazzo incident' see Ramírez (1989), pp. 102–3.
130. Commission for the Investigation of the Situation of the Disappeared and Related Events. See: DSCRROU (1985g).
131. Investigating Commission on the Kidnapping and Assassination of National Representatives Zelmar Michelini and Héctor Gutiérrez Ruíz. See: DSCRROU (1987), pp. 523–99. 589–99. 'Desaparecidos: Durante la Dictadura Militar en Uruguay se Cometió Genocidio', *Brecha*, 25 Oct. 1987; 'Informe Final Sobre el Caso Michelini-Gutiérrez Ruíz', *Alternativa Socialista*, 20 Aug. 1987.
132. 'No Tienen Facultades Para Investigar', *Compañero*, 13 June 1985; 'President Podría Ordenar la no Comparecencia de Militares: Diputados Aprobó Ampliación de Facultades a Investigadoras', *Búsqueda*, 17 July 1985. For the opposition see: Edison Rijo, 'A Propósito de Comisiones Investigadoras', *El Día*, 14 Apr. 1985; 'Discrepancias Entre Ferreira Aldunate y el Diputado Alem García por Iniciativa de Citar a Militares a Declarar Ante el Parlamento', *Búsqueda*, 14 Aug. 1986.
133. On the difficulties of establishing conclusive proof of otherwise 'proven' facts see: 'Sin Pruebas de Intervención de Uruguayos en Asesinatos de Gutiérrez Ruíz y Michelini', *Búsqueda*, 4 July 1985; 'En 25 Casos Existe SemiPrueba de que Efectivos de las FF.CC Tendrían Responsabilidad', *Las Bases*, 21 July 1985; 'Convicción de Coordinación Entre Militares Uruguayos y Argentinos en la Represión', *Búsqueda*, 17 Oct. 1985; 'En Pre-Informe de la Investigadora

Se Señala Vinculación Directa de 46 Militares Uruguayos y 3 Extranjeros', *Búsqueda*, 1 Nov. 1985. For the contradictions in the report and the final statement see: 'Sólo 46 Culpables?', *Brecha*, 9 Nov. 1985. Also: DSCRROU (1985g) and AI (1988a).

134. See: 'Qué Otras Pruebas Pretende el Gobierno', *El Popular*, 5 Sept. 1986.
135. 'Por Iniciativa de SERPAJ y IELSUR: Se Trata de Establecer Que los Militares Comparezcan en los Juzgados Al Ser Citados', *Búsqueda*, 9 May 1985.
136. 'El Colegio de Abogados Contra el Proyecto del Poder Ejecutivo', *La Hora*, 29 Sept. 1986; 'Pacificación: Comisión Rechazó Proyecto de Poder Ejecutivo', *La Mañana*, 20 Sept. 1986; 'Asamblea del Claustro de la Universidad de la República: Rechazan la Amnistía Colorada', *Brecha*, 19 Aug. 1986; 'Importantes Conclusiones de SERPAJ, IELSUR y Familiares', *Aquí*, 8 July 1986.
137. 'IELSUR y SERPAJ: Proyecto Blanco Deja Sin Investigar Tortura y Desapariciones', *La Hora*, 1 Oct. 1986.
138. 'La Televisión da la Espalda a la Campaña por Derechos Humanos', *Búsqueda*, 1 Aug. 1986.
139. 'Defensores de Derechos Humanos Objetan Informe de Comisión de Diputados', *Búsqueda*, 14 Nov. 1985; *Comunicado de Prensa* of 11 Nov. 1985 and 15 Apr. 1986, mimeos.
140. 'Paz y Justicia: Sumario de Derechos Humanos', Jan.–Apr. 1989, IV, no. 17, p. 26, 'Paz y Justicia: Sumario de Derechos Humanos', Aug.–Sept. 1988, IV, no. 15, p. 3; SERPAJ (1989), p. 15.
141. Ibid., p. 13, pp. 363–405 and p. 18.
142. Ibid.
143. 'Paz y Justicia: Sumario de Derechos Humanos', Ano IV, no. 17 Apr. 1989, p. 16.
144. SERPAJ (1992), p. xix. For a comparative analysis of this and similar reports in Brazil, Argentina, and Chile see: Barahona De Brito (1991).
145. Article 79, no. 2.
146. See: 'Comunicaron a la Corte Electoral la Decisión de Realizar el Referendum', *La Hora*, 12 Jan. 1987; 'Referendum: Se Forma Comisión', *La Hora*, 24 Jan. 1987; 'Representamos la Indignación del Pueblo', *Brecha*, 30 Jan. 1987; 'María Ester Gatti: Ningun Sector o Partido es el Padre el la Convocatoria al Plebiscito', *La Hora*, 13 Jan. 1987.
147. 'PIT–CNT También Respalda el Plebiscito Contra la Impunidad', *La Hora*, 8 Jan. 1987; 'Los Estudiantes Van a Firmar', *La Hora*, 21 Jan. 1987; 'Elementos Para la Reflexión de una Comunidad Cristiana: Monseñor Gottardi of the Comisión Arquidiosesana de Pastoral Social: El Referendum es un Recurso Adecuado', *La Juventud*, 16 Mar. 1987; 'Monseñor Partelli Firmó Para Que el Pueblo Se Exprese', *La Hora*, 8 Sept. 1987; 'El SMU Apoya el Referendum e Instrumenta su Participación en la Campaña de Firmas', *La Hora*, 21 Mar. 1987.

Others included the CEFOPO, the Centro Cooperativo Uruguayo, the CIDC, UPFE, Paz y Bien, Programa Cardjin, Scouts Católicos del Uruguay, SERSOC, Unidad Técnica para Reinserción Laboral, and NOTAS. See: 'Organizaciones Sociales con Referendum', *La Hora*, 29 Mar. 1987; 'Plenario FA Resolvió Apoyo al Referendum', *La Hora*, 13 Feb. 1987; 'CBI: Sector de Vaillant Apoya a Referendum', *La Hora*, 11 Jan. 1987; 'MNR Decidió Por Ampla Mayoria Apoyar el Referendo Contra la Ley de Caducidad', *El Día*, 1 Feb. 1987; 'MNB: Nelson Sica: La Única Bandera del Referendum es la Nacional', *La Hora*, 21 Feb. 1987; 'Corriente Popular Nacional: Posicion de CPN: Verdad y Justicia Para Defender la Democracia', *Brecha*, 3 Oct. 1986.

148. See Seregni's letter to all militants instructing them on how to collect signatures: 'Cada Compañero una Firma Más', 23 July 1987; 'FA Recorre Todo el País Por Firmas', *La Hora*, 16 May 1987. 'Seregni: Firmar por el Referendum es un Deber de Todo Frenteamplista', *La Hora*, 7 May 1987.

149. For two opposing examples see: Dr Miguel A Semino, 'El Referendum Contra la Ley N. 15.848', *El Día*, 21–7 Feb. 1987; 'Diputado Sturla: El Referendum es Totalmente Inútil Porque el Efecto de la Ley Ya Se Consumó', *El País*, 8 Feb. 1987; 'Dr. Pérez: El Referendum Deja Sin Efecto la Ley Desde el Princípio', *La Hora*, 12 Feb. 1987.

150. 'El PC Rechazó la Campaña por el Referendo', *El Día*, 17 Feb. 1987; 'Congreso PLP Rechazó Referendo: Wilson Se Declaró Responsable de la Ley de Caducidad', *El País*, 9 Feb. 1987; 'Los Tupamaros Propícian Firmas Contra la Ley de Pacificación', *La Mañana*, 24 Dec. 1986. This campaign was seen to be the equivalent of the military's cataloguing of citizens according to A B and C. See: 'Registro de Vecindad', *El País*, 24 Jan. 1987; 'Aclaran Sobre Posible Efecto del Referendo. Paz Aguirre: Podría Derogarse Amnistía del 85', *El Día*, 24 Jan. 1987; 'Diputado Víctor Cortazzo: Es Justo y Lógico que la Amnistía También Se Revea', *El Día*, 27 Jan. 1987.

151. Speech on 31 Jan. 1986 in Colonia. Also: 'Sanguinetti Exhortó a Que Partidos en Clima de Superior Entendimiento Alcancen Solución Que el País Necesita', *El País*, 2 Dec. 1986.

152. 'Sanguinetti: Sería Una Vuelta al Pasado', *El Día*, 22 Feb. 1987. For similar statements made by other Colorado leaders see: 'Batlle: Los Tupamaros Plantearon Referendum Que no Conlleva a la Pacificación del País', *El País*, 7 Jan. 1987; 'Diputado Ruben Díaz: El Referendum Plantea Opción Entre Sanguinetti y Sendic', *El Día*, 6 Feb. 1987; 'Eduardo Paz Aguirre: Al Referendum lo Propícian Tupamaros y Comunistas', *El Día*, 21 Feb. 1987.

153. 'Sanguinetti: Sería Una Vuelta al Pasado', *El Día*, 22 Feb. 1987. See also: 'Canton: A Quien Se le Ocurre Pacificar Amnistiando un Solo Bando de los Que se Enfrentaron', *El País*, 31 Dec. 1987; 'La Ley de Caducidad es Medida Pacificadora', *El Día*, 20 Mar. 1987.

154. *La República*, 19 July 1988.

155. *Búsqueda*, 2 June 1988.
156. *La República*, 29 Oct. 1988.
157. *Búsqueda*, 2 Mar. 1989.
158. '634,702 Firmas Entregadas a la Corte Electoral', *La Hora*, 18 Dec. 1987. The minimum required were 555,701.
159. AI (1988c). Captain Bernardo Gastón Silberman was administratively detained in August and held for 60 days and Sub-Lieutenant Sergio Retamoso detained in September for 42 days: AW (1989c), p. 32. Also AW (1988c).
160. *La República*, 15 Aug. 1988; DSCSROU (1988). Medina was subsequently called by Senate to explain his sanction of officers supporting referendum, pp. 103–232.
161. Eduardo Galeano, 'Sign on the Invisible Line', *The Nation*, 27 Mar. 1989, pp. 411–12. DSCSROU (1989a), pp. 7–91 and (1989b), pp. 93–144 for the Electoral Court's ratification of the referendum's validity and on the proceedings of the vote.
162. *Búsqueda*, 20 Oct. 1987. For an account of the referendum campaign and vote see: Burt (1988) and (1989).
163. Gillespie and Arregui (1988).
164. Sposito (1989), p. 4.
165. Garretón (1990).
166. 'Zumarán: Antes del Club Naval Hubo Un Acuerdo por le Cual el PC y el Frente Dieron al Ejército Su Garantía Que los Militares No Serían Juzgados', *Búsqueda*, 2 Feb. 1987. For the FA and UC outraged responses see: 'Seregni, Ciganda y Young le Salen al Paso Alberto Zumarán: De Canallada Que Ensucia el Clima Político Calificó el Presidente del Frente Afirmaciones del Líder Blanco', *La República*, 4 Feb. 1989.
167. *La Democracia*, 30 Dec. 1986. For the meeting see: 'Pacificación: Extenso Diálogo Mantuvieron Batlle y Zumarán', *La Mañana*, 6 Oct. 1986. Both leaders had refused to comment on the meeting.
168. 'Sanguinetti: Amenaza de Desacato Militar Es Un Argumento Retórico', *Búsqueda*, 8 Jan. 1987.
169. 'General Medina: La Democracia Esta Bien Asentada', *Búsqueda*, 21 Mar. 1987.
170. 'Medina Expresó Reconocimiento A Legisladores que Votaron Ley de Caducidad y a Sanguinetti por "Apoyo Indescriminable a FF.AA"', *Búsqueda*, 6 Feb. 1987.
171. See: 'Anexo I: Efectos del No Cumplimiento de la Ley de Caducidad de la Pretensión Punitiva del Estado', *Paz y Justicia: Informe* (1989). For the different promotions see: *Búsqueda*, 6 Feb. 1986; 14 Mar. 1986 p. 1; 20 Mar. 1986, p. 8; 29 May 1986, p. 4; 11 Aug. 1986, p. 4; 18 Sept. 1986, p. 5.
172. Navarette (1989).
173. Pareja (1987), p. 35.
174. 'Sanguinetti: Amnistía y Caducidad Son el Precio Político de la Democracia', *El Día*, 9 Mar. 1987.

Chapter 6

1. 'Aylwin Picks His Ministerial Team', *Southern Cone Report*, RS-90-01, 8 Feb. 1990, p. 2. See also: 'Informe al Legislativo Pleno del Presidente Patricio Aylwin', 21 May 1990, p. IV.
2. 'Transición: Lo Que Terminó y lo Que Viene', *Página Abierta*, 19 Aug. to 1 Sept. 1991. See declarations by Francisco Cumplido, 'Se Acabó la Transición', *Ercilla*, 26 June 1991.
3. 'El Informe y los Militares', *La Época*, 10 Mar. 1991.
4. Brett (1992), p. 258.
5. Medina Quiroga (1992).
6. National Office for the Return of Exiles. See: 'Comité Nacional Pro-Retorno de Exiliados', *El Retorno*, no. 30, May–July 1991.
7. Command of Exonerated People. See: 'Agreement Between Government and Exonerados', *El Mercurio*, 7 June 1992.
8. 'Dictada Ley Que Beneficia a Exonerados', *El Mercurio Internacional*, 5–11 Aug. 1993. The law provides for different types of pensions and a bonus of two months for every year of antiquity for up to 36 months. Exonerations that occurred between September and December 1973 need no proof of political motivation, others need to be backed up by evidence.
9. 'La Semana de los Dos Enriques', *Hoy*, no. 829, 7–13 June 1993, pp. 10–13.
10. 'Una Historia Que Vuelve a Comenzar', *El Mercurio Internacional*, 10–16 June 1993.
11. 'Una Historia Que Vuelve a Comenzar', *El Mercurio*, 10–16 June 1993; 'Aylwin Reconoce Temas Pendientes En la Transición', *El Mercurio Internacional*, 17–23 June 1993.
12. See the declaration by the Socialist Minister of Public Works, Ricardo Lagos: 'La Transición a la Democracia aún no ha Terminado en Chile', *El País*, 21 Sept. 1995.
13. 'Programa de Gobierno, CPPD', *La Época*, special edition, July 1989, p. 3.
14. Editorial in *La Época*, 22 Apr. 1990. See also: *La Época*, 9 Feb. 1991.
15. 'La Diferencia de Hacer Justicia', *Hoy*, no. 665, 16–22 Apr. 1990, pp. 3–7. See also 'Chile's Next Government to Face a Balancing Act', *Washington Post*, 17 Dec. 1989, pp. D1–D2.
16. Brett (1992), p. 129.
17. The President had originally envisaged a parliamentary commission, but this idea was rejected by the right.
18. Interview with President Aylwin: *El Mercurio*, 15 Apr. 1990.
19. Loveman (1991). For debates on the Rettig Commission see: DSCD (1990a), pp. 705–9; DSCD (1990b), pp. 1008–10; DSCD (1990c), pp. 1059–71; DSCD (1991c), pp. 4336–84. On the right's criticism of Rettig for being too limited in historical scope see: DSCD (1990f), pp. 229–31.

20. *Hoy*, no. 665, 16–22 Apr. 1990, p. 5. See also: 'Destapar la Olla', *Análisis*, no. 329, 30 Apr. and 6 May 1990, pp. 6–8.
21. CNVR (1991), p. III. It was presided over by Raúl Rettig Guissen. Jaime Castillo Velasco, founder of the Chilean Human Rights Commission, Jose Luis Cea Engaña, a conservative constitutional lawyer, Mónica Jiménez de la Jara, a Christian Democrat, Ricardo Martín Díaz, an ex-minister of the Supreme Court under Pinochet, President of the military regime's Comisión de Derechos Humanos from 1986 to 1989 and a designated Senator from March 1990, Laura Novoa Vásquez, lawyer and personal friend of the President, Gonzalo Vial Correa, Jose Zalaquet Daher, international human rights lawyer and former Chair of Amnesty International's Executive Committee, and Jorge Correa were its other members. See: 'A Destapar la Olla', *Análisis*, no. 329, 30 Apr. and 6 May 1990, pp. 6–8.
22. 'Un Camino Pedregoso', *El Mercurio*, 29 Apr. 1990.
23. 'Rettig Enfatiza que la Comisión No Es un Tribunal', *La Época*, 6 May 1990.
24. 'Discrepancias Sobre Ambito de Competencia de Comisión', *El Mercurio*, 7 Apr. 1990.
25. According to Article 6 'the delay in the elaboration of a serious concept regarding human rights violations is an element which will disturb national reconcilations and conspires against fellowship among Chileans', CNVR (1991), p. VVI.
26. Interview with the President: *El Mercurio*, 15 Apr. 1990.
27. Garretón (1992), p. 168.
28. CNVR (1991), pp. 6, IV, 4, and 7.
29. Ibid., p. IV.
30. Ibid., p. IV.
31. Interview with the Secretary of the Commission, Jorge Correa: *La Nación*, 10 Mar. 1991.
32. Ibid., p. 7.
33. The other mass graves found were: at Colina, an old army base in March 1990; 20 bodies in Chihuio in July 1990; Copiapó in July 1990; a few weeks later Calama; 13 disappeared identified at Paine in September 1990; and 130 bodies in the Patio 29 of the Santiago Cemetery in September 1991. Other discoveries were made in Tocopilla, Talca, Concepción, and Temuco.
34. 'Diputada Matthei: No Hay Vinculación de mi Padre con esos Hechos', *El Mercurio*, 7 June 1990; 'Jarpa: Si Tuviera Algun Antecedente lo Entregaría de Inmediato', *Últimas Noticias*, 20 June 1990. For attacks on the right see: Sérgio Fernández over findings at *La Colina*: DSCD (1990e), pp. 68–92. For the debate generated by Pisagua see: DSCD (1990g), pp. 488–90; DSCD (1990h), pp. 541–63; DSCD (1990i), pp. 643–54.
35. 'Toda la Verdad', *Análisis*, no. 336, 18–25 June 1990, pp. 6–9. See also: 'El Impacto en la Derecha', *Hoy*, no. 674, 18–24 June 1990, pp. 13–15.

36. For RN see: 'Jarpa y Caso Osamentas', *El Mercurio*, 9 June 1990; 'Senadores Reclaman Verdad', *Fortín Mapocho*, 6 June 1990; 'RN y UDI Se Refieren a Caso Pisagua', *La Tercera*, Santiago, 10 June 1990.
37. 'Encontrarse con la Verdad', *Análisis*, no. 337, 25 June–1 July 1990, pp. 10–11.
38. Loveman (1991), p. 58.
39. The Civic Assembly for Human Rights. See: 'El Manejo del Gobierno', *Hoy*, no. 711, 4–10 Mar. 1991, pp. 8–10. For Propuesta por la Paz see: DSCS (1990d), pp. 2233–6.
40. See Luis Maira interview: *La Época*, 5 Feb. 1991.
41. Brett (1992), p. 115.
42. For high level of speculation regarding the report see: 'Por Quien Doblan las Campanas', *Hoy*, no. 713, 18–24 Mar. 1991, pp. 6–8; 'Qué Sucederá Después del 9 de Febrero?', *Hoy*, no. 705, 21–7 Jan. 1991, pp. 9–10; 'Cómo Se Moverá el Gobierno?', *Hoy*, no. 708, 11–17 Feb. 1991, pp. 4–7; 'Derechos Humanos: Punto Seguido', *Apsi*, no. 376, 11–24 Feb. 1991, pp. 6–9.
43. 'La Hora de la Verdad', *El Mercurio*, 3 Feb. 1991.
44. 'El Manejo del Gobierno', *Hoy*, no. 711, 4–10 Mar. 1991, pp. 8–10.
45. Statistical Annex, CNVR (1991), p. 883. The conclusions of the report were reinforced by the fact that they were approved unanimously by all members of the Commission. See: Correa (1992), p. 1470.
46. CNVR (1991), pp. 823–7.
47. Ibid., pp. 837–69.
48. *Discurso de S.E El Presidente de la República, Don Patricio Aylwin Azocar, Al Dar A Conocer a la Ciudadanía El Informe de la Comisión de Verdad y Reconciliación*, 4 Mar. 1991 and 'El Presidente Anunció 9 Medidas y Llamó a Fuerzas Armadas a Hacer Gestos de Reconocimiento del Dolor Causado', *La Época*, 5 Mar. 1991.
49. 'Crónica de la Nación', *La Nación*, 9 Feb. 1991. The titles mean: 'Chile will never Accept Impunity' and 'Where Are They?'.
50. For the approval of the Commission by the Conferencia de Obispos see: *Ultimas Noticias*, 29 Apr. 1990. See, for example, 'Vicaría: Jueces Fueron Negligentes Durante la Dictadura', *Fortín Mapocho*, 15 Feb. 1991.
51. See: *Hoy*, 16–22 Apr. 1990, p. 4.
52. 'Pamela Pereyra: Esto de la Reconciliación a Mí Me Satura', *Hoy*, no. 709, 18–24 Feb. 1991, pp. 10–12. The name of the Commission was a cause of worry in itself, since it seemed to indicate that truth would be followed by reconciliation without justice as an intermediary stage.
53. See: *Últimas Notícias*, 12 Feb. 1991.
54. For example: 'Planteamiento y Propuesta de la Asociación de Ejecutados Políticos a las Autoridades de Gobierno', Santiago, 8 May 1990.

55. See: *La Época*, 18 Jan. 1991. See also: Sola Sierra of the AFDD: *Fortín Mapocho*, 19 Feb. 1991, and Ricardo Lagos of the PPD: *El Mercurio*, 19 Feb. 1991.
56. 'Documento de Rettig Resulta Sesgado', *El Mercurio*, 10 Feb. 1991.
57. Garreton *et al.* (1993), p. 187.
58. Ibid. (1993), p. 183.
59. Interview with Sola Sierra, leader of the AFDD, critical of the Argentine Madres de la Plaza de Mayo: 'En Búsqueda de la Verdad', *Análisis*, no. 327, 16–22 Apr. 1990, pp. 11–13. 'Coordinadora de Presos Políticos: Disposición de Cooperar Con la Comisión Nacional de Verdad y Reconciliación', *El Mercurio*, 21 June 1990.
60. 'Esto de la Reconciliación a Mí me Tiene Saturada.' op. cit., pp. 10–12.
61. See, for example: 'Politicos Rechazaron Listado del Siglo', *El Mercurio*, 12 Mar. 1990.
62. 'Con Paro PC Presionará Para Juzgar a los Violadores de Derechos Humanos', *La Época*, 29 Jan. 1991; 'PC Exige Dar a Conocer Nombres de Informe Rettig', *Fortín Mapocho*, 29 Jan. 1991; 'Cómo se Moverá el Gobierno?', *Hoy*, no. 708, 11–17 Feb. 1991.
63. 'Unánime Apoyo de Partidos a Medidas de Reparación', *El Mercurio*, 5 Mar. 1991.
64. *La Época*, 9 June 1990.
65. See also, for example, the indignation expressed by Jose Luis Cea Engaña on the performance of the judiciary under the authoritarian regime: *La Época*, 9 Feb. 1991. On the Senate's approval of Rettig see: DSDS (1991a), pp. 3449–50. Deputies unanimous approval of Rettig see: DSCD (1991b), pp. 4164.
66. See: *La Segunda*, 28 Mar. 1991.
67. 'Encarar la Verdad', *La Época*, 4 May 1990.
68. See: 'A Tirones Con el Informe Rettig', *Analisis*, no. 376, 1–7 Apr. 1991.
69. See: *El Mercurio*, 17 Mar. 1991. Interestingly, the reaction of the terrorist organizations to the report was exactly the same. See: CCDH 'Proposiciones Para Una Política Sobre Violencia', Santiago, 16 Apr. 1991.
70. Throughout Aylwin's rule numerous similar incidents of defiance occurred, some of them humorous had they not been signs of a serious challenge to democratic civilian authority supremacy. In September 1991, for example, when MIR leader, Van Schowen, was found illegally buried in the Santiago General Cemetery together with another body, Pinochet congratulated the 'buscadores de cadáveres' and declared the combined burial 'una economía'.: 'El Ejército en Campaña Publicitaria', *Hoy*, no. 738, 9–15 Sept. 1991, pp. 13–15.
71. See: 'El Caso Charly El Espía: El Sumario del Ejército', *Hoy*, no. 734, 12–18 Aug. 1991; 'La Cortina de Humo Negro, Muy Negro', *La Época*, 7 July 1991; 'La Guaracha de los Espías', *Hoy*, no. 767, 30 Mar.–5 Apr. 1992, pp. 6–11; 'Ministro Ricardo Lagos Denunció Seguimiento',

El Mercurio, 6 June 1991; 'Ejército Admitiría Identidad de "Charly", Pero no Espionaje, Según Revista "Hoy"', *La Época*, 12 Aug. 1991; 'Que Oculta el Espionaje Político', *Hoy*, no. 731, 22–28 June 1991, pp. 6–9; Investigation Ordered of Spying of Chief of Justice', *El Mercurio*, 15 Apr. 1992. (CHIP)

72. 'El Desafío de Aylwin', *El Mercurio*, 10 Feb. 1991. General Pinochet's response to this suggestion was 'Hasta cuándo están con las mismas leseras. Tengan imaginación para otra cosa' ('How long will you insist upon the same stupidities. Have the imagination to think about something else.'), *El Diario*, 4 Feb. 1991.
73. In September 1991, the President brought charges against General Medina Lois for making insulting statements about his person, using the old security legislation of the Pinochet regime, in this case the Law of Internal Security of the State. See: 'El General Alejandro Medina Lois y La Nueva Tesis del Poder Militar', *La Época* 2 Sept. 1991. In the other case a general was retired for 'responsabilidad directa'. See: *La Época*, 21 Sept. 1991. In Loveman (1991), p. 39.
74. For a similar assessment of the relationship between Aylwin and Pinochet see: Maira (1991), p. 8. For resentments see Ch. 4, above. For Aylwin's good relations with Air Force Commander Matthei see: 'El Otoño de Matthei', *Hoy*, no. 726, 17–23 June 1991, pp. 20–2.
75. President Aylwin suggested this to Pinochet, but he did not agree. See: 'Ahora Han Aparecido Cadáveres Mutilados en Nuevas Excavaciones', *La Nación*, 10 June 1990; 'Gutenberg Martínez, Secretario General de DC: Pinochet Tiene Responsabilidad Militar y Política en Pisagua', *Fortín Mapocho*, 10 June 1990. For PPD call for his resignation see: 'Que Digan Dónde Están los Cuerpos de los Ejecutados', *Ultimas Notícias*, 10 June 1990. For the Church see: 'Oviedo Reiteró que un Jefe de Estado Responde por Actos', *La Nación*, 9 June 1990; 'Camus: Pinochet es Responsable de las Transgresiones a Derechos Humanos', *Fortín Mapocho*, 8 July 1990. For the others see: 'Jefe de Bancada de DC, Jorge Lavandero, El Mundo Civilizado Exige que Pinochet Sea Llamado a Declarar', *Fortín Mapocho*, 11 June 1990; 'Afirman Que Pisagua es un Crímen Contra la Humanidad', *Ultimas Notícias*, 8 June 1990; 'CChDH: El Deber del Estado es Juzgar a Responsables de Ejecuciones', *Fortín Mapocho*, 8 June 1990.
76. 'Guzmán: Es Un Ataque Político', *Ultimas Notícias*, 11 June 1990; 'Sergio Fernández: Ley de Amnistía el Pilar de Convivencia Política', *El Mercurio*, 13 June 1990; 'Allamand: Si no Se Asume Responsabilidad No Habrá Reconciliación', *El Mercurio*, 16 June 1990; 'Comisión Política de RN: Chile Necesita Saber la Verdad, Pero Completa', *El Mercurio*, 11 June 1990; 'Guzmán: Manipuleo Político por la Osamentas', *Ultimas Notícias*, 5 Aug. 1990; 'UDI Pidió Que Se Reconozca Que El Uso de la Fuerza Fue Necesario', *Ultimas Notícias*, 15 June 1990.
77. See: *La Nación*, 14 June 1990. The declaration that was made public

was the most conciliatory of the three drafts allegedly written. The prevailing consensus was that the right had encouraged Pinochet to tone down the delivery. See: 'Sigue la Guerra de Papel', *La Época*, 17 June 1990. On the right's defence of the military response see: DSCD (1990j), pp. 763–76. For an analysis of the Army's response see: DSCD (1990k), pp. 1120–3; DSDS (1990a), pp. 660–98.

78. On 13 June 1990, the General sat together for the first time with his counterparts at a military ceremony: 'Matthei Concordó Que Hubo un Estado de Guerra', *El Mercurio*, 17 June 1990; 'General Stange: Es Ridículo Pedir la Renuncia de Pinochet', *El Mercurio*, 12 June 1990; 'Comandante en Jefe de la Armada Sobre Pisagua y 1973: Almte. Martínez. El País Vivió un Estado de Guerra Interna', *La Tercera*, 13 June 1990. The only one to differ was General Toro of the Investigating Police: 'Dir. de Inv, Gen. Toro: Hallazgo de Pisagua es Dura Realidad', *La Tercera*, 13 June 1990.
79. 'Canciller Subrogante, Edmundo Vargas: Confiamos en que el Poder Judicial Podrá Esclarecer Trágicos Hechos', *La Nación*, 7 June 1990; 'Ministro Correa: Tribunales de Justicia Son el Camino Adecuado Ante el Hallazgo de Osamentas', *La Segunda*, 7 June 1990; 'Correa: Designación de Ministro en Visita Prueba que es Necesario Investigar', *La Época*, 8 June 1990.
80. See: 'Por Qué Ahora?', *Hoy*, no. 673, 11–17 June 1990, p. 16; 'Umberto, El Sena y los Militares', *Hoy*, no. 675, 25 June–1 July 1990, pp. 10–11. Minister Secretary General of the Government, Enrique Correa Rios: 'Los Soldados Nunca Inician Ellos la Violencia', *Hoy*, no. 675, 25 June–1 July, 1990, pp. 12–14; 'Gobierno Desaprueba los Desbordes Que Ofendan a Instituciones, dijo Correa', *La Época*, 21 June 1990; 'No Se Juzga Instituciones, Ministro de Defensa Rojas', *La Tercera*, 2 Aug. 1990; 'Lo Que Decía el Borrador', *Hoy*, no. 675, 25 June–1 July 1990, pp. 8–9.
81. See: 'AFDD: Justificar lo Injustificable', *El Mercurio*, 24 June 1990; 'PS Difiere del Ejército Sobre Existencia de Estado de Guerra', *La Tercera*, 13 June 1990.
82. See: 'La Comisión, RN y los Generales', *La Época*, 29 Apr. 1991.
83. See: *La Tercera*, 5 May 1990. Similarly, General Horacio Toro, director of the Investigating Police, under whose guidance the police had begun to purge the institution of human rights violators, was critical of the military regime's use of the police to repress dissidents, and had promised full co-operation with the Commission. See the interview with General Horacio Toro: *La Tercera*, 5 Feb. 1991.
84. See: 'Entre Una Audiencia y Un Almuerzo', *La Época*, 6 May 1990; 'Pinochet-Aylwin: El Encontrón', *Hoy*, no. 668, 7–13 May 1990; 'Los Secretos de la Guerra', *Análisis*, no. 328, 7–13 May 1990.
85. The army was by far the most aggressive. General Corbalan, the ex-head of the CNI, warned, 'Stop the harassment. remember that because a lion does not roar it does not mean it is sleeping.' See: 'Malestar en el Ejército: El Leon Insomne', *Apsi*, no. 373, 14–27 Jan.

1991, pp. 6–7. And Pinochet claimed: 'Tengo 80.000 hombres armados. Yo tengo la solución [a los derechos humanos].' See: 'La Dificultad de Hacer Justicia', *Hoy*, no. 665, 16–22 Apr. 1990, p. 3–7.

86. See: 'Aylwin Gives Pinochet a Dressing Down as Tensions Escalate', *Southern Cone Report*, RS-90-05, 5 July 1990, p. 1; 'La Batalla de las Imágenes', *La Época*, 3 June 1990; 'Como Ve el Ejército las Relaciones con el Gobierno', *Hoy*, no. 671, 28 May–3 June 1990, pp. 5–7.
87. 'La Sinopsis de la Comisión', *Hoy*, no. 672, 4–10 June 1990, pp. 12–13; 'Frente a la Comisión de Derechos Humanos Pinochet Prepara el Contraataque', *Hoy*, no. 667, 30 May–6 June 1990, pp. 7–8; 'Chile Army Isolated After Aylwin and Pinochet Clash Over Human Rights Probe', *Southern Cone Report*, RS-90-04, 31 May 1990, p. 1; 'Rico Tu Té', *Hoy*, no. 705, 21–7 Jan. 1991, pp. 5–6; 'Aylwin Gives Pinochet a Dressing Down as Government Army Tensions Escalate', *Southern Cone Report*, RS-09-05, 5 July 1990, p. 1.
88. 'Dijo General Fernando Matthei Sobre Documento Rettig: Informe No Puede Analizarse Sin Referirse a Crisis del 73', *El Mercurio*, 9 Mar. 1991.
89. For this and middle-level pressures for the replacement of General Stange by General Nuñez: 'Comisión Rettig: Las Respuestas de las Fuerzas Armadas', *Hoy*, no. 712, 11–17 Mar. 1991, pp. 16–19.
90. 'La Armada Objeta el Informe Por sus Comisiones', *La Época*, 28 Mar. 1991. A subsequent declaration by the admirals in retirement condemned the 'campaña de descrédito' and claimed that the work of the Commission had been 'viciado desde su origen'. See: *La Nación*, 26 Apr. 1991.
91. For the full text of all the official military responses see: 'Respuesta de las FF.AA. al Informe Rettig', *La Nación*, 28 Mar. 1991; 'Afirma El Ejército de Chile: Informe no Tiene Validez Histórica ni Jurídica', *El Mercurio*, 28 Mar. 1991; 'Hacia el Punto Final?', *La Época*, 31 Mar. 1991; 'Venganza de Allende', *La Época*, 17 Mar. 1991; 'Comisión Rettig: La Respuesta de las Fuerzas Armadas', *Hoy*, no. 712, 11–17 Mar. 1991, pp. 16–19; The army's retired generals also issued a statement claiming that the report presented a deliberately half-told truth: 'Generales en Retiro Critican a Informe', *Ultimas Notícias*, 16 Mar. 1991.
92. The only person who denied everything was General Manuel Contreras, director of the ex-DINA. Apparently, the Army's response to the report was toned down because of their failure to prevent Contreras from making his unbelievable declarations of denial on national television on 25 Mar. 1990. See: 'El Hombre Que Volvió del Frio', *Hoy*, no. 715, 1–7 Apr. 1991, pp. 6–7.
93. See: *El Mercurio*, 2 Apr. 1991; *El Mercurio*, 3 Apr. 1991 respectively. See also: 'El Terremoto en la Derecha', *Hoy*, no. 716, 8–14 Apr. 1991, pp. 4–8; 'El Forzozo Cambio de Librete', ibid., pp. 10–12; 'Crímen y Desafio', *La Epoca*, 7 Apr. 1991; 'Es Uno de los Más Violentos Golpes Contra la Transición', *Fortín Mapocho*, 3 Apr. 1991; 'Unánime Repúdio

de Políticos Ante Asesinato del Senador Jaime Guzmán', *El Mercurio*, 2 Apr. 1991.

94. 4.0% rated violence at the top, 1.5% terrorism, 5.5% human rights violations, 21.5% employment, and 15.4% health care provisions. See: CERC, *Informe de Encuesta Nacional*, Oct. 1989.
95. Ibid., 12–14 Apr. 1990.
96. 'Los Primeros 60 Días del Gobierno', *Hoy*, no. 673, 11–17 June 1990, pp. 10–13.
97. CERC, *Informe de Encuesta Nacional* in *La Época*, 16 July 1991.
98. Garretón *et al.* (1992). See also: 'Terrorismo es el Tema de Seguridad Con Mayor Cobertura en Canales de Television', *La Época*, 27 July 1991.
99. See: 'Lautas: Vanguardia o Cabezas de Pistola?', *Hoy*, no. 623, 26 June–2 July 1989, pp. 3–6; 'FPMR Autónomo: Pinochet Está Sentenciado', *Hoy*, no. 654, 29 Jan.–4 Feb. 1990, pp. 10–12; 'El Nuevo Terrorismo: Carabineros en la Mira', *Hoy*, no. 628, 31 June–6 July 1989, pp. 18–20; 'FPMR: El Frankenstein del PC', *Hoy*, no. 670, 21–7 May 1990, pp. 26–7.
100. See: 'El Desafío de la Violencia: Y no Había Trégua', *Hoy*, no. 662, 26 Mar.–1 Apr. 1990, pp. 3–4; 'La Guerra Sorda', *Hoy*, 26 Mar.–1 Apr. 1990, pp. 5–7.
101. It was often doubtful whether these assassinations had not in fact been committed by members of the old repressive apparatus. Coronel Fontaine, allegedly involved in the *degollados* case, was murdered after giving testimony to the Rettig Commission on 15 Apr. 1990. The FPMR specifically rejected responsibility when its normal practice was to call and claim responsibility for acts of terror. Moreover, the person who had claimed responsibility in the name of the FPMR was not the *portavoz* they invariably used. See: 'Cor. Luis Fontaine: El Hombre Que Sabía Demasiado', *Hoy*, no. 669, 14–20 Apr. 1990, pp. 13–15. The Guzmán murder was also explicitly rejected: 'El Video del FPMR', *Hoy*, no. 720, 6–12 May 1991, pp. 6–10. For the murder of MIR leader, Jecar Neghme, after he supported Aylwin's peaceful policy of reconciliation see: 'Crimen en Calle Bulnes: Para el MIR el Asesinato de Jecar Neghme Busca Una Respuesta Militar que Polarize la Política Nacional. Para las Organizaciones de Derechos Humanos el Aparato Represivo Envió un Mensaje: "Aún Estamos Aquí"', *Hoy*, no. 634, 11–17 Aug. 1989, pp. 8–10.
102. 'UDI: El Gobierno Cede a Presiones', *La Tercera*, 20 July 1990; 'RN Crítica Pasividad de Gobierno en Toma de Cárceles', *El Mercurio*, 27 July 1990. According to Alberto Espina of the RN: 'La condición de terrorista hoy tiene privilegios', *La Tercera*, 20 June 1990.
103. Only a month and a half before the transition, a massive gaolbreak occurred which increased the animosity between the right and the *Concertación* over the issue of the political prisoners. See: *La Segunda*, 30 Jan. 1990. Similarly, when an ex-political prisoner was arrested on suspicion of involvement in the kidnapping of the son

of a prominent industrialist in Feb. 1992, the right was quick to use this as an indictment of Aylwin's policy. The man was subsequently found to be innocent. See: 'Ex-Preso Político Liberado en Caso Edwards', *El Mercurio*, 27 Feb. 1992.

104. See interview with Andrés Aylwin: *Ultimas Notícias*, 28 Mar. 1990.
105. For the tensions between the PS and the DC see: 'Circunstancias Pueden Excluir la Culpabilidad', *El Mercurio*, 20 July 1990. For a defence and an attack on government terrorist policy see: DSCD (1990d), pp. 1197–202.
106. FASIC (1989), p. 26.
107. 'Presos Por Violencia no Saldrían en Libertad', *El Mercurio*, 5 Feb. 1990.
108. Most of the cases were sent to the Santiago court of appeals, and were dealt with not in order of 'urgency' but dossier by dossier. Since there were 4,000 cases pending in the courts, 3,500 of which were in the Santiago Court of Appeals, the political prisoners had a long wait ahead of them. See: FASIC (1991).
109. *Mensaje de S.E El Presidente de la República Con el Que Modifica Diversos Textos Legales a Fin de Garantizar en Mejor Forma los Derechos de la Persona*, Santiago, 11 Mar. 1990. For the Cumplido laws, 19.029, 19.027, and 19.047 see: *Bitacora Legislativa, Programa de Asistencia Legislativa*, 7–11 Jan. 1991 and 1–5 July 1991.
110. Its preferred solution for the political prisoners was to divide them into three categories: those who were to be immediately released, those who could chose exile instead of gaol, and those who, for having committed blood crimes, would have to fulfil their sentences. See: 'Derechos Humanos: El Segredo de RN', *Hoy*, no. 666, 23–9 Apr. 1990. See also: 'RN Propuso un Proyecto Nacional de Reconciliación en Derechos Humanos', *Ultimas Notícias*, 12 Apr. 1990.
111. 'Guzmán Destacó Plan de Reconciliación de RN', *El Mercurio*, 13 Apr. 1990; 'Restricción de Indulto Propone Guzmán', *La Nación*, 19 Mar. 1990; 'La UDI Condiciona Apoyo a una Nueva Ley de Amnistía', *La Nación*, 18 Apr. 1990.
112. The Framework Agreement between the members of the Constitutional, Legislation and Justice Commission to be Submitted to the Consideration of the Government and the Political Parties. The members of the Commission were the Christian Democrats, Andrés Aylwin, Carlos Bosselín, Aldo Cornejo, Gutenberg Martínez, and Hernan Rojo, the members of the PPD, Jorge Molina, Victor Rebolledo, and Jorge Schaulson. The UDI was represented by Andrés Chadwick and Víctor Pérez, and the RN by Alberto Espina, Federiko Mékis, and Teodoro Ribera.
113. For text: 'Pacto Político en Leyes Penales', *La Segunda*, 6 June 1990. This agreement would have permitted across-the-board reductions in sentences, with political crimes reduced from 15 years and life to 5 years, and the crime of torture from 3 and 5 years to 61 or 541 days.

114. Presentation by Jorge Molina: DSCD (1990n), pp. 1438–9. For the support of the Acuerdo Marco see: DSCS (1990b), pp. 1172–2215.
115. DSCD (1990n), p. 1475.
116. See: 'Declaración de la Asociación de Abogados de Presos Políticos', *Fortín Mapocho*, 8 June 1990. For a general debate see: *Análisis*, no. 333, 28 May–3 June 1990. For Cumplido's speech see: DSCD (1990), pp. 2268–9. On the President's opposition to Accord see: 'Leyes Cumplido en el Senado: La Negociación Que Viene', *Hoy*, no. 684, 27 Aug.–2 Sept. 1990, pp. 10–13. The President called it *una amnistía encubierta* in parliament: 'Congreso a Dieta: El Pacto y las Osamentas', *Hoy*, no. 736, 11–17 June 1990, pp. 20–1.
117. According to the UDI's Andrés Allamand, two weeks before Pisagua the PS had been in agreement with it, but after it they had opted out, taking the PD with them. For PS rejection see: *Declaración Pública del Partido Socialista*, 12 June 1990. See also: 'Congreso a Dieta: El Pacto y las Osamentas', *Hoy*, no. 736, 11–17 June 1990, pp. 20–1.
118. DSDS (1990m), pp. 2002–13; 'Las Leyes Cumplido en el Senado', *Hoy*, no. 674, 18–24 June 1990, pp. 22–3.
119. Interview with Jarpa: *El Mercurio*, 6 Nov. 1990; 'RN Aprobó Formula Para Tema de Presos Políticos', *Ultimas Notícias*, 30 Oct. 1990; 'Jarpa Dispuesto a Estudiar Ampliación de su Propuesta', *El Mercurio*, 6 Nov. 1990.
120. Jarpa interview: *El País*, 31 Oct. 1990.
121. Law 19.055. voted through by 131 votes to 23, with 1 abstention. For the passage of constitutional reforms on *indulto* and *libertad provisional* see: DSDS (1991b), pp. 4–23; DSCD (1991a), pp. 3766–3802.
122. In May 1990, Law 19.029 on the death penalty had been passed in the Chamber of Deputies. In December 1990, it was rejected by the Senate. The Chamber had voted for the death penalty only for cases of wartime military offences. Although the five-member CCLJ Commission had voted for capital punishment for 20 offences, the Senate retained this penalty for 37 offences. All crimes were placed under the jurisdiction of the ordinary courts. However, crimes of political violence, of membership in an armed organization, of attacks on military personnel, and possession of firearms were kept under military jurisdiction. Those accused of terrorist charges were also excluded from early release and bail benefits. Finally, the proposal to reform the composition of the military courts of appeal was also defeated: CCDH, 'Cartilla Relativa a la Ley Anti-terrorista 1991: Area de Accion Juridica', 1991.
123. Since the first pardons in March 1990, only four more had been pardoned at the end of 1990.
124. See: 'PP: Coletazos de una Fuga', *Análisis*, no. 190, 31 Aug.–6 Sept. 1987, pp. 26–7; 'PPs en Huelga de Hambre: Empieza la Etapa Crítica', *Cauce*, no. 100, 23 Mar. 1987, p. 15; 'PPs en Huelga de Hambre: Todo Puede Suceder', *Cauce*, no. 101, 31 Mar. 1987, p. 12; 'Fin de

Huelga de Hambre: Primer Gesto de Reconciliación', *Cauce*, no. 103, 13 Apr. 1987, pp. 14–15; 'Nueva Huelga de Hambre', *Cauce*, no. 114, 29 June–5 July 1987, p. 38.

125. The Commission was presided over by Andrés Aylwin, Bishop Carlos González, Socialist leader Jorge Arrate, and Maximo Pacheco, senator for the Christian Democrats and a key figure of the CCD.
126. See: 'UDI Rechaza Nuevos Benefícios Legales a Presos Políticos', *El Mercurio*, 24 June 1991.
127. Out of the initial total, 47 had escaped in a massive gaol-break in 1990. For the slowness of releases see: 'El Más Malo de Todos: Guillermo Rodríguez Mirista y Preso Político', *Hoy*, no. 728, 1–7 July 1991, pp. 6–8.
128. AW (1994c), p. 28.
129. CNVR (1991), p. 823.
130. 'The fallen'.
131. AFDD (1990).
132. 'Construyen Memorial a Desaparecidos Detenidos', *El Mercurio Internacional*, 22–28 July 1993.
133. Correa (1992), p. 1479.
134. Inter-Ministerial Commission of Under-Secretaries for Reparation Measures.
135. Interview with Pamela Pereyra: 'El Gobierno Optó por la Confrontación', *Analisis*, no. 376, 1–7 Apr. 1991.
136. For the proposals see: *Presiciones de la AFEP al Proyecto de Ley Sobre Reparaciones Enviado al Parlamento por el Poder Ejecutivo*, 15 Apr. 1991 (mimeo); 'La Reparación no Cierra el Capítulo de los Derechos Humanos', *Análisis*, no. 397, 26 Aug.–1 Sept. 1991. The Congress's Human Rights Commission agreed to eliminate the clause on presumed death.
137. Sola Sierra in an interview in *La Época*, 1 Feb. 1992.
138. Law no. 19.123. 'President Aylwin Signs Reparations Bill', *El Mercurio* (CHIP), 1 Feb. 1992. See also: Brett (1992), p. 258.
139. *Bases Programáticas Institucionales de la CPPD* 1989 (mimeo).
140. Aylwin had wanted to call it 'de Reconciliación' and the AFDD 'de Reparación'. Both words were adopted. The Commission was directed by Alejandro González of the Vicaría and was created by DL 19.123.
141. *CPPD: Programa de Gobierno. La Época Documentos*, July, 1989, p. 4.
142. See: Sanhuenza (1989); 'El New Look de la Corte', *Hoy*, no. 688, 24–30 Sept. 1990, pp. 9–12.
143. See the speech of Minister Maldonado, President of the Supreme Court: *El Mercurio*, 1 Mar. 1991.
144. For the content of the bills see: 'Objecciones de Corte Suprema a Reforma Judicial', *El Mercurio*, 10 Aug. 1991; Brett (1992), pp. 213 ff.
145. The discovery of a plot by the FPMR to attack the ministers of the Court contributed to the climate of confrontation. See: 'La Dura Convivencia de los Poderes', *Hoy*, no. 664, 9–15 Apr. 1990, pp. 9–11.

146. The president was careful to point this out after numerous declarations by Concertacion representatives which equally emphasized the commitment to truth and justice. See: AW (1991a), p. 5.
147. See: 'Discurso de S.E el Presidente de la Republica al dar a la Ciudadania el Informe de la Comisión Verdad y Reconciliación', Santiago, 4 May 1991.
148. 'Los Caminos de la Justicia', *El Mercurio*, 17 Mar. 1991.
149. The case which led to this decision was an appeal by a group of lawyers on 70 disappearances in January 1990. In its justification, the Supreme Court contradicted a previous ruling, by stating that Article 3 of the Geneva Convention did not apply because there had been no state of internal war in Chile at the time.
150. 'Jaime Guzmán: Posée Pleno Valor Constitucional', *La Nación*, 26 Aug. 1990. For the more sympathetic attitude of RN deputy Alberto Espina see: 'Amnistía de 1978 no Alcanza a Casos de DD', *Fortín Mapocho*, 3 June 1990. On the debate over the Supreme Court's amnesty decision see: DSDS (1990c), pp. 2215–2223.
151. 'Ministro de Interior, Enrique Krauss: Ley de Amnistía No Impide Investigar', *Fortín Mapocho*, 26 Aug. 1990; 'Zaldívar: Una Resolución Completamente Equivocada', *La Nación*, 26 Aug. 1990; 'Vicaría: Fallo de la Corte Suprema Contiene Graves Errores', *La Nación*, 28 Aug. 1990; 'CChDH: Hay Que Enmendar la Plana a los Supremos Que Fallaron en Amnistía', *Fortín Mapocho*, 31 Aug. 1990.
152. It was thus consistent with its past rulings in similar cases. See, for example, the case of Lonquén in 1978 and of Patio 29 of Santiago Cemetery, Yumbel and Mulchen, in 1979.
153. 'Tribunales Militares Acumulan Casos de Fosas Clandestinas', *La Nación*, 23 Jan. 1991.
154. 'Krauss Prevé Un Conflicto de Competencia con el Poder Judicial', *El Mercurio*, 14 July 1991.
155. *El Mercurio*, 8 June 1992.
156. The bill was rejected in June 1990. It was argued that it was the priority of the Senate and not of the Chamber of Deputies to initiate such reforms: 'Zaldívar Sobre Amnistía: Gobierno Deber Tener Inciativa', *La Tercera*, 9 June 1990. Numerous such attempts were made throughout the first two years of the government: *El Mercurio*, 3 Mar. 1992, 9 Apr. 1992.
157. Approval of ACHR: DSCD (1990), pp. 2698–730.
158. *El Mercurio*, 2 June 1992.
159. 'Government Prohibits Information on Human Rights Case', *El Mercurio* (CHIP), 3 June 1992; 'Press Ban Lifted on Corbalan Case', *El Mercurio*, 15 May 1992 (CHIP).
160. The first announcement of the intention of all the human rights organizations and ten deputies to bring a Constitutional accusation against the Supreme Court had been in December 1990. See: 'Acusarán, Firme a la Corte Suprema', *Fortín Mapocho*, 18 Dec. 1990.

161. 'La Acusación Atenta Contra Institucionalidad', *El Mercurio Internacional*, 24–30 Dec. 1992.
162. 'Senado Aprobó la Destitución de Ministro Hernán Cereceda', *El Mercurio Internacional*, 21–7 Jan. 1993.
163. 'Acusación Fue un Climax de Campaña Contra el Poder Judicial', *El Mercurio Internacional*, 25 Feb.–3 Mar. 1993.
164. 'Time Limit to Present Denouncements Extended', *Andean Newsletter of the Andean Commission of Jurists*, no. 76, Lima, 22 Mar. 1993, p. 4.
165. The statute of limitation expired on 21 Aug. 1991 and the men were arrested two days later.
166. 'Caso Letelier: Como Intenta Defenderse Contreras', *Hoy*, no. 746, 4–10 Nov. 1991, pp. 10–12; 'Caso Letelier: Se Hara Justicia', *Hoy*, no. 747, 11–17 Nov. 1991, pp. 12–15; 'Indictment of Chile's Police Chiefs', *New York Times*, 19 Nov. 1991, p. A 12; 'Twelve Year Term For Assassin of Chilean Envoy', *New York Times*, 13 Aug. 1991, p. A 10.
167. This case involving the brutal murder of three men had been investigated by Judge Cánovas. The Supreme Court had dismissed the evidence collected by the Judge which had established the guilt of the Carabineros' DICOMCAR. In May 1989 the case had been passed on to another judge, but the case had remained inactive until the new government came to power.
168. See: 'Ex-Junta Member Arrested', *El Mercurio* (CHIP), 3 Apr. 1992, 'Police to Defend Their Men in "degollados" Case', *La Nacion*, (CHIP) 4 Apr. 1992; 'Charges Against Mendoza Confirmed', *El Mercurio*, (CHIP), 10 Apr. 1992; 'Mendoza Indictment Upheld', *El Mercurio* (CHIP), 22 Apr. 1992.
169. Brett (1992). For the *Cutufa* case see the following section.
170. 'Pinochet Tambalea', *Hoy*, no. 686, 10–16 Sept. 1990, pp. 4–5; 'Efecto Cutufa: Terremoto en el Ejército', *Análisis*, no. 360, 3–9 Dec. 1991, pp. 4–7; 'El Enredo de los Augustos', *Hoy*, no. 700, 17–23 Dec. 1990, pp. 6–11.
171. 'Aylwin: Gobierno no Alienta Campaña Contra Fuerzas Armadas', *La Época*, 21 Jan. 1991; 'El Destino de la Comisión', *Hoy*, no. 704, 14–20 Jan. 1991, pp. 10–12; 'El Sinuoso Camino de los Cheques', *La Época*, 27 Jan. 1991; 'Caso Cheques: Giro Doloroso', *Análisis*, no. 365, 14–20 Jan. 1991, pp. 4–7; 'Padre y Hijo Están Hasta el Cuello Con Pinocheques', *Fortín Mapocho*, 26 Jan. 1991.
172. 'Relaciones Gobierno-Ejército: Algo Vuelve a Oler Mal', *Hoy*, no. 750, 2–8 Dec. 1991, p. 13.
173. 'El Ejército y los Poderes', *La Época*, 13 Jan. 1991; 'Ejército Reclama for Infamante Campaña', *La Nación*, 9 Jan. 1991; 'La Mala Posición', *La Época*, 6 Jan. 1991; 'La Fiebre Cívico-Militar', *Hoy*, no. 688, 24–30 Sept. 1990, pp. 4–8.
174. 'El Sinuoso Camino de los Cheques', *La Época*, 27 Jan. 1991.
175. For two interpretations of the *acuartelamiento* see: 'Que Pasó Según

el Gobierno', pp. 4–7 and 'Que Pasó Según el Ejército', *Hoy*, no. 701, 24–30 Dec. 1990, pp. 7–8.

176. 'Adivina Quien Viene a Almorzar', *La Época*, 9 June 1991. Pinochet accepted the retirement of two Generals, Carlos Parera Silva and Ramon Castro Ivanovic, whose promotion Aylwin had vetoed, in exchange for the abandonment of the Pinocheques case: 'Ejército: En Pie de Negociación', *Hoy*, no. 743, 14–20 Oct. 1991, p. 13.
177. This section of the thesis was completed in late September 1993. It therefore lacks perspective given that it was written precisely as events continued to unfold.
178. 'Reiteró Ministro Enrique Correa: Gobierno no Está Dispuesto a Promover Ley de Punto Final', *El Mercurio Internacional*, 24–30 June 1993.
179. 'Cuantifican en 200 Procesos a Militares', *El Mercurio Internacional*, 17–23 June 1993; 'Reiteró Ministro Enrique Correa', ibid. The discrepancy stems from the fact that the military calculate the number of cases on the basis of each charge. Since a number of individuals are charged for multiple crimes, each charge counts as one case.
180. See: 'La Sombra', *La Época*, 24 Nov. 1991; 'Reiteró Ministro Enrique Correa', ibid; 'Gobierno Reitera Voluntad de Acortar Procesos a Militares', *El Mercurio Internacional*, 24–30 June 1993.
181. 'Gabriel Valdéz Planteó Fin a Juicios en Plazo de Tres Meses', *El Mercurio Internacional*, 17–23 June 1993.
182. 'Reiteró Ministro Enrique Correa', ibid.
183. 'Gobierno Pide Una Mayor Colaboración del Ejército', *El Mercurio Internacional*, 8–14 July 1993.
184. 'Solución Para Casos de Derechos Humanos no Tiene Plazos', *El Mercurio Internacional*, 22–8 July 1993; 'Gobierno Rechaza Dictar Ley de Muerte Presunta', *El Mercurio Internacional*, 22–8 July 1993.
185. 'Juicios Rápidos y Discretos Propuso Presidente Aylwin', *El Mercurio Internacional*, 29 July–4 Aug. 1993.
186. 'La Ley del Presidente: Cadena de Errores?', *Hoy*, no. 841, 30 Aug.–5 Sept. 1993, pp. 19–23; 'Ley Aylwin: El Disparo Letal', *El Mercurio Internacional*, 2–8 Sept. 1993.
187. 'Suma Urgencia Pidió Ejecutivo Para Proyecto' and 'Amplio Debate Genera Proyecto Que Agiliza Juicios a Militares', *El Mercurio Internacional*, 5–11 Aug. 1993.
188. 'Sin El Secreto Fue Aprobada "Ley Aylwin"', *El Mercurio Internacional*, 19–25 Aug. 1993; 'Aylwin Cazado por su Propia Ley', *El Mercurio Internacional*, 19–25 Aug. 1993.
189. 'Camara Aplazó Votación Sobre Proyecto Derechos Humanos', *El Mercurio Internacional*, 12–18 Aug. 1993; 'Persisten Discrepancias Por Diferencias en "Ley Aylwin"', *El Mercurio Internacional*, 19–25 Aug. 1993. The President requested that Townley's TV interview be postponed until after the presentation of the law, a request which caused much controversy: 'Lo Que Dijo Townley a TVN Sobre el

Asesinato de Letelier' and 'Los Fantasmas Regresaron Para Quedarse', *El Mercurio Internacional*, 12–18 Aug. 1993.

190. 'Persisten Discrepancias Por Diferencias en "Ley Aylwin"', *El Mercurio Internacional*, 19–25 Aug. 1993.
191. For all of above: 'Sorpresas Te Da la Vida', *Hoy*, no. 842, 6–12 Sept. 1993, pp. 10–12; 'Jefe de Estado Se Desistio de "Ley Aylwin"', *El Mercurio Internacional*, 2–8 Sept. 1993; 'Ley Aylwin: El Disparo Letal', *El Mercurio Internacional*, 2–8 Sept. 1993.
192. 'Los Mandos del Ejército Chileno re Reúnen y Callan tras la Condena de Contreras', *El País*, 3 June 1995.
193. It appears that the *Concertación* will survive this crisis in the medium term, since the will to patch up differences seems to override the desire for emphasizing programmatic and ideological differences between its component parts: 'Gutenberg Martínez, Presidente de la Democracia Cristiana: No Hay Quiebre el la Concertación', *El Mercurio Internacional*, 26 Aug.–1 Sept. 1993; 'Andrés Zaldívar: Aquí Todos Metímos la Pata', *Hoy*, no. 842, 6–12 Sept. 1993, pp. 24–8.
194. The *Concertación* retained a majority in the Chamber of Deputies with 70 seats; 50 were won by the right wing coalition, *Unión por el Progreso*. Each bloc won nine of the 18 Senate seats up for election. The eight non-elected senators remain. For an analysis of the election campaign see: Angel and Pollack (1994a).
195. 'Sorpresas Te Da la Vida', and 'Ley Aylwin: El Disparo Letal'.
196. The money is to be paid from public funds. See: AW (1994c), p. 18.
197. 'Carabinero Chief Stange Bows Out', *Latin American Weekly Reports*, 19 Oct. 1995, p. 478; 'Pinochet, Único Militar en Activo de la Junta de la Dictadura Chilena', *El País*, 9 Oct. 1995.
198. AW (1994c), pp. 5 and 18. In December 1994, the Supreme Court also decided to increase the sentence of Lieutenant Fernandez Dittus to 600 days for the murder of Rodrigo Rojas and the burning of Carmen Gloria Quintana following an appeal by the family. See: 'Chile: Human Rights', *Oxford Analytica Daily Brief*, 19 Dec. 1995.
199. 'A la Espera del "Cúmplase"', 'Contreras a la Cárcel', 'Es Una Batalla de Todos', *El País*, 1 June 1995. The sentence was very clear as regards the involvement of others in the assassination: 'the highest government authorities of the day and the army did not participate, either institutionally or personally, in the events which which culminated in the death of Letelier, although the participation of other parties is not excluded.'
200. 'El Jefe de la Policía Secreta de Pinochet Advierte de no Aceptará in a la Cárcel', *El País*, 29 May 1995; 'El General Manuel Contreras se Niega a Ir a la Cárcel', *El País*, 1 June 1995; 'Mis Camaradas de Armas me Apoyan', *El País*, 2 June 1995; 'Chilean General Vows to Defy Jail Sentence', *The Financial Times*, 1 June 1995.
201. Yet another case is being heard, this time in Italy, where the DINA is accused of the assassination attempt on Christian Democratic Senator, Bernardo Leighton.

202. 'Visitas Militares al General Contreras Ante la Inminente Sentencia por el "Caso Letelier"', *El País*, 30 May 1995.
203. 'Chilean Troops Sent to Guard Convicted General', *The Financial Times*, 30 May 1995.
204. 'El Gobierno Chileno Afirma que el Ejército Acatará la Sentencia del "Caso Letelier"', *El País*, 29 May 1995.
205. According to retired General Alejandro Medina, Director of the Parachuters School, 'if they don't stop pulling the lion's tail it will at least roar if not hit out'. See, 'Pinochet Garantiza al Gobierno Chileno que el Ejército Acata la Condena de Contreras', *El País*, 3 June 1995.
206. 'El General Contreras Ingresa en Prisión Tras 5 Meses de Desafío al Gobierno', *El País*, 22 Oct. 1995; 'Symbolic Justice in Chile', *International Herald Tribune*, 26 Oct. 1995.
207. Between May and October 1995, a total of 25 cases were dismissed in this way. See: 'Suddenly, Rights Cases Speed Up', *Latin American Weekly Report*, 9 Nov. 1995, p. 514.
208. 'Congress Passes Covert "Punto Final" Law', *Latin American Weekly Report*, 18 May 1995, p. 207.
209. The bill also ensures the 'privacy, integrity and honour of the members of the armed forces who may be called to testify in the trials.' See: 'Frei Strikes "Reform" Deal with Allamand', *Latin American Weekly Report*, 16 Nov. 1995, p. 562.
210. 'Row Over Rights Goes Public', *Latin American Weekly Report*, 30 Nov. 1995, p. 549.
211. 'PS Takes Rights Battle to Senate', *Latin American Weekly Report*, 7 Dec. 1995, p. 562.
212. While Allamand and his 'juvenile patrol' have majority support on the RN's national council, the Jarpa-led old guard have seven of the RN's 11 senators and 21 of its 29 deputies. The fate of the reforms is therefore unclear. The Communist Party, while not represented in Congress, is also opposed. See: 'Frei Strikes "Reform" Deal with Allamand', *Latin American Weekly Report*, 16 Nov. 1995, p. 526; 'Frei Presses on with Reform Agenda', *Latin American Weekly Report*, 28 Dec. 1995, p. 6.
213. Another case which may produce renewed conflict is that of the assassination of Carmelo Soria, a Spanish citizen who worked for the United Nations and whose case may not be covered by the amnesty law given his diplomatic status. The Supreme Court has applied the amnesty, but the family may appeal. See: 'Que se Haga Justicia', *El País*, 9 Nov. 1995; 'El Supremo de Chile Archiva la Investigación sobre el Asesinato del Español Carmelo Soria', *El País*, 22 Dec. 1995.
214. See: 'Informe a Su Excelencia el Presidente de la República Sobre las Actividades Desarrolladas Hasta 31 de Enero de 1994', *Corporación Nacional de Reparación y Reconciliación* (Santiago: March, 1994). See also: Ensalaco (1994).

215. 'Feelings Boil Over at Annual Parade', *Latin American Regional Reports: Southern Cone*, RS-95-08, 19 Oct. 1995, p. 2.

Chapter 7

1. Pareja (1987). The phrase means 'Coming to terms with a bunch of lazy myths'.
2. Quijano (1987b), p. 10. For a second quote: Pareja (1987), p. 35.
3. Gillespie (1990), pp. 104–91.
4. 'Un Poder en Ruinas Al Que Se Le Exige Justicia', *Brecha*, 18 Feb. 1986.
5. 'Unico Riesgo: Que No Se Haga Todo Lo Que Pueda Hacerse en Los Primeros Seis Meses', *Búsqueda*, 21 Feb. 1985.
6. Juan Pablo Terra, leader of the Christian Democratic Frente *sublema*: 'Parlamento del Pueblo', Radio Centenario CX 36, 19 Jan. 1987.
7. For support of truth and justice see, for example: 'Monseñor Partelli: Perdonar no es Canonizar la Impunidad', *Búsqueda*, 27 Feb. 1985; 'Monseñor Marcelo Mendihart, Obispo de Salto: El Perdón Cristiano Si Se Basa en la Justicia y la Verdad de lo Contrario es una Claudicación', *Aquí*, 9 Apr. 1985; 'Gottardi Arzobispo de Montevideo: La Sociedad Tiene Que Saber Toda la Verdad', *Brecha*, 12 Sept. 1986; 'Elementos Para la Reflexión', *Comisión Arquidiosesana de Pastoral Social*, 24 July 1986, mimeo.
8. Garretón *et al.* (1993), pp. 187 and 189.
9. Interview with Jorge Insunza, *El Diario*, 11 May 1990.
10. See the interview with Andrés Aylwin: 'La Democracia Debe Ser Sin Presos Políticos', *La Nación*, 9 Apr. 1990 and interview with Carillo Novoa: *El Mercurio*, 6 Mar. 1990.
11. Paz Aguirre in 'No Provocaría Escisiones en Partidos el Tema de Amnistía', *El País*, 28 Feb. 1985. For the failure of the pact see: Rial (1990).
12. Juan Pablo Terra: *Aquí*, 23 Dec. 1986.
13. Pareja (1987).
14. Gillespie (1990), p. 22.
15. Ibid., p. 185.
16. Tribunal Permanente de los Pueblos (1990), pp. 55–6.
17. Arocena and Quijano (1987b), p. 55.
18. Arocena and Quijano (1987a), p. 70.
19. 'Plebiscito de Resignados', *Aquí*, 13 Jan. 1987.
20. 'Uruguay Vive una Redemocratización Que Fue Sonada Hacia el Pasado', *Brecha*, 19 Sept. 1986.
21. In July 1988, despite Seregni's efforts to patch up the differences caused by the human rights battle, Batalla's Partido Por el Gobierno del Pueblo, and the Christian Democrats split from the Frente and joined with the Unión Cívica to form a new coalition, Nuevo Espacio.

22. Interview by Rial with Sanguinetti in Rial (1990), p. 42.
23. Rial (1986a), p. 49; Rial (1986b), p. 37.
24. Rial (1986a), p. 49.
25. Quijano (1987b), p. 10.
26. Senator Juan Martín Posadas in Navarrete (1989), p. 27.
27. 'So that you don't disobey, I won't tell you what to do'.
28. Arocena and Quijano (1987b), pp. 53–7.
29. 'Wilson Ferreira Aldunate: Medina Me Dijo Que Si Sanguinetti Pedía la Amnistía El Ejército No Podía Pedir Menos', *El País*, 5 Feb. 1987.
30. For an account of Medina's role in under Sanguinetti's rule see: Del Huerto Amarillo (1988b).
31. Ramírez (1989), p. 101.
32. For this view see: 'Personal Militar Afectado por Razones Políticas e Ideológicas: La Ley de Caducidad no Reparó la Injusticia con los Militares Demócratas', *Alternativa Socialista*, 8 Jan. 1987.
33. Del Huerto Amarillo (1988a), p. 22.
34. The higher the reliance of the new democratic government on the military, the lesser the chances for an activist human rights policy. See the case of Sarney in Brazil in: Stepan (1988), p. xv.
35. Pareja (1987).
36. Editorial by Cardoso in *Semanario Jaque*, 1 Nov. 1984.
37. Ramírez (1989), p. 94.
38. Tribunal Permanente del los Pueblos (1990), pp. 55–6.
39. '"Armistício" en el Verano', *La Época*, 3 Feb. 1991.
40. 'Los Primeros Apuros', *Hoy*, no. 661, 19–25 Mar. 1990, pp. 10–11.
41. For 'democracia de acuerdos' see: Maira (1991), p. 38.
42. This was the opinion of the owner of *Análisis*, Juan Pablo Cárdenas: 'The Press in Chile Has Lost its Critical Capacity', *La Nación*, 20 Apr. 1992 (CHIP).
43. The exception to this was the reduction of budget which got rid of financing for the CNI. Of the 69 legislative projects presented to the legislature from March 1990 to April 1991, only four emerged from the legislature itself. See: 'Tortuosa Relación', *Hoy*, no. 717, 15–21 Apr. 1991, pp. 16–17.
44. 'Los Corcoveos del Ejército', *Hoy*, no. 653, 22–8 Jan. 1990, pp. 7–8.
45. Equipos Consultores, *Información de Opinión Pública Sobre Derechos Humanos*, Montevideo, 16 June 1986.
46. 'El Momento Político en Materia de Violaciones a los Derechos Humanos Ocurridas Durante la Dictadura: Declaración del Plenario Nacional del Frente Amplio', Montevideo, 6–7 Dec. 1986; in Centro Uruguay Independiente (1987), p. 27.
47. 'Homenaje Al Día de los Caídos', *El Soldado*, no. 130, Nov. 1990–May 1991.
48. 'Teniente General Medina: Si el al Elecciones de 1971 el Frente Amplio Hubiera Ganado, No lo Habriamos Dejado Asumir el Poder', *Búsqueda*, 7 Mar. 1991.
49. See: CERC, Santiago, *Informe de Encuesta Nacional*, Apr. 1989.

50. 'El Informe Final no Va a Estar Sujeto a Negociación: Jorge Correa, Secretario Ejecutivo de la CNVR', *Hoy*, no. 688, 24 Sept. 1990.
51. The notable exception to the third general rule was, unsurprisingly, General Manuel Contreras. In a television interview in April, the director of the DINA told reporters that 'los vencedores no se defienden.' He claimed that there were no disappeared in a *guerra sucia*, that the military had not buried anyone clandestinely, but merely put them in 'cementerios de campaña.' Finally he stated that Pinochet knew everything that the DINA did. These declarations were rejected by everyone, including members of the armed forces. See: 'Contreras Rompe Silencio en Entrevista Con Canal 13', *El País*, 26 Apr. 1991.
52. Garretón *et al.* (1992).
53. 'Human rights seem to have created a universalist political culture . . . a fluid and open communication, a process of collective confrontation with trauma and the creation of a space to deal with it, to construct a "WE" which transcends social and ideological affiliations.' Garreton *et al.* (1993), p. 196.
54. See: 'Ex-Generales Criticaron a Matthei Por Sus Frecuentes Vacilaciones', *La Época*, 9 July 1991.
55. 'La Ley Votada Groseramente Inconstitucional, Asegura Impunidad de los Violadores de Derechos Humanos', *La Hora*, 22 Dec. 1986. For a list of the problems of the law see: 'Siete Preguntas de Amnistía Internacional Sobre la Aplicación de la Ley de Impunidad', *Alternativa Socialista*, 5 Feb. 1987.
56. 'Efectos No Alcanzan a los Mandos', *La Razón*, 2 Apr. 1987.
57. Article 3 of the law stated that if military or police officers were not involved, the investigation should continue. Article 3 of the Orden General del Comando of 3 Sept. 1978 stated that 'No obstante lo manifestado prededentemente, es decisión de este Comando General, que cuando surjan las pruebas se revisarán todos aquellos casos para sancionar con todo el peso de la ley y el desprecio, a los que lograron prebendas, beneficios personales y familiares o llenaron sus bolsillos de oro, a la sombra de los soldados y oficiales que morían luchando contra la subversión.' ('Whatever was stated before, it is the decision of this General Command that when evidence arises, all cases will be reviewed to apply punitive measures with the full weight of the law and to show disdain for those who gained favours, personal or family benefits, or who filled their pockets with gold in the shadow of the soldiers and officers who died fighting against subversion.') In 'Los Militares Son Inocentes Pero Los Perdonamos Por la Duda', *Brecha*, 30 Oct. 1987. For a critique of the law see: Cassinelli Muñoz (1987).
58. See the speech by the Foreign Minister, Hector Gros Espiell, in *Búsqueda*, 3 Jan. 1992. For subsequent case closed by Uruguayan courts: AW (1991c).
59. There has only been one case to date of a military court sentencing a military officer for human rights violations. On 17 December 1991,

a military court condemned two officers for the torture and murder of a worker from La Serena in 1984. It was a unanimous conviction, and the increase in the sentence requested by the family was passed by 3 to 2. The accused fled to Argentina but is to be extradited. See: Brett (1992).

60. Garretón *et al.* (1992).
61. 'Un Momento de Peligro', *La Época*, 10 June 1990.
62. 'Gobierno: Lo Que Encontraron los Ministros', *Hoy*, no. 662, 26 Mar.–1 Apr. 1990, pp. 12–16.
63. 'Un Tema Que Aprisiona', *El Mercurio*, 1 Apr. 1990.
64. Equipos Consultores, *Informacion de Opinion Publica Sobre Derechos Humanos*, Montevideo, 16 June 1986.
65. 21% did not answer or did not know. See: Equipos Consultores, *Derechos Humanos*, Montevideo, 24 June 1986.
66. See respectively: Equipos Consultores, *Informacion de Opinion Publica Sobre Derechos Humanos*, Montevideo, 16 June 1986; Equipos Consultores, *Derechos Humanos*, Montevideo, 24 June 1986 and Equipos Consultores, no title, Montevideo, 16 Sept. 1986 and Equipos Consultores, *Derechos Humanos*, Montevideo, 24 June 1986.
67. Equipos Consultores, no title, Dec. 1986.
68. 'Ampla Mayoria Contra Impunidad', *La Hora*, 7 Jan. 1987, p. 3. The Frente had been 100% opposed, while those of other party loyalties had been 75% opposed.
69. Equipos Consultores, *Evaluación de la Ley de Caducidad*, Jan. 1987.
70. These latter areas of influence were human rights violations and intelligence operations. See: Equipos Consultores, no title, Montevideo, 16 Sept. 1986.
71. Domingo Namuncura, 'Se Abre el Camino a la Verdad', *La Nación*, 2 May 1990.
72. Tomás Moulian and Irene Agurto, *Evolución de Demandas Politicas y Sociales en un Contexto de Democratización* vi (Santiago: FLACSO, 1992).
73. 'Volodia Teitelboim: Éste País Está Amarrado de Pies y Manos', *Análisis*, 1–7 July 1991, pp. 4–7.
74. 'Balance y Perspectivas de la AFEP', Internal Circular, Santiago, May 1990.
75. Aylwin received a prize from the United Nations University of Peace, set up in 1980. See: 'Aylwin to Receive Human Rights Award', *El Mercurio*, 27 Feb. 1992 and later 'Aylwin Receives Award for Contribution to Democracy', *El Mercurio*, 7 Mar. 1992.
76. Among the right this number increased to 57.7%. See: CERC, *Informe de Encuesta Nacional*, 12–14 Apr. 1990.
77. See: Encuesta SA Básica, in *La Tercera*, 8 Mar. 1991.
78. Encuesta SA Básica, *La Tercera*, 8 Mar. 1991.
79. 4.4% did not have an opinion. See: Encuesta Diagonos, May 1987.
80. See: CERC, *Informe de Encuesta Nacional*, Apr. 1989.

81. See: Encuesta SA Basica, *La Tercera*, 8 Mar. 1991.
82. Manuel Antonio Garreton, *et al.*, 'Orientaciones y Evaluaciones de la Democracia en la Sociedad Chilena, 1991–1992', *Participa*, 1992.
83. 13.3% did not know and 1.3% did not answer. See: Encuesta Diagonos, May 1987.
84. It should be noted, however, that 30.8% blamed problems on lack of material resources: Garreton, *et al.* (1992).
85. 6.6% thought there was no remaining problem and 16% did not answer: Garreton *et al.* (1992).
86. 'Feelings Boil Over at Annual Parade', *Latin American Regional Reports-Southern Cone*, RS-95-08, 19 Oct. 1995, p. 2.
87. See: Encuesta SA Basica, *La Tercera*, 8 Mar. 1991.
88. 'Sola Sierra, Presidente de Familiares de Detenidos Desparecidos: La Pregunta Sigue Siendo Dónde Están', *Hoy*, no. 712, 11–17 Mar. 1991, pp. 20–1.

Conclusions

1. As in Chile, however, the demand for the location of the bodies and an account of the cause of death remains pending. See: 'Hope for Relatives of Disappeared', *Brazil Regional Report*, RB-95-05, 8 June 1995, p. 2.
2. Sartori (1987), pp. 68–70.
3. Lechner (1992), p. 33.
4. Zalaquett (1994). For a contrary view see: Méndez (1994b); Smulovitz (1995), pp. 56–65.
5. Whitehead (1989), p. 81.
6. *Búsqueda*, 15 Aug. 1985.
7. 'Mães Regressam à Praça de Maio', *O Público*, 9 Mar. 1995; 'Disappeared But Not Forgotten', *Financial Times*, 28 Mar. 1995; 'Dead Return to Haunt Menem', *Southern Cone Report*, RS-95-03, 20 Apr. 1995, p. 3.
8. 'The PP and the Generation of 27', *El País*, 28 Aug. 1995.
9. See: 'El PPD Fuera del Libreto', *Hoy*, no. 109, 16 Feb. 1991 and 'Tortuosa Relación', *Hoy*, no. 717, 15–21 Apr. 1991, pp. 16–17.
10. See: 'Ésta No Es Una Democracia de Consensos', *Análisis*, 12–18 Aug. 1991, pp. 14–16
11. See: Garreton (1994).
12. Ibid., pp. 116–17. Lack of civilian trust in the military was also demonstrated in a December 1986 poll. When asked if they thought whether, were the military to come to power again, they would commit the same mistakes, 64% thought that they would and only 17% believed they would not.
13. Maria Irene Soto, 'El Trance de Volver a Interior', *Hoy*, 7–13 Jan. 1991, pp. 10–12, and Cavallo, Ascanio, 'Terrorismo: Dos Enfoques', *La Epoca*, 14 Apr. 1991 and id., 'La Oficina', *La Epoca*, 21 Apr. 1991,

pp. 6–9. In April 1990, following the murder of Jaime Guzmán, the government formed the Oficina Coordinadora de Seguridad Pública to co-ordinate the anti-terrorist activities of the Carabineros and Investigaciones and to design new security policies. It was placed under the direction of the former under secretary of the Air Force and the military were given an advisory capacity on the commission: Brett (1992), p. 184.

14. In April 1990, Investigating Police Director General Horacio Toro, sacked 25 chiefs and police officers for corruption and violations. In September 1990 a further 36 were sacked. See: 'Algo Huele Mal en Investigaciones', *Apsi*, 23 May–5 June, 1990; Brett (1992) p. 183.
15. For successive attempts to reform the law see: 'Relaciones Gobierno-Ejército: Algo Vuelve a Oler Mal', *Hoy*, no. 750, 2–8 Dec. 1991, p. 13, and *El Mercurio*, 2 Mar. 1992, 4 Mar. 1992, 23 May 1992 and 24 May. 1992.
16. See: 'A Search for a new Raison d'Être', *Latin American Regional Reports-Southern Cone*, RS-95-08, 19 Oct. 1995, p. 3; 'Budget Cuts "Leave Country Helpless"', *Latin American Regional Reports-Southern Cone*, RS-95-10, 28 Dec. 1995, p. 6, For internal reforms see: 'Argentina Cleans Up', *International Herald Tribune*, 28 Oct. 1995.
17. See: 'Pinochet Shows Old Soldiers Never Die', *Financial Times*, 29 Nov. 1995.
18. Loveman (1994) p. 155.
19. In June 1995 Fujimori promulgated an amnesty law, placing the military and police beyond the reach of the law. All previous cases of violations had been dealt with by military courts and any punishments had been symbolic. See: 'Peru: Impunity Debate', *Oxford Analytica Daily Brief*, 20 June 1995; Crabtree (1995), pp. 13–24.
20. Acuña and Smulovitz (1991).
21. 'Armed Forces Will not Apologize', *Latin America Weekly Report*, 18 May 1995, p. 209.
22. 'Dirty War Chief Wins in Tucumán', *Latin American Weekly Report*, 13 July 1995, p. 303.
23. 'Acusaciones de un Terrorista Confeso', *El País*, 21 July 1995.
24. Panizza (1993), pp. 210–11; AW (1988d). For Colombia see: Lee (1995); for Peru see: Crabtree (1995); for Guatemala see: Zur (1995); for Brazil see: AI (1988d), (1992).
25. The military are involved in many of these actions. See: HRW (1995a), pp. 79–83.
26. 'Military Ordered to Provide Support', *Caribbean and Central America Report*, RC-95-03, 6 Apr. 1995; 'UN Leaves with Praise and Warning', *Caribbean and Central America Report*, RC-95-04, 18 May 1995, p. 2.
27. Panizza (1993), pp. 211 and 212.
28. Ibid., p. 212. For the assassination of street children in Brazil see: AW (1994d); AI (1992). In Colombia see: HRW (1995), p. 81; AW (1994e).

29. The division between past and contemporaneous is made by Hampson (1995), pp. 7–12.
30. The political will to deal with abuses is critical, particularly under democracy, where often it is not lack of resources but lack of will which permits continued impunity. Lee (1995), pp. 25–31, argues that this is the case in Colombia.
31. Panizza (1993), p. 213.
32. 'Los Brasileños Aprueban la 'Ejecución' en la Calle de un Ladrón por un Policía', *El País*, 7 Mar. 1995.
33. AW (1994c), p. 5; AI (1991b); HRW (1995a), p. 78.
34. See: 'Menem Destituyó al Oficial que Denunció Atroces Crímenes de la "Guerra Sucia"', *El País*, 8 Mar. 1995; in June 1995, Alfredo Astíz, one of the most notorious participants in the dirty war, was proposed for the rank of full captain. See: 'Who is Astíz?' *Latin American Weekly Report*, 8 June 1995, p. 243. It is only due to French diplomatic pressure that Astíz has been dismissed because of his participation in the disappearance of two French nuns.
35. See: 'Argentine Army Chief Apologizes', *The Financial Times*, 27 Apr. 1995; 'The End Never Justifies the Means', *Southern Cone Report*, RS-95-04, 1 June 1995, p. 6; 'El Jefe del Ejército Argentino Certifica que ha no es "La Reserva Moral de la Nación"', *El País*, 21 July 1995.
36. See: Romania: HW (1991a); Bulgaria: HW (1991b); Czech Republic (1992b); Hungary: (1993c).
37. 'Brasil Reconhece Violações', *O Público*, 8 Feb. 1995.
38. HRW (1995a), pp. 79–83. In September 1995, Brigadier General Velandia became the first general to be dismissed from the Armed Forces by President Samper for the torture, disappearance, and death of a member of the M-19 guerilla group: 'First General Kicked Out for Torture in Colombia', *El País*, 13 Sept. 1995.
39. See: 'Crowd Bays for González's Blood', *The Financial Times*, 14 Sept. 1995. See also: 'Dos Desaparecidos de la Democracia', *El País*, 22 Mar. 1995, p. 1; 'Madrid Orders "Torture" Probe', *The Financial Times*, 23 Mar. 1995. 'Spanish Premier "Knew of Death Squads"', *The Financial Times*, 21 July 1995; 'González Faces New Pressure on "Dirty War"', *The Financial Times*, 8 Sept. 1995.
40. For Honduras see: HRW (1994); for El Salvador see: 'Statement of Secretary Christopher on Mar. 24, 1993', *US Department of State Dispatch*, vol 4. no. 13, 29 Mar. 1993, p. 188; 'Reagan Hid Salvador Abuses, Files Show', *International Herald Tribune*, 22 Mar. 1995. For Guatemala see: 'Un Militar Guatemalteco al Servicio de la CIA Ordenó el Asesinato de un Ciudadano Norteamericano', *El País*, 24 Mar. 1995, p. 9; 'CIA Agent Ordered Deaths', *The Financial Times*, 24 Mar. 1995; 'Clinton Exige Toda La Verdad Sobre el Papel de la CIA en Guatemala', *El País*, 25 Mar. 1995, p. 8. If the Salvadorean case is a good indicator, it seems impunity will reign in the US. The panel appointed to investigate the charges stated in mid-July 1993 that the

State Department's personnel had acted creditably throughout the period: AW (1993*a*) pp. 33–6.

41. HRW (1995*a*), p. xxi.
42. See: Andreu (1995).
43. For French reaction to the promotion of Astíz see: 'A Victim of the Argentine Dictatorship Beats up Captain Astíz, Accused of Being a Torturer', *El País*, 18 Sept. 1995; 'Retiro Anticipado para Alfredo Astíz, Símbolo de la Represión Militar Argentina', *El País*, 4 Dec. 1995.
44. Jelin and Hershberg (1996).

References

Books, Articles, and Papers

ACUÑA, CARLOS and SMULOVITZ, CATALINA (1991), '*Ni Olvido Ni Perdón? Derechos Humanos y Tensiones Civico-Militares en a Transición Argentina*' (Buenos Aires: CEDES).

AFDD (Agrupación de Familiares de Detenidos Desaparecidos) (1990), 'Recuento de Actividades 1990' (Santiago: mimeo).

AGOR, DOMINGO (1971), *Latin American Legislatures: Their Role and Influence* (London: Praeger).

AGOSIN, MARJORIE (1987), 'The Generals' Bonfires: The Death of Rodrigo Rojas in Chile', *Human Rights Quarterly*, 9: 423–5.

AGUERO, FELIPE (1990), 'Democratic Consolidation and the Military in Southern Europe and Latin America', paper presented to the Conference on Democratic Consolidation in Southern Europe, Social Science Research Council (Rome).

AGUIAR, CESAR (1980), '*Estado Aislado; Sociedad Inmovil*' (Montevideo: CIEDUR).

AGUIAR, ELINA (1988), *Terrorismo de Estado en Família y Pareja* (Montevideo: Archivo CID-SERSOC).

AGUIRRE BAYLEY, MIGUEL (1985), *El Frente Amplio: Historia y Documentos* (Montevideo: Ediciones de la Banda Oriental).

AHUMADA, EUGENIO, AFRIA, RODRIGO, ENGAÑA, JAVIER LUIS, GONGORA, AUGUSTO, QUESNEY, CARMEN, SABALL, GUSTAVO, VILLALOBOS, GUSTAVO (1989), *La Memória Prohibida: Las Violaciones a los Derechos Humanos 1973–1988* (Santiago: Péhuen).

ALDUNATE, JOSÉ *et al.* (1984), *Los Derechos Humanos y la Iglesia Chilena* (Santiago: Eco).

ANDERSON, MARTIN EDWIN (1993), *Dossier Secreto: Argentina's Desaparecidos and the Myth of the Dirty War* (Boulder Colo.: Westview Press).

ANDREU, FEDERICO (1995), 'The International Community in Haiti: Evidence of the New World Order', in Seider, Rachel (ed.), *Impunity in Latin America* (London: Institute of Latin American Studies), 33–43.

ANGELL, ALAN (1990), 'International Support for Political Democracy in Contemporary Latin America: The Case of Chile', in Whitehead, Laurence (ed.), *International Dimensions of Democratization* (Oxford: 1996).

—— (1994a), 'The Chilean Elections of 1993: From Polarization to Consensus' (Liverpool: Institute of Latin American Studies, unpublished paper).

ANGELL, ALAN (1994b), 'Incorporating the Left into Democratic Politics', paper presented at the Inter-American Dialogue Conference on Democratic Governance in the Americas (Washington DC, Sept. 1994).

—— and CARSTAIRS, SUSAN (1987), 'The Exile Question in Chilean Politics', *Third World Quarterly*, 9(1): 148–69.

—— and POLLACK, BENNY (1990), 'The Chilean Elections of 1989 and the Politics of Transition to Democracy', *Bulletin of Latin American Research*, 9(1): 1–23.

APPLEMAN (1954), *Military Tribunals and International Crimes* (Indianapolis: Bobbs Merril).

ARAÚJO, GERMÁN (1989), *Impunidad: Y Sé Todos los Cuentos Diálogo Con Chury Iribarne* (Montevideo: Talleres Gráficos Coopren).

ARENDT, HANNAH (1968), *The Origins of Totalitarianism* (London: Meridian Press).

—— (1985), *Eichmann in Jerusalem: A Report on the Banality of Evil* (London: Penguin).

AROCENA, FELIPE (1989), *Violencia Política en el Uruguay de los Sesenta: El Caso de los Tupamaros* (Montevideo: CIESU).

—— and QUIJANO, JOSÉ MANUEL (1987a), 'Entrevista a Líber Seregni: La Oposición Contra la Pared', *Cuadernos de Marcha*, III: II(17): 69–79.

—— —— (1987b), 'Entrevista a Wilson Ferreira Aldunate: La Hora Más Difícil', *Cuadernos de Marcha*, III: II(17): 40–68.

ARRATE, JORGE (ed.) (1987), *La Renovación Socialista* (Santiago).

ARRIAGADA, GENARO (1979), *Violencia Política, Seguridad Nacional y Derechos Humanos* (Santiago: Instituto de Estudios Internacionales de la Universidad de Chile).

—— (1980), 'Ideology and Politics in the South American Military: Argentina, Brazil, Chile and Uruguay', *Wilson Center Latin American Papers: Working Paper* no. 55 (Washington DC).

—— (1985), *La Política Militar de Pinochet* (Santiago: Salesianos).

—— (1986a), *El Pensamiento Político de los Militares* (Santiago: Editorial Aconcagua).

—— (1986b), 'The Legal and Institutional Framework of the Armed Forces in Chile', in Valenzuela, Arturo and Valenzuela, Samuel (eds.), *Military Rule in Chile: Dictatorship and Oppositions* (Baltimore: Johns Hopkins University Press) 117–43.

ARTUCIO, ALEJANDRO (1982), *La Justicia Militar en Carceles Uruguayas: Represión y Resistencia* (Madrid: Comité de Solidaridad con la Lucha del Pueblo Uruguayo).

Asociación Americana de Juristas (1988), 'Argentina: Juicio a los Militares, Documentos, Secretos, Decretos Leyes y Jurisprudencia' (Buenos Aires: Rama Argentina de la AAJ).

ASTORI, DANILO (1989), *El Uruguay de la Dictadura 1973–1985: La Política Económica de la Dictadura*, iv (Montevideo: Ediciones de la Banda Oriental).

AYLWIN, PATRICIO (1995), 'Commissions of Truth and Reconciliation: Chile', in Boraine, Alex and Levy, Janet (eds.), *The Healing of a Nation* (Capetown: Justice in Transition), 38–43.

Backzo, Bronislaw (1989), *Comment Sortir de la Terreur: Thermidor el la Revolución* (Paris: Gallimard Editions).

Barahona de Brito, Alexandra (1991), 'The *Nunca Más* Reports of Brazil, Argentina, Uruguay and Chile', unpublished paper.

Barrán, José Pedro and Nahúm, Benjamín (1979), *El Uruguay del Novecientos* (Montevideo: Ediciones de la Banda Oriental).

Barrera, Manuel and Valenzuela, Samuel (1986), 'The Development of the Labour Movement in Opposition to the Military Regime', in Valenzuela, Arturo and Valenzuela, Samuel (eds.), *Military Rule in Chile: Dictatorship and Oppositions* (Baltimore: Johns Hopkins University Press), 230–69.

Barros Lémez, Álvaro (1987), *Seregni: Entrevista de Álvaro Barros Lémez* (Montevideo: Colección Protagonista).

Baumgartner, Jose Luis (1986), *Desparecidos* (Montevideo: CEDAL).

Benomar, Jamal (1993), 'Confronting the Past: Justice After Transitions', *Journal of Democracy*, 4(1): 3–14 (January).

Bitar, Sergio (1988), *Isla Diez* (Santiago: Editores Péhuen).

Bloche, Maxwell Gregg MD (1987), *Uruguay's Military Physicians* (Washington: Committee on Scientific Freedom and Reponsibility for the American Association for the Advancement of Science).

Boeker, Paul (1990), *Lost Illusions: The Latin American Struggle for Democracy as Recounted by its Leaders* (New York: Marckus Weiner Publishing Company).

Bolentini, Coronel (1977), *El Pensamiento de las Fuerzas Armadas en su Intervención en el Proceso Político* (Montevideo: Ministerio de Relaciones Exteriores, Instituto Artigas del Servicio Exterior).

Boraine, Alex and Levy, Janet (eds.) (1995), *The Healing of a Nation* (Capetown: Justice in Transition).

—— —— and Scheffer, Ronel (eds.) (1994), *Dealing with the Past: Truth and Reconciliation in South Africa* (Capetown: Institute for Democracy in South Africa).

Bordaberry, Juan María (1980), *Las Opciones* (Montevideo: Imp. Rosgal).

Brackman, Arnold (1987), *The Other Nuremberg* (New York: William Morrow Company Inc).

Branch, Taylor and Propper, Eugene (1982), *Labyrinth* (London: Penguin).

Brett, Sebastian (1992), *Chile: A Time of Reckoning: Human Rights and the Judiciary* (Geneva: International Commission of Jurists).

Bruschera, Oscar (1962), *Los Partidos Políticos Tradicionales* (Montevideo: Editorial Rio de la Plata).

—— (1986), *Las Décadas Infames: Análisis Político 1967–1983* (Montevideo: Libería Linardi y Risso).

Buergenthal, Thomas (1994), 'The United Nations Truth Commission for El Salvador', *Vanderbilt Journal of Transnational Law*, 27(3): 497–554.

BURT, JO MARIE (1988), *The Current Status of the Campaign For the Referendum on the Ley de Caducidad in Montevideo* (Montevideo: SERPAJ).

—— (1989), *El Pueblo Decide: A Brief History of the Referendum Against Impunity In Uruguay* (Montevideo: SERPAJ).

BURTON, MARY (1994), 'Amnesty and Transition in South Africa', in Borraine, Alex, Levy, Janet, and Scheffer, Ronel (eds.), *Dealing With the Past: Truth and Reconciliation in South Africa* (Capetown: Institute for Democracy in South Africa), 120–4.

CAETANO, GERARDO (1983), *La Agonia del Reformismo*, i, ii. Serie Investigaciones 37–8 (Montevideo: CLAEH).

—— and RILLA, JOSE PEDRO (1985), 'El Sistema de Partidos: Raíces y Permanencias', in Caetano, Gerardo *et al.* (eds.), *De la Tradición a la Crisis: Pasado y Presente de Nuestro Sistema de Partidos* (Montevideo: CLAEH).

—— —— (1989), *El Uruguay de la Dictadura 1973–1985: La Era Militar*, i (Montevideo: Ediciones de la Banda Oriental).

CAMPS, RAMÓN (1983), *El Poder en la Sombra* (Buenos Aires: Ro.Ca Producciones).

CARRIÓ, MIGUEL (1987), *Pais Vaciado: Dictadura y Negociados 1973–1985* (Montevideo: Monte Sexto).

CARVER, RICHARD (1990), 'Called to Account: How African Governments Investigate Human Rights Violations', *African Affairs*, 89(356).

CASSELL, DOUGLAS, JR. (1993), 'International Truth Commissions and Justice', *Aspen Quarterly*, Summer: 5(3): 69–90.

CASSINELLI MUÑOZ, HORACIO (1987), 'La Caducidad Del Ejercício de la Pretensión Penal Del Estado', *Cuadernos de Marcha*, III: II(17): 15–20.

CASTAGNOLA, JOSÉ LUIS and MIERES, PABLO (1989), *El Uruguay de la Dictadura 1973–1985: La Ideología Política de la Dictadura*, iii (Montevideo: Ediciones de la Banda Oriental).

CASTILLO, CARMEN (1986), *Un Día de Octubre en Santiago* (Santiago: Editora Sin Fronteras).

CAULA, NELSON and SILVA, ALBERTO (1986), *Alto El Fuego: Militares y Tupamaros* (Montevideo: Monte Sexto).

CAVALLO, ASCANIO, SALAZAR, NAULE, and SEPÚLVEDA, OSCAR (1988), *La Historia Oculta del Régimen* (Santiago: Editorial La Epoca).

CAVAROZZI, MARCELO (1992), 'Patterns of Elite Negotiation and Confrontation in Argentina and Chile', in Higley, John and Gunther, Richard (eds.), *Elites and Democratic Consolidation in Latin America and Southern Europe* (Cambridge: Cambridge University Press), 208–36.

CCDH (Comisión Chilena de Derechos Humanos) (1987), 'Declaración y Compromiso Con los Derechos Humanos', (Santiago: CCDH).

—— (1988), *Documentos Socio-Políticos, Centro de Informaciones y Orientación* (Santiago: CCDH).

—— (1989), *Gracias al Mundo: Orientaciones y Criterios Para la Elaboración de Una Propuesta de Derechos Humanos para el Transito a la Democracia: Declaración y Compromiso Con los Derechos Humanos* (Santiago: CCDH).

Centro Uruguayo Independiente (1989), *Uruguay 1985–1989: Impulso Democrático Bloqueo Conservador* (Montevideo: CUI).

CLAUDE, RICHARD (1983), 'Torture on Trial: The Case of Joelito Filártiga and the "Clinic of Hope"', *Human Rights Quarterly*, 5: 275–95.

CNVR (1991), *Informe de la Comisión Nacional de Verdad y Reconciliación* (Santiago: Ediciones del Ornitorrinco).

Comando General del Ejército Uruguayo (1976), *Las Fuerzas Armadas al Pueblo Oriental: La Subversión* (Montevideo: Junta de Comandantes en Jefe).

—— (1978a), *Testimonio de Una Nación Agredida* (Montevideo: Universidad de la República).

—— (1978b), *Las Fuerzas Armadas al Pueblo Oriental: El Proceso Político* (Montevideo: Junta de Comandantes en Jefe).

COMBLIN, JOSÉ (1979a), *Dos Ensayos Sobre Seguridad Nacional* (Santiago: Estudios: Vicaría de la Solidaridad).

—— (1979b), *The Church and the National Security State* (Maryknoll, NY: Orbis Books).

Comisión Arquidiosesana de Pastoral Social (1987), *Elementos Para la Reflexión Sobre la Ley de Caducidad de la Pretensión Punitiva del Estado* (Montevideo: Mimeo).

CONADEP (1984), *Nunca Más Argentina: Informe Sobre la Desaparición Forzada de Personas* (Buenos Aires: CONADEP).

CONOT, ROBERT (1983), *Justice at Nuremberg* (London: Weindenfield and Nicholson).

CONSTABLE, PAMELA and VALENZUELA, ARTURO (1991), *Chile Under Pinochet: A Nation of Enemies* (New York: W. W. Norton and Co).

CORRADI, JUAN (1992), 'Towards Societies Without Fear', in Corradi, Juan, Wells Fagen, Patricia, and Garreton, Manuel Antonio (eds.), *Fear at the Edge: State Terror and Resistance in Latin America* (Berkeley, Calif.: University of California Press), 167–92.

CORREA, ELIZABETH and VIERA-GALLO, JOSÉ ANTÓNIO (1985), *Iglesia y Dictadura* (Santiago: Cesoc).

CORREA, JORGE (1992), 'Dealing With Past Human Rights Violations: The Chilean Case After Dictatorship', *Notre Dame Law Review*, 67: 1455–1485.

CORREA, RAQUEL and SUBERCASEAUX, ELIZABETH (1989), *Ego Sum Pinochet* (Santiago: Editorial Zig-Zag).

CORTES RENCORET, CORONEL GERARDO (1976), *Introducción a la Seguridad Nacional* (Santiago: Cuadernos del Instituto de Ciencia Política, Universidad Católica de Santiago).

CORTIÑAS, LEÓN (1982), *El Poder Ejecutivo y Su Función Jurisdiccional* (Mexico: UNAM).

COSTA PINTO, ANTÓNIO (1994), 'Dealing with the Legacy of Authoritarianism: Political Purges and Radical Right Wing Movements in Portugal's Transition to Democracy 1974–1980s', in Larsen, Stein U *et al.* (eds.), *Modern Europe After Fascism*.

Crabtree, John (1995), 'Militarization, Impunity and the New Constitution in Peru', in Seider, Rachel (ed.), *Impunity in Latin America* (London: Institute of Latin American Studies), 13–25.

CRAHAN, MARGARET E. (1982), 'National Security Doctrine and Human Rights', in Crahan, Margaret E. (ed.), *Human Rights and Basic Needs in the Americas* (Washington DC: Georgetown University Press), 100–27.

CRAWFORD, KATHRYN LEE (1990), 'Due Obedience and the Rights of Victims: Argentina's Transition to Democracy', *Human Rights Quarterly*, 12: 17–52.

CRONIN, THOMAS (1989), 'Foreword', in Rosenbach, William, *Contemporary Issues in Leadership* (Boulder, Colo.: Westview Press).

CUMPLIDO, FRANCISCO and BALBOTÍN, IGNÁCIO (1978), 'Proyectos de Cambio y Institutionalidad Jurídico-Política: Chile 1964–1973', *Estudios Sociales*, 17: 57–95.

DAHL, ROBERT (1971), *Polyarchy: Participation and Opposition* (New Haven, Conn.: Yale University Press).

DANOPOLOUS, CONSTANTINE (ed.) (1992), *From Military to Civilian Rule* (London: Routledge).

DASSIN, JOAN (1986), 'Time up for Torturers: A Human Rights Dilemma for Brazil', *Nacla Report on the Americas*, 20(2).

DELGADO, MARTA (1988), 'Respuestas de las Organizaciones Sociales a la Represión', *Cuadernos Paz y Justicia*, iv.

DEL HUERTO AMARILLO, MARÍA (1981), *El Proceso de Militarización del Estado en el Uruguay* (Madrid: Centro de Estudios Constitucionales).

—— (1986), 'El Ascenso al Poder de las Fuerzas Armadas', *Cuadernos Paz y Justicia*, i (Montevideo: SERPAJ).

—— (1987), 'El Proceso Continua . . .', *Cuadernos de Marcha*, III: III(17): 21–32.

—— (1988a), 'Estratégia Democrática de Seguridad Nacional', *Cuadernos de Marcha*, III: IV(32): 39–46.

—— (1988b), 'La Visión del General Medina', *Cuadernos de Marcha*, III: IV(32): 47–8.

—— and SERRENTINO, ANTÓNIO SABELLA (1986), *Movimiento de Derechos Humanos en el Uruguay* (Montevideo: IELSUR).

—— and RIAL, JUAN (1988), 'Fórum Con María del Huerto Amarillo y Juan Rial', *Cuadernos de Marcha*, III: IV(138): 19–41.

DE RIZ, LILIANA (1986), 'Uruguay: La Transición Desde Una Perspectiva Comparada', in Gillespie, Charles, Goodman, Louis, Rial, Juan, and Winn, Peter (eds.), *Uruguay y la Democracia*, iii (Montevideo: Ediciones de la Banda Oriental), 121–38.

DE SIERRA, GERONIMO (1985), 'La Izquierda en la Transición', in Gillespie, Charles, Goodman, Louis, Rial, Juan, and Winn, Peter (eds.), *Uruguay y la Democracia*, ii (Montevideo: Ediciones de la Banda Oriental), 149–60.

DETZNER, JOHN (1989), *Después del Plebiscito: Nuevas Estratégias para la Protección de Derechos Humanos en Chile*, Cuadernos de Trabajo 9 (Santiago: Academia de Humanismo Cristiano).

—— (1991), 'Utilización de Mecanismos Internacionales en la Protección de los Derechos Humanos,' in Frühling, Hugo (ed.), *Derechos Humanos y Democracia: La Contribución de las Organizaciones No Gubernamentales* (Santiago: Instituto Interamericano de Derechos Humanos), 85–109.

De Zurilla, William (1981), 'Individual Responsibility for Torture Under International Law', *Tulane Law Review*, 56: 186–226.

Díaz, José Pedro and Wettstein, Germán (1989), *Exilio-Inxilio: Dos Enfoques* (Montevideo: Testimonios de las Comarcas del Mundo).

Dinamarca, Hernan (1989), *Dónde Están? La História de los 13 Niños Uruguayos Desaparecidos* (Montevideo: La República).

Dinges, John and Landau, Saul (1980), *Assassination on Embassy Row* (London: Publishers and Readers Publishing Co.).

Dooner, Patricio (1989a), *Periodismo y Política: La Prensa de Derecha y de Izquierda 1970–1973* (Santiago: Editorial Andante).

—— (1989b), *Iglesia Reconciliación y Democracia* (Santiago: Editorial Andante).

Duhalde, Eduardo (1983), *El Estado Terrorista Argentino* (Barcelona: Argos Vergara SA).

Du Toit, Andre (1994), 'Amnesty and Transition in South Africa', in Borraine, Alex, Levy, Janet, and Scheffer, Ronel (eds.), *Dealing With the Past: Truth and Reconciliation in South Africa* (Capetown: Institute for Democracy in South Africa), 130–3.

—— (1995), 'The Task for Civil Society', in Boraine, Alex and Levy, Janet (eds.), *The Healing of a Nation* (Capetown: Justice in Transition), 94–8.

Dworkin, Ronald (1995), 'The Unbearable Cost of Liberty', *Index on Censorship*, 3: 43–6.

Echevarría, Andrés and Frei, Luis (1974), *La Lucha Por la Juricidad en Chile* (Santiago: Editorial El Pacífico).

Egeland, Jan (1982), *Humanitarian Initiatives Against Political 'Disappearances': A Study of the Status and Potential of International Humanitarian and Human Rights Instruments and the Role of the International Red Cross in Protecting Against the Practise of Disappearances* (Geneva: Henry Dunant Institute).

Ensalaco, Mark (1994), 'Truth Commissions for Chile and El Salvador: A Report and Assessment', *Human Rights Quarterly*, 16: 656–7.

Espínola, Mercedes *et al.* (1986), *La Vida Diaria en una Cárcel Política Como Sistema de Tortura* (Montevideo: Comisión Reecuentro de los Uruguayos).

Faraone, Roque and Fox, Elizabeth (1988), 'Communication and Politics in Uruguay', in Fox, Elizabeth (ed.), *Media and Politics in Latin America: The Struggle for Democracy* (London: Sage), 150–61.

FASIC (Fundación de Ayuda Social de las Iglesias Cristianas) (1989), *Presos Políticos en Chile, Nómina y Cuadros Estadísticos, al 30 Junio de 1989* (Santiago: FASIC).

Faúndez, Julio (1988), *Marxism and Democracy in Chile: From 1932 to the Fall of Allende* (New Haven, Conn.: Yale University Press).

FERNÁNDEZ HUIDOBRO, ELEUTÉRIO (1990), *La Fuga de Punta Carretas* (Montevideo: Editorial Túpac Amaru).

FERREIRA ALDUNATE, WILSON (1986), *El Exílio y la Lucha* (Montevideo: Ediciones de la Banda Oriental).

FINCH, HENRY (1990), *A Political Economy of Uruguay Since 1870* (London: Macmillan).

FITZGIBBON, RUSSELL (1954), *Uruguay: Portrait of a Democracy* (New Brunswick, NJ: Rutgers University Press).

FLEET, MICHAEL (1985), *The Rise and Fall of Chilean Christian Democracy* (Princeton, NJ: Princeton University Press).

FONSECA, MANUEL (1951), *La Política de Coparticipación* (Montevideo: Editorial Medina).

FOXLEY, ALEJANDRO (1986), 'The Neo-Conservative Experiment in Chile', in Valenzuela, Arturo and Valenzuela, Samuel (eds.), *Military Rule in Chile: Dictatorship and Oppositions* (Baltimore: Johns Hopkins University Press), 13–50.

FRONTALINI, DANIEL and CAIATI, MARÍA CRISTINA (1984), *El Mito de la Guerra Sucia* (Buenos Aires: CELS).

FRÜHLING, HUGO (1980), 'Poder Judicial y Política en Chile', FLACSO 3 (Santiago: FLACSO).

—— (1981a), 'Disciplinando a la Sociedad: Estado y Sociedad Civil en Chile 1973–1978', Conferencia General de la Asociación Chilena de Investigaciones para la Paz (Santiago).

—— (1981b), 'Limitando la Acción Coercitiva del Estado: La Estratégia Legal de Defensa de los Derechos Humanos en Chile', FLACSO 12 (Santiago: FLACSO).

—— (1982), 'Fuerzas Armadas, Orden Interno y Derechos Humanos', in Frühling, Hugo, Portales, Carlos, and Varas, Augusto (eds.), *Estado y Fuerzas Armadas* (Santiago: FLACSO), 35–58.

—— (1984), 'Repressive Policies and Legal Dissent in Authoritarian Regimes: Chile 1973–1981', *International Journal of the Sociology of the Law*, 12: 351–74.

—— (1985a), 'Derechos Humanos y Problemas de la Transición', *Cuadernos de Trabajo*, 115 (Santiago: Academia de Humanismo Cristiano).

—— (1985b), 'Autoritarismo y Defensa de los Derechos Humanos: Estudio de la Vicaría de la Solidaridad en Chile', *Cuaderno de Trabajo*, 2 (Santiago: Academia de Humanismo Cristiano).

—— (ed.) (1986a), *Represión Política y Defensa de los Derechos Humanos* (Santiago: Ediciones Chile America).

—— (1986b), 'La Defensa de los Derechos Humanos en el Cono Sur: Dilemas y Perspectivas Hacia el Futuro', in Frühling, Hugo (ed.), *Represión Política y Defensa de los Derechos Humanos* (Santiago: Ediciones Chile America), 18–32.

—— (1987), *Justicia y Violación de Derechos Humanos in Chile* (Santiago: CED).

—— (1988), *Poder Judicial y Política en Chile* (Santiago: FLACSO).

—— (1991a), 'El Movimiento de Derechos Humanos y la Transición en

Chile y Argentina', *Cuadernos de Trabajo*, 11 (Santiago: Academia de Humanismo Cristiano).

—— (ed.) (1991b), *Derechos Humanos y Democracia: La Contribución de las Organizaciones No Gubernamentales* (Santiago: Instituto Interamericano de Derechos Humanos).

—— and SÁNCHEZ, DOMINGO (1988), *La Realización de Justicia por la Violación de Derechos Humanos en Chile: Una Descripción de las Posiciones Sostenidas a Este Respecto Por Diversos Actores Sociales y Políticos* (Santiago: FLACSO).

—— ALBERTI, GLORIA, and PORTALES, FELIPE (1989), *Organizaciones No Gubernamentales de Derechos Humanos en el Cono Sur* (San José: Instituto Americano de Derechos Humanos).

GABAY, MARCOS (1988), *Política Información y Sociedad*, Serie Estudios no. 4 (Montevideo: Centro de Estudios Independientes).

GALEANO, EDUARDO (1983), *Days and Nights of Love and War* (New York: Monthly Review Press).

GARCÍA VILLEGAS, JUEZ RENÉ (1990a), *Soy Testigo: Dictadura, Tortura, Injusticia* (Santiago: Amerinda).

—— (1990b), *Pisagua! Caín, Qué Has Hecho Con Tu Hermano?* (Santiago: Editorial Emisión).

GARRETÓN, MANUEL ANTÓNIO (1982), 'Tensiones Entre los Derechos Humanos y Los Nuevos Regimenes Autoritarios de America Latina', paper presented at XII Congress of Political Culture (Rio de Janeiro).

—— (1986a), 'The Political Evolution of the Chilean Military Regime', in O'Donnell, Guillermo, Schmilter, Philippe, and Whitehead, Laurence (eds.), *Transitions from Authoritarian Rule: Latin America* (Baltimore: Johns Hopkins University Press), 95–122.

—— (1986b), 'Political Processes in an Authoritarian Regime: The Dymanics of Institutionalization and Opposition 1973–1980', in Valenzuela, Arturo and Valenzuela, Samuel (eds.), *Military Rule in Chile: Dictatorship and Oppositions* (Baltimore: Johns Hopkins University Press), 153–214.

—— (1987), *Reconstruír la Política: Transición y Consolidación Democrática en Chile* (Santiago: Editorial Andante).

—— (1988), *El Plebiscíto de 1988 y la Transición a la Democracia en Chile* (Santiago: FLACSO).

—— (1989a), *Propuestas Políticas y Demandas Sociales*, iii (Santiago: FLACSO).

—— (1989b), *The Chilean Political Process* (Boston: Unwin Hyman).

—— (1990), 'Las Condiciones Socio-Políticas de la Inauguración Democrática en Chile', *Kellogg Working Paper* no. 142 (Notre Dame: University of North Carolina).

—— (1991), 'The Political Opposition and the Party System Under the Military Regime', in Drake, Paul and Jaksic, Ivan (eds.), *The Struggle For Democracy in Chile 1982–1990* (Lincoln: University of Nebraska Press), 211–51.

—— (1992), 'Fear in Military Regimes: An Overview', in Corradi, Juan,

Weiss Fagen, Patricia, and Garreton, Manuel Antonio (eds.), *Fear at the Edge: State Terror and Resistance in Latin America* (Berkeley: University of California Press), 13–25.

—— (1994), 'Human Rights and Processes of Democratization', *Journal of Latin American Studies*, 26: 221–34.

—— Moulián, Tomás, and Agurto, Irene (1992), 'Orientaciones y Evaluaciones de la Democracia en la Sociedad Chilena 1990–1992', *Participa* (Santiago).

—— —— —— (1993), *Orientaciones y Evaluaciones de la Democracia en la Sociedad Chilena 1990–1993* (Santiago; mimeo).

—— Lagos, Marta, and Méndez, R. (1992), 'Orientaciones y Evaluaciones de la Democracia en la Sociedad Chilena 1990–1992', *Participa* (Santiago).

Garro, Alejandro (1990), 'Panel Discussion: Crime and Punishment: Accountability for State Sponsored Mass Murder', *New York Law School Journal of International and Comparative Law*, Fall: 11: 361–90.

—— and Dahl, Henry (1987), 'Legal Accountability for Human Rights Violations in Argentina: One Step Forward and Two Steps Backward', *Human Rights Law Journal*, Spring-Fall: 5: 283–344.

Gauck, Joachim (1994), 'State Security Files and Disqualification: Germany', in Borraine, Alex, Levy, Janet, and Scheffer, Ronel (eds.), *Dealing With the Past: Truth and Reconciliation in South Africa* (Capetown: Institute for Democracy in South Africa), 71–4.

Gil, Daniel (1990), *El Terror y la Tortura* (Montevideo: Editorial Eppal).

Gillespie, Charles (1982), 'Regime Instability and Partisan Endurance: Authoritarianism and Opposition in Uruguay', paper presented at the International Political Science Association Conference (Rio de Janeiro).

—— (1984), 'The Breakdown of Democracy in Uruguay: Alternative Political Models', paper presented at the International Political Science Association Conference (Rio de Janeiro).

—— (1985), 'From Suspended Animation to Animated Suspension: Political Parties and the Difficult Birth of Uruguay's Transition', Documento de Trabajo 94 (Montevideo: CIESU).

—— (1986a), 'Uruguay's Transition form Collegial Military-Technocratic Rule', in O'Donnell, Guillermo, Schmitter, Philippe, and Whitehead, Laurence (eds.), *Transitions From Authoritarian Rule: Latin America* (Baltimore: Johns Hopkins University Press), 173–95.

—— (1986b), 'Activists and Floating Voters: The Unheeded Lessons of Uruguay's Primaries', in Drake, Paul and Silva, Eduardo (eds.), *Elections and Democratization in Latin America 1980–1985* (San Diego, Calif.: University of California Press), 215–44.

—— (1990), *Negotiating Democracy: Politicians and Generals in Uruguay* (Cambridge: Cambridge University Press).

—— (1992), 'The Role of Civil-Military Pacts in Elite Settlements and Elite Convergence: Democratic Consolidation in Uruguay', in Higley, John and Gunther, Richard (eds.), *Elites and Democratic Consolidation in Latin America and Southern Europe* (Cambridge: Cambridge University Press), 178–207.

—— and ARRÉGUI, MIGUEL (1988), 'Uruguay: A Solution to the Military Question?', in Lowthenthal, Abraham (ed.), *Latin American and Caribbean Contemporary Record* vi (New York: Holmes and Meier).

——, GOODMAN, LOUIS, RIAL, JUAN, and WINN, PETER (eds.) (1985), *Uruguay y la Democracia*, iii (Montevideo: Ediciones de la Banda Oriental).

GILLIO, MARÍA ESTER (1970), *Tupamaros: Conspiración o Revolución?* (Montevideo: Editorial Voz Obrera).

GIRARDET, RAOUL (1986), *Mythes et Mythologies Politíques* (Paris: Sevil).

GITLI, EDUARDO, SIÁZARO, JUAN CARLOS, COSTA BOMNO, LUIS, DEL HUERTO AMARILLO, MARIA, RIAL, JUAN (1987), *La Caída de la Democracia: Las Bases del Deterioro Institucional 1966–1973* (Montevideo: Ediciones de la Banda Oriental).

GOLDFARB, JEFFREY (1989), *Beyond Glasnost: The Post-Totalitarian Mind* (Chicago: University of Chicago Press).

GÓMEZ, LEÓN (1990), *Trás la Huella de los Desaparecidos* (Santiago: Ediciones Calueche).

GONZÁLEZ, ALEJANDRO (1990), 'La Experiencia de la Vicaría de la Solidaridad del Arzobispado de Santiago de Chile', *Persona y Sociedad*, 1: 6(2–3), 153–66.

GONZÁLEZ, LUIS EDUARDO (1983a), 'Uruguay 1980–1981: An Unexpected Opening', *Latin American Research Review*, 18(3): 63–76.

—— (1983b), *The Legitimacy Problems of Bureaucratic Authoritarian Regimes: The Cases of Chile and Uruguay* (New Haven, Conn.: Yale University Press).

—— (1984), 'Political Parties and Redemocratization in Uruguay', Working Paper no. 163 (Washington DC: Woodrow Wilson Center Latin American Programme).

—— (1985a), 'Transición y Restauración Democrática', in Gillespie *et al.* (eds.), *Uruguay y la Democracia*, iii (Montevideo: Ediciones de la Banda Oriental), 101–20.

—— (1985b), 'Transición y Partidos en Chile y Uruguay', Documento de Trabajo no. 93 (Montevideo: CIESU).

—— and NOTARO, JORGE (1980), 'Alcances de una Política de Estabilización Heterodoxa', Working Paper no. 45 (Washington, DC: Woodrow Wilson Latin American Programme).

—— and GILLESPIE, CHARLES (1989), 'Uruguay: The Survival of Old and Autonomous Institutions', in Linz, Juan, Diamond, Larry, and Lipset, Seymour Martin (eds.), *Democracy in Developing Countries: Latin America* iv (London: Adamantine Press).

GROISMAN, ENRIQUE (1985), 'El Sistema Jurídico Frente a las Secuelas del Proceso de Reorganización Nacional', in Rouquié, Alain and Schvarzer, Jorge (eds.), *Como Renascen las Democracias* (Buenos Aires: Emece).

GUEST, IAN (1990), *Behind the Disappearances: Argentina's Dirty War Against Human Rights and the United Nations* (Philadelphia, Pa.: Pennsylvannia University Press).

GUNTHER, RICHARD (1992), 'Spain: The Very Model of the Modern Elite Settlement', in Higley, John and Gunther, Richard (eds.), *Elites and*

Democratic Consolidation in Latin America and Southern Europe (Cambridge: Cambridge University Press), 38–80.

HAKIM, PETER and LOWENTHAL, ABRAHAM (1991), 'Latin America's Fragile Democracies', *Journal of Democracy*, Summer 2(3): 16–29.

HAMPSON, FRANÇOISE (1995), 'Impunity and Accountability', in Seider, Rachel (ed.), *Impunity in Latin America* (London: Institute of Latin American Studies), 7–13.

HANDELMAN, HOWARD (1979), 'Economic Policy and Elite Pressures in Uruguay', American University Field Staff Reports no. 27.

—— (1981a), 'Politics and Plebiscites: The Case of Uruguay', Working Paper no. 89 (Washington DC: Woodrow Wilson Center Latin American Programme.

—— (1981b), 'Labour Industrial Conflict and the Collapse of Uruguayan Democracy', *Journal of Inter American Studies and World Affairs*, 23(4): 371–94.

—— (1986), 'Prelude to Elections: The Military Legitimacy Crisis and the 1980 Constitutional Plebiscite in Uruguay', in Drake, Paul and Silva, Eduardo (eds.), *Elections and Democratization in Latin America 1980–1985* (San Diego, Calif.: University of California Press), 203–14.

HAUSER, THOMAS (1978), *Missing* (New York: Simon and Schuster).

HAYNER, PRISCILLA B. (1994), 'Fifteen Truth Commissions—1974 to 1994: A Comparative Study', *Human Rights Quarterly*, 16: 597–655.

HERTZ, JOHN (ed.) (1978), 'Comment and Opinion: On Re-Establishing Democracy After the Downfall of Authoritarian or Dictatorial Regimes', *Comparative Politics*, 10(4): 559–62.

—— (1982), *From Dictatorship to Democracy: Coping With the Legacies of Authoritarianism and Totalitarianism* (Westport, Conn.: Greenwood Press).

—— (1988), 'An Historical Perspective', in Henkin, Alice (ed.), *State Crimes: Punishment or Pardon* (Queenstown, Md.: Aspen Institute), 11–23.

HUNTINGTON, SAMUEL (1991), 'Democracy's Third Wave', *Journal of Democracy*, Summer 2(2): 12–34

HUTCHINSON QUAY, ELIZABETH (1991), 'El Movimiento de Derechos Humanos en Chile Bajo el Régimen Autoritario', in Orellana, Patricia and Hutchinson Quay, Elizabeth (eds.), *El Movimiento de Derechos Humanos en Chile 1973–1990* (Santiago: Centro de Estudios Latino Americanos Simon Bolívar), 69–198.

ICLASAOCP (International Commission of the Latin American Studies Association to Observe the Chilean Plebescite) (1989), 'Report by the ICLASA to Observe the Chilean Plebescite', *Bulletin of Latin American Research*, 8(2): 275–305.

IELSUR (1984), 'El Rol de los Derechos Humanos en el Re-establecimiento de un Régimen Democrático en el Uruguay', paper presented at the Congreso Interamericano de Organismos de Derechos Humanos (Zaragoza).

Index on Censorship (1995), *Rewriting History*, iii (Index on Censorship London: Writers and Scholars International).

IRELA (1995), *Guatemala: Elections and Pacification* (Madrid: Irela Briefing).

IRIBARNE, DANIEL (1990), *Los Infiernos de la Libertad* (Montevideo: Vintén Editor).

JELIN, ELIZABETH (1994), 'The Politics of Memory: The Human Rights Movement and the Constitution of Democracy in Argentina', *Latin American Perspectives*, no. 81.

—— and HERSHBERG, ERIC (1996), *Contructing Democracy: Human Rights, Citizenship and Society in Latin America.*

KAPLAN, SUSAN (1980), *The Legal Response to Disappearances: Habeas Corpus and Amparo* (New York: Lawyers Committee for International Human Rights).

KAUFMAN, EDY (1979), *Uruguay in Transition: From Civilian to Military Rule* (New Brunswick, NJ: Transaction Books).

—— (1993), 'The Role of the Political Parties in the Redemocratization of Uruguay', in Sosnowski, Saul and Popkin, Louise (eds.), *Repression, Exile and Democracy: Uruguayan Culture* (Durham, NC: Duke University Press), 17–58.

KRITZ, NEIL J. (1994), *Transitional Justice: How Emerging Democracies Reckon with Former Regimes* (US Institute of Peace).

KROG, ANTJIE (1995), 'To Remember and Acknowledge: The Way Ahead', in Boraine, Alex and Levy, Janet (eds.), *The Healing of a Nation* (Capetown: Justice in Transition), 112–19.

LANGGUTH, A. J. (1978), *Hidden Terrors: The Truth About US Police Networks in Latin America* (New York: Pantheon Books).

LARTEGUY, JEAN (1961), *The Centurions* (Paris: Presses de la Cité).

—— (1979), *La Guerre Nue: Reflections on Men and Combat* (Indianapolis: Bobbs Merrill).

LA RUE, FRANK (1995), 'The Right to Truth in Central America', in Seider, Rachel (ed.), *Impunity in Latin America* (London: Institute of Latin American Studies), 73–81.

LECHNER, NORBERTO (1992), 'Some People Die of Fear: Fear as Political Problem', in Corradi, Juan, Weiss Fagen, Patricia, and Garreton, Manuel Antonio (eds.), *Fear at the Edge: State Terror and Resistance in Latin America* (Berkeley, Calif.: University of California Press), 26–5.

LEE, SUSAN (1995), 'Colombia: A Case Study in Impunity', in Seider, Rachel (ed.), *Impunity in Latin America* (London: Institute of Latin American Studies), 25–33.

LEE GARDO, MAURICIO (1987), *Confesiones Para un Genocídio: Antologia de la Represión en America Latina* (Montevideo: TAE Editorial).

LEGASPI DE ARISMENDI, ALCIRA and RICO, ALVARO (1989), *La Resistencia a la Dictadura 1973–1975: Construir la Memoria Popular Sobre la História Reciente del Uruguay* (Montevideo: Editorial Problemas).

LIJPHART, AREND (1977), *Democracy in Plural Societies: A Comparative Exploration* (New Haven, Conn.: Yale University Press).

LINDAHL, GORAN (1962), *Uruguay's New Path: A Study in Politics During the*

First Colegiado (Stockholm: Library and Institute of Ibero-American Studies).

—— (1964), 'Uruguay: Government by Institutions', in Needler, Martin (ed.), *Political Systems of Latin America* (Princeton, NJ: Princeton University Press).

LINZ, JUAN (1964), 'An Authoritarian Regime: The Case of Spain', in Allard, Eric and Littunen, Yrjo (eds.), *Cleavages, Ideologies and Party Systems* (Helsinki: Westermark Society), 291–341.

—— (1978), *The Breakdown of Democratic Regimes: Crisis Breakdown and Reequilibration* (Baltimore: Johns Hopkins University Press).

—— (1988), 'Political Regimes and Respect for Human Rights: Historical Cross National Perspectives', paper presented at the Symposium on Human Rights at the Nobel Institute (Stockholm), ed. Bernt Hagtvet.

—— (1990), 'The Transition from Authoritarian Political Regimes to Democratic Political Systems and the Problems of the Consolidation of Political Democracy', paper presented at the Roundtable of the International Political Science Association (Tokyo).

—— and STEPAN, ALFRED (1989), 'Political Crafting of Democratic Consolidation or Destruction: European and South American Comparisons', in Pastor, Robert (ed.), *Democracy in the Americas: Stopping the Pendulum* (New York: Holmes and Meier), 41–61.

—— DIAMOND, LARRY, and LIPSET, SEYMOUR MARTIN (eds.) (1989), *Democracy in Developing Countries: Latin America*, iv (London: Adamantine Press).

—— —— —— (eds.) (1990), *Democracy in Developing Countries: Comparing Experiences with Democracy*, v (London: Adamantine Press).

LIPSET, SEYMOUR MARTIN and ROKKAN, STEIN (1967), 'Cleavages, Structures, Party Systems and Voter Alignments: An Introduction', in Lipset, Seymour Martin and Rokkan, Stein (eds.), *Party Systems and Voter Alignments* (New York: Doubleday), 1–64.

LÓPEZ DAWSON, CARLOS (1986), *Justicia y Derechos Humanos* (Santiago: Instituto Para El Nuevo Chile).

LÓPEZ GOLDARACENA, OSCAR (1986), *Derecho Internacional y Crímenes Contra la Humanidad Concepto y Evolución: No Admisibilidad de la Amnistía Particular Referencia al Caso Uruguayo* (Montevideo: Asociación Americana de Juristas).

LOVEMAN, BRIAN (1991), 'Misión Cumplida? Civil Military Relations and the Chilean Political Transition', *Journal of Interamerican Studies and World Affairs*, 33(3): 35–74.

—— (1993a), 'The Political Left in Chile 1973–1990', in Carr, Barry and Ellner, Steve (eds.), *The Latin American Left From the Fall of Allende to Perestroika* (Bonlder, Colo.: Westview Press and London: Latin American Bureau).

—— (1993b), *The Constitution of Tyranny: Regimes of Exception in South America* (Pittsburgh: University of Pittsburgh Press).

—— (1994), 'Protected Democracies and Military Guardianship: Political Transitions in Latin America, 1978–1993', *Journal of Interamerican Studies and World Affairs*, 36(2): 105–75.

LOWDEN, PAMELA (1996), *The Vicariate of Solidarity: Moral Opposition to Authoritarian Rule in Chile 1973–1990* (Oxford: Macmillan).

LUJÁN, CARLOS (1993), 'El Rol de los Principales Actores Internacionales en los Procesos de Democratización del Cono Sur. El Caso Uruguayo', in AIETI, *El Apoyo Internacional a la Democracia en América Latina* (Madrid: AIETI), 277–312.

MACRIDIS, ROY (1982), 'France: From Vichy to The Fourth Republic', in Hertz, John (ed.), *From Dictatorship to Democracy: Coping With the Legacies of Authoritarianism and Totalitarianism* (Westport, Conn.: Greenwood Press), 162–76.

MCSHERRY, PATRICE (1992), 'Military Power, Impunity and State-Society Change in Latin America', *Canadian Journal of Political Science*, 25(3): 463–88.

MAGGIOLO, OSCAR (1988), *La Universidad Uruguaya Bajo la Dictadura* (Montevideo: Universidad de la República: Facultad de Humanísticas y Ciencias).

MAGNON, CRO (1987), *Humanos Humanoides* (Santiago: Editorial Aconcágua).

MAIRA, LUIS (1991), *Notas Sobre la Transición Chilena* (Santiago: Centro Para el Análisis y Transformación de la Sociedad Chilena (CENAT)).

MALAMUD-GOTI (1989), 'Trying Violators of Human Rights: The Dilemma of Transitional Democratic Governments', in Henkin, Alice (ed.), *State Crimes: Punishment or Pardon* (Maryland: Aspen Institute), 71–87.

MARAN, RITA (1989), *Torture: The Role of Ideology in the French Algerian War* (New York: Praeger).

MARRAS, SERGIO (1988), *Confesiones: Entrevistas de Sergio Marras* (Santiago: Ediciones del Ornitorrinco).

—— (1989), *Palabra de Soldado: Generales Medina Lois, Horacio Toro, Ernesto Baeza and Luis Danus* (Santiago: Ediciones del Ornitorrinco).

MARTINEZ MORENO, CARLOS (1986), *La Junta Militar en el Uruguay* (Montevideo: Librosur).

—— (1988), *El Infierno* (London: Readers International).

MARTINS, LUCIANO (1986), 'The Liberalization of Authoritarian Rule in Brazil', in O'Donnell, Guillermo, Schmitter, Philippe and Whitehead, Laurence (eds.), *Transitions From Authoritarian Rule: Latin America* (Baltimore: Johns Hopkins University Press), 72–94

MARTIRENA, DR. GREGORIO (1988), *Uruguay: La Tortura y los Médicos* (Montevideo: Ediciones de la Banda Oriental).

MASLIAH, LEO (1993), 'Popular Music: Censorship and Repression', in Sosnowski, Saul and Popkin, Louise (eds.), *Repression, Exile and Democracy: Uruguayan Culture* (Durham, NC: Duke University Press), 108–19.

MEDINA QUIROGA, CECILIA (1988), *The Battle For Human Rights: Gross Systematic Violations and the Inter-American System* (Utrecht: Netherlands Institute For Social and Economic Law Research).

MÉNDEZ, JUAN (1994a), 'Acknowledgement, Truth and Justice', in Borraine, Alex, Levy, Janet, and Scheffer, Ronel (eds.), *Dealing With the Past: Truth and Reconciliation in South Africa* (Capetown: Institute for Democracy in South Africa), 35–40.

MÉNDEZ, JUAN (1994b), 'Prosecution: Who and For What', in Borraine, Alex, Levy, Janet and Scheffer, Ronel (eds.), *Dealing With the Past: Truth and Reconciliation in South Africa* (Capetown: Institute for Democracy in South Africa), 88–93.

—— and VIVANCO, JOSÉ MIGUEL (1990), 'Disappearances and the Inter-American Court: Reflections in a Litigation Experience', *Hamline Law Review*, Summer: 13: 507–77.

MENESES, ALDO (1989), *El Poder del Discurso: La Iglesia Católica y el Gobierno Militar 1973–1984* (Santiago: ILADES-CISOC).

MERA, JORGE (1986), 'La Aplicación de Justicia en Una Futura Institucionalidad Democrática', (Santiago).

—— GONZÁLEZ, ALEJANDRO, and VARGAS, JUAN (1989), *La Protección de los Derechos Humanos en el Orden Jurídico Interno*, Cuadernos de Trabajo no. 10 (Santiago: Academia de Humanismo Cristiano).

MERCADER, ANTONIO (1969), *Tupamaros: Estratégia y Acción Militar* (Montevideo: Alta).

MFDD (Madres y Familiares de Desaparecidos Detenidos en Uruguay) (1984), *Desaparecidos: Los Ninos* (Montevideo: Graphis).

—— (1985), *Uruguayos Desaparecidos en Argentina* (Montevideo: MFDD).

—— (1986), *La Desaparición Forzada en el Uruguay* (Montevideo: Ediciones Uno).

MICHELINI, ZELMAR (1975), 'Accusations Against Uruguay', in Jerman, William (ed.), *Repression in Latin America: A Report on the First Session of the Second Russell Tribunal, Rome, April 1974* (London: Spokesman Books).

MICHNIK, ADAM (1994), 'Why Deal with the Past', in Borraine, Alex, Levy, Janet, and Scheffer, Ronel (eds.), *Dealing With the Past: Truth and Reconciliation in South Africa* (Capetown: Institute for Democracy in South Africa), 15–18.

MIERES, PABLO (1983), *Opciones Políticas en 1982: Un Intento de Clasificación Documento de Trabajo*, no. 10 (Montevideo: Taller de CIEDUR).

—— (1988), *Cómo Votan Los Uruguayos: Análisis o Interpretación de las Elecciones de 1984* (Montevideo: CLAEH).

MIGNONE, EMÍLIO (1992), 'Beyond Fear: Forms of Justice and Compensation', in Corradi, Juan *et al.* (eds.), *Fear at the Edge: State Terror and Resistance in Latin America* (Berkeley: University of California Press), 250–66.

—— ESTLUND, CYNTHIA, and ISSACHAROFF, SAMUEL (1984), 'Dictatorship on Trial: Prosecution of Human Rights Violations in Argentina', *Yale Journal of International Law*, 10(119): 118–49.

MIGUENS, JOSÉ ENRIQUE (1986), *Honor Militar, Consciencia Moral y Violencia Terrorista* (Buenos Aires: Sudamericana Planeta).

MIRANDA, PEDRO (1988), *Terrorismo de Estado: Testimonio del Horror en Chile y Argentina* (Buenos Aires: Colección Expediente Negro).

MONCKEBERG, MARÍA OLÍVIA, CAMUS, MARÍA EUGENIA, and JILES, PAMELA (1986), *Crímen Bajo Estado de Sitio* (Santiago: Editorial Emisión).

MOYANO, MARÍA JOSÉ (1991), 'The Dirty War in Argentina: Was it a War and How Dirty Was It?', in Werner Tobler, Hans and Waldman, Peter (eds.), *Stäachliche Und Parastäatliche Gewalt in Lateinamerika* (Frankfurt: Vervuert Verlag).

MUÑOZ, HERALDO (1986), 'Chile's External Relations Under the Military Government', in VALENZUELA, ARTURO and VALENZUELA, SAMUEL (eds.), *Military Rule in Chile: Dictatorship and Oppositions* (Baltimore: Johns Hopkins University Press), 304–22.

NAVARRETE, MARGARITA (1989), 'La Cuestión Militar y los Derechos Humanos', *Paz y Justicia Sumario de Derechos Humanos*, 6(19): 25–30.

NEIER, ARYEH (1994), 'Why Deal With the Past', in Borraine, Alex, Levy, Janet, and Scheffer, Ronel (eds.), *Dealing With the Past: Truth and Reconciliation in South Africa* (Capetown: Institute for Democracy in South Africa), 2–8.

NINO, SANTIAGO (1985), 'The Human Rights Policy of the Argentine Constitutional Government: A Reply to Mignone, Estlund and Issacharoff', *Yale Journal of International Law*, 11: 217–230.

—— (1991), 'The Duty to Punish Past Abuses of Human Rights Put Into Context: The Case of Argentina', *Yale Journal of International Law*, 100(8): 2619–43.

NUNCA MAIS (1985), *Nunca Mais: A Tortura no Brasil* (Petrópolis: Editora Vozes).

NUNN, FREDERICK (1976), *The Military in Chilean History: Essays on Civil Military Relations 1810–1973* (Albuquerque: University of New Mexico Press).

O'DONNELL, GUILLERMO (1989), 'Transition to Democracy: Some Navigation Instruments', in Pastor, Robert (ed.), *Democracy in the Americas: Stopping the Pendulum* (New York: Holmes and Meier), 62–75.

—— SCHMITTER, PHILIPPE, and WHITEHEAD, LAURENCE (eds.) (1986a), *Transitions From Authoritarian Rule: Comparative Perspectives* (Baltimore: Johns Hopkins University Press).

—— —— —— (eds.) (1986b), *Transitions From Authoritarian Rule: Latin America* (Baltimore: Johns Hopkins University Press).

—— —— (1986c), *Tentative Conclusions About Uncertain Democracies* (Baltimore: Johns Hopkins University Press).

OMAR, DULLAH (1995), 'Building a New Future', in Boraine, Alex and Levy, Janet (eds.), *The Healing of a Nation* (Capetown: Justice in Transition), 2–8.

ORELLANA, PATRICIA (1991), 'Los Organismos de Derechos Humanos en Chile Hacia 1985', in Orellana, Patricia and Hutchinson Quay, Elizabeth, *El Movimiento de Derechos Humanos en Chile 1973–1990* (Santiago: Centro de Estudios Latino Americanos Simon Bolivar), 9–68.

—— and FRÜHLING, HUGO (1991), 'Organizaciones no Gubernmentales de Derechos Humanos Bajo Régimenes Autoritários en la Transición a la Democracia: El Caso Chileno Desde una Perspectiva Comparada', in Frühling, Hugo (ed.), *Derechos Humanos y Democracia: La Contribución de las Organizaciones No Gubernamentales* (Santiago: Instituto Interamericano de Derechos Humanos), 25–85.

ORENTLICHER, DIANE (1991), 'Settling Accounts: The Duty To Prosecute

Human Rights Violations of a Prior Regime', *Yale Law Journal*, 100(8): 2537–615.

OSIATYNSKI, WIKTOR (1994), 'Reconciliation and Amnesty', in Borraine, Alex, Levy, Janet, and Scheffer, Ronel (eds.), *Dealing With the Past: Truth and Reconciliation in South Africa* (Capetown: Institute for Democracy in South Africa), 59–63.

OSIEL, MARK (1987), 'The Making of Human Rights Policy in Argentina: The Impact of Ideas and Interests on a Legal Conflict', *Journal of Latin American Studies*, 18: 135–78.

OSORIO VARGAS, JORGE (1985), 'El Movimiento de Derechos Humanos en Chile', *Documento de Trabajo*, no. 1 (Santiago: Academia de Humanismo Cristiano).

PACHECO, MÁXIMO (1980), *Lonquén* (Santiago: Péhuen).

PANIZZA, FRANSISCO (1990), *Uruguay Batllismo y Después: Pacheco, Militares y Tupamaros* (Montevideo: Ediciones de la Banda Oriental).

—— (1993), 'Human Rights: Global Culture and Social Fragmentation', *Bulletin of Latin American Research*, 12(2): 205–14.

PAREJA, CARLOS (1987), 'Los Infortunios de Una Salida Mentirosa', *Cuadernos de Marcha*, 3: 2(17): 43–56.

PASQUALUCCI, J. (1994), 'The Whole Truth and Nothing But the Truth: Truth Commissions, Impunity and the Inter-American System', *Boston University International Law Journal*, 12(2): 321–70.

PAUST, JORDAN *et al.* (1990), 'The Role of International Law and Supervision in Strenghtening Democratic Transitions: Transitions to Democracy and the Rule of Law', *American University Journal of International Law and Policy*, Summer: 5: 1063–86.

PEREIRA, MARCELO (1986), *1980–1985 Operación Sanguinetti* (Montevideo: Centro Uruguay Independiente).

PERELLI, CARINA (1984), *25 de Noviembre: Los Programas Partidários: Análisis y Comparación* (Montevideo: Cuaderno 4 de Historia y Politica CIEP).

—— (1985), 'El Proyecto Ideológico Batllista', *Documento de Trabajo*, no. 110 (Montevideo: Notas de CIESU).

—— (1987a), *Someter o Convencer: El Discurso Militar* (Montevideo: Ediciones de la Banda Oriental).

—— (1987b), *Perception of Threat and the Political Thinking of the Miltary in South America* (Montevideo: Peitho).

—— (1987c), *The Legacies of the Transition to Democracy in Argentina and Uruguay* (Montevideo: Peitho).

—— (1987d), *Amnistía No, Amnistía Sí, Amnistía Puede Ser: La Constitución Histórica de un Tema Político del Uruguay en la Transición* (Montevideo: Ediciones de la Banda Oriental).

—— (1992), 'Youth, Politics and Dictatorship in Uruguay', in Corradi, Juan, Weiss Fagen, Patricia, and Garreton, Manuel Antonio, *Fear at the Edge: State Terror and Resistance in Latin America* (Berkeley: University of California Press), 212–35.

—— (1993), 'The Power of Memory and the Memory of Power', in Sosnowski, Saul and Popkin, Louise (eds.), *Repression, Exile and*

Democracy: Uruguayan Culture (Durham, NC: Duke University Press), 147–59.

—— and RIAL, JUAN (1986), *De Mitos y Memorias Políticas: La Represión, El Miedo y Después* (Montevideo: Ediciones de la Banda Oriental).

PÉREZ, ALBERTO PÉREZ (1971), *La Ley de Lemas* (Montevideo: Fundación de Cultura Universitaria).

PÉREZ AGUIRRE, LUIS (1986), 'Derechos Humanos: Un Relato Militante de Su Defensa y Promoción en el Uruguay', *Cuadernos Paz y Justicia*, 2.

—— (1987), 'Ley de Caducidad: Crónica de un Punto Final Largamente Anunciado', *Servicio de Paz y Justicia*, Jan.–Mar.: 12–22.

—— (1989), *Opción Entrañable* (Montevideo: Editorial Trilca).

—— (1991), 'Vale la Pena: Diez Años Por la Paz y los Derechos Humanos', (Montevideo: SERPAJ, mimeo).

PÉREZ ANTÓN, ROMEO (1985), 'La Izquierda en la Fase Post-Autoritária', in Gillespie, Charles, Goodman, Louis, Rial, Juan, and Winn, Peter (eds.), *Uruguay y la Democracia*, ii (Montevideo: Ediciones de la Banda Oriental), 129–48.

PETROVA, DIMITRINA (1994), 'State Security Files and Disqualification: Bulgaria', in Borraine, Alex, Levy, Janet, and Scheffer, Ronel (eds.), *Dealing With the Past: Truth and Reconciliation in South Africa* (Capetown: Institute for Democracy in South Africa), 73–80.

PINOCHET, GENERAL AUGUSTO (1991), *Camino Recorrido: Memórias de Un Soldado*, ii (Santiago: Instituto Geografico Militar de Chile).

PION-BERLIN, DAVID (1989), *The Ideology of State Terror: Economic Doctrine and Political Repression in Argentina and Peru* (London: Lynne Reinner Publishers).

POLITZER, PATRICIA (1985), *Miedo en Chile* (Santiago: Ediciones Chile y America).

Presidencia de la República del Uruguay (1990), *Cinco Años de Democracia* (Montevideo: Imprenta del Ejército).

PSOMIADES, HARRY (1982), 'Greece: From the Colonel's Rule to Democracy', in Hertz, John (ed.), *From Dictatorship to Democracy: Coping With the Legacies of Authoritarianism and Totalitarianism* (Westport, Conn.: Greenwood Press), 245–65.

QUIJANO, JOSÉ MANUEL (1987a), 'La Política de Alianzas: Entrevista a Alberto Zumarán', *Cuadernos de Marcha*, III: II(17): 61–8.

—— (1987b), 'La Consolidación de un Proyecto Conservador', *Cuadernos de Marcha*, III: II(17): 9–13.

RAMA, GERMÁN (1987), *La Democracia en el Uruguay: Una Perspectiva de Interpretación* (Montevideo: Editorial Arca).

RAMÍREZ, GABRIEL (1988), *El Factor Militar: Genesis, Desarollo y Participación Política* (Montevideo: Arca).

—— (1989), *La Cuestión Militar: Democracia Tutelada o Democracia Asociativa?* (Montevideo: Arca).

REAL DE AZÚA, CARLOS (1964), *El Impulso y Su Freno: Tres Décadas de Batllismo* (Montevideo: Ediciones de la Banda Oriental).

—— (1971), *Política, Poder y Partidos en el Uruguay de Hoy: Conyuntura y Prognósticos* (Buenos Aires: Siglo XXI).

Real de Azúa, Carlos (1984), *Uruguay: Una Sociedad Amortiguadora* (Montevideo: Ediciones de la Banda Oriental).
Regino Burgueño, Coronel (1983), *Guerra No Convencional y Acciones Irregulares*, 67 (Montevideo: Centro Militar Departamento Editorial General Artigas).
Remmer, Karen (1989), *Military Rule in Latin America* (Boston: Unwin Hyman).
—— and Merkx, G. W. (1982), 'Bureaucratic Authoritarianism Revisited', *Latin American Research Review*, 17(2): 3–40.
Rey Piuma, Daniel and García Rivas, Hugo (1984), *Los Crímenes del Río de la Plata: Confesiones de un Ex-Torturador* (Buenos Aires: El Cid).
Rial, Juan (1983), 'Acuerdos Interpartidarios e Intrapartidarios en las Salidas a los Procesos Autoritários: Uruguay', *Documento de Trabajo*, no. 5 (Montevideo: Taller de CIEDUR).
—— (1984a), 'Los Partidos Políticos y la Democracia en la Conyuntura Uruguaya', *Documento de Trabajo*, no. 67 (Montevideo: CIESU).
—— (1984b), *Uruguay: Elecciones 1984 Un Triunfo de Centro* (Montevideo: Ediciones de la Banda Oriental).
—— (1984c), *Partidos Políticos, Democracia y Autoritarismo*, i (Montevideo: Ediciones de la Banda Oriental).
—— (1985a), 'Los Militares en Tanto "Partido Político Sustituto" Frente a la Democratización', (Montevideo: CIESU).
—— (1985b), 'Los Partidos Tradicionales: Restauración o Renovación?', in Gillespie, Charles, Goodman, Louis, Rial, Juan, and Winn, Peter (eds.), *Uruguay y la Democracia*, i (Montevideo: Ediciones de la Banda Oriental), 193–213.
—— (1985c), 'Concertación y Gobernabilidad: Proyecto, Acuerdo Político y Pacto Social: La Reciente Experiencia Uruguaya', *Documento de Trabajo*, no. 124 (Montevideo: CIESU).
—— (1986a), *Las Fuerzas Armadas: Soldados Políticos Garantes de la Democracia?* (Montevideo: CIESU).
—— (1986b), 'Militares y Redemocratización', *Cuadernos de Marcha*, III: II(8): 26–39.
—— (1990), 'Los Partidos Políticos Uruguayos en el Proceso de Transición a la Democracia', *Kellogg Working Paper*, no. 145 (Notre Dame: North Carolina University Press).
—— (1992), 'Makers and Guardians of Fear: Controlled Terror in Uruguay', in Corradi, Juan, Weiss Fagen, Patricia, and Garreton, Manuel Antonio, *Fear at the Edge: State Terror and Resistance in Latin America* (Berkeley: University of California Press), 90–103.
—— (1993), 'The Social Imaginary: Utopian Political Myths in Uruguay: Change and Permanence During and After the Dictatorship', in Sosnowski, Saul and Popkin, Louise (eds.), *Repression, Exile and Democracy: Uruguayan Culture* (Durham, NC: Duke University Press), 59–82.
Rickard, Lisa (1981), 'Filártiga vs. Peña-Irala: A New Forum For Violations of International Human Rights', *American University Law Review*, Spring, 30: 807–33.

RODRIGO, FERNANDO (1992), 'The Politics of Reconciliation in Spain's Transition to Democracy', paper presented at the Justice in Times of Transition Conference (Salzburg, Austria).

ROGERS, GEORGE (1990), *Argentina y la Tortura: Obligación de Juzgar a los Responsables, Cuadernos de CELS*, no. 2 (Buenos Aires: CELS).

ROHT-ARRIAZA, NAOMI (1990), 'State Responsibility to Investigate and Prosecute Grave Human Rights Violations in International Law', *California Law Review*, 78: 449.

—— (1995), *Impunity and Human Rights in International Law and Practise* (Oxford: Oxford University Press).

ROJAS, ALVARO (1989), *Los Secretos de Colonia Dignidad* (Santiago: Editorial Las Notícias de Chile).

ROJAS, MARÍA EUGENIA (1988), *La Represión Política en Chile: Los Hechos* (Madrid: Iepala).

ROSENBERG, TINA (1994a), 'Latin America: Reconciliation and Amnesty', in Borraine, Alex, Levy, Janet, and Scheffer, Ronel (eds.), *Dealing With the Past: Truth and Reconciliation in South Africa* (Capetown: Institute for Democracy in South Africa), 66–8.

—— (1994b), 'Prosecution: Who and For What', in Borraine, Alex, Levy, Janet, and Scheffer, Ronel (eds.), *Dealing With the Past: Truth and Reconciliation in South Africa* (Capetown: Institute for Democracy in South Africa), 93–9.

—— (1995), *The Haunted Land: Facing Europe's Ghosts After Communism* (London: Random House).

ROSENCOFF, MAURICIO (1993), 'On Suffering and Song and White Horses', in Sosnowski, Saul and Popkin, Louise (eds.), *Repression, Exile and Democracy: Uruguayan Culture* (Durham, NC: Duke University Press), 120–32.

ROUQUIÉ, ALAIN (1987a), 'De-Militarization and Military Dominated Polities in Latin America', in O'Donnell, Guillermo, Schmitter, Philippe, and Whitehead, Laurence (eds.), *Transitions From Authoritarian Rule: Comparative Perspectives* (Baltimore: Johns Hopkins University Press), 108–37.

—— (1987b), *The Military and the State in Latin America* (Berkeley: University of California Press).

ROVIRA, ALEJANDRO (1981), 'Subversión, Terrorismo, Guerra Revolucionaria: La Experiencia Uruguaya', paper presented to a Conference Given by Minister of Interior to US Delegates on Security (Montevideo).

SACHS, ALBIE (1994), 'Amnesty and Transition in South Africa', in Borraine, Alex, Levy, Janet, and Scheffer, Ronel (eds.), *Dealing With the Past: Truth and Reconciliation in South Africa* (Capetown: Institute for Democracy in South Africa), 126–30.

SAJO, ANDRAS (1994), 'Reconciliation and Amnesty', in Borraine, Alex, Levy, Janet, and Scheffer, Ronel (eds.), *Dealing With the Past: Truth and Reconciliation in South Africa* (Capetown: Institute for Democracy in South Africa), 64–5.

SÁNCHEZ, DOMINGO (1990), 'Las Resoluciones Internacionales Sobre Chile:

Un Desafío Para la Futura Democracia', *Revista Chilena de Derechos Humanos*, 12: 61–103.

SANDERS, THOMAS (1981a), 'Decompression', in Handelman, Howard and Sanders, Thomas (eds.), *Military Government and the Movement Towards Democracy in Latin America* (Bloomington: Indiana University Press), 145–63.

—— (1981b), 'Human Rights and Political Process', in Handelman, Howard and Sanders, Thomas (eds.), *Military Government and the Movement Towards Democracy in Latin America* (Bloomington: Indiana University Press), 181–206.

SANHUENZA, MANUEL (1989), 'Organización y Funcionamiento del Poder Judicial', in Comisión Chilena de Derechos Humanos, *Cómo Hacer Justicia en Democracia: Segundo Encuentro Internacional de Magistrados y Juristas* (Santiago: CCHDH), 211–29.

SARTORI, GIOVANNI (1987), *The Theory of Democracy Revisited*, i (Chatham, NJ: Chatham House Publishers).

SCHLEMMER, LAWRENCE (1995), 'The Domestic Contexts: South Africa', paper presented at the Conference on a Comparative Analysis of Transitions in Chile and South Africa (Capetown: Nov. 1995).

SCHMITTER, PHILIPPE (1980), 'Speculations About the Perspective of Demise of Authoritarian Regimes and its Possible Consquences', Working Paper no. 60 (Washington, DC: Woodrow Wilson Center Latin American Programme).

SCHOULTZ, LARS (1981), *Human Rights and US Policy Towards Latin America*, (Princeton, NJ: Princeton University Press).

SCHULL, JOSEPH (1992), 'What Is Ideology: Theoretical Problems and Lessons From Soviet-Type Societies', *Political Studies*, 60: 728–41.

SCHWARZENBERG, KAREL (1994), 'State Security Files and Disqualification: Czech Republic', in Borraine, Alex, Levy, Janet, and Scheffer, Ronel (eds.), *Dealing With the Past: Truth and Reconciliation in South Africa* (Capetown: Institute for Democracy in South Africa), 81–5.

SEONE, MARÍA and NUÑEZ, HECTOR RUÍZ (1986), *La Noche de los Lápices* (Buenos Aires: Editorial Contrapunto).

SERPAJ (1982), *Informe Sobre El Estabelecimiento Militar de Reclusion EMR-1 Libertad* (Montevideo: SERPAJ).

—— (1983), *Amnistía y Reconciliación Nacional: Propuesta del Serpaj-Uruguay* (Montevideo: SERPAJ).

—— (1989), *Nunca Más Uruguay: Informe Sobre las Violaciones a Los Derechos Humanos 1972–1985* (Montevideo: SERPAJ).

—— (1992), *Uruguay Nunca Más: Human Rights Violations 1972–1985* (Philadelphia: Temple University Press).

SÉSNIC, RODOLFO (1985), *Tucapel: La Muerte de un Líder* (Santiago: Editorial Bruguera).

SIGNORELLI-WILSON, ALDO (1986), *Quién Mató a Tucapel?* (Santiago: Editorial Ariete).

SIKKINK, KATHRYN (1991), 'The Effectiveness of US Human Rights Policy:

Argentina Guatemala and Uruguay', paper presented to the International Political Science Association Conference (Buenos Aires).

SIMPSON, JOHN (1985), *The Disappeared and the Mothers of the Plaza de Mayo: The Story of 11,000 Argentinians Who Disappeared* (New York: St. Martins Press).

—— and BENNET, JANA (1985), *The Disappeared: Voices From a Secret War* (London: Robson).

SKIDMORE, THOMAS (1988), *The Politics of Military Rule in Brazil 1964–1985* (Oxford: Oxford University Press).

SMITH, BRIAN (1982), *The Church and Politics in Chile* (Princeton, NJ: Princeton University Press).

—— (1986), 'Old Allies New Enemies: The Catholic Church as Opposition to Military Rule in Chile', in Valenzuela, Arturo and Valenzuela, Samuel (eds.), *Military Rule in Chile: Dictatorship and Oppositions* (Baltimore: Johns Hopkins University Press), 270–303.

—— (1990), 'The Catholic Church and Politics in Chile', in McKeogh, Dermot (ed.), *The Church and Politics in Latin America* (London: Macmillan).

SMULOVITZ, CATALINA (1995), 'Commissions of Truth and Reconciliation: Argentina', in Boraine, Alex and Levy, Janet (eds.), *The Healing of a Nation* (Capetown: Justice in Transition), 56–65.

SOSNOWSKI, SAUL and POPKIN, LOUISE (eds.) (1993), *Repression, Exile and Democracy: Uruguayan Culture* (Durham, NC: Duke University Press).

SPOSITO, RAFAEL (1989), 'Elecciones 1989: Lecciones y Perspectivas', *Cuadernos de Marcha*, III: V(50): 3–10.

STAHLER-SCHOLK, RICHARD (1994), 'El Salvador's Negotiated Transition: From Low-Intensity Conflict to Low-Intensity Democracy', *Journal of Inter-American Studies and World Affairs*, 36(4): 1–59.

STEPAN, ALFRED (1971), *The Military in Politics: Changing Patterns in Brazil* (Princeton, NJ: Princeton University Press).

—— (1976), 'The New Professionalism of Internal Warfare and Military Role Expansion', in Lowenthal, Abraham and Fitch, J. Samuel (eds.), *Armies and Politics in Latin America* (New York: Holmes and Meier), 134–50.

—— (1988), *Rethinking Military Politics: Brazil and the Southern Cone* (Princeton, NJ: Princeton University Press).

STOVER, ERIC and NIGHTINGALE, ELENA (eds.) (1985), *The Breaking of Bodies and Minds: Torture, Psychiatric Abuse and the Health Profession* (New York: W H Freeman).

TAPPATÁ DE VALDEZ, PATRICIA (1995), 'Commissions of Truth and Reconciliation: El Salvador', in Boraine, Alex and Levy, Janet (eds.), *The Healing of a Nation* (Capetown: Justice in Transition), 66–78.

TARIGO SCHECK, PABLO (1985), *Cómo Nuestra Vida Fue Pasando* (Montevideo: Ediciones de la Plaza).

TAYLOR, PHILIP (1952), 'The Uruguayan Coup D'Etat of 1933', *Hispanic American Historial Review*, 33(3): 301–20.

TAYLOR, PHILIP (1960), *Government and Politics of Uruguay* (New Orleans: Tulane University Press).
TIMMERMAN, JACOBO (1979), *Chile: Death in the South* (New York: Vintage).
—— (1981), *Prisoner Without a Name, Cell Without a Number* (New York: Vintage).
TOBIN, JACK *et al.* (1990), 'Accountability and the Transition to Democracy: Transition To Democracy and the Rule of Law', *American University Journal of International Law and Policy*, Summer, 5: 1033–63.
Tribunal Permanente de los Pueblos (1990), *Sesión Uruguay: April 1990* (Montevideo: Graphis).
TRINQUIER, ROGER (1975), *Guerra, Subversión, Revolución* (Buenos Aires: Rioplatense).
TROBO, CLAUDIO (1986), *Quién Mató a Michelini y Gutiérrez Ruíz?* (Buenos Aires: Ediciones Teoria y Práctica).
VALDÉZ, HERNÁN (1975), *Tejas Verdes: Diario de un Campo de Concentración* (Barcelona: Editorial Ariete).
VALENZUELA, ARTURO (1978), *The Breakdown of Democratic Regimes: Chile* (Baltimore: Johns Hopkins University Press).
—— (1991), 'The Military in Power: The Consolidation of One Man Rule', in Drake, Paul and Jaksic Ivan (eds.), *The Struggle For Democracy in Chile 1982–1990* (Lincoln: University of Nebraska Press), 21–73.
—— and VALENZUELA, SAMUEL (eds.) (1986a), *Military Rule in Chile: Dictatorship and Oppositions* (Baltimore: Johns Hopkins University Press).
—— —— (1986b), 'Party Oppositions Under the Chilean Authoritarian Regime', in Valenzuela, Arturo and Valenzuela, Samuel (eds.), *Military Rule in Chile: Dictatorship and Oppositions* (Baltimore: Johns Hopkins University Press), 184–229.
VANGER, MILTON (1963), *José Batlle y Ordoñez of Uruguay: The Creator of His Times 1902–1907* (Cambridge, Mass.: Harvard University Press).
—— (1980), *The Model Country: José Batlle y Ordoñez of Uruguay* (Waltham, Mass.: Brandeis University Press).
VARGAS, CARLOS (1989), 'Entrevista a Luis Eduardo González: Por Qué Pierde el Partido Colorado?', *Cuadernos de Marcha*, III: V(49): 3–9.
VARGAS, JUAN ENRIQUE (1990), 'El Caso Chileno Ante el Sistema Inter-Americano de Protección de los Derechos Humanos', *Revista Chilena de Derechos Humanos*, 12: 11–31.
VARGAS, MARÍA CAROLINA (1990), 'El Caso Chileno en la Asamblea General y la Comisión de Derechos Humanos de la ONU', *Revista Chilena de Derechos Humanos*, 12: 31–61.
VASCONCELLOS, AMÍLCAR (1987), *Febrero Amargo: Uruguay 1973* (Montevideo: Monte Sexto).
VEIL, SIMONE (1986), *Disappeared: Technique of Terror: A Report For the Independent Commission of International Humanitarian Issues* (London: Zed Books).
VERDUGO, PATRICIA (1986), *Rodrigo y Carmen Gloria: Quemados Vivos* (Santiago: Editorial Aconcagua).

—— (1989), *Los Zarpazos del Puma* (Santiago: Ediciones Chile America).
—— (1990), *Tiempo de Días Claros* (Santiago: Ediciones Chile America).
VERGARA, PILAR (1986), 'Changes in the Economic Functions of the State Under the Military Regime', in Valenzuela, Arturo and Valenzuela, Samuel (eds.), *Military Rule in Chile: Dictatorship and Oppositions* (Baltimore: Johns Hopkins University Press), 85–116.
VEVERKA, KAREN (1992), 'El Salvador: A Year After the Accords', *Life and Peace Review*, 4: 9–11.
Vicaría de la Solidaridad (1990), *Dónde Están*, i–vii (Santiago: Talleres Graficos Corporación).
—— (1993), 'Informe Global Sobre las Violaciones a los Derechos Humanos,' (Santiago: mimeo).
VICTOR, J. (1981), *Confesiones de Un Torturador: Entrevista a Hugo Walter García Rivas* (Barcelona: Laia).
VIERA-GALLO, JOSÉ ANTÓNIO and RODRÍGUEZ, TERESA (1987), 'Ideologías, Partidos Políticos y Derechos Humanos: Democracia Cristiana', *Cuadernos de Trabajo*, no. 6 (Santiago: Academia de Humanismo Cristiano).
—— (1988), 'Ideologías, Partidos Políticos y Derechos Humanos: La Derecha', *Cuadernos de Trabajo*, no. 7 (Santiago: Academia de Humanismo Cristiano).
VIGNAR, MARCELO and MAREN (1989), *Exil et Torture* (Paris: Denouel).
WALTER, KNUT and WILLIAMS, PHILIP J. (1993) 'The Military and Redemocratization in El Salvador', *Journal of Interamerican Studies and World Affairs*, 35/1: 39–88.
WEINSTEIN, EUGENIA (1987), *Trauma Duelo y Reparación* (Santiago: FASIC).
WEINSTEIN, MARTIN (1975), *The Politics of Failure* (Westport, Conn.: Greenwood Press).
—— (1988), *Uruguay: Democracy at the Crossroads* (Boulder, Colo.: Westview Press).
—— (1993), 'The Decline and Fall of Democracy in Uruguay: Lessons For the Future', in Sosnowski, Saul and Popkin, Louise (eds.), *Repression, Exile and Democracy: Uruguayan Culture* (Durham, NC: Duke University Press), 83–100.
WEISS FAGEN, PATRICIA (1992), 'Repression and State Security', in Corradi, Juan, Weiss Fagen, Patricia and Garreton, Manuel Antonio (eds.), *Fear at the Edge: State Terror and Resistance in Latin America* (Berkeley: University of California Press), 39–71.
WEISSBRODT, DAVID and BARTOLOMEI, MARÍA (1991), 'The Effectiveness of International Human Rights Pressures: The Case of Argentina', *Minnesota Law Review*, 75: 1009–35.
—— and FRASER, PAUL W. (1992), 'Report of the Chilean National Commission on Truth and Reconciliation', *Human Rights Quarterly*, 14(4).
WESCHLER, LAURENCE (1990), *A Miracle, A Universe: Settling Accounts With Past Torturers* (New York: Pantheon Books).

WHITEHEAD, LAURENCE (1989), 'The Control of Fragile Democracies: A Discussion With Illustrations', in Pastor, Robert (ed.), *Democracy in the Americas: Stopping the Pendulum* (New York: Holmes and Meier), 76–95.

WILDE, ALEXANDER *et al.* (1990), 'Civil Miitary Relations in the Western Hemisphere and Human Rights: Transitions to Democracy and the Rule of Law', *American University Journal of International Law and Policy*, Summer: 5: 1019–33.

WITKER, ALEJANDRO (1977), *El Compañero Tohá* (México: Casa de Chile en México).

WOETZAL, ROBERT (1960), *The Nuremberg Trials in International Law* (New York: Stevens and Praeger).

YANEZ, RÚBEN (1993), 'The Repression of Uruguayan Culture: A Response to People's Reponse to the Crisis', in Sosnowski, Saul and Popkin, Louise (eds.), *Repression, Exile and Democracy: Uruguayan Culture* (Durham, NC: Duke University Press), 133–46.

ZABEL, WILLIAM, ORENTLICHER, DIANE, and NACHMAN, DAVID (1987), *Human Rights and the Administration of Justice* (New York: Bar Association of the City of New York and the International Bar Association).

ZAGORSKY, PAUL (1992), *Democracy vs. National Security: Civil Military Relations in Latin America* (Boulder, Colo.: Lynne Rienner Publishers).

ZALAQUETT, JOSÉ (1988), 'Confronting Human Rights Violations by Former Governments: Principles Applicable and Political Constraints', in Henkin, Alice (ed.), *State Crimes: Punishment or Pardon* (Queenstown, Md.: Aspen Institute), 23–71.

—— (1994), 'Why Deal with the Past', in Borraine, Alex, Levy, Janet, and Scheffer, Ronel (eds.), *Dealing With the Past: Truth and Reconciliation in South Africa* (Capetown: Institute for Democracy in South Africa), 8–14.

—— (1995), 'Commissions of Truth and Reconciliation', in Boraine, Alex and Levy, Janet (eds.), *The Healing of a Nation* (Capetown: Justice in Transition), 44–55.

ZUBILLAGA, CARLOS and PÉREZ, ROMEO (1988), *El Uruguay de la Dictadura 1973–1985: La Democracia Atacada*, i (Montevideo: Ediciones de la Banda Oriental).

ZUR, JUDITH (1995), 'The Psychological Effects of Impunity: The Language of Denial', in Seider, Rachel (ed.), *Impunity in Latin America* (London: Institute of Latin American Studies), 57–72.

International Human Rights Organizations Reports

Africa Watch

Africa Watch (1992a), *Accountability in Namibia: Human Rights and the Transition to Democracy*.

—— (1992b), *South Africa: Accounting for the Past: The Lessons for South Africa from Latin America*.

Americas Watch

AW (1983), *Chile Since the Coup: Ten Years of Repression.*
—— (1987a), *Human Rights Concerns in Chile.*
—— (1987b), *Truth and Partial Justice in Argentina.*
—— (1988a), *Closing the Space: Human Rights in Guatemala.*
—— (1988b), *Chile: Human Rights and the Plebiscite.*
—— (1989a), *Chile in Transition: Human Rights and the Plebiscite 1988–1989.*
—— (1989b), *Carnage Again: Preliminary Report on Violations of the Laws of War by Both Sides in the November 1989 Offensive in El Salvador.*
—— (1989c), *Challenging Impunity: The Ley de Caducidad And the Referendum Campaign in Uruguay.*
—— (1989d), *Honduras: Without the Will.*
—— (1989e), *Nicaragua: A Human Rights Chronology July 1979 to July 1989.*
—— (1990a), *A Year of Reckoning: El Salvador a Decade After the Assassination of Archbishop Romero.*
—— (1990b), *Violations of Fair Trial Guarantees by the FMLN's Ad Hoc Courts.*
—— (1990c), *Honduras: The Inter American Court of Human Rights Wraps Up First Adversarial Case.*
—— (1991a), *Human Rights and the 'Politics of Agreements': Chile During President Aylwin's First Year.*
—— (1991b), *El Salvador: The Jesuit Trial.*
—— (1991c), *Judiciary Bars Steps to Identify Kidnapped Child.*
—— (1991d), *Fitful Peace: Human Rights and Reconciliation in Nicaragua under the Chamorro Government.*
—— (1991f), *Truth and Partial Justice in Argentina: An Update.*
—— (1992a), *Chile: The Struggle for Truth and Justice For Past Human Rights Violations.*
—— (1992b), *Bolivia, Trial of Responsibilities: Nine Years and No Verdict.*
—— (1992c), *Paraguay: An Encouraging Victory in the Search for Truth and Justice.*
—— (1993a), *El Salvador: Accountability and Human Rights: The Report of the UN Commission on the Truth for El Salvador.*
—— (1993b), *Bolivia: The Trial of Responsibilities: The García Meza Tejada Trial*
—— (1994a), *Nicaragua: Separating Facts from Fiction: The Work of the Tripartite Commission in Nicaragua.*
—— (1994b), *Human Rights in Guatemala During President De León Carpio's First Year.*
—— (1994c), *Chile: Unsettled Business: Human Rights at the Start of the Frei Presidency.*
—— (1994d), *Final Justice: Police and Death Squad Homicides of Adolescents in Brazil.*
—— (1994e), *Generation Under Fire: Children and Violence in Colombia.*

——(1995), *Disappeared in Guatemala: The Case of Efraín Bámaca Velásquez.*

Amnesty International

AI (1975a), *A Report on Torture.*
——(1975b), *Torture in Greece: The First Torturers' Trial.*
——(1975c), *Annual Report.*
——(1983a), *Report on Human Rights Violations in Uruguay.*
——(1983b), *Memorandum to the Government of Uganda on an Amnesty International Mission to Uganda in January 1982 and Further Exchanges Between the Government and Amnesty International.*
——(1983c), *Chile: Evidence of Torture.*
——(1986), *Nicaragua: The Human Rights Record.*
——(1987), *Argentina: The Military Juntas and Human Rights: Report of the Trial of the Former Junta Members.*
——(1988a), *Uruguay: Official Investigations Fail to Establish the Fate of the Disappeared.*
——(1988b), *Testimony on Secret Detention Camps in Argentina.*
——(1988c), *Naval Officers Released But Concern Continues About Virtual Impunity of Human Rights Violators.*
——(1988d), *Brasil: Violencia Autorizada en el Medio Rural.*
——(1991a), *Argentina: Presidential Pardon to Military Officers Before Trial.*
——(1991b), *Chile: La Tortura Desde Marzo 1990.*
——(1992), *Brazil. Impunity and the Law: The Killing of Street Children in Rio de Janeiro.*
——(1995), *Sri Lanka: Time For Truth and Justice.*

Helsinki Watch

HW (1990), *Trials in Romania: A Rush to Appease . . . And to Conceal.*
——(1991a), *Destroying Ethnic Identity: The Persecution of Gypsies in Romania.*
——(1991b), *Destroying Ethnic Identity: The Persecution of Gypsies in Bulgaria.*
——(1991c), *Yugoslavia: Human Rights Abuses in the Croatian Conflict.*
——(1992a), *Czechoslovakia: DeCommunization Measures Violate Freedom of Expression and Due Process Standards.*
——(1992b), *The Struggle for Ethnic Identity: Czechoslovakia's Endangered Gypsies.*
——(1992c), *War Crimes in Bosnia-Hercegovina, i.*
——(1993a), *Procedural and Evidentiary Issues for the Yugoslav War Crimes Tribunal: Resource Allocation, Evidentiary Questions and Protection of Witnesses.*

——(1993b), *Decommunization in Bulgaria.*
——(1993c), *The Struggle for Ethnic Identity: The Gypsies of Hungary.*
——(1993d), *War Crimes in Bosnia-Hercegovina, ii.*
——(1994), *The Former Yugoslavia the War Crimes Tribunal: One Year Later.*

Human Rights Watch

HRW (1994), *The Facts Speak for Themselves: The Preliminary Report on Disappearances of the National Commissioner for the Protection of Human Rights in Honduras.*
——(1995a), *Human Rights Watch World Report.*
——(1995b), *Playing the 'Communal Card': Communal Violence and Human Rights.*

International Commission of Jurists

ICJ (1972), 'Uganda: A Lawless State', *The Review*, 9(18).
——(1974a), *Report of the Mission to Chile in April 1974 to Study the Legal System and the Protection of Human Rights.*
——(1974b), *Report of the Mission to Uruguay: April to May 1974.*
——(1976), *Report on the Mission to Uruguay 1976.*
——(1991a), *The Trial for the Assassination of the Jesuits.*
——(1991b), 'The Failed Promise: Human Rights in the Phillipines Since the Revolution of 1986', *The Review*, 27(125): 232–49.
——(1983), *States of Emergency: Their Impact on Human Rights.*

Organization of American States–Interamerican Commission of Human Rights

OAS (1981), *Report of the Situation of Human Rights in Nicaragua.*

United Nations

UNECOSOC (1975), *UNECOSOC Report of the Economic and Social Council: Ad Hoc Working Group on Chile* (New York: A/10285).
UN (1993), *Report of the Truth Commission for El Salvador: De la Locura a la Esperanza: Informe de la Comision de la Verdad para El Salvador.*

Washington Office on Latin America

WOLA (1988), *Conditions for Chile's Plebiscite on Pinochet: WOLA Delegation to Chile 3–10 September 1988.*
——(1989), *Chile's Transition to Democracy.*

Legislative Sessions: Chamber of Deputies and Senate

Uruguay

DSCSROU (1968–1970), Diario de Sesiones de la Cámara de Senadores de la República Oriental del Uruguay: 'Informe de la Comisión Especial Investigadora Sobre Violación de los Derechos Humanos and Comisión de Actos de Torturas a Detenidos y Regimenes de Detención Vejatorios a la Dignidad Humana.' Montevideo: Cámara de Senadores, Carpeta no. 1368 (1968), Repartido no. 146 (1970), Distribuido no. 216, 6 Oct. 1970.

—— (1985a), Diario de Sesiones de la Cámara de Senadores de la República Oriental del Uruguay (DSCSROU): tomo 287, Sessions 14 Feb.–11 Mar. 1985; tomo 287, 15 Feb. 1985, 1a Sesión Ordinária.

—— (1985b), Diario de Sesiones de la Cámara de Senadores de la República Oriental del Uruguay (DSCSROU): tomo 287, Sessions 14 Feb.–11 Mar. 1985; tomo 287, 20 Feb. 1985, 2a Sesión Ordinária.

—— (1985c), Diario de Sesiones de la Cámara de Senadores de la República Oriental del Uruguay (DSCSROU): tomo 287, Sessions 14 Feb.–11 Mar. 1985; tomo 287, 5 Mar. 1985, 5a. Sesión Ordinária.

—— (1985d), Diario de Sesiones de la Cámara de Senadores de la República Oriental del Uruguay (DSCSROU): tomo 287, Sessions 14 Feb.–11 Mar. 1985; tomo 287, 7–8 Mar. 1985, 7a Sesión Extraordinaria.

DSCRROU (1985e), Diario de Sesiones de la Cámara de Representantes de la República Oriental del Uruguay: tomo 616, no. 1796, XLII Legislatura, 4a Sesión Extraordinaria, 28 Feb. 1985.

—— (1985f), Diario de Sesiones de la Cámara de Representantes de la República Oriental del Uruguay: tomo 616, no. 1797, XLII Legislatura, 5a Sesión Extraordinaria, 4 Mar. 1985.

—— (1985g), Cámara de Representantes de la República Oriental del Uruguay: Comisión de Investigación de la Cámara de Diputados, Carpeta no. 253. Montevideo.

—— (1986a), Diario de Sesiones de la Cámara de Representantes de la República Oriental del Uruguay (DSCRROU): tomo 618, Sessions 19–21 Dec. 1986.

DSCROU (1986b), Diario de Sesiones de la Cámara de Senadores de la República Oriental del Uruguay (DSCSROU): tomo 304, Sessions 18–23 Dec. 1986, no. 165, 74a Sesión Extraordinária, 18–19, Dec. 1986.

—— (1986c), Diario de Sesiones de la Cámara de Senadores de la República Oriental del Uruguay (DSCSROU): tomo 304, Sessions 18–23 Dec. 1986, no. 166, 75a Sesión Extraordinaria, 19–20 Dec. 1986.

—— (1986d), Diario de Sesiones de la Cámara de Senadores de la República Oriental del Uruguay (DSCSROU): tomo 304, Sessions 18–23 Dec. 1986, no. 167, 76a Sesión Extraordinaria, 20–1 Dec. 1986.

—— (1986e), Diario de Sesiones de la Cámara de Senadores de la República Oriental del Uruguay (DSCSROU): tomo 304, Sessions 18–23 Dec. 1986, no. 168, 77a Sesión Extraordinaria, 22–3 Dec. 1986.

DSCRROU (1987), Diario de Sesiones de la Cámara de Representantes de la República Oriental del Uruguay (DSCRROU): no. 1968, tomo 631, XLII Legislatura, 51a Sesión, 13 Oct. 1987.
—— (1988), Diario de Sesiones de la Cámara de Senadores de la República Oriental del Uruguay (DSCSROU): no. 277, tomo 317, XLII Legislatura, 40a Sesion Extraordinaria, 30–1 Dec. 1988.

Chile

DSCD (1990a), Diario de Sesiónes de la Cámara de Diputados (DSCD): Sesiones Extraordinárias, 18 Apr.–15 May 1990, pp. 560–1202, Sesión 12a, 25 Apr. 1990.
—— (1990b), Diario de Sesiones de la Cámara de Diputados (DSCD): Sesiones Extraordinárias, 18 Apr.–15 May 1990, pp. 560–1202, Sesión 17a, 8 May 1990.
—— (1990c), Diario de Sesiones de la Cámara de Diputados (DSCD): Sesiones Extraordinárias, 18 Apr.–15 May 1990, pp. 560–1202, Sesión 18a, 9 May 1990.
—— (1990d), Diario de Sesiones de la Cámara de Diputados (DSCD): Sesiones Extraordinárias, 18 Apr.–15 May 1990, pp. 560–1202, Sesión 20a, 15 May 1990.
—— (1990e), Diario de Sesiones de la Cámara de Diputados (DSCD): Sesiones Ordinárias, 29 May–8 Aug., pp. 68–2730, Sesión 2a, 29 May 1990.
—— (1990f), Diario de Sesiones de la Cámara de Diputados (DSCD): Sesiones Ordinárias, 29 May–8 Aug., pp. 68–2730, Sesión 3a, 30 May 1990.
—— (1990g), Diario de Sesiones de la Cámara de Diputados (DSCD): Sesiones Ordinárias, 29 May–8 Aug., pp. 68–2730, Sesión 5a, 6 June 1990.
—— (1990h), Diario de Sesiones de la Cámara de Diputados (DSCD): Sesiones Ordinárias, 29 May–8 Aug., pp. 68–2730, Sesión 6a, 12 June 1990.
—— (1990i), Diario de Sesiones de la Cámara de Diputados (DSCD): Sesiones Ordinárias, 29 May–8 Aug., pp. 68–2730, Sesión 7a, 13 June 1990.
—— (1990j), Diario de Sesiones de la Cámara de Diputados (DSCD): Sesiones Ordinárias, 29 May–8 Aug., pp. 68–2730, Sesión 8a, 19 June 1990.
—— (1990k), Diario de Sesiones de la Cámara de Diputados (DSCD): Sesiones Ordinárias, 29 May–8 Aug., pp. 68–2730, Sesión 11a, 27 June 1990.
—— (1990l), Diario de Sesiones de la Cámara de Diputados (DSCD): Sesiones Ordinárias, 29 May–8 Aug., pp. 68–2730, Sesión 23a, 8 Aug. 1990.
—— (1990m), Diario de Sesiones de la Cámara de Diputados (DSCD): Sesiones Extraordinárias, Sesión 17a, 4 Dec. 1990.

——(1990n), Diario de Sesiones de la Cámara de Diputados (DSCD): Sesiones Ordinárias, 320a, Legislatura Ordinária, Sesión 13a, 13 June 1990.

——(1991a), Diario de Sesiones de la Cámara de Diputados (DSCD): Sesiones Extraordinárias, 11 Oct.–14 Mar. 1991, pp. 370–4384, Sesión 31a, 22 Jan. 1991.

——(1991b), Diario de Sesiones de la Cámara de Diputados (DSCD): Sesiones Extraordinárias, 11 Oct.–14 Mar. 1991, pp. 370–4384, Sesión 35a, 8 Mar. 1991.

——(1991c), Diario de Sesiones de la Cámara de Diputados (DSCD): Sesiones Extraordinárias, 11 Oct.–14 Mar. 1991, pp. 370–4384, Sesión 36a, 14 Mar. 1991.

DSDS (1990a), Diario de Sesiones de la Cámara de Senadores (DSDS): Sesiones Ordinárias, 19 June–5 Sept. 1990, pp. 660–2226, Sesión 9a, 19 June 1990.

——(1990b), Diario de Sesiones de la Cámara de Senadores (DSDS): Sesiones Ordinárias, 19 June–5 Sept. 1990, pp. 660–2226, Sesión 17a, 17 July 1990.

——(1990c), Diario de Sesiones de la Cámara de Senadores (DSDS): Sesiones Ordinárias, 19 June–5 Sept. 1990, pp. 660–2226, Sesión 30a, 5 Sept. 1990.

——(1990d), Diario de Sesiones de la Cámara de Senadores (DSDS): Sesiones Extraordinárias, 12 Dec. 1990–23 Mar. 1991, pp. 1778–3450, Sesión 27a, 19 Dec. 1990.

——(1991a), Diario de Sesiones de la Cámara de Senadores (DSDS): Sesiones Extraordinárias, 12 Dec. 1990–23 Mar. 1991, pp. 1778–3450, Sesión 36a, 5 Mar. 1991.

——(1991b), Diario de Sesiones de la Cámara de Senadores (DSDS): Sesión Congreso Pleno, 23 Mar. 1991.

Newspapers

Uruguay

La República
El Día
El País
Búsqueda
Brecha
Zeta
Alternativa Socialista
El Diario
Paz y Justicia
Cuadernos de Marcha
Las Bases

Chile

Análisis
Hoy
Apsi
Qué Pasa
Epoca
El Mercurio
La Nación
La Tercera
La Segunda
Cauce
Caras
Fortín Mapocho

Other Countries

The Financial Times (London)
International Herald Tribune (USA)
Latin America Weekly Reports (UK)
Mail and Guardian (South Africa)
Le Monde (France)
New York Times (USA)
El País (Spain)
O Público (Portugal)
Southern Cone Reports (UK)

Interviews (Chronological)

Uruguay

Carlos Baraibar, Political Secretary, FA: 27 May 1991.
Luis Pérez Aguirre, SERPAJ: 27 May 1991.
Francisco Bustamante, SERPAJ. *Uruguay Nunca Más team*: 27 May 1991.
Dr Nelson Nicollielo, Minister of the Supreme Court: 28 May 1991.
Dr Julio M. Sanguinetti, President of Uruguay 1985–1989: 28 May 1991.
Efraín Olivera, SERPAJ: 28 May 1991.
Dr Torriello, Supreme Court: 28 May 1991.
Mitíl Ferreira, Director, Asociación Sindical del Uruguay: 29 May 1991.
Dr Francisco Ottonelli, IELSUR: 29 May 1991.
Elisa Michelini, Wife of Zelmar Michelini: 30 May 1991.
Pablo Mieres, CLAEH: 31 May 1991.
Germán Araújo, Parliamentarian, FA 1985–6: 3 June 1991.
Rafael Michelini, Parliamentarian, FA: 3 June 1991.
Gonzalo Carámbula, Parliamentarian, FA: 4 June 1991.

Dr Lapinn, Director, Colegio de Abogados, 4 June 1991.
Ope Pasquett, Parliamentarian, CP: 4 June 1991.
Fernando Urioste, Academic and lawyer: 5 June 1991.
Belela Herrera, ANCUR and FA: 5 June 1991.
Luis Eduardo González, Director, Equipos Consultores: 6 June 1991.
Dr Marchesano, Sanguinetti Administration: 6 June 1991.
Hugo Batalla, Parliamentarian, FA: 7 June 1991.
Carlos Julio Pereyra, Leader of MNR: 10 June 1991.
Alberto Pérez Pérez, Leader, Referendum Campaign: 10 June 1991.
Héctor Acosta, Political Committee, FA: 11 June 1991.
Dr Claudio Williman, Blanco Party, Commission of Jurists: 11 June 1991.
Officer Malán, Oficiales Retirados Por Razones Políticas: 11 June 1991.
Gastón Silberman, Ex-Navy Officer: 11 June 1991.
Víctor Vaillant, Leader, CBI: 12 June 1991.
Dr Adiego, Supreme Court: 13 June 1991.
Danilo Astori, Parliamentarian, FA: 13 June 1991.
Dr Schurmann Pacheco, Jurist: 13 June 1991.
General (R) Paulós, Director, Centro Militar del Ejército: 13 June 1991.
Korzeniak, Parliamentarian, FA: 14 June 1991.
Roger Rodríguez, Journalist, *Brecha*: 16 June 1991.
General (R) Licandro, purged from armed forces: 17 June 1991.
Almirante (R) Márquez, one of planners of the coup within the Navy: 18 June 1991.
Linj Cardoso, Journalist, *Búsqueda*: 18 June 1991.
Romeo Pérez, *Centro Latinoamericano de Economía Humana*: 20 June 1991.
Major (R) Círio, purged from armed forces: 20 June 1991.

Argentina

Augusto Conte McDonnell, Christian Democrat, father of disappeared: 24 June 1991.
Dr Emílio Mignone, Centro de Estudios Sociales y Legales, father of disappeared: 24 June 1991.
Réné Eppelbaum, Leader, Abuelas de la Plaza de Mayo: 25 June 1991.
Graciela Fernández Mejide, Asamblea Permanente de Derechos Humanos: 25 June 1991.
Luis Moreno Ocampo, Assistant Prosecutor of Junta Trials: 28 June 1991.

Chile

Rodolfo Rodríguez, Political Prisoner, MIR: 17 July 1991.
Ignacio Walker, Christian Democrat: 18 July 1991.
Eugenio Ahumada, Vicaría, author *La Memória Prohibída*: 18 July 1991.
Comandante Arriagada, Air Force: 20 July 1991.
Capitán Mesa, Air Force: 20 July 1991.

Domingo Namuncura, Director, SERPAJ: 23 July 1991.
Jorge Correa, Secretary of the CNVR: 23 July 1991.
Coronel Villalobos, CEADE, Academia de Guerra Aérea: 24 July 1991.
Hugo Ocampo, CODEPU: 24 July 1991.
Hugo Cárcamo, AFEP: 24 July 1991.
Alejandro Salinas, AI-Chilean Section: 24 July 1991.
Máximo Pacheco, CChDH, Christian Democrat, 26 July 1991.
Sola Sierra, President, AFDD: 26 July 1991.
Andrés Domínguez, CChDH: 29 July 1991.
María Maluenda, Parliamentarian, PPD, mother of disappeared: 30 July 1991.
Roberto Garretón, HR Department, Foreign Ministry: 1 Aug. 1991.
Réné García Villegas, Judge, Disbarred under Pinochet: 1 Aug. 1991.
Sergio Bitar, PPD, Author *Isla Diez*: 5 Aug. 1991.
Carlos Fresno, Ministry of Justice, 9 Aug. 1991.
Eugenio Velasco, CChDH, 13 Aug. 1991.
Ernesto Illanes, UDI: 13 Aug. 1991.
Hugo Frühling, expert on human rights issues: 16 Aug. 1991.

Index